Guidance Services in the Modern School

MERLE M. OHLSEN
UNIVERSITY OF ILLINOIS

Guidance Services
IN THE
Modern School

UNDER THE GENERAL EDITORSHIP OF

WILLARD B. SPALDING
COORDINATING COUNCIL FOR HIGHER EDUCATION,
CALIFORNIA

HARCOURT, BRACE & WORLD, INC.
NEW YORK · BURLINGAME

To Helen, Marilyn, Linda, Barbara, and Ronald

PREFACE

THIS revision of *Guidance: An Introduction* has the same purposes as the original edition: to help teachers, administrators, counselors, and prospective counselors to understand the basic guidance services and the relationships among these services; to define essential positions for guidance workers; and to help all these persons to discover and use more effectively all available personnel resources in improving the school adjustment of pupils. The point of view is the same as in the original text, but the revision is organized quite differently in order to focus attention on each of the basic guidance services.

Guidance Services in the Modern School presents the principles of guidance within the framework of a consistent, child-centered philosophy and suggests how those principles may be applied by a teacher working with pupils, a faculty sponsor or a student leader working with a group, a counselor working with clients, and an administrator working with pupils and faculty.

The revision incorporates up-to-date research and reflects nine additional years of experience in counseling pupils and their parents, supervising prospective counselors in the guidance practicum, teaching guidance courses, and undertaking research. Among the new topics dealt with are the ethics of testing, the underachiever, the exceptional child, theories of vocational choice, problems girls face in achieving vocational maturity, the implications of theory and research for vocational counseling, and the nature of social and leadership development in guidance programs. In addition, this revised edition reviews relevant research for each of the basic services.

I am grateful to clients, graduate students, and colleagues for case material, and to several users of the first edition who suggested topics which should be deleted and others which should be added. Especially helpful were suggestions made by those who scrutinized early versions of this revision. Finally, I am grateful to Willard Spalding for editing the entire manuscript, and to my wife, Helen, for her editoral work on the manuscript and her typing of its various versions.

MERLE M. OHLSEN

November 1963
Champaign, Illinois

EDITOR'S FOREWORD

THE author of a beginning text in guidance needs a scholarly knowledge of the subject and wide experience of the problems of students, teachers, parents, counselors, and school administrators involved in guidance programs. This revision of *Guidance: An Introduction* reflects its author's continuing scholarship and experience.

Dr. Ohlsen is widely recognized as a leader in the development of principles and practices in student personnel work. He has directed four cooperative research projects in these fields, has been active in the American Personnel and Guidance Association, and has recently written a chapter called "Interpretation of Test Scores" for the Sixty-second Yearbook of the National Society for the Study of Education. As in all his writings, references here are up-to-date, and often acquaint the reader with little-known but important research.

During most of his college teaching, Dr. Ohlsen has been primarily concerned with counselor-teacher education. Almost every semester he has taught at least one section of the course for which his guidance book is designed as a text. In addition he always has a few counseling clients. The progression of chapters in this revision is logically related to the increasingly complex tasks of counselors and teachers. Material on testing is briefer than in the original edition and is more closely tied to the use of tests in guidance. The new chapter on Information Services with the two which follow—Educational-vocational Planning, and Vocational Placement and Follow-up—provide thorough information about sources and procedures for use in guiding young people as they decide about their careers, and in securing feedback to improve guidance operations.

Guidance Services in the Modern School should fill a definite need in the beginning course.

WILLARD B. SPALDING

CONTENTS

LIST OF FIGURES

LIST OF TABLES

Guidance Services in the Modern School

The Role of Guidance in the Modern School

G UIDANCE is a cooperative effort of the counselor and his colleagues to help a pupil improve his adjustment to school, and to help him develop skills for dealing more successfully with the problems he encounters after he leaves school. The young person has particular need of help in understanding himself and his environment. He needs assistance not only in solving his immediate problems but in developing his resources for solving future problems. To achieve these goals the school must help the pupil to recognize, accept, develop, and use his various potentialities while he is in school. When he is confronted by problems which he cannot solve by himself, it is essential for him to realize that someone is interested in him and to believe that he can obtain help from that person when he needs it. This book describes the various guidance services, presents techniques which may be used to help the young person, and discusses the roles which various school personnel can play in giving this help.

Although guidance is often thought of as limited to giving tests, building cumulative student records, planning extra-class activities, prescribing courses, and assigning readings in vocational pamphlets, it actually involves much more. Guidance focuses attention on the individual pupil. Recognizing that all problems are peculiar to the individual facing them, it considers these problems in relation to the continuous history of that individual and in relation to all the many phases of his life. It recognizes that the solution to any of the particular problems which may arise from a pupil's frustrating and irritating experiences, in school or out, requires an understanding of the whole picture of his activities, and that the solution to any particular problem will influence the total development of the individual's personality.

Since guidance attempts to deal with problems which must be analyzed and solved within the context of a student's whole life, many people must take part in solving the problems of a single individual. The construction of the complete picture involves a pooling of information provided by parents, classroom teachers, guidance specialists, and school administrators. Each observes the pupil from a somewhat different point of view: (1) parents notice how he responds to his siblings and peers, and to them, and they see how he accepts his responsibilities at home, at school, and in the community; (2) teachers observe how he relates to peers, how he relates to the teacher as another authority figure, how he responds to classroom limits and responsibilities, and how well he uses his potentialities; (3) administrators usually see a global picture of the school and the individual's various roles within it; and (4) finally, from his conferences with the pupil the counselor obtains a picture of the pupil's private life. The counselor also has special information which he secures from tests and nontest techniques in an effort to get still a better understanding of the pupil.

Though each of the persons mentioned above sees a child in a different setting, those who help him most have much in common: (1) they accept him; (2) they listen to him and try to understand him; (3) they are genuinely concerned about his welfare; (4) they are able to convey to him the feeling that they are concerned about his welfare and that he does not have to be perfect to be a good erson; (5) they help him to capitalize on his strengths and to correct those weaknesses which he can correct with a reasonable effort; (6) they respect him as an individual; (7) they have confidence in his ability to choose what is best for him; and (8) they try to teach him to take increasingly greater responsibility for himself.

What Is Adjustment?

IMPROVED adjustment is the primary objective of guidance. Adjustment may briefly be defined as a dynamic process in which an individual gradually becomes better acquainted with himself, discovers what he would like to be, determines how he can achieve his goals, and improves his ways of meeting life's crises. Good adjustment includes the ability to give and accept love, to accept oneself and others, to work cooperatively with others and be concerned about their welfare, to enjoy work and play, and to face reality. The well-adjusted person realizes that he is gradually becoming more like his wished-for self.

Marie Jahoda [1] recently completed a careful analysis of mental health concepts. In Chapter 2 of this excellent report she discusses some of the unsuitable conceptualizations of mental health. She points out, for example, that the absence of mental illness is certainly not an adequate criterion for mental health. Neither is the concept of normality an adequate criterion. The culture, and groups within the culture, determine what is normal behavior.

From her inspection of the diverse concepts of mental health, Jahoda developed six major criteria, discussed in her third chapter, which she finds acceptable:

1. "Positive attitudes of an individual toward his own self." The person who meets this criterion is self-accepting, self-confident, self-reliant, and independent. He has learned to live with himself rather comfortably, accepting both his limitations and his potentialities. He sees himself realistically and objectively, and he knows who he is.

2. "Growth, development, and self-actualization as criteria for mental health." To satisfy these criteria a person must have values, interests, and long-range goals which are meaningful to him, and he must be able to maintain and to find pleasurable the tensions that motivate him to use his potentialities for achieving his goals.

1 Marie Jahoda, *Current Concepts of Positive Mental Health* (New York: Basic Books, Inc., 1958).

Mere survival and tension reduction are not sufficient for him. His investment in living extends beyond his own needs to genuine concern for others.

3. "Integration as a criterion for mental health." When this condition exists in a person, the various components of his personality function together harmoniously. A person is integrated when there is within him a balance of psychic forces. Some claim that the individual must also be conscious of the unifying outlook that gives meaning and purpose to his life.

4. "Autonomy as a criterion for mental health." To satisfy this criterion a person exhibits independence and self-determination. When called upon to make a decision, he makes it on the basis of his internalized standards and takes independent action. His behavior is regulated from within.

5. "Accurate perception of reality as a criterion for mental health." What the mentally healthy person sees corresponds closely to what is there. Besides avoiding distortion of what he observes, a person who meets this criterion treats the inner life of other people as a matter worthy of his concern and attention, and he arrives at conclusions about others that are free from distortion. A healthy person seeks evidence and accepts it even when it disagrees with what he wants to believe.

6. "Environmental mastery as a criterion for mental health." Relevant literature discusses this criterion in terms of two common themes: the theme of success and the theme of adaptation to the environment.

In the mental health literature adaptation and environmental mastery are treated on different levels of specificity. Ordering these emphases roughly from most to least specific forms of human functioning, these aspects can be distinguished: (1) ability to love; (2) adequacy in love, work, and play; (3) adequacy in interpersonal relations; (4) efficiency in meeting situational requirements; (5) capacity for adaptation and adjustment; (6) efficiency in problem solving.[2]

The process of efficient problem solving involves the following: When the well-adjusted person senses a problem, he tries to define it more precisely, seeks appropriate information, identifies alternative solutions, selects one, and then takes action (although he does

2 *Ibid.*, p. 53.

not always proceed in just this sequence).[3] Hopefully he would, at least most of the time, evaluate his choice and his problem-solving techniques in order to improve his ability to solve future problems. When he fails he attacks the problem again. When, however, he retraces his steps in the problem-solving process, he defines the problem more carefully the second time, he seeks new alternatives, and he carefully appraises each of them. Though he realizes that he should try to get the facts before making a decision, he also realizes that rarely, if ever, is there clearly a single best answer. He also realizes that he must commit himself to a plan with the knowledge that it may fail.

The History of the Guidance Movement [4]

FROM the beginning of the guidance movement, its leaders have been concerned about the mental health of pupils and about the development of human resources. Originally, however, the spokesmen for these objectives tended to focus on one or the other. Today most scholars in the field of guidance believe that helping an individual recognize, accept, and develop his potentialities is one of the necessary conditions for mental health. Recently Gardner Murphy developed his case for this point of view as follows:

A healthy personality involves fulfillment rather than frustrations of potentials, and if potentials are not studied, fulfillment and therefore health is unreachable. Discovery, all too late, of earlier potential is a very common source of regret. Most serious people are happier in doing what they can do with some degree of skill and finesse. Most mental illness is at least colored by sense of failure, inadequacy, inferiority. A built-in sense of adequacy and fulfillment is only possible on a realistic basis, that is, by enabling people to do actually what they really can do.[5]

The fulfillment of talents as well as of intellectual potential is the goal set here. It represents a great challenge to education, and especially to guidance.

3 Those who are really interested in this process should see John Dewey, *How We Think* (New York: D. C. Heath and Company, 1933).

4 Those who are interested in a scholarly history of vocational guidance in the United States will want to read John M. Brewer, *History of Vocational Guidance* (New York: Harper & Row, Publishers, 1942).

5 Gardner Murphy, "Self-Realization and Mental Health," *Bulletin of the Menninger Clinic*, XXIII (1959), 84.

The leading spokesmen for the two different approaches published their classic books at about the same time: Frank Parsons [6] presented the case for vocational guidance and Clifford Beers [7] described the conditions in mental hospitals and urged Americans to attack the mental health problem.

Parsons founded the Vocational Bureau of Boston and wrote *Choosing a Vocation.*[8] Both of these achievements very quickly attracted national attention. Of them Hutson recently commented:

> Leaders in American education very early caught the social significance of Parson's contribution. They acclaimed the value of vocational guidance for the individual and for society. Helpful and illuminating literature [9] in the field of vocational guidance today are the papers and the addresses given between 1910 and 1915 by President Eliot and Professor Hanus of Harvard, President MacLaurin of the Massachusetts Institute of Technology, Professor Mead of the University of Chicago, F. E. Spaulding, then superintendent of schools in Minneapolis, and Professor Thorndike of Teachers College . . .[10]

Unfortunately, schools were slow to employ well-qualified personnel to provide vocational guidance.

Beers' autobiography attracted the attention of many who were genuinely concerned about conserving human resources. This concern for human welfare was expressed in another important movement in American life: the mental hygiene movement. Its leaders have tried to help men from all walks of life to understand mental illness, to alert them to the conditions which seem to cause it, to enlist their assistance in alleviating those conditions, and to improve the facilities for treating mental illness. Like the heads of many other such movements, the leaders of this one were quick to see the advantages of enlisting the aid of school personnel. The influence of these efforts to prevent mental illness can be seen today in teacher-education programs, in the academic content of in-service

6 Frank Parsons, *Choosing a Vocation* (Boston: Houghton Mifflin Company, 1909).

7 Clifford Beers, *A Mind That Found Itself* (New York: Doubleday & Company, Inc., 1908).

8 *Op. cit.*

9 Meyer Bloomfield, *Readings in Vocational Guidance* (Cambridge: Harvard University Press, 1915).

10 Percival W. Hutson, *The Guidance Function in Education* (New York: Appleton-Century-Crofts, 1958), p. 7.

education programs, in the nature and content of instructional materials, and in the psychological services offered by schools and community agencies. The influence of the mental hygiene movement has been great, and yet its work is just begun.

Prior to World War I, guidance lacked adequate instruments for the study of the individual. With the war and the problem of selecting personnel for special military assignments, the need for better methods became clear, and some advances in testing procedures emerged. Faith in the promise of tests and concern for the conservation of human resources encouraged psychologists, after the war, to adapt military tests for school use. These psychologists believed that tests offered great promise for improving educational placement, educational planning, and vocational planning. Unfortunately, many who first used them assumed that these tests were better instruments than they were. Rothney, Danielson, and Heiman have concluded that this problem is still a serious one. They state their analysis of the problem as follows:

If one were to take 1916, the year in which the Stanford Binet was published, as a base year, and appraise the accomplishments in testing for counseling since that time, the results would be discouraging. The measurement in the guidance movement that began with such promise has failed to meet the expectations that had been raised by its auspicious start. When counselors seek tests that meet the standards measurement experts have themselves called essential, the quest is generally unrewarding. Currently they get only an approximation of what they need . . . Tests and use of tests may be improved as a result of increasing sophistication and consequent demands for higher standards by users. The discouraging lack of progress to date may have occurred because test users have not learned what to seek from test publishers. Their failure to require high quality tests has resulted in huge production and sales of instruments that cannot possibly do what is claimed for them. It does not seem likely that there will be a significant improvement until the level of sophistication of test users has been raised. . . .[11]

Unwise use of tests by poorly qualified workers accounts, in part, for the failure of tests to make the contribution to guidance which was at first expected of them. Scores obtained from tests were too frequently accepted as precise measures and used to solve students'

11 J. W. M. Rothney, P. W. Danielson, and R. A. Heiman, *Measurement for Guidance* (New York: Harper & Row, Publishers, 1959), p. 320.

problems when they should have been perceived as crude measures to be used only along with other data to help students to understand themselves.

Other guidance workers used tests to fortify their authoritarian relationship with their clients. They used test scores to support their judgments and to impress students and parents with their expert knowledge. When their judgments proved to be wrong they criticized the tests. This same authoritarian attitude was reflected in such a popular discussion topic as "How to Get Students to Abandon Unrealistic Vocational Goals." Though many of them gave lip service to the idea that youths be permitted to decide such matters for themselves, these authoritarian workers really believed that they knew what was best for students, and that many students were not capable of making their own decisions.

On the other hand, during this same period tests provided researchers with effective tools for appraising the success with which subject matter was mastered when different teaching methods were used, for diagnosing learning problems, and for studying individual differences. Thus, we see that in spite of their weaknesses, tests helped qualified workers to understand human behavior.

This same period produced many of America's leading psychologists and psychiatrists. Frequently they used the clinical data which they obtained from their patients to better understand human growth and development and to formulate personality theories. Because of the tremendous impact of Freud and the influence of the mental hygiene movement in developing material for laymen, psychiatrists and psychologists also attracted the attention of laymen during this period. Parents, especially, were inclined to give serious attention to these specialists' advice on child-rearing practices. This influence quickly spilled over into the schools, as was noted in the discussion of the mental hygiene movement.

Toward the end of this period a number of psychologists produced texts designed for school people who were concerned with counseling and the use of tests. One of the books, Carl R. Rogers' *Counseling and Psychotherapy*,[12] deserves special attention because it challenged the counselor's authoritarian relationship with clients. Rogers' work also deserves special recognition because he and his colleagues introduced the systematic use of the recorder for im-

12 Carl R. Rogers, *Counseling and Psychotherapy* (Boston: Houghton Mifflin Company, 1942).

proving supervised practice in counseling, and for research in both the study of the counseling process and the growth achieved by clients.

With World War II the need once again arose for quick recruiting and selecting of specialized personnel for industry and military services. At first some leaders turned to tests for a quick answer. But others used all the data at their command to screen candidates for especially responsible, difficult tasks. The latter made some substantial contributions to helping man understand man.[13]

As the war progressed, military leaders became more and more concerned about rehabilitating casualities with mental illness. Significant results were achieved by mental-health teams. Within these mental-health teams psychologists were given increasingly greater responsibility for psychotherapy. This practice carried over into the treatment of veterans in Veterans Administration hopitals after the war. It also changed the emphasis in graduate education programs for clinical psychologists and encouraged the development of a new branch of psychology: counseling psychology. Psychologists' increased interest in counseling and psychotherapy is evidenced by the large number of counseling books written by psychologists in the decade following the war. This change in the psychologists' perception of his role also caused the school counselor to reevaluate and to redefine his professional competencies and job role.[14]

At the close of the war special attention was given to educational and vocational planning at military separation centers. The Veterans Administration provided veterans with counseling and insisted that they present reasonable vocational plans when they applied for vocational training and college programs. These veteran centers made college administrators aware of the need for counseling service in their own institutions.

Since World War II there have been two significant trends in the field of guidance: increased interest in research, and increased interest in the development of special professional education for the guidance workers. Today, most recognized professional journals in guidance and counseling psychology have a backlog of acceptable professional papers; and the proportion of papers concerned with

13 Offices of Strategic Services Assessment Staff, *Assessment of Men* (New York: Holt, Rinehart & Winston, Inc., 1948).

14 *Counselor Preparation* (New York: National Vocational Guidance Association, 1949).

research is much higher now than it was fifteen years ago.[15] In addition, many new professional journals have been introduced since 1945: *American Journal of Psychotherapy, Group Psychotherapy, International Journal of Group Psychotherapy, International Journal of Social Psychiatry, Journal of Counseling Psychology, Journal of College Student Personnel, Vocational Guidance Quarterly, Journal of Student Personnel Association for Teacher Education,* and *Counselor Education and Supervision.*

Accompanying these changes has come substantial strengthening of the professional organizations which attract guidance and student personnel workers. For example, the American Personnel and Guidance Association was formed in 1952 from four independent organizations. Today it is a powerful organization with over eighteen thousand members. In 1945 the American Psychological Association had only approximately four thousand members; today it has over twenty thousand members.

Finally, we must take cognizance of the National Defense Education Act. Obviously, it is too early to assess the full impact of this act, but already it has provided financial aid for college students, professional education for many guidance workers who were inadequately prepared for their duties, and financial assistance for schools to expand guidance services. Although it was designed primarily to improve the identification, guidance, and education of gifted youth, it also should encourage school personnel to give more attention to the problems of individuals from every learning level.

The Present Situation

WHAT is the counseling situation in the United States today? This is a difficult question to answer because we lack comprehensive research evidence and because the evidence we have suggests that the quality of guidance services varies considerably from one school to another. However, published descriptions of guidance practices and other sources suggest that much progress has been made since the end of World War II. For example, schools today appear to be employing better qualified guidance workers, people who know what they should be expected to do and who are insisting that their role be properly defined. Guidance services seem to be better.

15 Fortunately, funds for research in this area also have been increased substantially during this period.

Graduate programs for school counselors appear to be markedly improved. More funds are available for research, and the quality of research has improved.

On the other hand, there is need for more improvement in every one of the areas listed above. More and better qualified people are needed to meet the needs of youth. In many instances, job descriptions should be reexamined and redefined to insure that duties assigned to a given individual are compatible and that the school is making the best use of each worker's qualifications. Adequate standards must be developed for the evaluation and accreditation of graduate programs for the preparation of guidance workers. Finally, as Chapter 17 will indicate, there is a great need for systematic evaluation of guidance services.

Guidance workers today are faced with a number of problems that are caused at least in part, and in some instances primarily, by conditions outside of the school. If, however, the school experiences are to have meaning for the pupils who are influenced by these adverse conditions, the school personnel must assume an important role in rehabilitating these youngsters and in developing their potentialities. For example, although we have always had some neglected, unwanted children, there seems to be an increase in recent years in children who are reared in the slums by irresponsible unwed mothers. Many of these children are also the ones who feel rejected at school and drop out at the earliest possible moment. Usually they have no real ego-involvement anywhere. This kind of person, as Gordon Allport points out, is forced to be reactive against constant threats and deprivations:

When the ego is not actively engaged the individual becomes reactive. He lives a life of ugly protests, finding outlets in complaints, strikes, above all in scapegoating; in this condition he is ripe prey for a demagogue whose whole purpose is to focus and exploit the aggressive outbursts of non-participating egos.[16]

For these neglected youth, the leader of the delinquent gang assumes the role of the demagogue. The large number of these youngsters, and others who are less inclined to be delinquent but who dropped out of school without salable job skills, has led to the

16 Gordon W. Allport, "The Psychology of Participation," *Psychological Review*, LII (1945), 126.

recognition of the problem as a serious one even by national political leaders. Obviously guidance workers cannot solve this problem by themselves, but they can try to identify these youngsters early in their school career,[17] and to enlist the assistance of teachers and administrators in trying to make school more meaningful for them. Prevention appears to be much more promising than rehabilitation. If, however, really effective preventive measures are to be taken, the parents must be helped to become more responsible and conditions within the community must be improved. A thorough program would involve legislation and legal action that even the most courageous political leaders are reluctant to push. For the present both prevention and rehabilitation are needed, and both require the cooperation of school staff, therapists in community treatment centers, and political leaders.

The notion of identifying potential problems early and preventing them from developing into serious ones is not limited to the kinds of youngsters described above. Consider the following examples of two youngsters who were identified early and helped before their problems became serious ones. Although change in their attitudes toward their teachers, and school in general, led to their referral, there are many other clues that suggest a student's need for referral to a counselor; such clues are discussed in Chapter 9.

Betty was a fourth-grader who had been very interested in school, had done very well, and had seemed to like her teacher. When she quite suddenly exhibited a change in attitude, the teacher discussed her case with the school counselor and made a referral. During a matter of five or six sessions the counselor dealt with a serious conflict Betty had had with her mother, a conflict which developed out of the death of Betty's dog, and the death of her grandmother who had lived with the family. Apparently the grandmother had been a wonderful mother to Betty's mother, but because of illness and old age she became for Betty a cantakerous, inconsiderate woman for whom Betty saw little reason to grieve. However, Betty did grieve for her lost dog. Both had died at about the same time so that Betty and her mother were grieving together. As they cried and talked about their loss, the mother was horrified to learn that Betty was grieving not for her grandmother but for her dog. Her mother's immediate reaction, and subsequent behavior, created a real conflict between the two. This conflict was carried over into Betty's re-

17 See the section on sociometric methods in Chapter 9.

lations with her teacher. When Betty learned, with a competent counselor's help, to express these feelings, she came to understand them better and to understand why her mother reacted as she did. With the counselor's assistance she also was able to reestablish communication with her mother, and she soon returned to her normal school behavior.

The case of Jim, an eleventh-grader, was more difficult because the source of the conflict was not detected so soon. Over a period of twelve to eighteen months Jim had changed from a cooperative, and perhaps overconforming, boy to a hostile, uncooperative one. Though never a top student, he had always done average or better work; by the time his father asked for help, Jim was failing in one subject and doing poorly in the others. The request for help was precipitated by a brawl in which the father's nose was broken. When the father sought help, he indicated that he felt Jim's case was hopeless. During eight sessions (the counselor felt these were not sufficient, but Jim did not wish to have more) the boy described what appeared to be a good father-son relationship prior to this period, expressed his hostile feelings toward his father, discovered many positive feelings toward his father which he thought he had lost, learned through role playing with his counselor how to tell his father how he felt toward him and what the father did that turned Jim against him, and began developing a better relationship with his father. With Jim's knowledge and permission the counselor also met with Jim's teachers to discuss his case and to ask for their assistance in helping Jim rehabilitate himself. Obviously, the situation was not immediately corrected, but it did improve markedly over a period of seven or eight months. The point is that Jim was helped, that his problem was caught before it drove him to more serious trouble, and that perhaps he could have been helped more easily had the problem been discovered still earlier.

Although counselors are usually assigned to secondary schools, they also are needed in the elementary schools if the earliest stages of a pupil's development are to be guided and if pupils in need of help are to be identified early and serious problems be prevented. For the same purpose, schools will need remedial teachers, school psychologists, and school social workers. Remedial teachers are needed to help teachers diagnose and treat learning problems, and to assist with the development of study skills. School psychologists are needed to help teachers assess school readiness, to help classroom and remedial teachers diagnose certain learning problems, to help teachers appraise social and emotional adjustment, and to help teachers develop school policies and make decisions with reference to educational placement. Finally, school social workers are needed to work with pupils and their parents on family problems, to interpret the school program to parents, and to explain to the school staff how forces outside the school may be affecting a pupil's school adjustment.

The above emphasis on prevention suggests that guidance workers must be concerned about all the pupils, not just the physically handicapped, the mentally handicapped, the emotionally disturbed, the asocial, and the gifted. Still, the preoccupation with these special groups is understandable. The intellectually gifted have been the subject of particular concern in recent years. Though they were regarded as a neglected group in the past, society's need for college-educated manpower has encouraged many schools to develop or reintroduce programs for the intellectually gifted. However, that problem is still by no means solved.

Today business, industry, educational institutions, and the professions are competing for the services of college-educated persons. Fortunately, the United States is producing enough youth capable of earning college degrees to satisfy this demand. Unfortunately, however, that capacity is not always realized.

Some time ago the National Manpower Council described the situation as follows:

Today, less than half of those capable of acquiring a college degree enter college. About two-fifths of those who start college—many with superior ability—do not graduate. For every high school graduate who eventually earns a doctoral degree, there are twenty-five others who have the intellectual ability to acquire that degree but do not.[18]

The committee which prepared the Fifty-Seventh Yearbook of the National Society for the Study of Education asked, "Why does the system not produce more highly literate and professionally trained people to meet the demands for engineers, research scientists, and school and college teachers?" They answered their own question as follows:

18 *National Manpower Council: A Policy for Scientific and Professional Manpower* (New York: Columbia University Press, 1953), p. 83.

Although one could answer with truth that the American educational system today does produce a higher proportion and also a greater absolute number of such people than it has ever done before, and than any other nation has ever done, yet many educators are loath to make this kind of answer because they feel that American education does not do as good a job with gifted children as it might and should.[19]

Doing better than others gives us little comfort when we know that we can, and that we must, do much better still.

But, however important the gifted child is to our nation's welfare, school personnel are expected to help every pupil develop his potentialities. Though even laymen recognize that this is a very difficult goal to achieve, few, if any, would advocate that schools give it up as an objective. C. Gilbert Wrenn notes that this goal is what makes the American teacher's task the toughest in the world:

He is asked to see each student as a distinct individual who represents the hope of continued progress in the future and who is not to be submerged in the group. The goal is to understand the various phases of development that affect the student's intellectual growth and to assist him in making appropriate adjustments and choices along the way. This emphasis is seen in both public and private schools, and at all educational levels.[20]

To fulfill these expectations teachers need the assistance of the guidance specialist.

What is more, it is this same concern for the development of each individual's potentialities that has committed our nation to educating all the children of all the people. Our very way of life is dependent, in part at least, on this great experiment in mass education. For citizens to act as intelligent free men, the best is required of everyone. Therefore, schools must try to help each pupil discover and develop his potentialities. Since emotional problems tend to interfere with efficient learning, schools must be concerned about each pupil's mental health in order that he may develop his potentialities.

19 *Education for the Gifted*, Fifty-Seventh Yearbook of the National Society for the Study of Education (Chicago: University of Chicago Press, 1958), p. 4.
20 C. Gilbert Wrenn, *The Counselor in a Changing World* (Washington, D.C.: American Personnel and Guidance Association, 1962), p. 2.

Guidance Services

THE preceding discussion established the need for guidance in our schools. The following discussion demonstrates how each of the basic guidance services meets the needs of youth.

Counseling services are needed when a reasonably well-adjusted pupil encounters problems that he cannot solve either by himself or with the assistance of such important other people as parents or teachers. At least most experts agree that a pupil can profit from the help of a qualified counselor when he is in such situations as these: (1) he feels that those whose love and affection he has relied on have let him down; (2) he loses someone dear to him; (3) he feels unsure of love and affection from those whom he loves; (4) he feels guilty about letting others down or hurting them; (5) he does something which he believes is wrong and feels guilty about it; (6) he knows what he should do, and feels guilty about not doing it; (7) he cannot, or will not, do what those whose recognition he seeks expect; (8) he is placed in a situation where he is unsure what he is expected to do; (9) he has the necessary prerequisite knowledge, skills, and abilities to do what is expected, but he doubts his ability to succeed; (10) he must make a decision which will please some whose recognition he seeks and disappoint others; (11) he is faced with a problem for which he sees several alternative solutions, and he cannot decide which to choose. These are but a few of the problems which everyone faces at one time or another. Some of them are very difficult for even healthy, mature adults to solve; little wonder then that they interfere with children's learning efficiency.

The *child study* service is needed: (1) to determine a pupil's readiness for a school experience or a next phase in the school program—e.g., to begin formal instruction in reading; (2) to help pupils and their teachers determine whether the pupils are making satisfactory progress in their school work; (3) to identify and to diagnose learning problems and to plan appropriate remedial programs for individuals; (4) to identify pupils for special programs involving exceptional children, including both the gifted and the talented as well as the various types of handicapped children; (5) to help individuals discover what they feel they need to know about themselves in order to make intelligent educational and vocational plans; (6) to help pupils to identify and to cope with those distracting and disturbing forces which are interfering with efficient learning and healthy living.

Orientation is designed to help pupils prepare for and adjust to new situations as they progress through the schools—e.g., from home to kindergarten, elementary to junior high school, and senior high school to college or to employment.

The *information service* is a cooperative effort of teachers, counselors, and librarians to obtain appropriate materials, to organize them for the pupils' most efficient use, and to help pupils understand the significance of the materials for them when they cannot do so by themselves. The need for educational and vocational information is obvious. Social information is needed, too. As children grow up, their questions suggest that they want and need a great variety of information.

Educational and vocational planning is especially important in the United States where we have a strong tradition that every man has the right to choose his life work. To choose well a pupil must understand his abilities, aptitudes, and interests, and be familiar with vocational opportunities available to him. He also must be able to relate this information to his perception of himself and to his other important life goals. Similar knowledge of himself and of the opportunities available to him is needed to make intelligent educational plans. For most students these are difficult decisions, and for many the assistance of well-qualified counselors is needed.

Job placement can help a student avoid drifting into a job, often obtained with the assistance of friends and relatives, that has little or no relationship to his most salable skills. For best vocational placement, most youngsters need assistance in identifying and in developing their salable skills, in identifying appropriate jobs for these skills, and in selling themselves to a prospective employer.

A good *follow-up service* can provide a high school's students with helpful information on what they may expect when they leave school, and provide the staff with suggestions that they can use to improve the school's program. Both types of information are needed by every school.

A carefully planned program for *leadership and social development* provides for the identification and training of prospective leaders, encourages school activities which provide leadership experience, and assists in the development of meaningful social and extra-class activities. It also enlists pupils' assistance in planning and developing meaningful social experiences.

Except for educational and vocational planning, job placement, and follow-up services, which are not essential for most pupils below grade seven, the basic services described above are needed by all youth. However, those who work with elementary-school pupils must recognize that the children are less independent than older students are, and therefore guidance workers must involve parents more in the treatment process than they would with older pupils. Though teacher participation should be encouraged at every level, it is especially important at the elementary level. Even when excellent results are obtained from work with the children, pupils usually need the assistance of their parents and teachers in order to change their behavior. Usually help must be provided for parents at the same time it is being provided for a pupil. Parent-education seminars and group work for parents should be encouraged, especially for parents of elementary-school children. Where this cannot be provided by school personnel, it should be encouraged by appropriate community agencies. Both elementary and secondary schools should give more attention to the prevention of mental health problems.

Obviously, a youth's way of expressing his need for help will vary with his maturity, and his ability to profit from verbal treatment methods will be limited by his verbal skills. This means, for example, that those who counsel elementary pupils must understand children of this age and know how to communicate with them in order to adapt the basic principles of counseling to the child's maturity. This understanding and skill is required at every other level, too. Guidance workers also must understand the school setting in which they function.

In each of these guidance services, attention is focused on the individual pupil. Even when guidance is provided in groups, its purpose is to help the individual. And this is as it should be, for the particular problems that the pupil has arise out of circumstances which are peculiar to him. Furthermore, these same experiences which make the individual's problems unique also shape his perception of himself and his environment, influence how he attacks a problem, and determine the extent to which he can use in the future what he learns from solving a problem. By focusing on the individual, guidance helps the pupil to become increasingly more proficient in recognizing and using his own resources in problem solving.

The Essentials of a Guidance Program

Now that we have defined guidance and adjustment, reviewed the history of the guidance movement, examined our present situation, and described briefly the guidance services, we are ready to consider the essentials of a good guidance program.

Guidance services must be accepted as an essential part of the school program. Failure to provide these services suggests that the school is not committed to helping youngsters to improve their adjustment and to develop their potentialities. With respect to developing the potentialities of the gifted, Lewis Terman recently wrote as follows:

Finally, any serious attempt to provide special opportunities for gifted children will require the services of well-trained psychologists and school counselors. Psychologists are necessary to supervise the testing program that identifies those who are superior in intelligence or have special talents, and counselors are needed in the junior high school and beyond for educational and vocational guidance. . . . In fact, more and better counselors are imperative for the encouragement of talents at all levels.[21]

The support of the school administration is necessary in initiating and carrying out a good guidance program. Both the superintendent and the principal must recognize guidance as one of the school's important responsibilities: they should take an active part in the guidance program, give recognition to the staff for their services in the program, and secure financial support for it.

Cooperation among teachers, administrators, and specialists is essential. When several persons attempt to help a child independently, they may confuse him instead of help him. Cooperation also is necessary in initiating a guidance program, in coordinating guidance services, and in formulating guidance policies.

Everyone must recognize that the classroom teacher plays an important role in the guidance program. The teacher sees pupils regularly, observes them in a variety of situations, and can, therefore, help them with certain problems and refer them to appropriate sources for other assistance. Even without the assistance of a spe-

21 Lewis M. Terman, "What Education for the Gifted Should Accomplish," *Education for the Gifted,* Fifty-Seventh Yearbook of the National Society for the Study of Education (Chicago: University of Chicago Press, 1958), p. 19.

cialist he can do much to help his pupils by cooperating with colleagues in case conferences.

There is no substitute for a good educational program staffed by competent teachers who are genuinely interested in their pupils' welfare.

Every pupil should feel that there is someone in his school to whom he can turn for help when he is troubled. Moreover, the staff should realize that a pupil cannot be helped until he recognizes that he has a problem and wants to do something about it.

There is a place in the guidance program for qualified specialists who have time set aside for guidance. It is a fundamental need of every school to have a counselor who can counsel pupils and help teachers appraise school progress, intellectual growth, social development, and emotional adjustment. For a good guidance program a school also needs remedial teachers, school psychologists, and school social workers.

Essential guidance services should be available to every child when he needs them.

Guidance services must be carefully defined. Until they are understood by pupils, parents, and teachers, they will not be used effectively.

Responsibilities for guidance services must be carefully assigned. In addition to making certain that individuals are professionally qualified to provide a service, the administrator must, when assigning several responsibilities to one person, ascertain whether these various services are compatible.

Guidance services alone cannot be expected to insure good adjustment for all pupils. If a school is to make its maximum contribution, teachers, administrators, and guidance specialists must understand and accept the basic principles of positive mental health and use them as guides in defining school objectives and school policies, in developing curricula, in planning special school programs, in developing an adequate guidance program, and in defining criteria for evaluating not only the guidance services but also the entire school program.

SUGGESTED READINGS

1. GORDON, IRA J. *The Teacher as a Guidance Worker*. New York: Harper & Row, Publishers, 1956.

> *As the title suggests, this book was designed to guide the teacher in his daily work of helping boys and girls live more richly. Chapter 1.*
> a] What is guidance?
> b] Why must teachers be concerned about the uniqueness of the individual?
> c] In what ways should guidance be concerned with instruction?

2. HUTSON, P. W. *The Guidance Function in Education*. New York: Appleton-Century-Crofts, 1958.

> *This book was written for the entire professional staff in a school. Its author believes that guidance is a responsibility of teachers and principals as well as counselors and deans. Chapters 1–5.*
> a] To what extent does the United States have an open-class structure? How may this condition influence a student's choice of vocation?
> b] How has the development of social work in the United States affected the guidance movement?
> c] What are the implications of child-centered teaching for guidance?
> d] What research evidence can you cite to prove the need for improved guidance services?
> e] What are the basic purposes of guidance?

3. JAHODA, MARIE. *Current Concepts of Positive Mental Health*. New York: Basic Books, Inc., 1958.

> *The first in a series of publications sponsored by the Joint Commission on Mental Illness and Health, this book examines the current assumptions about the nature of man and society, and presents a scholarly definition of positive mental health. Chapters 2 and 3.*
> a] Why is absence of mental illness an unsatisfactory criterion for mental health?
> b] How does a well-adjusted person perceive himself?
> c] What is unique about Maslow's self-actualizing people?

4. KORNER, IJA N. "Mental Health vs. Mental Illness," *Mental Hygiene*, XLII (1958), 315–20.

> a] How does the healthy person differ from the mentally ill in ability to use help offered him?
> b] How does the author differentiate between the mentally ill and the handicapped? How can the teacher make use of this distinction?

5. McDANIEL, H. G., J. E. LALLAS, J. A. SAUM, and J. L. GILMORE. *Readings in Guidance*. New York: Holt, Rinehart & Winston, Inc., 1959.

This is a compilation of important and practical professional papers. Sections I, III, and IV from Part One.
a] How did John Dewey influence the vocational guidance movement?
b] What defense do these scholars offer for the college professor teaching values as well as knowledge in pre-Civil War days?
c] How can the teachers assist the counselor?
d] How can the counselor assist the teachers?

6. MAY, ROLLO. "A Psychologist Looks at Mental Health in Today's World," *Mental Hygiene*, XXXVIII (1954), 1–11.

The author describes those people who need psychological or psychiatric services.
a] What percentage of our society will require some psychological or psychiatric aid in order to cope with their problems?
b] What kinds of people need psychological services?

7. PETERS, HERMAN J. and GAIL F. FARWELL. *Guidance: A Developmental Approach*. Chicago: Rand McNally & Co., 1959.

This is a beginning text in guidance which encourages the reader to examine himself and to search for underlying guidance principles. Chapter 1.
a] What is guidance?
b] What can guidance do for those who seek it?
c] On what basic principles should the guidance program be developed?

8. SHOBEN, E. J. "Toward a Concept of Normal Personality," *American Psychologist*, XII (1957), 183–89.

a] What is the person like who has learned to fulfill his distinctively human potentialities?

9. WRENN, C. GILBERT. *The Counselor in a Changing World*. Washington, D.C.: American Personnel and Guidance Association, 1962.

One of the most significant guidance publications of the sixties, this book should be read by every prospective counselor.
a] Why is guidance primarily an American phenomenon?
b] What changes in American society may we expect in the near future? How will these changes influence the schools and guidance services?

2

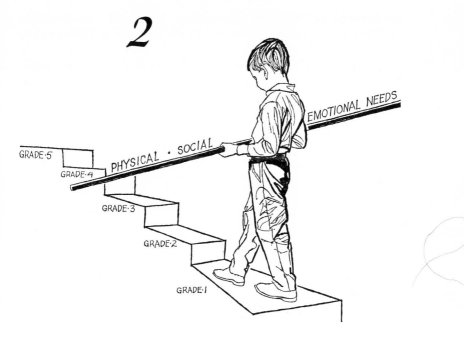

Understanding Pupils' Needs

BEFORE a graduate student learns about counseling, it is important that he have adequate knowledge of human behavior. For this reason, the study of pupils' needs and their methods of satisfying these needs is discussed as background for Chapter 3, on the counseling relationship.

But understanding the pupil whom he attempts to help is essential not only for the counselor but also for those who provide the other guidance services. In fact, the classroom teacher, especially at the elementary level, is often the one who first recognizes unmet needs of his pupils and helps them find ways of satisfying these needs. Furthermore, it is the counselor's job to help teachers in this task; therefore, most of the case materials for this chapter are taken from the classroom.

That children have basic needs is an accepted fact. Some needs are common to all members of the human race. Other needs are acquired in the process of growing up; these latter are often the products of our culture. When needs are not met and the process of growth is thwarted, problems develop. Every guidance worker must be sensitive to children's needs, contribute to their satisfaction with the resources available to him, recognize serious problems when they arise, and seek the help of other professional workers when he is unable to provide the necessary assistance.

Most students of child development in this country agree that the children in our modern culture have the following needs:

1. Essential physical requirements
2. Understanding of physical and emotional changes
3. Self-acceptance
4. Acceptance, understanding, and love from others
5. Recognition from others
6. Understanding of responsibilities to others
7. Development of independence
8. Management of fear and guilt feelings
9. Ability to face reality

These categories of needs are *not* mutually exclusive; they do not function independently of one another. Neither is the present-day occurrence of a need sharply separated from its occurrence in the past. Into each situation each child carries his whole personal history. In one situation this backlog of experience helps him solve a problem. In another situation this same background interferes with his solving a problem. Sometimes the new situation exposes old emotional wounds, bringing out fears, guilt feelings, or disappointments that prevent the child from using all his resources to meet the situation.

Because he had been punished for forgetting his lines in the Christmas program when he was in second grade, Danny, for example, was afraid to participate in the skit which his fourth-grade class agreed to do for the school's PTA program. However, he did not say that he was afraid when selected for the leading role. Instead, he merely refused to do it, and he spoke so sharply that the teacher became annoyed with him. Fortunately, she did not reprimand him before the group; later, when she spoke with him privately, she discovered the real reason he had refused to participate. Acting on this information, she gradually reduced Danny's fear by providing him with a series of small-scale experiences, speaking to or performing before the group, in which he gained satisfaction of his need for recognition from others. Thus, one need was worked with indirectly through the satisfaction of another.

Needs are differently related to each other in different situations. Though a number of needs may be motivating behavior at a given time, some of them usually have priority over others. Again, the satisfaction of one need may give rise to another, or the satisfaction of one need may interfere with the satisfaction of another. Or a single response can sometimes satisfy several needs at once.

When a child's needs are not satisfied, he may become anxious or disappointed. He may feel that he has been a failure and withdraw, he may become aggressive, or he may simply be baffled and not know what to do. The condition of a child when he fails to satisfy these basic needs is sometimes called frustration.

Marjorie, for example, had often wished that her family could afford a piano, for she and her friends had had a great deal of fun at parties singing together and playing musical games. She knew that her parents liked to play and she wanted to learn to play too. Then one day, when a neighbor got a job in a distant city, her parents bought the neighbor's piano. She asked to take lessons, and her parents granted her request. But before long Marjorie noticed that her parents often interrupted her practice to correct her mistakes. One evening Marjorie's mother overheard her talking with Sally, her best friend. She said, "They think I should play like they do. They tell me to practice when I want to play with you. When I want to practice, they nag at me about all my mistakes. Is it that way at your house, Sally?"

Marjorie was unhappy because she felt her parents did not understand her. Of course, this eight-year-old had to be reminded of her responsibility to practice regularly to make her lessons worthwhile, but she resented nagging. Instead, she wanted praise and recognition from her parents. Marjorie's parents could not sense all her needs and could not help her perform well because they were too much concerned with their own need for recognition through Marjorie's skill. Then, too, Marjorie had looked upon the piano as an attraction for group activity in her home, but she now felt that it was taking her away from her friends. As a result, she was disgusted and unhappy. Once her parents learned how she felt, it was much easier for them to understand her behavior and to help her.

Martha, another elementary-school child, one Friday evening forgot a book which she planned to take home, and returned to the classroom to pick it up. Leaving the room, she noticed Mrs. Murphy's new pen and took it without knowing why she did so, for she owned a good pen. She felt so afraid, ashamed, and guilty Friday night that she could not sleep. On Saturday she was in an unhappy turmoil of guilt. Then in Sunday school her class happened to talk about the Ten Commandments! On her way home alone Martha cried hard.

Mrs. Murphy was searching for her pen to make out some reports on Monday morning when Martha came into the room. Although she noticed that Martha was unusually quiet, she did not pay much attention to her since she was momentarily concerned about her own needs. When class began, she asked the children to help find her pen and then borrowed a pupil's pen for her work.

By the time school was out on Monday, Martha felt miserable. She had not been able to accomplish anything all day. She was one of the last to finish putting away her books. Mrs. Murphy had noticed that Martha had had a bad day and said, "Would you like to help me a few minutes?" She felt she should try to find out what was bothering Martha. Martha said "Yes" but wondered to herself how she had been caught. When the last child had left, she began crying. Between sobs she said, "How did you find out that I took your pen? I'm so sorry. I don't know why I did it."

Sensibly and perceptively, Mrs. Murphy gently helped relieve Martha's feelings of guilt and fear. She concluded that there were other needs involved in the problem. Further study by Mrs. Murphy and the school social worker revealed that the serious illness of Martha's father had forced the girl's mother to take a job. Martha's act was her way of revealing her feeling that she had been forgotten.

When a child behaves as Martha did, there is a good reason for it, but the reasons for the behavior are not always as easily discovered as Martha's reasons were. Arthur Jersild explains the relationship between need satisfaction and behavior as follows:

The more wholesome, healthy, and spontaneous the person is in his relations with others, and in his capacity to be himself and to draw on his own resources, the less he probably will need to cheat others or to steal from them, to be cruel to them, or to take advantage of them in other ways. His good moral conduct would be a feature of his own integrity rather than a calculated kind of conformity to an external code of conduct. He would have no need to use honesty as a "policy" to curb his dishonest tendencies, for the more genuinely he was true to himself the less occasion there would be to play false with others.

. . . By virtue of being accepted and respected from the earliest period of his life, he will have the freedom to experiment with life, to test his powers, to discover the limits and boundaries of his abilities, to explore and experiment in his relations with others, and to express his feelings, including feelings of affection, anger, fear, without danger of humiliation or risk of status. In such an atmosphere he is free to discover himself, to develop his potentials, to find a place for himself in relation to others, and to develop ideas and attitudes concerning his own worth in a healthy and unencumbered way.

. . . They [failures, reminders of limitations, and rejection] may have the effect of humiliating the child by depreciating his worth in a manner that does no good to society and does him a great harm. Much of the failure at school is contrived. Much of the depreciation children encounter there is based upon false evaluations. Some of it rests upon a primitive approach to education which in some schools has a savage intensity. The cards are stacked against many children. They are stacked when teachers, in league with the prevailing competitive pressures in our society, attach greater importance to certain school achievements than they merit, and apply pressures which make the child feel that he is worthless in all respects because he does not happen to be a top performer in some respects.[1]

Hopkins further defines the relation between the child's need and his performance.

It makes a lot of difference whether a school is organized around the needs of teachers or those of children. Adults can, if they wish, work cooperatively with children on their needs, but children cannot, even if they wish, work cooperatively with adults on their needs. Since need begins and sustains action, the depth of need-tension determines the amount of energy released. The understanding the individual has of himself determines the level at which such energy will function. If the schools expect children to release much energy operating at high levels, they must be organized around the needs of the learner.[2]

Only when the teacher is genuinely concerned about his pupils' welfare can the goal described in the previous paragraph be

1 Arthur T. Jersild, *In Search of Self* (New York: Bureau of Publications, Teachers College, Columbia University, 1952), pp. 35, 62, 91.

2 L. Thomas Hopkins, *The Emerging Self* (New York: Harper & Row, Publishers, 1954), p. 125.

achieved. To achieve it, the teacher must understand his pupils' needs, know how they satisfy these needs, and realize that he can discreetly adapt school experiences to meet an individual pupil's needs. Obviously, he can succeed best if he has the moral support and assistance of an understanding principal and competent guidance specialists.

Although counselors must take account of how well a pupil's basic needs are met in all phases of his life, they are particularly concerned about his school adjustment. To determine the extent to which a pupil's basic needs are being met in school and to improve his school adjustment, counselors must work very closely with the pupil's teachers. This chapter will define each of the basic needs, describe teacher behavior which contributes to the satisfaction of each need, and describe teacher behavior which interferes with the satisfaction of each need. Examples of both elementary- and secondary-school pupils' behavior are used.

Essential Physical Requirements

THE basic physical requirements include those of health, diet, balance of rest and activity, clothing and housing, and sex.

HEALTH

Tired, undernourished, and sickly children have difficulty using their mental powers efficiently. Therefore, teachers should be trained to detect signs of physical neglect and poor health, as well as the first symptoms of contagious diseases. Upon discovering these special cases, teachers should refer the children to their family physicians. Moreover, teachers and school administrators should encourage (if they cannot require) every pupil to have a thorough physical examination each fall prior to the opening of school. Not only does the medical report acquaint the teacher and parent with the child's general health, but it often helps each better to understand the child's behavior. The examination also encourages the parent to seek medical care for the child when such care is needed. Through their follow-up contacts with parents, the teachers and guidance personnel also learn which parents are not financially capable of providing medical care. At this point, they should seek the assistance of city or county welfare agencies which have funds for providing such care.

DIET

Quality of diet is an important factor for guidance workers to consider in studying pupils. For example, many pupils come to school with little or no breakfast. Knowing which pupils fall in this category helps the teacher understand why some become irritable and restless during the forenoon. Since a good breakfast helps the child get off to a good start each day, school administrators might well consider substituting a school breakfast for the customary school lunch if they do not have adequate funds to support both. Since the child is less tired in the forenoon than in the afternoon, and since the forenoon session is longer, a good breakfast should contribute more to learning efficiency than a good lunch. Of course, some children who do get their meals at home have a poorly balanced diet at every meal. This, too, is important to know.

A study of diet in school, under conditions which make the child feel free to confide in the group, sometimes reveals stories which the teacher finds almost unbelievable. Patty's report was such a story. Her fourth-grade friends were talking about the meals they had had the day before. After listening for a while, she asked, "Do you really sit down around a table and eat your meals?" Her teacher's private reactions were, "What is she talking about? What does she mean?" The teacher's own childhood experiences had convinced her that the other children's experiences were commonplace: unconsciously she had assumed that all her pupils were living in homes much like her own. She did not know that there was a very poor tenement-house section on the edge of that school district.

Fortunately, she stayed out of the discussion until she was able to accept Patty's questions as reasonable. While she was listening, she heard Patty tell about the eating habits in her home. She found that Patty's family never really had a family meal. Patty and her younger brother just shifted for themselves, and ate whatever they could prepare until the parents returned from work about seven in the evening. Then they ate with their parents, but not around the table. Each person made his own sandwiches; usually soda pop or milk was available for the children to drink.

BALANCE OF REST AND ACTIVITY

A balance of rest and activity, in addition to adequate sleep during the night, aids the pupil's learning efficiency while he is at school.

Too often, even when one activity has been the source of unrest in the classroom, teachers fail to recognize the need for change of activity. They also may fail to provide rest periods when needed, especially for young children. Obviously, if teachers are to avoid such mistakes, they must know what they can expect of their pupils in order to adjust the learning activities to the pupils' maturity.

Some teachers fail to teach with continual awareness of the relationship between the child's maturity and the assigned school tasks. Unfortunately, some still assign tasks which make demands beyond the physical and mental maturity levels of at least part of the class. For example, they often expect too much of the large teen-age pupil —both in mental tasks and in tasks which require unusual physical coordination. However, even a young child can tolerate some tedious or strenuous activities when teachers adjust periods of work to the child's maturity. For example, most first-graders can write with an ordinary pencil in doing relatively fine work, for short periods of time, without becoming tense. In this way the problem of selecting appropriate tasks is related to the problem of balancing rest and activity.

Most parents realize that children need adequate sleep to do their best work in school, but many fail to define and enforce rules which insure proper sleep. This problem exists especially for high school students. Some are involved in so many activities that they must study late to maintain good grades. Others keep late hours to convince themselves and their friends that they are grown-up. Hence, knowing what a pupil does between the time school is out in the afternoon and the time it resumes in the morning helps the teacher to understand him. Although most pupils will provide the teacher with this information, the parents' cooperation is usually needed when a pupil's routine should be changed.

CLOTHING AND HOUSING

Teachers should not expect to solve health problems through use of either counseling or remedial instruction. Neither should they expect to solve, within the classroom, problems of inadequate clothing and poor housing. Some people question whether the school should be concerned at all with these problems, and this is a reasonable criticism: educators have been inclined to accept responsibility for more services than they are adequately staffed to provide. Nevertheless, the teacher cannot avoid his responsibility to identify clothing and housing problems which affect the child's learning efficiency. The least the teacher can do is to refer these problems to appropriate community agencies; even this is not easy, since he must know something about the agencies and their services before he can make intelligent referrals.

The satisfaction of housing and clothing needs usually represents something more than protection from the elements. For example, Roger's shabby clothes, and especially his ill-fitting shoes, did not seem to worry Roger, but they did worry his sister Mabel. Every time she met Roger when she was with her ninth-grade friends she was embarrassed, and she was eventually driven to save money to buy him some decent clothes. Reasonably attractive clothes were important to Mabel, as they are to most teen-age girls—and boys. In general, a child's clothes are important to him because they determine whether he appears to be like others or different from them.

The kind of house in which the child lives is important in a similar way: of course, the way in which he is protected from the elements may affect the child's health but further, the place in which he lives may determine with whom he associates and where he associates with them. Housing, like clothing, is particularly important to the adolescent because it identifies him—both to himself and to his group.

SEX

Sex drives develop gradually as the child matures, and children develop at different rates. The fact that some children mature early and others late complicates the pupil's relationships with his classmates. Upper-grade elementary-school teachers and junior high school teachers certainly must take cognizance of the preadolescent's increasing need for varying degrees of sexual satisfaction.

Problems growing out of sex drives intensify as the adolescent matures, and are certainly complicated by the fact that the adolescent's sex drives are increasing during the period in which he is also striving for independence from adults and their imposed standards. From his parents, his church, and his friends, a child learns a moral code which governs his sexual behavior. In our social order parents usually, and churches always, frown upon sexual intercourse before marriage. Homosexual activities are generally rejected. At the same time the child hears his peers boast about their sex experiences; he wants both to be accepted by them and to satisfy his strong drives.

He also may have observed that some adults ignore that part of their moral code which prohibits the direct satisfaction of sex drives out of wedlock.

All of this confuses him. When presented with an opportunity for direct sexual satisfaction, he finds it difficult to refuse. If he takes advantage of the opportunity, at the same time feeling that sexual intercourse prior to marriage is wrong, then he develops guilt feelings. Many times these guilt feelings later interfere with his happiness during marriage. Too frequently good information which has been prepared to help the young person meet these situations is not made available to him, and he acts without understanding the consequences of his acts.

In addition to all this moral confusion, his own physical nature and the degree of his physical maturity may seem abnormal to him. If his needs are either more or less intense than he perceives those of his peers to be, he becomes concerned about being different. Both early-maturing and late-maturing youth face this problem.

If his questions about physical and emotional changes are answered when he asks them during the process of growing up, if the persons who answer his questions can understand his need for answers, and if they can help him understand the answers they give him, if he lives in an emotional climate in which he feels that he is accepted and that his associates are willing to help him discover his responsibilities to others, almost every youth can find a satisfactory solution to the problem of meeting his sex needs. Some young people, however, experience many unhappy moments because someone fails to understand them and their needs. Then they create tensions in themselves through not knowing what to do, or they satisfy these needs through approaches which create still other problems.

Helping young people understand and accept their sex drives should be the parents' responsibility. Since many parents either do not know how to meet this responsibility or choose to avoid it, many pupils turn to teachers, counselors, and school administrators for assistance. School personnel should not ignore this problem. Neither should they encourage staff to attempt to help when they are improperly prepared to do so. However, within the limits of their competencies, the staff should try to be of use to both parents and pupils. Teachers may help children answer their questions about physical and emotional changes by talking with them, providing appropriate reading material, and making referral to appropriate school and community personnel. Teachers and administrators should plan classroom and extra-class activities in which boys and girls can learn to work and play together. Furthermore, school personnel can in some cases provide for adult classes to help parents become better qualified to shoulder this and other responsibilities.

Unfortunately, some teachers and counselors have difficulty accepting their pupils' sex needs, especially the sex needs of elementary-school children. Such workers feel that the child's sex needs have been exaggerated, and that they are therefore justified in ignoring them. Other workers have never felt comfortable when discussing the topic. Because they are embarrassed, and sometimes poorly informed, they tend to handle their pupils' questions about sex badly. With the help of an understanding principal or supervisor both these types of teachers and counselors can increase their proficiency in dealing with these needs.

The problem of answering questions and providing pupils with information will be discussed in greater detail in the following section. It also will be discussed in Chapters 4 and 10.

Understanding of Physical and Emotional Changes

As indicated earlier, the nine categories of pupils' needs are not mutually exclusive. In particular, there is considerable overlap in the following categories: need for knowledge and understanding of his physical and emotional changes; need for acceptance of himself; need for acceptance, understanding, and love from others; need for recognition from others; and need for understanding of responsibility to others. When, for example, the pupil asks about physical and emotional changes, he usually is not only trying to understand the changes which are occurring within himself and to accept the new self, but is also trying to learn what others expect from him so that he may win recognition and acceptance from them. Moreover, the pupil who cannot accept others probably cannot accept himself. Nevertheless, these need-categories must be studied separately to understand each fully and to learn how each relates to the others.

The need for knowledge and understanding of physical and emotional changes involves such a wide variety of problems for youth that only a few examples will be discussed here. Young people are often concerned about their size, posture, personal grooming, condition of skin, appetite, health, menstruation, and sex organs. They are also concerned, while they are changing from the child to the young adult stage, about such problems as their relations with their peers, with the opposite sex, with their family, and with their church. They also struggle to assess their aptitudes.

The school working by itself, of course, cannot help its pupils work out these problems fully. However, by trying to accept each pupil for what he is and by trying to help him understand the factors which influence his behavior, teachers and counselors can often do a great deal. Further, the counselor often has an opportunity to serve as a resource person who can help both the pupil and his parents. Parents find it comparatively easy to work with their child when they realize that he is going through a change which is normal for him at that age. Sometimes teachers feel that they can do little more than try to discover what role other agencies are playing; this much in itself is important.

Pupils often have questions about these changes in their behavior. They appreciate having parents, teachers, and counselors make it easy for them to ask their questions. In helping pupils find answers, adults should look carefully at their own responses. The following questions may help the adult evaluate the way in which he answers a child's questions:

—Did I take into account the child's emotional readiness for the information requested? Did I understand how he felt, and how strongly he felt, about the question before I answered it?
—Did I show the good sense to stop talking when the child expressed satisfaction with my answer to his questions?
—Did I take cognizance of the child's sensitivity in choosing a place in which to answer his questions?
—Did I make the facts meaningful to the child? Did he understand what I attempted to explain? How do I know that he understood what I said?
—Did I help him consider how he may use the facts? When, for example, he asked questions about his interests and aptitudes, did I realize that adult answers alone are not sufficient? Did I also help him examine how he can use these facts in defining his life goals?
—Did I inject my own prejudices into the answers?
—Was I really equipped to help him find the answers? Did I recognize when I lacked the facts to answer his questions?
—Was I aware of the serious implications involved in pursuing questions which should be answered by special personnel? Did I know the resource

people who could be called upon to help? Did I know how to make the referral to the appropriate person and make it in a manner so as to increase the effectiveness of his services for the child?

No one need be embarrassed because he does not know how to help a pupil find the answers to his questions or because he does not have all the skills needed. He must, however, recognize his inadequacies and know when and where to seek help. The above questions should help him discover what his current shortcomings are so that he may try to correct them. He may obtain further help from Chapter 4, which discusses ways of helping a pupil accept and use personal information.

Self-Acceptance

WHILE we readily agree that we never seem to understand fully those around us, we are inclined to believe that, as adults, we do understand ourselves. Yet in an emergency, when we do things which we cannot explain, we realize that we do not even fully understand ourselves. If this is true of relatively stable adults, then we should understand why the child has so much difficulty in understanding and accepting his ever changing, gradually maturing self.

Even as adults, we often wish that we were better or different from what we are. Frequently we find it difficult to accept our own weaknesses and limitations. Sometimes we disregard our strengths. In general, however, the healthy individual lives in the present and plans for the future in accordance with what he really is. He realizes that he does not have to be perfect to be a good person. Though he still does many things which he believes are wrong, and he fails to do other things which he believes he should do, he recognizes that he is gradually becoming the kind of person he would like to be.

Attitudes toward self [3] begin developing in the home before the child enters school. If his experiences with parents, siblings, other relatives, and friends are wholesome, he discovers that he is accepted; this helps him in turn to accept others and to accept himself. From these important other people he also learns to give and accept love. As he works and plays with them he discovers that he does some tasks very well with a minimum of effort, that other tasks

3 For our purposes here, self is defined as the combination of all the characteristics which make the individual a distinct person at any particular time.

require considerable effort on his part for success, and that there are still other tasks in which he fails. Some things which the healthy child learns about himself he likes and accepts, while other things he dislikes and either rejects or accepts reluctantly. He corrects those elements in the latter category which can be corrected with a reasonable effort; he learns to live with the other weaknesses. Until he accepts these, they disturb him, especially when they interfere with his achieving goals which mean much either to him or to others whose recognition he seeks. Not only does he become acquainted with his strengths and weaknesses, but he takes cognizance of both in defining his life goals.

If, on the other hand, a child has been reared in a home in which he is not accepted, or at least where he feels that he is not accepted, he is unlikely to think well of himself. Even when he receives recognition and acceptance elsewhere, he may not be able to accept it. For example, he may have such a low opinion of himself that he cannot believe he deserves recognition; or he may have been deceived so often that he is suspicious of those who appear to accept him; or he may have had so little experience with people who accept him that he does not know how to react. But if he does not discover that someone does accept him, he tends either to become aggressive and hostile or to withdraw.

Many understanding, accepting teachers contribute to the development of the child's wholesome acceptance of self as he moves through school. However, Jersild's evidence indicates that the child finds too little support of this kind in the schools:

> There is a need of staggering magnitude for doing something in our educational program to help children and youth acquire realistic attitudes of self-acceptance. A large proportion of the young people now entering adulthood are burdened with anxiety, hostility, defensive attitudes toward themselves and others, feelings of guilt, inferiority, or other forms of self-disparagement and self-distrust. They struggle not only with the real dangers and thwartings in our troubled world but with unresolved childhood problems.[4]

The following examples reveal the kinds of goals which the student, and the adults who guide him, should work toward to diminish self-disparagement and to encourage self-acceptance.

4 *Op. cit.*, p. 5.

Satisfactory adjustment between what he wishes he were and what he is. Both children and adults often have difficulty accepting themselves when they fail to measure up to what they wish they were. This sense of failure may occur in striving toward any given goal or any combination of goals. The teacher may reduce the number of such conflicts by expecting from each pupil only that classroom behavior and that level of school success which is reasonable for him. The teacher should also be able to identify those pupils whose conflicts between real self and ideal self create problems too difficult for the teacher to handle alone, and he should seek help from specialists for such pupils.

Unrealistic expectations of success in school create problems with which the teacher can be of assistance. Sometimes parents create the problem by expecting too much from their child. Occasionally, a child may have a physical defect which interferes with success. A less apparent defect is immaturity.

In any case the teacher should accept the child as he is and work with colleagues in diagnosing the sources of the difficulty. He should recognize too that he may not be doing the child a favor if he makes it seem that the child is doing better work than he really is. There is a difference between letting the child know that it is all right for him to read at second-grade level when he is in fourth grade, and giving the child the impression that he is a good fourth-grade reader. In addition to accepting the fact that the child reads below grade level, the teacher should try to find out why the child reads at this level and to determine whether or not he is in a position to improve the child's work at the given time. If the child is ready emotionally, physically, and academically to do better work, the teacher should of course give him the help he needs.

Deciding what he cherishes most in life and examining how these values relate to his goals. Unfortunately, many adults have had unhappy experiences because they failed to determine what they value most and to examine the relationship between these values and their life goals. As a consequence, many an adult finds himself working with people, or even marrying someone, whose primary values he cannot accept.

Parents, teachers, and counselors should help students discover what they value most and examine the relationship between these values and their life goals. Through social problems classes, homeroom discussions, and other group guidance activities, teachers and counselors have an opportunity to help students discover their values. In helping them select courses and make educational and vocational plans, teachers and counselors also may help students examine the relationship between values and life goals. Later chapters will present in detail the avenues by which guidance workers approach this problem.

Developing acceptable relationships with his teachers and classmates. When the child starts school, he faces new problems. A strange new adult, the teacher, suddenly becomes an important person in his life. He no longer is the "hub of the universe"; he is just one among many. His new peers are both competitors and friendly associates. Naturally he wonders where he stands in this new situation. Here the teacher has an opportunity to help each child make new friends and discover acceptable avenues for earning recognition. In extending such help, however, he should recognize that children from different types of home will have these needs satisfied through different kinds of response.

In spite of the fact that the young child may find it difficult to tell how he feels, the early school period may be the easiest time for the child to examine his relationships with his peers. At least this was true in the case of six-year-old Jimmy, who frequently fought in the playground. He was a stable little boy but he had had limited experience with children of his own age. He needed help in discovering what his peers expected from him and in letting them know what he expected from them. On the way in from recess one day his teacher commented, "You have a pretty tough time getting along on the playground, don't you?" The boy quickly responded with the comment, "Yes, the other kids always tease me. They make me mad, and then I hit 'em." This gave his teacher a chance to help Jimmy tell how he felt and to tell him how the other pupils felt. As a consequence of this and several similar conferences, Jimmy gradually accepted what his peers expected from him and learned how to make friends in the group.

Finding friends and developing an understanding of friendship. Since a pupil's acceptance by others is very important in helping him accept himself, teachers can greatly aid the pupil by helping him discover what friendship means and how to make friends—that is, how he affects others, and what he can do to establish better relationships with them.

One way for him to learn to relate to others is through participation in planning worthwhile school activities. As he works in a group, he learns that individuals make many more suggestions than the group can use. He learns that the group chooses some of these ideas and not others. This experience helps him to accept similar consideration, and possible rejection, of his ideas by the group. It also helps him accept himself as a contributor to the group. Should he not know how to contribute, the teacher can help him learn how.

In a permissive classroom atmosphere, teachers also help children learn to evaluate each child's contribution to the solution of problems and to select the best alternatives for their use. Through these group experiences the child learns what others expect from him, and comes to feel that he is a part of the group, and that the group needs him. This helps him accept himself.

Clarifying his feelings toward others in his family and learning to understand and accept their feelings toward him. It is normal for the child to have negative feelings and ambivalent feelings toward parents, siblings, teachers, peers, and other associates. These persons limit his activities; they take what he wants, and they fail to notice things which he does to win recognition. Inasmuch as many parents and teachers find it difficult to accept the child's negative feelings, the child also has difficulty in accepting himself because he has these feelings. These adults make the child feel guilty and ashamed because he has such feelings.

Instead, adults should help the child learn to express his negative feelings at the appropriate times and places, when the child is with someone who can help him understand these feelings, and where no one will be seriously hurt as a consequence of their being expressed. When the child learns that others have such feelings too, and learns what he can do to resolve these conflicts, he finds it increasingly easy to accept himself.

Support for the point of view presented within this section can be found in A. H. Maslow's study of self-actualizing people—persons who have developed or are developing to the full status of which they are capable. With reference to acceptance of self he described his subjects as follows:

The first and most obvious level of acceptance is at the so-called animal level. Those self-actualizing people tend to be good and lusty animals, hearty in their appetites and enjoying themselves mightily without regret or shame or apology. They seem to have a uniformly good appetite for food; they seem to sleep well; they seem to enjoy their sexual lives without unnecessary inhibition and so on for all the relatively physiological impulses. They are able to accept themselves not only on these low levels, but at all levels as well; e.g., love, safety, belongingness, honor, self-respect. All of these are accepted without question as worthwhile, simply because these people are inclined to accept the work of nature rather than argue with her for not having constructed things to a different pattern. This shows itself in relative lack of the disgusts and aversions seen in average people and especially in neurotics, e.g., food annoyances, disgust with body products, body odors, and body functions.

Closely related to self-acceptance and to acceptance of others is (1) their lack of defensiveness, protective coloration, or pose, and (2) their distaste for such artificialities in others. Cant, guile, hypocrisy, front, face, playing a game, trying to impress in conventional ways: these are all absent in themselves to an unusual degree. Since they can live comfortably even with their own shortcomings, these finally come to be perceived, especially in later life, not as shortcomings at all, but simply as neutral personal characteristics.[5]

Acceptance, Understanding, and Love from Others

THE child wants to feel that he is accepted, understood, and loved. He tries to achieve this end by eating, dressing, and behaving as his classmates do, as well as by seeking general acceptance from them. The child feels that he can realize his desire through membership and true acceptance in peer groups. So also he desires love and affection from his family and from a few intimate friends.

The child acquires a sense of personal worth and a feeling of belonging by discovering that his peers and his family really want him around, that they enjoy his company and miss him when he is absent. Telling a child that he is a part of things at school and that he is loved at home is not enough. He must develop security by being treated in ways that are consistent with such statements. Sometimes he may feel rejected even when he is accepted by his parents, teacher, and classmates, if acceptance is not communicated to him.

Sometimes adults try to hide negative feelings and overcompensate for them. Because they cannot accept the fact that they reject those whom they are supposed to love, they act in an opposite manner from the way they feel. For example, a "doting" parent may try

5 A. H. Maslow, *Motivation and Personality* (New York: Harper & Row, Publishers, 1954), pp. 207, 208.

to conceal basic rejection of his child by being unusually attentive to him. In such situations the adult may seem to say and do the right things, yet the child senses that "the words are sung to the wrong emotional tune." Confused, the child cannot attack the problem because everything appears all right on the surface. Usually he even hesitates to inquire why all is not well.

Another example of this kind of behavior is noticeable in some teachers who really possess deep racial intolerance. To comfort themselves, such teachers frequently will give extra help to pupils of the rejected race. Sometimes these children are confused by such action, much as the rejected child of a doting parent is confused. At other times they recognize this "helpfulness" as rejection of them as inferior people, people who cannot succeed by themselves.

Children also try to hide negative feelings. The older child who goes out of his way to help care for the baby and to express affection for it may be trying to offset his own guilt feelings. When he becomes aware of his strong feelings of rejection for a baby sister or brother, he may find them very disturbing. To salve his conscience he does special chores and looks for chances to show publicly his affection for the baby.

Although surface demonstrations of acceptance may be a mask for very different kinds of feeling, it is important that true acceptance be made apparent to the child. What can the teacher do to help his pupils feel that they are loved and accepted?

The teacher can make an effort to understand himself. Frequently he will find within himself unresolved conflicts [6] which account for his difficulties in accepting or communicating his acceptance of certain pupils. He also may discover some of his own unresolved conflicts while he is trying to understand why he rejects certain pupils and overprotects others. Usually a case conference with colleagues will help a teacher to empathize with a pupil and to understand better how he really feels toward that pupil. Though no teacher can be expected to understand fully each of his pupils, he should try gradually to improve his understanding of each and try to see things as his pupils see them. It is practically impossible for a healthy teacher to reject any pupil whom he is trying to understand.

The teacher should be aware of his overtures to his pupils. For example, whom does he encourage to walk with him on a field trip?

---

6 Arthur T. Jersild, *When Teachers Face Themselves* (New York: Bureau of Publications, Teachers College, Columbia University, 1955).

Whom does he invite to sit next to him during the school program?

The teacher should recognize and accept the fact that the young child will expect affection from this new and important adult, the teacher. He should watch for these overtures and respond to them.

The teacher can let the child know that he is missed when he is absent. When, for example, Ralph returned to school after a long illness, he hesitated at the door. Miss Larson did not fuss over the excuse. Instead, she let him know that she and the pupils were glad he was back in school and that they had missed him.

The teacher can try to help the pupil understand that he is accepted even when his behavior is not. If, for example, it is necessary to take paints away from a child because he broke the rule about keeping paints off others' clothes, the teacher should try to differentiate between not liking the violation of the rule and not loving the child.

When the child makes a contribution worthy of special recognition, the teacher should help the group express their feelings so that the child will understand that they appreciate him and his contribution. Dana, for example, rarely said anything in his second-grade class; but when his teacher read a story about bringing milk to the city, he invited the class to his parents' dairy farm. The class made the trip and enjoyed it. Though the boys and girls thanked Dana's father for the excursion, no one said anything special to Dana that day; but on the way home they told the teacher that they enjoyed the trip. When she suggested they tell Dana, they did; and he liked it. The next day, in class, she made a special point of telling Dana that she had enjoyed the trip and that the children had, too. She also asked him whether he would help her answer the children's questions about the farm, thus again helping him find a place in the group.

The teacher can try to protect the child from becoming embarrassed because the group expects something from him which he cannot do. For example, a school drive for funds, calling attention to those who give, puts those who cannot give in a bad light. Or a pupil who cannot sing well is embarrassed because he is asked to perform before the group, and he dreads looking bad in the eyes of his peers.

The teacher can try to learn how a child's parents feel about the child and how they treat him. Knowing how the child is treated in the home helps the teacher understand the way in which the child expresses his needs in school, and suggests cues to the teacher for helping the child become accepted in school. Getting acquainted with parents also opens the way for cooperation between home and school, which may result in better understanding of the child on the part of both the parents and the teacher. Sometimes a school social worker's services are needed to help them with this task.

The teacher can find out how a child's peers feel about the child. Sociometric tests, described in Chapter 8, can help him obtain this information.

The teacher can try to find out how the child sees himself in his school groups. Methods for obtaining this information are also described in Chapter 8.

The teacher can try to help the child make friends with his classmates. Once a sociometric test has told the teacher whom the child wants as a friend, the teacher can try to help the child. Opportunity to sit near the other child or to work with him may be sufficient. Or the teacher may, without stressing it, mention to the other child that the first one likes him and wants to know him better. Most children are pleased to learn that they are liked; occasionally, the second child does not accept the friendship, but then another reference to the sociometric test will reveal others whose friendship the first child seeks. Usually one of these will accept the child.

The teacher can try to help the child earn recognition from his peers. Almost every child can do something which will be of interest to his classmates.

Whenever classmates reject a child, one of the obvious ways a teacher can be of use is to help the pupil determine what his classmates expect from him, and where he failed to meet their expectations. To accomplish this end, the teacher may help him participate in sessions in which the entire group discusses what members expect from one another. The teacher also may analyze his sociometric test responses and observe him in his group to note how he relates to classmates and how they relate to him.

The healthy person seeks acceptance from others, and wants to accept others, but he does not allow these wishes to interfere with being honest with himself and others and with developing his own potentialities. He does not say "yes" when he means "no." When, for example, he is asked by a female friend how he likes a hat that he feels is atrocious, he does not say that he likes it. Neither is he cruel. While he responds as he feels, he also conveys consideration for the other's feelings. Early in life he learned that when he feels "no" and says "yes," he usually conveys "no" anyway. He also realizes that when he falsifies his feelings, he loses some respect for himself and conveys lack of respect for the individual who asked the question.

Maslow's [7] unusually well-adjusted research subjects dared to be themselves—to express their real feelings without fear of losing friends. Though he found that they had greater compassion for their fellow men than most men, they also had greater need for solitude and privacy than most men. They seemed to need to pull themselves out of the turmoil of life in order to think for themselves and to make their own analysis of a situation rather than to rely on others' impressions. They did not need other men in the ordinary sense.

By contrast, the ordinary friendship relationship is more clinging, more demanding, more desirous of reassurance, complement, support, warmth, and exclusiveness.—The usual picture is of our subject being kind and pleasant when forced into these relationships, but ordinarily trying to avoid them as gracefully as possible.

Self-actualizing people have deeper and more profound interpersonal relations than other adults (although not necessarily deeper than those of children). They are capable of more fusion, greater love, more perfect identification, more obliteration of the ego boundaries than other people would consider possible . . . self-actualizing people have these especially deep ties with rather few individuals. Their circle of friends is rather small. The ones that they love profoundly are few in number. Partly this is for the reason that being very close to someone in this self-actualizing style seems to require a good deal of time.[8]

Recognition from Others

THE importance which our culture places upon individual success creates in youth a strong need for personal achievement. Not all children, however, feel the urge for recognition to the same degree or desire recognition from the same sources. Some children will work hard to get gold stars on their arithmetic papers; others will not. Some boys like to be known as good baseball players or good fighters. Some girls like to be recognized as models for pretty clothes, as graceful dancers, or as good companions. Each child tries to learn

7 *Op. cit.*, pp. 206–19.
8 *Ibid.*, pp. 213, 219, 218.

what he can do that will be approved *by those persons whose recognition he seeks.* But even after he discovers what wins recognition, he may not be able to do it well.

Whose recognition does the child seek? Though this varies with the child's maturity, he always seeks recognition from those whom he loves most. When he enters school, this list of persons is extended beyond his family and a few intimate friends to include his teacher and at least selected classmates. As he approaches adolescence, recognition from peers becomes very important. Sometimes he will try to please others, even though he is not especially fond of them, in order to earn recognition which he feels he needs in achieving an important goal.

Sometimes those whose recognition the child seeks hold conflicting standards. Then he is caught in a dilemma, because he is forced to please the one person and disappoint the other. Occasionally he will try to avoid this conflict by withdrawing from the situation entirely rather than displease someone.

Through experiences in their homes and neighborhoods some pupils learn to value and to do well the same activities which won recognition for their teacher when he was a child in school. These children adjust easily and tend to like school. Still other pupils learn to value and to do well activities which the teacher never even notices. Some of these pupils find that the other pupils value their work, and thus their need for recognition is at least partially met. Others in this last group prefer to get into trouble rather than be ignored and left out by both pupils and teacher.

In giving the child recognition for school achievement, the teacher should take into account the child's family background and community mores. He should be conscious that differences in values may make it difficult for him to reward certain pupils. Even though the teacher does give recognition to behavior which he feels is worthy of it, the child will get little satisfaction if the recognition is associated with an activity which has low prestige in his social group. For example, to motivate the child to do well academically, the teacher must help the child to discover value in this work. However, the work must have some prestige value in the child's social group, too, if the teacher is to be successful in motivating the child; thus, the teacher must know what is honored by the child's family and peers.

Betty, for example, was a science professor's only child. She did average work in her fifth-grade group. Betty's teacher felt that Betty was doing about the caliber of work that should be expected from a child with her ability. But average work was not satisfactory achievement for her proud, academically famous father. Betty did well in art, and especially well in singing, which she enjoyed. Yet she knew from her father's remarks about her report card and her creative work that he was impressed only by good results in traditional academic subjects. The extreme pressure at home may well have reduced her school efficiency somewhat; beyond that, she was beginning to cut herself off from her friends in order to spend more time studying. She was also beginning to stutter.

Ken's problem in school was quite different. His family had moved from another part of the country where his father had worked as a farm laborer. All eight members of the family worked whenever they could. Neither of the parents had gone beyond the fifth grade. To Ken, their discussion about financial matters and about children's doing their share suggested that they were more interested in what he could contribute to the family income through his paper route and odd jobs than they were in his school work. Though his parents frequently asked if he was well-behaved in school, he felt that they never cared about his grades. As a result, whenever there was a choice between working and going to school, he concluded that they wanted him to work.

While both of these children were in the same classroom, the total social settings in which each was being reared created some very different needs for school recognition. Even those needs for recognition which the two children had in common were colored by their social backgrounds; for instance, both sought recognition from their peers, yet they expected to give and receive very different reactions with peers. Such differences in the need for recognition are widespread.

Keeping in mind that pupils express the need for recognition differently, let us look at some of the things a teacher can do to help his pupils satisfy this need:

—By observing his pupils in a variety of situations, the teacher can discover from what sources of recognition each pupil achieves most satisfaction.
—The teacher can help each pupil discover those tasks which he can do well and for which he may expect recognition.

—The teacher can define standards of school work which are flexible enough to provide some success for each child, working at his own pace, on his own level. At the same time, the teacher should recognize that the child cannot fully satisfy his need for recognition unless the tasks which he perfoms well are challenging. While unrealistic demands may hinder academic progress and damage personality development, no pupil can develop good work- and study-habits when he operates a "twelve-cylinder brain on a one-cylinder job."

—The teacher can examine his criteria for selecting the work which is exhibited. Some teachers plan to provide every child with some success experience, yet always exhibit the work of only certain children.

—The teacher can reward the child in a manner that is meaningful to him. He can do this by supplementing the academic report with comments on superior performances in activities which are very important to the child. He can also look for improvement in a child's work and point out *exactly* where this improvement was made.

—The teacher can encourage a child to seek help when the child feels he needs it. (But at the same time, the teacher should watch for opportunities to teach independence to the dependent child.)

—The teacher can make sure that each pupil knows what the teacher expects him to do. Teachers often criticize children for not doing assignments which the pupils have not understood. Pupils resent such criticism; they feel that the assignment should be clarified.

—The teacher can involve his pupils in teaching. Pupils tend to help each other anyway, but this assistance is more effective, and students feel more at ease about it, when the teacher accepts their efforts to help each other. Such a procedure can also be useful in teaching students to differentiate between doing work for another and helping him learn how to do it for himself. In order to make most effective use of pupils' assistance, some teachers name pupils to serve as assistants. Teachers may invite pupils to help select assistants by having them answer a sociometric test item like "Which of the pupils who are good in arithmetic would you like to have help the teacher teach arithmetic to you?" Besides avoiding the problem of preadolescents and adolescents being labelled as teacher's pets, this approach gives pupils recognition from peers for scholarship.

Understanding of Responsibilities to Others

WHILE our way of life encourages the individual to become independent to the extent of developing his own personal code of behavior, our community, our state, and our nation have found it necessary to limit individual behavior with appropriate laws. But living within these limits is not sufficient. Democracy requires that most citizens assume responsibility for improving the nation. They must help define the problems and take an active part in solving them. They should not fear change. Neither should they accept the new just because it is different. Instead, they should examine the issues involved, debate the merits associated with each solution, and express their preference on a secret ballot in free elections.

Thus, on the largest scale, the mature adult balances his responsibilities to others with his need for independence. The same sort of balance is required of him at all levels of formal and informal organization of society. The child must learn how to achieve that balance, and thus the school has partial responsibility for guiding his understanding of responsibilities to others, on the one hand, and, on the other, for guiding his developing independence.

Through his experiences in the home, school, and community the child learns his responsibility to others. He learns to serve others and to live by the rules of his group. In each new situation, he tries to find out what the members of his group expect from him. Sometimes he asks what they expect; at other times he tests limits and discovers by trial what they expect.

On the one hand, a teacher should encourage his pupils to become independent; on the other hand, he should recognize that individually they must develop a sense of responsibility to others. However, independence from others and responsibility to others should not conflict; certainly a pupil can learn to do things for himself without neglecting his responsibilities to others.

Worry and overconcern about himself interfere with the pupil's achieving happiness. Service to others not only tends to take the pupil's thoughts away from himself, but also gives him a sense of personal worth and a feeling that he is needed.

Pupils develop a general understanding of responsibility to others through experiences like the following, which bring out specific areas of responsibility:

—Every class should devote ample time to discussing what pupils have a right to expect from each other, what they can expect from their teacher, and what their teacher can expect from them. Failure to achieve this kind of understanding is a source of many discipline problems.

—The social studies teacher can help his pupils study school regulations and the reasons for them. He may also help them analyze the social and political significance of local, state, and national laws which attract the attention of his pupils.

—Every teacher can help his pupils discover opportunities for participating in school activities. Some pupils even require special help in learning how to contribute to class discussion. Frequently, they need help in selecting and becoming affiliated with extra-class activities. Sometimes this requires the assistance of a counselor.

—Most teachers can provide pupils with opportunities to assist one another with school work. At the same time, teachers should remember that part of the value of such cooperation will be lost if pupils fail to differentiate between doing work for a classmate and helping him learn how to do it himself.

—Most teachers have opportunities to help their pupils discover how they can give aid to someone who needs it.

Development of Independence

THE child should learn to make decisions, to act on his own, and to assume responsibility for his own actions. Children want to try new things and to accept new responsibilities; they want to be independent. Sometimes when they show interest in assuming new responsibilities, the adult ignores them because he finds it easier to do the work himself. It is difficult for the adult to remember that children assume responsibility gradually—that they need help and encouragement in doing things for themselves.

Sometimes the adult will suddenly recognize that a child is old enough to take on responsibilities; he will expect the child to assume full responsibility without even a reminder of the job to be done. Adults are also inclined to nag rather than to remind, to hold children to adult standards, to forget to compliment children when they do well. Adults often fail to let children know how much their help is needed and appreciated, they expect children to do tasks the adult way rather than the child's way, and they fail to give children help in experimenting with their own ideas.

As some adults expect a child to take on responsibilities very suddenly, some parents and teachers have personal needs that make it difficult, if not impossible, for them to help children to "cut the apron strings." Persons of this type satisfy their own needs for affection and recognition by keeping youngsters dependent upon them. They enjoy the attention they receive from dependent children. In order to avoid this tendency, every parent and teacher should make sure that his own needs are not obstacles to his teaching of independence to children.

In our society, we want our children to learn how to think and act upon independent judgment. We also want them to develop a sense of responsibility to their associates and, even more broadly, to society. In fact, the child needs to learn to integrate the two complex action theories of "doing things by and for one's self," and "doing things for and with others." The latter is part of the child's need for understanding his responsibilities to others. The teacher can best help his pupils satisfy both of these needs by creating a democratic classroom atmosphere in which children can make real choices and learn how to use their freedom to make such choices.

Every member of the school staff may use the following questions to evaluate his teaching of independence:

—How do I teach the child to assume responsibility for such things as dressing himself, keeping himself clean, and getting his work done on time?
—How do I involve my pupils in classroom planning?
—What do I do when my pupils plan an activity which I have difficulty in accepting?
—What kinds of decision do I permit my pupils to make?
—How do I help my pupils examine the limits within which they may make choices?
—How do I react when values other than my own are presented to the class?
—What kinds of problem do I present to the student council? How do I react when they discuss other problems? How do I react to the council when its members become involved in activities which I feel are beyond their jurisdiction? How are these limits defined?
—What do I do when a pupil makes an unrealistic choice? Do I allow him to make such a choice? Under what conditions could I justify interference with his plans? Does my interference really change his actions? How can failure which results from his unrealistic choices best be used in helping him learn to choose better?

Just as there is little likelihood that the counselor will change the behavior of a pupil by telling him what he should do, so there is little likelihood that a staff member's behavior will be changed by specifically answering the above questions. But generally, if he wishes to teach independence, he will not tell the child what to do. Instead, he will help the pupil find the needed information and will help him use this information in formulating an independent judgment.

Management of Fear and Guilt Feelings

INTENSE fear about harmful things which may happen to him, and painful guilt feelings over what he believes were wrong acts, make a child unhappy and create within him tensions which interfere with his school success.

Almost all fears are learned attitudes. A child often learns them in a situation where he is hurt or comes close to it, or where he sees someone else hurt. Fears may also be taught to the child when he hears others describe their frightening experiences. Sometimes he develops fears by being placed in an embarrassing situation which he is not prepared to meet.

A child feels guilty when he realizes that some act of his does not agree with what he believes he should do. Parents, teachers, and peers all help the child gradually formulate the prohibitions and positive guides which will eventually govern his behavior as a self-disciplined person. Some adults, not realizing that the child's formulation takes time and must come from many sources, try to shame the child when he does not act exactly as they would like. The child may ignore or resist such pressure, but he may become quite disturbed if he cannot meet the demands of an adult whose respect and affection he seeks. In some cases, a child may be discouraged because behavior is demanded which he cannot achieve; at other times, he may be confused simply because he has not been clearly shown what he is expected to do.

Unfortunately, some adults try to control children by deliberately creating unwholesome fears and guilt feelings. But enforcing limits in this way can frequently create problems more serious than the child's failure to observe the limits. It is much better for teachers and parents to teach the child what dangerous experiences he must avoid and to develop cooperatively with him the realistic limits.

Since deep feelings of fear and guilt may involve very serious problems, a teacher should approach the discussion of these feelings with discretion. Though a teacher may let a pupil talk about his fears and guilts, it is very dangerous to probe into these feelings.

As suggested in Chapters 3 and 4, such probing is always a doubtful practice, but here it is especially dangerous because of the likelihood that questions will uncover problems which the child is not prepared to handle; should this happen, the child will be hurt, not helped. When dealing with fears and guilt feelings, the teacher should know his own professional limitations and he should also know where he may turn for help.

In helping children manage feelings of fear and guilt, teachers should keep four questions in mind:

What fears have I created and what others have I reinforced?
Teachers should, for example, try to avoid doing things like these:

—Some teachers make the child afraid to speak before a group by asking him to make a speech before he is prepared and thus embarrassing him.
—Some teachers encourage children to criticize and belittle each other's contributions, until only the more aggressive are willing to contribute to a class discussion. Some teachers may even join in the hurtful criticism and belittling.
—Some teachers embarrass a child when he sings poorly or paints badly, until he is afraid to express his feelings through music and art.
—Some teachers tease a child or allow his peers to tease him about personal fears, thus adding embarrassment to the tension that is already associated with the fear.
—Some teachers may also tell children such things as "big boys and girls" are not afraid of mice, snakes, and the dark; then if, in emergency conditions, the teacher reveals that he, too, is afraid of these, he reinforces old fears and teaches new ones.
—Some teachers describe frightening experiences with such deep feeling that they teach a child to be afraid.
—Some teachers may even fail to answer a child's question about his fears or belittle the fears, thus destroying any opportunity for helping him later. No matter how unrealistic fears appear to be, they are real to the child. Belittling of his fears tends merely to make him ashamed of them so that he cannot seek help in coping with them.

What can I do to reeducate the child about his fears?

—The teacher can use group methods to help children discuss and evaluate their fears; but unless he is thoroughly familiar with the methods outlined in Chapters 3, 4, and 5, he should approach the discussion of fears with care.

A 4
B 5
C 6
D 7
E 8
F 9
G 0
H 1
I 2
J 3

—The teacher may help the child discover the cause for his fears.

—The teacher can provide his pupils with opportunities to make pleasant associations with harmless objects or with situations about which the child has unrealistic fears.

How do I create feelings of guilt and reinforce previously engendered feelings of guilt?

Teachers should try to avoid using responses like the ones, all too typical, quoted below: such remarks create guilt feelings or cause the child to reject the teacher, or both.

"I try so hard to be nice to you and still you treat me this way."

"If you really liked me, would you do a think like that?"

"How do you suppose God feels about a little boy who cheats on an examination?"

"Then it is your own fault that you failed. And to think both your mother and father were honor students in this very school."

"How do you suppose your parents would feel if I were to tell them what I just caught you doing?"

"I always thought I could count on you. Even you let me down when I left the room."

"What in the world was the matter with you, Sally? Didn't you know the answer? You know how much it means to me to have you children do well when the principal visits our room."

How can I help free a child of guilt feelings?

—The teacher should try to see with the child's eyes. If he understands how the child feels and what he values most, then it will be comparatively easy to avoid actions which create guilt feelings in the child.

—The teacher should remember that his expectations may be unrealistic for some of his pupils. What the teacher expects may be based on values which are quite different from the child's.

—The teacher should try to accept the child for what he is, realizing that most children misbehave at times.

—The teacher should realize that obscene notes and pictures express pupils' curiosity and their need for satisfactory answers to their questions.

—The teacher should not look upon misbehavior as a personal attack upon him. Usually children do not mean to hurt the teacher personally. Frequently, they are attacking a symbol of authority. When the teacher interprets pupil behavior as a personal attack upon him, he makes pupils feel ashamed and fails to help them understand why they behaved as they did.

Complete freedom from guilt is abnormal, and perhaps undesirable. If a person is to correct his shortcomings, he must be aware of his failures to live up to the expectations which he sets for himself and he must be motivated to correct those weaknesses which he can correct. But at the same time he must have reasonable expectations for himself and he must try to manage his guilt so that it does not become debilitating. Though Maslow found that his self-actualizing people learned to live with their shortcomings, they were not completely freed of sadness, guilt, shame, anxiety, and defensiveness. However, they rarely suffered from unnecessary guilt.

What healthy people do feel guilty about (or ashamed, anxious, sad, or defensive) are (1) improvable shortcomings, e.g., laziness, thoughtlessness, loss of temper, hurting others; (2) stubborn remnants of psychological ill health, e.g., prejudice, jealousy, envy; (3) habits, which, though relatively independent of character structure, may yet be very strong, or (4) shortcomings of the species or of the culture or of the group with which they have identified. . . .[9]

Ability to Face Reality

IF the child is to make a good adjustment to life he must learn to identify his problems, define alternative modes of behavior for each, choose an alternative, and take positive action. In contrast, the emotionally sick person retreats into his imaginary world where he has no problems or can solve his problems with little discomfort.

Daydreaming is a way to escape from reality. The world of phantasy is safer and happier, usually, than the actual present. Of course most well-adjusted persons also dream of better things ahead and look forward to the realization of their special plans. Sometimes it is difficult to differentiate between thinking through plans for the future and daydreaming about success. The well-adjusted person, however, does not confuse his dreams of the future with his present situation. He distinguishes between phantasy and reality.

While, for most people, daydreaming is simply a matter of wasting time, it becomes a serious problem for the individual who achieves

9 *Ibid.*, p. 208.

most of his satisfactions from this escape activity. The teacher can help a child through discovering when the child uses this escape and why. Moreover, the teacher should determine whether the child uses it excessively. Eventually, he should help the child achieve some success experience while facing reality. This may mean finding something that the child can do to earn recognition in his group. Occasionally such children require treatment by a specialist to whom the teacher should make a referral.

Learning to avoid retreat into a world of daydreams is an important part of learning to face reality; differentiating between truth and fiction is another. Even before the child enrolls in kindergarten, he has had the experience of having adults and older children question his stories. He knows what it means to have others doubt what he claims to have seen and done. Of course, he may have exaggerated the size of the dog, or he may have stretched the distance that his father hit the baseball. Yet the practice of exaggerating is not confined to the preschool child; in fact, the child himself can probably recall several instances in which he detected that an adult sacrificed the truth for a good story. The point is that the adult usually knows when he fabricates, but the child often fails to discriminate between what happened and what he wanted to happen.

Then too, there are observational errors. Even adults may gain different impressions from observing the same scene. What any one individual perceives in a situation is colored by his own peculiar vision. Even more than an adult, the young child has trouble differentiating between what happened and what might have happened.

The child learns to distinguish between phantasy and reality step by step as he grows up. Parents and teachers should help him make these distinctions without embarrassing him. If adults accept the child for what he is, and stand by ready to help him by demonstrating the difference between phantasy and reality in the experiences in their daily lives, they can help him face reality and struggle with the problems which result.

To function efficiently everyone must understand himself and his environment: he must understand his strengths and weaknesses and be able to describe accurately the conditions within his environment. Once he is able to do all this, he can decide whether he should accept certain weaknesses in himself and certain undesirable elements in his environment, or whether he should do what is required to change either himself or his environment.

SUGGESTED READINGS

1. ALLPORT, GORDON W. *Becoming: Basic Considerations for a Psychology of Personality.* New Haven: Yale University Press, 1955.

The subtitle describes this little book very well. The book certainly should help teachers and counselors to understand human behavior.
   a] How do the young child's strivings differ from the adult's strivings?
   b] What consequences follow a child's failure to satisfy affiliative needs during preschool years?
   c] What is the source of conscience?
   d] Where has psychoanalytic theory erred in interpreting the role of religion in personality development?

2. ALLPORT, GORDON W. "Scientific Models and Human Morals," *Psychological Review,* LIV (1947), 182–92.

There are many good ideas in this paper, but the teacher will be particularly interested in what he sees as the basic goodness of the child's nature.

3. GORDON, IRA J. *Human Development: From Birth Through Adolescence.* New York: Harper & Row, Publishers, 1962.

This volume describes the development of self and sets forth some hypotheses on the nature of this process. Chapters 1, 6, 10, and 16.
   a] To what extent can adults use normative data about what to expect from a child without ignoring his unique nature?
   b] How does the ability to evaluate self develop? When does it develop?
   c] How does the child differentiate between right and wrong? How are these decisions made? What factors seem to influence the decisions at various periods in a child's life?

4. HILGARD, ERNEST R., and DAVID H. RUSSELL. "Motivation in School Learning," Chapter 2 in *Learning and Instruction,* National Society for the Study of Education, Forty-Ninth Yearbook, Part I. Chicago: University of Chicago Press, 1950.

Hilgard and Russell described the motives of children as follows: (1) the need for affiliation, (2) the need for approval—to impress others favorably, (3) aggression—to find some way to give expression to anger, hostility, and destructiveness, (4) sexual needs—a continuity from earliest childhood to adult experience, (5) ambivalence—a combination of positive and negative attitudes; e.g., children both like and hate school; they like and hate parents and teachers.

a] State at least one example of child behavior that demonstrates Hilgard and Russell's concept of ambivalence.

5. JENKINS, GLADYS GARDNER, HELEN SHACTER, and WILLIAM A. BAUER. *These Are Your Children.* Chicago: Scott, Foresman & Co., 1953.

This book deals with the various influences on the child within the family, the school, and the community. Its well-chosen and meaningful case material adds much to the book.

a] Note how the need for acceptance, understanding, and affection from others expresses itself in different ways from year to year as the child grows up.

b] Do the same for the need for independence.

c] How does a teacher's or parent's taking offence at signs of disrespect affect the preadolescent?

d] What can adults do to build confidence and self-respect in the child?

6. MARTIN, WILLIAM E., and CELIA B. STENDLER. *Child Behavior and Development.* New York: Harcourt, Brace & World, Inc., 1959.

Readers will find this book interesting as well as scholarly. It provides a framework within which to evaluate the behavior of a given child. Chapters 9, 10, 11 and 12.

a] How do early learnings sometimes interfere with later learnings?

b] How do democratic and autocratic child-rearing practices seem to influence a child's behavior?

c] Why is the rejected child not always easily identified?

d] What values do middle-class teachers teach?

e] How does the peer group influence a child's behavior?

7. MASLOW, A. H. *Motivation and Personality.* New York: Harper & Row, Publishers, 1954.

This very readable book presents its author's views of personality development and the principles which seem to explain human motivation. Chapters 5, 6, and 12.

a] To what extent is behavior motivated by unconscious needs?

b] What phenomena seem to determine basic need gratifications?

c] What is unique about self-actualizing people?

8. NIXON, ROBERT E. *The Art of Growing: A Guide to Psychological Maturity.* New York: Random House, Inc., 1962.

In this book the author tries to show how youth's potential for rich living can be developed.

a] What can be done to help the child make the transition from the home into the world?

b] With respect to helping people cope with negative feelings, how have the teachings of Christ been misinterpreted to the detriment of man's mental health?

9. RATHS, LOUIS E. *An Application to Education of the Needs Theory.* Published by author, 157 West 13th Street, New York 11, 1949.

In addition to giving the teacher an outline for studying the environmental factors predisposing to various emotional disturbances, Raths also explains in this pamphlet how children behave when their needs are not met.

a] Which of the activities suggested by Raths have you tried in helping your pupils meet their needs?

b] Among the disturbing actions of teachers, of which are you guilty?

3

The Counseling Relationship

THE PRIMARY objective of this chapter is to describe the unique nature of the counseling relationship. It has two other objectives as well, which it shares with the following two chapters: to give the prospective counselor the basic information about counseling which he can use in deciding whether or not to become a counselor, and to give the rest of the school staff sound information about what a counselor should do.

There are two reasons for beginning the discussion of guidance services with the counseling service: its great importance to the pupil and the fact that it best exemplifies the point of view that should be exhibited in pupil-staff relationships for all the guidance services. A genuine concern for the pupil, an effort to try to understand the pupil as a unique individual, and a nonjudgmental attitude—all the necessary equipment of the counselor—should be fostered in every guidance worker. For greatest effectiveness, not only counselors but also all other guidance workers must try to see things from the pupil's point of view. That is why the discussion of pupils' needs in Chapter 2 directly precedes the discussion of the counseling relationship in this chapter.

What happens when a pupil comes in for an interview? After the pupil and the counselor exchange greetings, the conversation gets started, perhaps by the pupil's discussing the problems that bother him most, perhaps not; the pupil pauses, needs help in resuming the conversation, asks questions, expresses feelings in sudden outbursts or with painful slowness, makes a decision, talks some more, perhaps makes an appointment for another interview, and leaves. Meanwhile the counselor listens, tries to understand how the pupil feels, tries to reflect these feelings (to mirror his understanding of what the pupil is saying), tries to help the pupil feel accepted and understood, helps the pupil to talk yet tries not to interrupt productive pauses, makes notes, constantly considers whether he is following what the pupil is saying, determines whether he should continue working with the pupil or refer the pupil to a colleague who is better qualified to help, perhaps reminds the pupil of the time limits, and, when the pupil has left, organizes his interview notes.

Counseling is an intimate, trusting relationship. If it is to work, the pupil must feel that the counselor accepts him as a person despite his faults and shortcomings, and that the counselor is making a sincere effort to see things as he does. The youngster must believe that the counselor is capable of makng an enormous investment in him as a person, and that somehow this process will help him learn how to cope with his problems.

When the prospective counselor first observes an effective counselor working with a client, he is impressed with how hard the counselor works at trying to understand his client—with the amount of psychic energy he invests in the process. The counselor draws upon all his professional resources, both his understanding of human behavior and his knowledge of counseling techniques, in an effort to understand life, and its varied problems, *as his client sees it,* and to help his client understand the disturbing forces within himself and within his environment. He knows how to reach beneath mere talk to help his client discover and deal with relevant material. As he tries to walk beside his client emotionally (or, as the teenager would say, "to get with him"), the counselor's behavior reveals that he realizes things are not always what they seem. For example, a pupil who goes out of his way to tell a counselor what a wonderful person his dad is may, in reality, be very angry with his father; perhaps he cannot admit it even to himself or, if he does recognize how he really feels, he may be ashamed to say it. The effective counselor, by noticing both his client's nonverbal behavior and his manner of saying what he says, detects his client's real feelings and helps him discuss these feelings. Sometimes it is necessary to lead a pupil to examine why he has had difficulty talking about certain topics before he can discuss them; when counseling is successful, the pupil talks about problems which heretofore he had not been able to discuss adequately. During the process he comes to see himself and his situation more realistically, obtains the information he needs, develops the self-confidence and the will to act, and takes positive action. From these experiences the client gains new understanding of himself and his situation, learns to accept himself and others better, assumes increasingly greater responsibility for his actions, and learns how to attack future problems more skillfully.

A counselor is often tempted to take responsibility for a client, but there are several reasons why he must try to avoid doing so. When the counselor thinks, decides, or acts for a client, he makes his client increasingly dependent upon him; he also implies that his client lacks the resources to solve his own problems. Those who seek a counselor's assistance may seem to lack the resources for solving their own problems, but if they are to be treated by school counselors—rather than by psychotherapists—they should have the potential for solving those problems. The counselor must develop these potentialities rather than teach dependency.

At one time or another, most pupils face problems similar to those described in the section on guidance services in Chapter 1. On such occasions the pupil should be able to feel there is someone in the school to whom he can turn for the type of assistance described in this and the following two chapters. Though few pupils will require long-term counseling (especially in those schools which provide good guidance services and emphasize prevention of mental illness), most will require more than one interview. For example, one of the most common problems for which the high school student seeks a counselor's assistance is choice of a vocation. When he seeks aid with this problem, he usually needs help in answering for himself such questions as: (1) Where have I done my best work (both in school- and in work-experiences)? (2) Where have I done my poorest work? (3) From which of these experiences have I achieved the greatest personal satisfactions? and (4) From which of these experiences have I received least satisfactions, and why? The counselor ordinarily uses most of the first session to try to understand the student and the student's perception of his problem. If the counselor is fortunate, he may be able to help the student begin thinking about questions of the kind listed above. Usually several additional conferences are needed to help the student formulate the questions he has about himself and about the vocations which appeal to him, and to help him obtain the information that he needs. Frequently, those who seek help in selecting a vocation have doubts about themselves which they must discuss before they can make a vocational choice and take the necessary steps to prepare for the vocation. There also are outside pressures for particular choices with which the student must learn to cope before he can make *his own choice*.

Obviously, choosing a vocation touches on many phases of a student's life which he is reluctant to discuss with a counselor until he is relatively certain that the counselor can be trusted. The counselor must not only provide the good conditions described above, but he must also convince the pupil that his counselor understands and keeps confidences. Sometimes a school counselor fails his clients by discussing confidential information with colleagues or parents. Very rarely does he do this to hurt clients; usually he is merely doing what he believes is expected of him: making information available to his principal or discussing material with his colleagues which the students feel should be kept confidential.[1]

Knowing that confidences will be kept is important to all clients, but it is especially important to adolescents. Actually many of them have good reasons for doubting adults. In their experiences few adults listen to them or try to understand them. Some adults criticize adolescents unfairly; often they believe that adolescents should be forced to do what adults think is best. When one also considers

---

1 *Counseling Services in the Secondary Schools of Illinois,* Allerton House Conference on Education, Study Group IX, Role of the Counselor (Urbana: University of Illinois, 1958), p. 17. The following two questions were presented first to a group of school administrators, teachers, and guidance workers—and then to a group of students: Is the information (from interview with counselors) available to the principal on his request? Is the information used by counselors in aiding other members of the staff? Approximately three out of four principals, teachers, and counselors answered the questions "yes," whereas the students felt that these questions should be answered "no."

that adolescents are trying to achieve independence from adults, that many of them are required to see their counselors periodically whether they want help or not, that many of them are referred to counselors because they misbehave in class, and that many are referred by persons who fail to try to understand them or to help them see how counseling may be of use to them, it is remarkable that even effective counselors win their confidences.

Despite the above conditions most adolescents will try to trust the counselor when they seek his help, especially when they realize that the counselor can understand and accept their doubts about him. Of course, some young people, perhaps because they have had unsatisfactory experiences with counselors, or perhaps because they are not certain what counselors do or how they can help, find it difficult to approach a counselor for help. Still other pupils may be reluctant to talk about their problems because of natural reticence, shame and guilt feelings, fear that they may get others into trouble, or for many other personal reasons. But when a pupil seeks help he usually has already given considerable thought to his difficulties. He recognizes that he has problems; he wants to talk about them and to do something about them; and he realizes that he needs help. He may already have sought the help of a personal friend or trusted teacher, and such experiences with other adults sometimes lead him to expect that the counselor will solve his problems for him, telling him exactly what to do. Indeed, the adult who makes the referral to the counselor frequently helps to develop this feeling of dependence. On the other hand, many adults, by the very nature of their referrals, increase readiness for counseling and understanding of what may be expected from it.

The Counselor's Attitude Toward His Client

How the counselor feels toward a client is of first importance. If he is attempting to help a pupil whom he likes very much, he may have difficulty allowing the pupil to struggle through the painful steps involved in achieving insight and finding his own solution to his problem. He may let the client lean on him while he tries to find an easy shortcut. If, on the other hand, the pupil represents a stereotype which the counselor rejects, he may unconsciously let the pupil suffer unnecessarily. In each case the counselor must remember that he is dealing with a person who has sought his help and wants his understanding. The counselor must discover for himself, therefore, how he feels toward the person whom he is trying to help. If he finds either that he has trouble accepting a client or that he is too anxious to help him, then the counselor should evaluate his own behavior.

This consideration of attitudes applies also to the teacher. Since pupils often discuss their personal as well as their academic problems with their favorite teacher, teachers may become involved in pupils' difficulties. A teacher may be inclined, when a youngster comes for help, to tell him what to do rather than to listen to his story. Or sometimes he thoughtlessly belittles the pupil's problem, when he intends to reassure the pupil, by telling him that his problem is not serious and that it will take care of itself shortly. In these instances the teacher forgets that some of the same problems were very serious to him when he was the pupil's age. The fact that the pupil seeks help proves that he believes the problem is a serious one; moreover, what appears at first to be a simple problem may not be simple when the teacher obtains the full story and understands fully how the pupil feels about it. The pupil needs help in discovering for himself what the situation is and what he can do about it. Neither a counselor nor a teacher can immediately transfer from himself to the pupil that which is obvious to an adult; rather the pupil has to wrestle with the problem in order to discover and synthesize the relevant data for himself, to understand the alternatives, and to take positive action.

When the counselor's or teacher's feelings about a pupil affect him to the extent that he cannot accept the pupil as he is and allow him the opportunity to solve his problems in his own way, the relationship is unwholesome. At this point the counselor has a strong personal investment in the choices being made by the client. The term for this personal investment is "counselor involvement."

For example, consider a counselor's relation to Herman, who had made an excellent high school record with particularly good grades in science. As Herman talked about his plans to become a science teacher, he felt that his counselor, Mr. Tiederman, weighed every word he said. When they finished talking about teaching and began discussing Herman's choice of college, Mr. Tiederman pointed out that the college which Herman had chosen also had a very good premedical program, and he indicated that Herman could follow the premedical course for two years if he would specialize in either biology or general science. Then Mr. Tiederman caught himself asking Herman whether he had ever thought about studying medicine.

At that point he realized that he had been reliving his own life and was once again choosing between science teaching and medicine. Herman's record and his interests reminded Mr. Tiederman of himself when he was Herman's age, and he realized that he had been encouraging Herman to study medicine so that *he* could achieve success in medicine through Herman's success in it. Mr. Tiederman, once he realized his involvement, frankly admitted what had happened and asked whether Herman would like to talk further about *his own plans*.

Fortunately Mr. Tiederman was able to recognize his own involvement. Korner [2] has described various symptoms of counselor involvement in the behavior of the counselor; his description of these danger signals may be summarized as follows:

—The counselor has difficulty concentrating on what the client is saying.
—He suddenly finds that he cannot understand the client.
—He may find himself suddenly thinking about something which appears to be in no way connected with the client's statements.
—He may feel personally disturbed. He may feel uncomfortable and recognize that he is not functioning normally.
—He may conclude that the interview is not moving along as fast as it should.
—He may resent the client and feel that the client is not telling everything.
—He may find himself pushing a specific point.
—On a certain day he may be surprised to learn that many of his clients appeared to have similar problems with similar dynamics.
—He may develop strong emotional ties with the client and consequently dislike to see him suffer.

Some maintain that involvement is a problem only for directive and eclectic counselors. But involvement may also be a problem for nondirective counselors. Although the nondirective counselor takes less responsibility for his clients than do either of the other two, even he must make choices among the feelings to which he will respond. If he becomes personally involved, he will, in making his choices, respond only to those feelings associated with a particu-

2 Ija N. Korner, "Ego Involvement and the Process of Disengagement," *Journal of Consulting Psychology*, XIV (1950), 206–09.

lar problem area, and overlook other relevant material. He may select this way because he has decided that the client's real problem lies within this area, but he may also select according to his own needs.

Every good counselor thinks first of his client's needs, and tries not to let his own needs interfere with helping his client improve his adjustment. Though counselors who hold different views disagree on what they can expect from their clients and what their clients should expect from them, *effective counselors from each school of thought* seem to help their clients. Fred E. Fiedler [3] found that counselors who hold different points of view nevertheless seem to agree on the behaviors most characteristic of an ideal counseling relationship. He also found that the ability to describe the ideal relationship was more a matter of expertness and experience than a matter of allegiance to any philosophical orientation. He reports that the following conditions were named as most characteristic of an ideal therapeutic relationship:

—There is an empathic relationship.
—The therapist and patient relate well.
—The therapist sticks closely to the patient's problems.
—The patient feels free to say what he likes.
—An atmosphere of mutual trust and confidence exists.
—Rapport is excellent.
—The patient assumes an active role.
—The therapist leaves the patient free to make his own choices.
—The therapist accepts all feelings which the patient expresses as completely normal and understandable.
—A tolerant atmosphere exists.
—The therapist is understanding.
—The patient feels most of the time that he is really understood.
—The therapist is really able to understand the patient.
—The therapist really tries to understand the patient's feelings.

In the same paper Fiedler lists the following descriptions as *least characteristic* of the ideal therapeutic relationship:

—The therapist is punitive.
—The therapist makes the patient feel rejected.

3 Fred E. Fiedler, "The Concept of an Ideal Therapeutic Relationship," *Journal of Consulting Psychology,* XIV (1950), 239–45.

—The therapist seems to have no respect for the patient.
—There is an impersonal, cold relationship.
—The therapist often puts the patient "in his place."
—The therapist curries favor with the patient.
—The therapist tries to impress the patient with his skill and knowledge.

Good counselors seem to agree on the characteristics which they place at the extreme ends of this scale. Nevertheless, individual practices may still vary, either because counselors cannot apply all of these guides for counselor behavior or because not all counselors accept each guide with equal enthusiasm. And there is also a good possibility that representatives from these various schools do behave at least somewhat differently with their clients than their words suggest. Barker and Sunderland's [4] recent research report supports this opinion. They divided their subjects into three major groups: Freudian, Sullivanian, and Rogerian. Each group was composed of equal numbers of experienced (six years or more) and inexperienced (five years or less) therapists. The persons from the three schools differed at the .01 level of significance on eleven of their sixteen dimensions. Experienced and inexperienced therapists differed on only one dimension. The Freudians differed from the other two groups on the importance which they attributed to experiences in childhood, unconscious motivation, conceptualization, therapist's training, and therapist's goals, planning, and objectivity; they also stressed the importance of the therapist's suppressing his spontaneity. The Rogerians were at the opposite end of the continuum on these dimensions. Though the Sullivanians usually occupied the middle position, they were nearer the Freudians in stressing the necessity for conceptualization, for inhibition of spontaneity, for planning, and for having therapeutic goals; and they were closer to Rogerians in seeing the therapist as personally involved, and in emphasizing the importance of the therapist's personality. The researchers also found that inexperienced therapists were a more heterogeneous group than were the experienced therapists.

Inasmuch as counselors differ from one another in their attitudes toward their fellowmen, their values, their temperament, their abilities and aptitudes, their job experience, and their professional prep-

4 Edwin N. Barker and Donald M. Sunderland, *The Methods and Attitudes of Psychotherapists* (Columbus, Ohio: Psychiatric Clinic, Columbus State Hospital, mimeographed, 1960).

aration, it is natural for them to disagree on the philosophy of counseling and to use different procedures with their clients. Such differences have led to the development of many philosophies of counseling. Though it is interesting to argue about the merits of the various theories, it is more profitable to acquaint the prospective counselor with a number of the philosophies and to help him select from each the techniques which are consistent with his values, attitudes, and professional competencies. The discussion of several points of view also helps the newcomer to the field understand why the various counselors behave as differently as they do. Furthermore, the three points of view discussed here—nondirective, directive, and eclectic—are often mentioned in the professional literature and in courses for school counselors, and therefore persons interested in guidance should understand them.

Nondirective Counseling

THE nondirective counselor believes that the client has within himself all the resources for solving his own problems, but that emotional blocks prevent him from using these resources properly. The role of the counselor, according to this view, is to help the client remove the emotional blocks. The nondirective counselor also believes that the client has a strong drive to become well adjusted socially, that the client wants to become independent and to accomplish for himself the changes necessary to achieve a happier life. Therefore, the client is not only permitted but encouraged to focus attention on the issues which are important to him.

PUPIL'S PERCEPTION OF THE RELATIONSHIP

When a pupil seeks the counselor's help, he soon discovers that the counselor accepts him as he is and believes in his ability to solve his problem in his own way. He also learns that he can talk about whatever he chooses, and sometimes he finds, even to his own surprise, that he can talk about topics which heretofore he could not discuss even with his closest friends.

Though previous experiences with counselors may have taught him that the counselor is a "giver of advice," he now finds himself talking with a person who tries to understand him, tries to follow what he is saying and feeling, tries to help him understand himself. He observes that this counselor neither gives advice nor attempts to manipulate him into making a decision which the counselor believes is best. Although the pupil must occasionally restate and attempt to clarify something that the counselor does not understand, he can make inconsistent statements without being challenged. He feels that the counselor understands why he sees things differently at different times. And he learns that if he wishes, he can terminate the relationship without solving the specific problem that brought him to the counselor.

Occasionally, the pupil wants advice and resents not receiving it. At such times he may feel that he is not getting the help he needs. On these occasions the counselor helps the pupil express his disappointment and talk about his dependency feelings. There are also times when the pupil becomes aggressive and wants to attack the counselor. He finds numerous faults with the counselor's way of doing things. Instead of scolding him, the counselor accepts these aggressive feelings and again helps the pupil to express them. When the pupil finds it difficult to talk, the counselor helps him tell why he is finding it difficult to talk about the issues involved.

After an interview is over, the pupil thinks about what went on. This may be when he really achieves insights, when the subjects he has discussed and the things he has seen in himself take on new meanings. However, such illuminations may come at any time, either during the interviews or between them. In a subsequent interview, the pupil may want to explore the significance of this self-examination. He may want to talk about how upsetting or how satisfying these discoveries about himself were. He also may want to explore their immediate significance for him.

On the other hand, as the pupil thinks about the counseling periods between counseling sessions, he may conclude that they are not worthwhile. In that case he may terminate the relationship. If he does so, and sometime later feels he needs more counseling, he makes an appointment. The responsibility for continuing the relationship resides with the pupil. He decides when he has received the help he needs for working out his problem to his own satisfaction.

COUNSELOR'S PERCEPTION OF THE RELATIONSHIP

The nondirective counselor is more concerned about the pupil's development as an individual than about the solution of the pupil's immediate problems. However, he is interested in the pupil's immediate problems. He works toward his objective by helping the pupil talk freely about matters that bother him. He tries to detect what the pupil is feeling from what the pupil is saying and doing. As he tries to follow the pupil, he checks on himself by asking, "Is this what you are saying . . . ?" or "Am I following you? You feel . . . ?" or "Is . . . what you mean?" Or he may accomplish this purpose with responses like, "Then you are pretty bothered over what your parents think about you?" or "You are wondering whether you have what it takes to go to college?" or "You would like very much to know how your classmates feel about you?" In assisting the pupil to express these feelings, the counselor helps him realize that he may discuss whatever bothers him and that his counselor wants to understand him.

The counselor devotes his full attention to the pupil during the counseling session. He tries to put aside his own needs and enter the pupil's world. He tries indeed to be "another self" for the pupil, to comprehend the pupil's views of life and the problems he faces in living within the boundaries those views impose. At the same time he tries not to influence the pupil's choices. Rather than give advice or force information on the pupil, his task is to free the pupil from the emotional blocks that impede his use of his own potentialities. By creating an empathic, permissive climate, the counselor is able to help the pupil talk freely about any experiences and feelings, even some for which he had not previously found words.

The nondirective counselor believes that under these circumstances he need not probe into the pupil's past to obtain the pertinent information. He feels that the pupil, encouraged to speak freely, will reveal what is pertinent or raise questions about pertinent information which he needs.

When the pupil raises questions about himself that can best be answered through the use of tests, the counselor refers the pupil to the appropriate person for testing. He will, but prefers not to, interpret test scores and obtain data from the cumulative folder for the pupil. He does not want to become involved in any relationship in which the pupil could picture him as making judgments for and about the pupil.

During the interview he tries to record, as best he can, what the pupil says and does, so that he may use these notes to orient himself for subsequent counseling sessions. However, he tries not to make diagnostic judgments in writing these notes. His purpose is to record

enough of the content and the emotional tone of the client's comments to be able to follow the client's discussion in subsequent
sessions.

COUNSELOR'S RELATIONSHIP WITH THE STAFF

The nondirective counselor accepts the other members of the
school staff and recognizes their important contributions, as do good
counselors of any type. However, he does not impose his services
on them. Even though he lets the staff know, through the principal's description of his job at the time of employment, that he is
expected to assist teachers in the study of their pupils, he feels that
teachers should initiate the request for help. As with the pupils, he
feels he can help teachers best when they recognize the need for help
and seek his assistance.

When a teacher seeks assistance, the nondirective counselor tries
to help him understand how he feels about his pupil, and help him
also discover and describe how the pupil feels. The nondirective
counselor is pleased to help teachers arrange a case conference
which a teacher initiates. He himself would hesitate to initiate a
case conference to enlist the staff's help in getting a pupil, who he
feels needs his help, referred to him. If, however, he felt he needed
the assistance of certain staff members, he would not hesitate to
enlist it. In other words, he simply feels that the one needing
the help should request it.

Directive Counseling

WHEREAS the nondirective counselor is primarily interested in
helping the pupil learn to cope with himself, the directive counselor
appears to be primarily interested in helping the pupil solve the
problems which he presents to the counselor. But the directive
counselor is also interested in helping the pupil achieve better
overall adjustment. He believes that persistent unsolved problems
account for the pupil's present inadequacies, and that as the pupil
solves these immediate problems he will gradually acquire greater
effectiveness. He also believes that the satisfaction which the pupil
achieves from solving his immediate problems increases his confidence in himself and his counselor, and that this confidence enables
the pupil to attack his less obvious problems with increased success.

Directive counselors give more emphasis to the counselor's role, stress the importance of case histories on clients, adequate test data, diagnosis, prognosis, and interpretation, and question whether the pupil has within himself the power to solve his own problems. Though they recognize that information can help the pupil only when it is meaningful to him and when he realizes that he needs it, they believe that the counselor may have to create awareness of the need for information when the pupil needs information and fails to request it. They also believe that counselors may give advice.

Many directive counselors believe that some pupils who need help will not seek it. Whenever they discover such a pupil, they arrange to see him. Many such pupils are contacted through the school counselor's periodic interview with all the pupils for whom he is responsible; others are either referred by the staff or contacted by the counselor for some specific purpose.

Directive counselors contend that the counselor should question the pupil's inappropriate decisions and take the initiative in helping him reexamine the implications of these questionable choices. At the same time they believe that the *pupil* should select from the alternatives the one which he believes is best for him and, by encouraging him to do so, they do help the dependent client to achieve independence. They present him with real choices which they believe he is able to make.

PUPIL'S PERCEPTION OF THE RELATIONSHIP

In directive counseling the pupil soon discovers that he can talk about whatever he chooses and that the counselor makes it easy for him to talk about himself. Of course the counselor asks questions to bring out points which the pupil forgets to mention: nothing can be overlooked; the counselor must secure the complete picture before he can provide his best help. Usually the pupil accepts without difficulty the fact that he must cooperate by providing the counselor with all the information which the counselor requests. Sometimes he does not understand why the counselor asks him to fill out personal data sheets concerning his past and why occasionally he even requires him to take a number of tests. Nevertheless, since he finds that the counselor is friendly and helpful, he assumes that the procedure is all right. As a matter of fact, the businesslike way in which the counselor obtains facts reminds the pupil of his visits to the family doctor. Usually the pupil concludes that his counselor knows about people and about helping them solve their problems.

Though the pupil at times feels a little resentful about some of these questions, still he goes on talking about himself, his past, his present, and his plans for the future. The counselor asks him all kinds of questions about his happiest moments, his unhappiest moments, his early childhood, his home, the members of his family and how he feels about them, his friends, the things he likes, and the things he does not like. However, this conversation runs along so smoothly that at times the pupil hardly realizes that he is answering so many personal questions.

The pupil, in getting to know the counselor, and gradually acquiring real faith in him and in his professional competency, does not worry about providing the counselor with the information requested. He feels so sure of help that he relaxes and lets the counselor do some of the worrying. He feels good knowing that his counselor not only is making it possible for him to understand himself better but also is not going to let him make many unnecessary mistakes in solving his problems.

Eventually, however, the pupil must make some decisions. If he cannot identify any good alternatives, he can always count on his counselor to suggest some. Sometimes both pupil and counselor need more facts before they can identify good alternatives; they may find the needed facts either through tests or through nontest techniques. They may also use other sources better to understand the setting in which the pupil's problem arose. After obtaining the necessary information and identifying several alternatives, the pupil realizes that it is his responsibility to choose one of the alternatives. When at times he feels that his counselor is trying to maneuver him into choosing one particular alternative, he resists a little. But faith in the counselor helps carry him over these periods in the interview.

The pupil and the counselor terminate the counseling sessions when both cooperatively conclude that they have solved the pupil's problems. However, some pupils stop coming to the counseling sessions before such a decision is arrived at. If the sessions are terminated through cooperative agreement, the pupil usually finds it easier to return to the counselor whenever he faces new problems that are too difficult for him to solve by himself.

COUNSELOR'S PERCEPTION OF THE RELATIONSHIP

Before the first interview, the directive counselor studies the story of the pupil's life and the important conflicts in it. Prior to subsequent interviews he reviews the counseling notes and the data in the cumulative folder in his search for possible solutions to the student's present problem. The better he knows the pupil, the more helpful he can be in interpreting for the pupil the forces which are creating his problems. And he plans ways to help the pupil see the relationship between his immediate problem and any other problems which the counselor may have discovered.

Though the counselor believes that the pupil should make the final decision, he feels free to help the pupil obtain the information which each needs for defining alternative solutions, and he also feels it proper for him to give the pupil advice that is consistent with the counselor's diagnosis. Should the pupil choose an alternative which the counselor's diagnosis leads him to believe is an unwise one, he raises questions to cause the pupil to reevaluate the choice.

Since the counselor needs as complete a picture as he can obtain, he must record interview notes. Some directive counselors take very complete notes while the interview is going on, trying to keep a running account of what they and their clients discuss. Others make notes immediately following the interview. They usually believe that note-taking may interfere with the building and maintaining of a good working relationship, and thus they prefer to run the risk of losing some pertinent facts. After the interview all of these counselors will try to sort out of their notes information which will help them make a good diagnosis.

Many directive counselors use "small talk" to become acquainted with pupils and to create a friendly atmosphere; they talk about school activities, the pupil's special interests that they have noticed, and any other topic which they believe will be interesting to the pupil and relax him. Rarely does it occur to the counselor that he may also be using "small talk" to find security for himself while creating a good counseling relationship; such "small talk" cannot be defended.

The directive counselor, like the nondirective counselor, must be able to create a friendly climate that encourages the pupil to tell his own story, revealing his feelings about himself and those elements in his life that he values most. The counselor tries, of course, to follow what the pupil is saying and feeling. He also tries to use both facts and feelings in making his diagnosis, by means of which he tries to show the pupil how his problems relate to what he has felt and spoken of.

The release of the pupil's feelings is important to the directive as well as the nondirective counselor, though for very different reasons. The nondirective counselor seeks to help the pupil clarify his feelings through expressing them, so that the counselor can follow what he is trying to say; the directive counselor tries to free the pupil of emotional tensions so that the pupil can attack his problems on a more logical basis and use the counselor's interpretation of his behavior to solve his problems.

Obviously directive counselors tend to make their clients dependent upon them. Competent ones recognize this danger and try to give each client as much responsibility as he can take. They also make a genuine effort to teach independence. For some dependent clients this is the most important part of the counseling experience.

COUNSELOR'S RELATIONSHIP WITH STAFF

The directive counselor also assumes much more responsibility than the nondirective counselor in working with the staff to develop a guidance program. He takes the initiative in helping them develop a testing program and a cumulative record. He teaches them how to contribute to the guidance records and how to improve their child study techniques. He enlists their assistance in his study of his pupils, he encourages them to seek his help in studying their pupils, and he may initiate a discussion of his own and teachers' limitations in attempting to help pupils.

When the directive counselor discovers a pupil who needs special help and does not seek it, he enlists the assistance of the staff in studying the pupil. He also may plan a case conference with the hope that someone in the group will know the pupil and will see value in referring the case to a counselor. If a thorough study of the child by the group supports the counselor's diagnosis, the counselor discusses openly with the staff his reasons for wanting a referral and the way in which someone from the staff could make the referral.

Eclectic Counseling

THEORETICALLY, the eclectic counselor chooses from the various schools the techniques that he believes most appropriate for him to use in order *to help each client*. He also feels it appropriate for him to change his role (varying the degree of responsibility he takes for the client) to meet the immediate needs of his client. On the surface, this approach makes good sense. Unfortunately, however, each counselor has only limited flexibility. He has certain attitudes toward people in general, and especially toward that part of the population from which most of his clients come. He may or may not believe, for example, that most of his clients have the capacity for solving their own problems or that most of them, left to their own good judgment, will make socially acceptable choices. Whatever he believes, these attitudes alone limit the extent to which he can play different roles and use techniques that are consistent with these roles.

Those individual qualities are peculiar to each counselor and may contribute to his unique successes but at the same time limit the roles that he can play. These are determined, as suggested above, in part at least, by his attitudes toward his clients, and also by his attitudes toward himself. For example, the eclectic counselor, in choosing methods from the various schools of counseling, probably will select those techniques that he believes he can apply effectively or can learn with a reasonable effort. He will avoid others because he does not think he can apply them effectively. Even the ability to make such judgments with reasonable accuracy will vary from counselor to counselor. One of the important functions of good supervision is to strengthen this ability. In addition to helping the counselor better to understand his clients, to examine his relationship with each, and to appraise the techniques used, good supervision helps the counselor better to understand himself and the techniques he can use most effectively in helping others.

Even if it were possible to place the leading spokesmen for all the various schools of counseling on a single continuum from very directive to very nondirective, few, if any, competent counselors would even pretend that they could play all these varied roles. Then what does it mean to be an eclectic counselor? The competent eclectic counselor selects those techniques (within the limits of his own values, personal qualifications, and professional competence) which will enable him best to help each client. As one might expect from this, eclectic counselors differ considerably from one another in their behavior. The behavior of each person tends to be more nondirective or else more directive—depending on the counselor's basic attitudes toward his clients and the amount of responsibility he encourages his clients to assume.

All eclectic counselors are required to make certain diagnostic judgments before they select the role they play, and they must use some criteria in order to make these judgments. The categories developed by Edward Bordin [5] and Harold Pepinsky [6] are perhaps the most useful which have been developed for this purpose. Bordin developed the following categories: (1) dependence, (2) lack of information, (3) self-conflict, (4) choice anxiety, and (5) no problem. While working as a colleague of Bordin in the Student Counseling Bureau at the University of Minnesota, Pepinsky studied the implications for using these categories in counseling college students. As an outgrowth of his research, Pepinsky retained Bordin's first four listings, and developed two new ones to replace the fifth: (5) lack of assurance and (6) lack of skill. In addition to defining these categories and citing meaningful case material to clarify their significance, the two researchers suggest treatment methods that the counselor may use with these various types of client. For example, Bordin defines the choice anxiety type as follows:

These individuals were faced with alternatives, all of which were unpleasant in that all would involve a disruption of their life plans. The student talking to the counselor was fully informed on all the alternatives open to him. He appeared to be coming to the counselor in the hope that he would be able to find some other alternative that would represent a way out without unpleasant consequences . . . [He also gives several examples of this type of client.]

The treatment that appears to be indicated for individuals with this type of problem is to enable them to face and accept the fact that they are "in for it." It is here assumed that once the individual has accepted the fact that he is in a situation from which there is no escape without unpleasantness, the psychasthenic symptoms will disappear and the individual will be able to make a decision. It is further assumed that many such individuals will be able to accept this statement of their problem when it is given to them directly after some "talking out" process . . .[7]

For the type 2 client (lack of information) Bordin again recommends directive treatment, perhaps even more counselor-centered than was true in the preceding case: "The treatment of such individuals would appear to be quite direct. They should be given information, referred to books or other individuals, and so on." [8]

5 Edward S. Bordin, "Diagnosis in Counseling and Psychotherapy," *Educational and Psychological Measurements*, VI (1946), 169–84.

6 Harold B. Pepinsky, *The Selection and Use of Diagnosis Categories in Clinical Counseling* (Stanford: Stanford University Press, 1948).

7 *Op. cit.*, pp. 180–81.   8 *Ibid.*, p. 178.

Bordin adds a warning that counselors be careful in such cases lest they foster dependency.

In contrast, he recommends nondirective counseling for the type 3 client (self-conflict). All three recommendations make sense, and it is very likely that Bordin is able to implement what he recommends. However, it seems questionable that either a very directive or a very nondirective counselor could follow Bordin's recommendations for counseling these three cases. The very nondirective counselor when he told the type 4 client what the situation was or when he gave information to the type 2 client, would feel that he was compromising on one of his basic principles—that the client has the resources for solving his problems. A very directive counselor would probably be unable to function as a nondirective counselor. Undoubtedly, competent counselors, even though they operated from these very different positions, could counsel all three types of client; however, they would have to counsel quite differently. Counselors can and do make some adjustments in their style of counseling to meet the needs of their clients, but few are likely to play successfully the diverse roles that are required for truly eclectic counselors.

Although counselors are limited in the techniques that they can apply effectively, they can use a variety of personality theories to enable them to understand their various clients. Leona Tyler illustrates this point as follows:

> Every personality has many facets. Different theories of personality are like spotlights focused on the individual from different directions. The same facets do not show up when one turns on the light labeled Freud that appear clearly when one throws on the Rogers switch. And while Freudian concepts may enable a counselor to understand and help Bill Amory, they may hinder him from seeing what is really the dominant factor in the life of Sarah Peele.[9]

When the counselor's diagnosis requires a shift in roles from either directive (counselor-centered) to nondirective (client-centered) or from nondirective to directive, his client often has difficulty in understanding the change. Sometimes a client will accept the change without an explanation, but even such a client often wonders why the counselor is treating him so differently. Usually such a basic change confuses the client. The eclectic counselor must be sensitive

---

9 Leona E. Tyler, "Theoretical Principles Underlying the Counseling Process," *Journal of Counseling Psychology,* V (1958), 3.

to this possibility, help the client talk about his confusion, and explain the changed roles. Obviously, a client has the right to know what he may expect from his counselor.

The confusion that results from switching roles is one of the basic arguments raised against eclectic counseling. Its critics contend that switching roles also interferes with the development of a wholesome counseling relationship. They further question whether the eclectic counselor really changes roles or whether he merely assumes some of the outward appearances of those roles that are not consistent with his own personality.

But failure to live the role that he has defined for himself is a problem not only for the eclectic counselor. Every counselor should be wary lest he fail to live the role to which he gives lip service. For example, a directive counselor warns his colleagues against interfering with a client's choice of alternatives, urging them merely to help the client define alternatives—and at the same time his recorded interviews reveal many instances in which he himself tried to influence his clients' choice.

One also can find instances of inconsistency between the behavior and the stated point of view of a nondirective counselor. Even though he may say that the counselor should help a client talk about whatever he chooses, one may find upon playing back one of his recorded interviews that he consistently responded to that part of the client's responses which highlighted one particular problem area—probably the area in which the counselor concluded the client's real problems lay. A reader should not infer from what has been said that most directive and nondirective counselors do not function within their philosophical framework. Many probably do. However, counselors must always maintain their efforts to understand their basic relationships with clients, and to note the very possible variance between their descriptions of the relationship and the actuality. This constant vigilance is especially important for the eclectic counselor because he tries to play such varied roles.

PUPIL'S PERCEPTION OF THE RELATIONSHIP

Pupils' perceptions of relationships with eclectic counselors vary, not only because the counselors use different methods but also because every individual observes and remembers different things.

With an eclectic counselor who has accepted most of the directive counselor's basic attitudes toward pupils, a pupil experiences much the same satisfaction and disappointment that he would have experienced with a directive counselor. And of course a similar statement may be made about the pupil with an eclectic counselor who has accepted most of the nondirective counselor's basic attitudes.

However, the pupil seeking help from an eclectic counselor who attempts to change roles while counseling will have experiences different from those of pupils with either directive or nondirective counselors. When the counselor shifts from a nondirective role to a directive role, the pupil usually wonders why this permissive person decided to assume more responsibility. If the pupil wants independence, he resents the shift, but if he wants to lean on someone, he likes it. Naturally, the pupil can accept this change more readily if it occurs early in the relationship.

Though the pupil can also accept the change from directive to nondirective, this change is more difficult than its counterpart mentioned above, since the counselor begins with a pattern similar to that of the pupil's other contact with adults, and thus the pupil tends to believe that the counselor will eventually return to it.

As was stated earlier, whenever the counselor changes his role, he confuses the pupil. The pupil feels he cannot count on the counselor —that he never knows what to expect from him. And of course the more frequently the counselor changes his role, the more he confuses the pupil.

COUNSELOR'S PERCEPTION OF THE RELATIONSHIP

On the basis of his knowledge of the client, the counselor decides what type of counseling would be most appropriate. During his early contacts with the client he assumes this role, and continues to play it unless further diagnostic information suggests that a switch in roles is necessary. Though he recognizes the need for considerable information on clients prior to counseling, he also recognizes the need for being flexible enough to use new information in changing his original diagnosis. Obviously, eclectic counselors differ considerably in their perceptions of the relationship. Consequently, their approaches also differ.

COUNSELOR'S RELATIONSHIP WITH THE STAFF

The eclectic counselor's role will be defined in part by his attitudes toward his colleagues. If he seeks their assistance in aiding his clients, they, in turn, are more inclined to seek his help in understanding their pupils. In this situation an atmosphere of mutual respect and confidence develops. He may, on the other hand, see himself as a specialist who may call on colleagues for assistance and also offer them assistance, but whose role as specialist gives him more status than teachers have. His own needs and the staff's prior perception of his role help determine which image finally prevails.

Author's Perception of Counseling

ALTHOUGH the author's perception of the counseling relationship is presented at the beginning of this chapter, the reader may wish to know precisely how that perception relates to the three points of view described above. Actually his perception does not agree entirely with any of the other three. He uses techniques from the various philosophies, but he cannot be labeled an eclectic because he makes neither the kind of diagnosis nor the change in roles that the eclectic does. However, he does vary the amount of responsibility which he assumes for a client according to the client's maturity and ability to assume responsibility for himself.

Over a period of twenty years he has *tried* to do what he encourages each student enrolled in supervised practice in counseling to do: to know himself and to select from various philosophies of counseling those techniques that are consistent with his competencies, values, attitudes toward people, and ways of relating to others. Though he has worked with adults, most of his clients have been reasonably well-adjusted elementary-school, secondary-school, and college students. In writing the following description of the counselor at work, he used public school clients for a frame of reference.

For the initial contact, it is usually the pupil who seeks the counselor's help. Because the pupil accepts responsibility for coming in on his own, he also finds it easier to accept responsibility during counseling. Occasionally the counselor invites a pupil to talk with him. However, he makes no effort to schedule conferences for all the pupils. When he invites a pupil to come in, the counselor indicates to the youngster what counseling is, what would be expected of him, and how the counselor might be able to help him; then it is the pupil's responsibility to decide whether he wishes to accept this help. Though some pupils who have not requested assistance will leave when given this choice, many will accept the assistance and others will return for the assistance later.

The pupil soon discovers that the counselor believes in him and in his potentialities for solving his own problems. He is helped to talk about his problems in his own way, and he finds that when he can make his points clear to the counselor, he himself understands them better. Furthermore, he feels that his counselor is especially sensitive to how he feels.

While the counselor actively helps the pupil obtain answers to his questions, the pupil has primary responsibility for determining the questions for which he needs answers. When some of the answers are to come from tests, the pupil has an important part in selecting the tests. He learns why he is taking the tests, learns something about what he can expect from them, and learns about some sources of information to supplement the test results. When a pupil seems to be worried about what he may learn from test results, the counselor tries to help him discuss these feelings. After the information is obtained, he tries to help the pupil not only to evaluate and use it, but also to discuss his feeling about it. Through such practices, the pupil feels responsible for his own actions and concludes that he must learn to decide things for himself. Finally, he terminates the sessions whenever he feels that he can proceed on his own. He knows, of course, that he can return to the counselor for help whenever he feels he needs it again.

As for the counselor, he makes no apology for using both the diagnostic skills of the directive counselor and the response-to-feelings techniques which are commonly associated with the nondirective counselor. Though he uses the directive counselor's diagnostic skills, he does not probe for facts in the pupil's past; rather he believes that the pertinent information and the relevant questions will emerge during counseling. At the same time, this counselor sees no reason why he should not obtain for the pupil that information which either is not readily available to the pupil or which the pupil could obtain only with very great effort. However, the counselor also considers whether getting information for the pupil will foster dependency.

The counselor does not force his understanding of the pupil into the pupil's thinking. Occasionally, he uses his understanding to speculate about how the pupil feels or to explain why the pupil feels and behaves as he does, making tentative statements with which the pupil can freely disagree. Usually he employs his knowledge of the pupil to help the pupil answer *his* own questions. He lets the pupil lead the way. He constantly checks to determine whether he is following what the pupil is saying and feeling. He tries to make sure that he is seeing the situation as the pupil does. Though some counselors reflect the pupil's feelings back to him in order to force the pupil to look at them again, that is not this counselor's reason for responding to feelings. Instead, he wants to make sure that communication channels are functioning properly. He believes that when the pupil expresses himself so that his words are meaningful to the counselor, the pupil probably is also improving his understanding of himself.

However, the counselor recognizes that even improved understanding of self is not sufficient, and neither is solving his immediate problems. As was suggested at the beginning of this chapter, the counselor must encourage the development of independence, help the pupil improve his problem-solving skills, and help him improve his overall level of adjustment.[10]

Though interested in improving teachers' guidance techniques, this counselor is more inclined to wait for the staff to ask for his assistance in developing an in-service training program than the directive counselor would be. On the other hand, he would be quick to ask the staff to help him understand a client.

Upon going into a new school, this counselor probably would not be as aggressive as the directive counselor, nor would he be as passive as the nondirective. All three probably would want their positions defined by the administration for the *staff*. While the nondirective counselor would probably stop there, this counselor would go to classes and activity groups to explain what counseling is and to answer *pupils'* questions about it. He would try to get acquainted with all of his clients and to help them understand counseling. On the other hand, he would try to avoid calling pupils in for conferences; he would use this method only as a last resort. If he discovered a pupil who could profit from counseling, he would enlist the help of the staff in studying the pupil—preferably in a case conference setting. If the session indicated that he was right, then he would describe the referral process and request help in bringing about the referral. If a referral did not follow within a reasonable period of time (defined in part by the urgency of the situation), he would again enlist the staff's help—to determine whether a refer-

10 Chapter 4 illustrates how this philosophy of counseling applies to some of the common problems that school counselors meet.

ral was still desirable, and then to decide whether to call the pupil in or wait longer for an opportunity for a natural referral. The counselor having presented the advantages and disadvantages of calling in the pupil, the case conference group would then make their recommendation; usually the counselor would abide by it. Through such experiences as these, the counselor demonstrates that he needs the help of his colleagues and that he respects their professional judgment.

Expectations from Counseling

WHEN a counselor defines the counseling relationship for either pupils or the staff he is usually expected to be able to tell what counseling can do for pupils. If the members of the staff are to make good referrals, they too must know what to expect from counseling. It is not sufficient for them to believe that counseling helps clients; they also should know how it helps. Moreover, they should understand these facts sufficiently to communicate the information to youngsters in meaningful language. The primary reason for attempting to show how counseling helps is to enable teachers and counselors to meet this responsibility.

Perhaps the best place to begin is with the goals of counseling. P. M. Symonds states them very well: [11]

—therapy consists not in giving the client the solution to his problems or even in helping him to discover the solution, but to change him in such a way that he is able to discover these solutions by himself. The adjustments themselves can be achieved only through the process of living. It is for this reason that the benefits of psychotherapy are never completely realized at the end of treatment, and the individual continues to work out more satisfactory adjustments for a considerable time after the treatment is completed.

In general the aims of psychotherapy can be boiled down to these two: in the first place, the therapist hopes that his clients will gain inner peace and freedom from anxiety, worry and stress. In the second, he hopes that his client will be able to effect certain changes in his behavior, leading to improved social relationships and more adequate functioning, both

11 Though Symonds speaks of goals for psychotherapy (or therapy), these are also appropriate goals for counseling. For this book, counseling is defined as a therapeutic experience for normal people treated in a nonmedical setting; psychotherapy, on the other hand, is defined as a therapeutic experience which is provided for emotionally disturbed people within a medical setting.

in his work, in his family and in his other social relationships. As a result of psychotherapy the client should become a better member of the human family. These two aims of psychotherapy are not unrelated, however, and as a person gains inner peace and freedom from anxiety he should also achieve improved social relationships.

Psychotherapy provides a situation in which a person, perhaps for the first time, can be completely honest with himself. Because he has nothing to fear from his therapist, he learns that he has nothing to fear from himself, and the false front which he has shown the world is no longer necessary in his relationships. When he discovers that what he has been concealing is not so terrible or so devastating and that he can afford to be himself quite naturally, much of the strain, tension, and anxiety of living is removed and he is then in a position to face life confidently and realistically.

To attempt to list the types of problems for which counseling services may be provided would be to list all the problems to which mankind is heir. First of all, any personal problem may be helped through counseling. Individuals suffering from feelings of inferiority, inadequacy, or immaturity may be helped by counseling, particularly with a nondirective approach, and such individuals, through the help of a sympathetic and accepting counselor, may be able to work through their own self-concepts with a minimum of assistance. However, in many instances, these inadequate self-evaluations point the way to neurotic difficulties. Other types of problems which may yield to counseling are feelings of inadequacy at work, the inability to concentrate or study, the inability to enjoy life's experiences or one's tasks, being cramped in personality expression and being unable to fit in with one's social group. Persons who suffer from feelings of stagnation, boredom, and emotional deadness and those individuals who find themselves without purpose should expect to benefit from counseling, although here again these apparently simple personality handicaps almost invariably lead to deeper problems involving emotional dislocation, neurotic difficulties, anxiety, and repression.[12]

There is evidence which suggests that the above goals are realistic. When successful, the following changes in attitudes and behavior have been noted in pupils who were counseled.

Improved school achievement for clients is one of the common goals of public school counselors. Research evidence indicates that: (1) third-graders treated with nondirective play therapy improved their reading ability—Bills; [13] underachieving, gifted ninth-graders

12 P. M. Symonds, *Dynamics of Psychotherapy* (New York: Grune and Stratton, Inc., 1956), pp. 9–11.

13 Robert E. Bills, "Nondirective Play Therapy with Retarded Readers," *Journal of Consulting Psychology*, XIV (1950), 140–49.

treated in group counseling improved their scores on a standardized achievement test—Broedel, Ohlsen, Proff, and Southard; [14] (3) antisocial junior high school age boys counseled in groups improved their grades—Caplan; [15] (4) delinquent boys improved their scores on a standard achievement test and on an individual mental test—Gersten; [16] (5) subsequent to counseling, college students made a better adjustment to college than a pair-matched control group—Williamson and Bordin; [17] (6) college students in academic difficulty improved their grades, and fewer dropped out of college than members of the control group who were enrolled in a study skills course but not counseling—Shelden and Landsman; [18] and (7) compared with other college students who had made a similar academic record at the time of the referral but did not accept counseling, the counseled students' performance was superior—Watson.[19]

Improved understanding of self was exhibited in clients in a variety of ways following counseling: (1) there was less discrepancy between high school students' interest scores and their self-estimates of interests—Singer and Steffle; [20] (2) college freshmen were more able to predict their probable achievement in college and to estimate their vocational interests—Berdie; [21] (3) mean gains in self-understanding by freshman clients appeared to be rather closely related to the mean client-participation index. (In other words, counselors who encouraged most client participation in test interpretations

14 John Broedel, Merle Ohlsen, Fred Proff, and Charles Southard, "The Effects of Group Counseling on Gifted Underachieving Adolescents," *Journal of Counseling Psychology*, VII (1960), 163–70.

15 Stanley W. Caplan, "The Effects of Group Counseling on Junior High School Boys' Concepts of Themselves in School," *Journal of Counseling Psychology*, IV (1957), 124–28.

16 Charles Gersten, "An Experimental Evaluation of Group Therapy with Juvenile Delinquents," *International Journal of Group Psychotherapy*, I (1951), 311–18.

17 E. G. Williamson and E. S. Bordin, "Evaluating Counseling by Means of a Central-Group Experiment," *School and Society*, LII (1940), 434–40.

18 William D. Shelden and Theodore Landsman, "Investigation of Nondirective Group Therapy with Students in Academic Difficulty," *Journal of Consulting Psychology*, XIV (1950), 210–15.

19 Gladys H. Watson, "An Evaluation of Counseling with College Students," *Journal of Counseling Psychology*, VIII (1961), 99–104.

20 Stanley Singer and Bufford Steffle, "Analysis of Self-Estimate in the Evaluations of Counseling," *Journal of Counseling Psychology*, I (1954), 252–54.

21 Ralph F. Berdie, "Changes in Self-Rating as a Measure of Evaluating Counseling," *Journal of Counseling Psychology*, I (1954), 49–54.

tended to help their clients achieve greatest increase in self-under-standing.)—Dressel and Matteson; [22] (4) there was a closer correlation between self- and other ratings—Sheerer; [23] and (5) according to the counselor-judgment criterion, there was a positive correlation between success of counseling and increasing awareness of self—Vargas.[24]

Increased acceptance of self is generally regarded as an essential element in improving the mental health of clients. Inasmuch as some laymen have become concerned lest counseling make clients conceited and self-centered, the nature of this change deserves clarification. First of all, this increased acceptance of self is usually associated with increased acceptance of others. Moreover, there seems little likelihood that successful clients will come to believe that they are good enough as they are—nor should they be encouraged to be completely satisfied with themselves as they are. Successful clients, on the contrary, seem to become increasingly aware of their own shortcomings, and increasingly committed to the correction of those weaknesses that they believe they can correct; at the same time, they feel that they do not have to be perfect to be good people. Maslow's [25] work with self-actualizing people supports this notion. He concluded that in spite of the discrepancies between their own human nature and their ideal image, the self-actualizing can accept themselves as they are. However, he also concluded that they feel guilty about their improvable shortcomings.

The following studies suggest that successful treatment does increase clients' acceptance of themselves: (1) unruly, antisocial junior high school boys showed increased correlation between perceptions of self and ideal self—Caplan; [26] (2) gifted, underachieving ninth-graders demonstrated increased acceptance of themselves in

22 P. L. Dressel and R. W. Matteson, "The Effect of Client Participation in Test Interpretation," *Journal of Educational and Psychological Measurement,* X (1950), 693–706.

23 Elizabeth T. Sheerer, "An Analysis of the Relationship Between Acceptance of and Respect for Self and Acceptance of and Respect for Others in Ten Counseling Cases," *Journal of Consulting Psychology,* XIII (1949), 169–73.

24 Manuel J. Vargas, "Changes in Self-Awareness in Client-Centered Therapy," Chapter 10 in *Psychotherapy and Personality Change,* ed. Rogers and Dymond (Chicago: University of Chicago Press, 1954), pp. 145–66.

25 A. H. Maslow, *Motivation and Personality* (New York: Harper & Row, Publishers, 1954), pp. 206–08.

26 *Op. cit.*

picture-test stories—Broedel, Ohlsen, Proff, and Southard;[27] (3) the greatest change in the subjects occurred in the areas of personal feelings toward self and in the amount of daydreaming (a fact which tends to support the theory that personal change precedes improved social adjustment)—Fleming and Snyder;[28] (4) college students' perceptions of self and ideal self moved closer to each other—Ewing;[29] (5) clients developed a more positive attitude toward themselves and their circumstances—Gibson, Snyder, and Ray;[30] (6) there was an increase in congruence between the self and the ideal self for the entire group, and the differences were reduced most for those who grew most—Butler and Haigh;[31] (7) in successful counseling there was a shift from a preponderance of disapproval of self to a preponderance of approval—Raimy;[32] (8) there was a marked and fairly regular increase in the measured acceptance or respect for self during counseling. (There also was a marked, but more uneven, increase in acceptance of others. A definite relationship was found between attitudes of acceptance of self and acceptance of others.)—Sheerer;[33] and (9) support for Raimy's findings was recently published by Todd and Ewing.[34]

Increased acceptance of others is supported by the following research evidence on benefits associated with counseling: (1) mean gain in acceptance of others (In the stories elicited in response to the picture-story test, the clients, after group counseling, demonstrated an increased ability to project affectivity into their stories. Not only was more affect introduced into the stories, but the identification figures as well as others were described in more positive

27 *Op. cit.*

28 Louise Fleming and William U. Snyder, "Social and Personal Changes Following Nondirective Group Play Therapy," *American Journal of Orthopsychiatry*, XVII (1947), 101–16.

29 Thomas N. Ewing, "Changes in Attitudes During Counseling," *Journal of Counseling Psychology*, I (1954), 232–39.

30 Robert L. Gibson, William U. Snyder, and William S. Ray, "A Factor Analysis of Measures of Change Following Client-Centered Therapy," *Journal of Counseling Psychology*, II (1955), 83–89.

31 John M. Butler and Gerald W. Haigh, "Changes in Relations Between Self-Concepts and Ideal-Concepts Consequent Upon Client-Centered Counseling," *Psychotherapy and Personality Change*, ed. Rogers and Dymond (Chicago: University of Chicago Press, 1954), 55–57.

32 V. C. Raimy, "Self-Reference in Counseling Interviews," *Journal of Consulting Psychology*, XII (1948), 153–63.

33 *Op. cit.*

34 William B. Todd and Thomas N. Ewing, "Changes in Self-Reference During Counseling," *Journal of Counseling Psychology*, VIII (1961), 112–15.

terms than previously. In stories produced after counseling, clients also increasingly depicted identification figures as demonstrating more warmth and affection for others, as well as being more willing recipients of affection.)—Broedel, Ohlsen, Proff, and Southard; [35] (2) increased acceptance of others also was reflected in these adolescents' improved interpersonal relations with others [36] (Independent judgments recorded on a behavior inventory by the father, the mother, and the members of a four-man observer team indicated that the clients had learned to live better with others); and (3) positive changes occurred in school administrators' attitudes toward themselves, other adults, and children—Zinet and Fine.[37] Zinet and Fine's work also showed that as an individual perceived himself, other adults, and children in a more favorable light, his behavior in a group setting also became more positive. As he exhibited less need to be in command and to win respect, he became more concerned about understanding, respecting, and aiding others.

Following counseling *the behavior of clients became more congruent with the behavior of well-adjusted persons.* For clients treated at the University of Chicago Counseling Center, Rogers [38] reported changes in personality structure which brought them closer to the well-functioning person. For junior high school pupils who were classified as major behavior problems in school by both teachers and administrators, Arbuckle and Boy [39] found that those pupils who were counseled made significantly greater change than their controls with reference to: (1) congruence between ideal self and actual self, (2) teachers' behavior ratings, (3) change in status of educational and/or vocational objectives, and (4) change in relation to peers (Counseled students were less rejected by peers, although there was no significant increase in acceptance). Gallagher [40] reported decrease in anxiety concomitant with client-centered therapy. Gibson, Snyder, and Ray [41] found that gains made by their

35 *Op. cit.*   36 *Ibid.*

37 Carl N. Zinet and Harold J. Fine, "Personality Changes with a Group Therapeutic Experience in a Human Relations Seminar," *Journal of Abnormal and Social Psychology,* LI (1955), 68–73.

38 Carl R. Rogers, "Personality Changes in Psychotherapy," *International Journal of Social Psychiatry,* I (1955), 31–41.

39 Dugald S. Arbuckle and Angelo V. Boy, "Client-Centered Therapy in Counseling Students with Behavior Problems," *Journal of Counseling Psychology,* VIII (1961), 136–39.

40 James J. Gallagher, "Manifest Anxiety Concomitant with Client-Centered Therapy," *Journal of Consulting Psychology,* XVII (1953), 443–46.

41 *Op. cit.*

clients were associated with three primary factors: (1) the kinds of change that trained observers noted: relief from tension, more positive or optimistic attitude about themselves and their situation, and less need to pour out their troubles; (2) data from Rorschach (the way a person changes in a relatively unstructured situation): greater emotional control and rapport and improved ability to utilize their reflective capacities; and (3) material principally from Minnesota Multiphasic Personality Inventory, but also from judges' ratings: less feeling of depression or anxiety, increase in activity, and increased feelings of independence. In a study which began with tenth-graders, Merenda and Rothney [42] compared those who received intensive counseling with those who received no counseling. They concluded that counseling seemed to produce increased educational, vocational, and personal adjustment, a more optimistic outlook toward the future, and greater persistency in post-high school endeavors.

In this instance the results obtained from individual and group counseling are presented separately. Results obtained from counseling individuals were presented in the previous paragraph. For individuals treated in groups the following changes were noted: (1) antisocial junior high school boys improved their school citizenship—Caplan; [43] (2) treating parents improved the school citizenship for misbehaving elementary-school children—Buchmueller, Porter, and Gildea; [44] (3) juvenile delinquents appeared to become less inhibited and evasive, more productive, more self-critical, and more responsive to mature promptings from within—Gersten; [45] and (4) prospective counselors increased acceptance of themselves and changed their manifest needs as follows: increased their need for autonomy, heterosexuality, and achievement, and decreased their need for abasement, succorance, and nurturance—Gazda and Ohlsen. [46]

42 Peter F. Merenda and John W. M. Rothney, "Evaluating the Effects of Counseling—Eight Years After," *Journal of Consulting Psychology,* V (1958), 163–68.

43 *Op. cit.*

44 A. D. Buchmueller, Francis Porter, and Margaret Gildea, "Group Therapy Project with Parents of Behavior Problem Children in the Public Schools," *Nervous Child,* X (1954), 415–24.

45 *Op. cit.*

46 George Gazda and Merle Ohlsen, "The Effects of Short-Term Group Counseling on Prospective Counselors," *Personnel and Guidance Journal,* XXXIX (1961), 634–38.

Who Is a Counselor?

THE counselor is a specialist in counseling pupils and helping teachers understand their pupils. He should be able to help teachers appraise a pupil's school progress, intellectual potential and growth, social development, and emotional adjustment. It also would be desirable for him to be able to help teachers diagnose learning problems and make plans for appropriate remedial instruction. He helps normal children solve their problems and identifies others who require more specialized treatment than he is qualified to give. He knows, too, how and where to refer children for the more specialized treatment.

WHAT KIND OF PERSON IS HE

The counselor is a well-adjusted person who works well with people. Teachers feel that he understands the problems which they encounter in the classroom and that he understands why they act and feel as they do in that setting. Pupils sense that he sees their problems as they see them. Both conclude that they can take any problem to him—that he is approachable. He demonstrates this approachability through his moment-to-moment contacts with students and staff from the day he arrives in the school. It is easy for students and staff to learn to trust the professional counselor. The counselor realizes when confidential matters are under discussion; he knows what information he may and may not discuss with teachers and with other counselors.

The counselor has a genuine interest in helping his clients resolve their own conflicts in their own ways, and he believes that they can reach solutions when they are given a chance to do so. He realizes that he does not know what is best for every client. Thus, he does not tell a client to "do as I would if I were in your spot."

He is fully conscious that if he fails to sense the importance of a client's problem as the client perceives it, he damages or interferes with the development of a good counseling relationship. Even when the counselor believes that the pupil's problem can be easily corrected, he avoids the temptation to say, "Oh, don't let this bother you; you will forget about it in a couple of days." He knows that such remarks make the pupil feel rejected, and that they do not reassure the pupil by persuading him that the whole thing will pass over quickly, but rather cause the pupil to say to himself, "That fellow doesn't understand kids. He doesn't know how it hurts to have a gal like Sally turn you down for a date."

The qualified counselor also understands himself and his own unresolved conflicts, and is aware of how these conflicts may impair his effectiveness as a counselor.[47] Though difficult for some to achieve, this understanding is necessary. Those with serious problems should be identified by the institution's program for screening prospective counselors and should be either rejected or referred for appropriate treatment. During their supervised practicum experience in counseling, others will discover how their own problems interfere with their ability to understand and help their clients. For some, this knowledge about themselves will be sufficient; most who discover such problems during the practicum will require the assistance of a competent counselor.

As the professional counselor recognizes his personal limitations, so too he recognizes his occupational limitations. He sees himself as no more than another worker in the school. Because he recognizes himself as a staff member whose work is of no more importance than that of the classroom teachers, he can honestly respect the judgments of his colleagues who live day in and day out with classrooms full of lively youngsters. Knowing that classroom teachers are specialists in their own right, the counselor can help create a working atmosphere which encourages teachers to participate in the guidance program and to develop policies appropriate for the school.

HOW DOES ONE BECOME A COUNSELOR?

Most public school counselors begin their careers as teachers. In fact, even with the present shortage of school counselors, most school administrators list teaching experience as one of the qualifica-

---

47 For example, Arthur Jersild [*When Teachers Face Themselves* (New York: Bureau of Publications, Teachers College, Columbia University, 1955)] reported that many teachers have not learned how to cope adequately with authority figures or with the topic of sex. Since adolescents often want to discuss these problems with a counselor, the counselor must learn to deal with the subjects. When clients tried to discuss topics which their counselor had not resolved, George Lawton ["Neurotic Interactions Between Counselor and Counselee," *Journal of Counseling Psychology* (1958), 28–33] found that the counselor became uncomfortable, and sometimes even hostile. Consequently, the counselor either discouraged discussion of certain problems or dealt with them in an authoritarian manner.

tions for counseling positions. They believe that classroom experience helps the counselor to relate to teachers—that such experience enables him to understand better how the teachers feel when things go well in the classroom, when things go wrong, and when the pupils put them on the spot.

Work-experience outside of teaching is also usually considered desirable. A number of states require it for counselor certification. Such experience gives the prospective counselor an opportunity to work with people from various socioeconomic levels—to talk with them and to learn about them and their personal values. While it is of course important that the counselor have read published materials on many kinds of work, it is equally important that he have firsthand experience in several ordinary jobs.

If a university student knows as an undergraduate that he wants to be a counselor, it would be profitable for him to select courses in psychology, sociology, social work, and business administration. Course work in child psychology, adolescent psychology, personality theory and/or dynamics, marriage and the family, community organization, business practices, labor organization and labor problems, and social psychology all provide useful background knowledge for the counselor. His teacher preparation should include work in child growth and development, curriculum, learning theory applied to the school setting, analysis of good classroom teaching practices, child study and evaluation techniques, and a well-planned sequence of supervised laboratory experiences with children.

Working from an opinion survey of members of the American School Counselor Association and the Association for Counselor Education and Supervision, David Lloyd [48] concluded as follows:

1. Any state which now possesses counselor certification or plans to adopt such certification for the first time should consider the following:

a. The certifying regulations should be mandatory and apply to all persons in the counseling field irrespective of the amount of time spent in counseling.

b. The counseling certificate should cover all grades, K-12, elementary through high school.

c. A teaching certificate valid for the level (elementary, junior high, or high school) on which the counselor is functioning should be required.

48 David O. Lloyd, "Counselor and Couselor-Trainer Attitudes Toward Counselor Certification in the United States," *Personnel and Guidance Journal*, XL (1962), 797, 798.

d. Adult work experience in addition to that of teaching should be required. The length of the experience should be one year.

e. The academic requirements should be stated in terms of broad general areas with specific courses. The broad general areas should include the following: counseling techniques; principles of guidance; educational and occupational information; analysis of the individual; supervised practice in guidance and counseling; organization and administration of guidance programs; statistics; group procedures in guidance; research and evaluation procedures; and human growth and development. . . .

f. Personal attributes such as emotional maturity, interest and ability in working with people, good personal adjustment, personality which invites and deserves confidence, pleasing appearance, and good physical health should be included as part of the certifying regulations.

g. The minimum degree program should be the master's degree for the first level, and, if two levels are used, the educational specialist degree (60 semester hours above the B.A.) program should be required for the second level.

h. Where there is only one level, the certificate should be renewed on the basis of either a period of every five years or a period of three years of successful counseling experience. . . .

2. The contribution of teaching and adult work experience to counselor certification should be further investigated as to the number of years of experience and type of experience desirable.

3. The feasibility of establishing uniform counselor certification in all states should be investigated. The results of this study indicate a marked agreement in all areas except that of levels.

4. There should be further study regarding the identification of desirable personal attributes for counselors and procedures for their assessment.

With reference to the academic requirements, Dorothy Clendenen,[49] C. G. Wrenn,[50] The American Personnel and Guidance Association's Committee on Professional Training, Licensing, and Certification,[51] and The American Psychological Association's Committee on Subdoctoral Education [52] all suggested similar preparation. The requirements of adult work experience and teaching experience have

49 Dorothy Clendenen, *Selection and Training of Counselors: New Prospectives in Counseling* (Minneapolis: University of Minnesota Press, 1955).

50 C. G. Wrenn, "The Selection and Education of Student Personnel Workers," *Personnel and Guidance Journal*, XXXI (1952), 9–14.

51 "APGA Committee Reports on Training, Licensing, and Certification," *Personnel and Guidance Journal*, XXXIII (1955), 356–57.

52 "The Training of Technical Workers at Subdoctoral Levels," *American Psychologist*, X (1955), 541–45.

been questioned, however, by some of the authorities mentioned above as well as by others.

In an article devoted to the discussion of six developmental tasks which school counselors will have to perform to achieve professional status, C. Harold McCully lists two tasks concerned with counselor education:

Standards for the selection and training of school counselors must be developed and such standards must be acceptable to the corporate group of qualified school counselors as well as to those professional schools offering counselor preparation of high quality. . . .

In order to make selection and training standards functional it will be necessary to develop a means of accrediting those institutions which meet such standards on at least a minimum basis.[53]

A number of years ago Joseph Samler[54] recognized that even good pre-service preparation for school counselors is not sufficient. In-service education is needed to maintain competence and to insure necessary professional growth on the job.

SUGGESTED READINGS

1. ARBUCKLE, DUGALD S. *Counseling: An Introduction.* Boston: Allyn and Bacon, Inc., 1961.

   This book describes the counselor and the counseling process for the beginner. It presents the client-centered point of view. Chapters 2, 3, and 6.
   a] What does the counselor need to know to fulfill his professional responsibilities?
   b] With what restrictions and contradictions are counselors often confronted?
   c] What are the critical elements in a good client-counselor relationship?

2. BORDIN, EDWARD S. *Psychological Counseling.* New York: Appleton-Century-Crofts, 1955.

   This book is addressed to counselors who are being trained to further the individual personality development of clients. Chapters 1, 2, and 3.
   a] How does Bordin define counseling?

53 C. Harold McCully, "The School Counselor: Strategy for Professionalization," *Personnel and Guidance Journal,* XL (1962), 685.
54 Joseph Samler, "Professional Training: End Goals or Kick Off Point?" *Personnel and Guidance Journal,* XXXI (1952), 15–19.

b] What are the objectives of personnel work?

c] Why is it important for the counselor to let the client know what is expected from him?

3. BRAMMER, LAWRENCE M., and EVERETT L. SHOSTROM. *Therapeutic Psychology.* Englewood Cliffs, New Jersey: Prentice-Hall, Inc., 1960.

Though parts of this book assume considerable background in psychology, Chapter 4 can be read profitably by the beginning student in guidance.

a] What are the steps in the therapeutic process?

b] What are the goals of psychological counseling?

4. FROEHLICH, CLIFFORD P. *Guidance Services in Schools.* New York: McGraw-Hill Book Co., Inc., 1958.

This is a book for the prospective guidance worker. Its primary focus is on guidance services. Chapter 10.

a] What arguments does Froehlich offer in support of the eclectic counselor?

b] What is the weak point in his plan for counseling failing students?

5. GOODSTEIN, LEONARD D., and AUSTIN E. GRIGG. "Client Satisfaction, Counselors, and the Counseling Process," *Personnel and Guidance Journal,* XXXVIII (1959), 19–26.

This paper presents one of the disputes concerning the role of the counselor. The dispute is between C. H. Patterson, a spokesman for client-centered counselors, and the authors listed above.

a] What are the primary arguments for using client satisfaction as a basis for evaluating counseling?

b] What are the arguments against it?

6. GORDON, IRA J. *The Teacher as a Guidance Worker.* New York: Harper & Row, Publishers, 1956.

The title describes the book well. Chapter 8.

a] How many teachers function as counselors?

b] What does Gordon believe to be essential for an effective counseling relationship?

7. McGOWAN, JOHN F., and LYLE D. SCHMIDT. *Counseling: Readings on Theory and Practice.* New York: Holt, Rinehart and Winston, Inc., 1962.

This book presents an unusually good collection of relevant papers for the school counselor. Chapters 2 and 3.

a] For what should an employer look in selecting a school counselor?

b] What is the place of values in counseling?

8. Moustakas, Clark E. *Psychotherapy with Children*. New York: Harper & Row, Publishers, 1959.

> *This book, written in language the beginner can understand, describes what goes on between a child and his therapist. Chapters 1 and 2.*
> a] What are the essential conditions for therapy?
> b] What are the primary goals of therapy?
> c] How does the therapist help the child achieve these goals?

9. Pepinsky, Harold B., and Pauline N. Pepinsky. *Counseling: Theory and Practice*. New York: The Ronald Press Company, 1954.

> *These authors contend that the counselor must be both scientist and practitioner. In developing important points they also raise many serious theoretical questions. The beginner may find some of their material too difficult, but he should encounter many useful ideas in Chapters 8 and 9.*
> a] What is the primary function of the interaction between counselor and client?
> b] What may a counselor do to build a good relationship?
> c] How does counseling help clients?

10. Porter, E. H. *Therapeutic Counseling*. Boston: Houghton Mifflin Company, 1950.

> *This book's unique value is in helping a counselor appraise his own counseling behavior. Chapters 2, 5, and 6.*
> a] How can one differentiate between an evaluative response and an interpretive one? between an interpretive response and an understanding one?
> b] Take the pre-test in Chapter 2 of Porter's book. Since the test is only to help you discover how you usually relate to persons who seek your assistance, please do not look at the key until you have finished.
> c] Try to locate a tape recorder in your school. Usually both the speech teacher and music teacher will have one. Record an instance in which a pupil seeks your help with a problem. Transcribe the interview and classify your responses in terms of Porter's five categories.

11. Rogers, Carl R. *On Becoming a Person: A Therapist's View of Psychotherapy*. Boston: Houghton Mifflin Company, 1961.

> *In this very interesting book Rogers talks about himself as well as about the counseling relationship and his research on counseling. The book is a collection of some of his best speeches and previously published papers. Chapters 2, 3, and 4.*
> a] What characteristics of the relationship foster growth?
> b] How can one build a helping relationship?

12. TYLER, LEONA E. *The Work of the Counselor.* New York: Appleton-Century-Crofts, 1961.

This book presents many good ideas for the beginning counselor. Chapters, 1, 2, and 12 present materials which are especially appropriate here.
a] What is counseling? How does it differ from psychotherapy?
b] What is unique about the counseling relationship?
c] What are the characteristics of a good counselor?

13. WILLIAMSON, E. G. *Counseling Adolescence.* New York: McGraw-Hill Book Co., Inc., 1950.

In this book the author, one of the early critics of Roger's nondirective counseling, describes his varied experiences in student personnel work. Chapters 1, 3, and 5.
a] How can counseling be viewed as education?
b] What significance does the author place on solving the client's immediate problem?
c] What does counseling contribute to the student personnel program?
d] What role should teachers play in the student personnel program?

SUGGESTED FILMS

1. *Counseling—Its Tools and Techniques,* 22 minutes, Vocational Guidance Films, 1948.

The script for this film was prepared by the staff of the Institute of Counseling, Testing, and Guidance at Michigan State University. It shows a trained class counselor working with an eleventh-grade boy who is about to quit school.
a] How did Mr. Jenkins help Bob talk about his problem?
b] Where do you think Mr. Jenkins was most effective?
c] Where do you think he was least effective?
d] What would you have done differently?
e] How did Mr. Jenkins project himself into Bob's life?
f] How do you think Mr. Jenkins would define his responsibilities in the counseling situation?
g] How do you think he would define Bob's responsibilities?
h] In which of the counseling groups would you place Mr. Jenkins?

2. *Client-centered Therapy,* two parts—30 minutes each, produced by Carl R. Rogers and Reuben Segel, Pennsylvania State University, 1953.

a] How did Rogers' work with the graduate student differ from his work with the middle-aged mother?
b] In what ways were his techniques different from Mr. Jenkins' in the Michigan State University Staff's film?
c] Where do you think he was most effective?
d] Where do you think he was least effective?
e] What would you have done differently?

3. *Psychotherapy I: The Counselor* and *Psychotherapy II: The Client—* approximately 30 minutes each, produced by Carl R. Rogers, Bureau of Visual Aids, University of Wisconsin, 1960.

In Part I Rogers tells how he feels while he is trying to help his clients; in Part II he discusses the client's side of the experience, demonstrating a number of the points with a young, adult, female client.

a] What does the client discover about herself as she deals with her problems?

b] What does the counselor contribute to client growth?

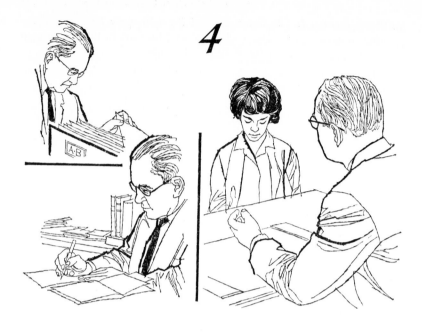

Counseling the Individual

THIS chapter describes the counseling process and shows how the counselor can meet some of his common problems. A few of these problems are of an emergency nature; they must be dealt with at once because they threaten the counselor and disturb the counseling relationship. But most are the more subtle problems which arise every day; these, though not so urgent or dramatic, must be well handled if the counselor is to understand his client, to develop a wholesome relationship with him, and to help him improve his adjustment.

Many of the problems encountered by the counselor are also problems for the teacher. For example, most teachers would like to understand their pupils better; they wish they knew how to talk with pupils more effectively, how to develop between themselves and their pupils an attitude of mutual trust, how to answer their pupils' questions with greater effectiveness, and how to teach their pupils to use pauses before speech for trying to clarify what they want to say. Teachers could use this knowledge and skill to improve private conferences with pupils and parents, to provide individual assistance with learning problems, to help high school students select school subjects, and to improve the classroom climate. On the other hand, a teacher should not be expected to serve as a school counselor. Counseling is a complex undertaking which should be reserved for the specialist.

Understanding the Client

USUALLY a counselor increases his chances of understanding a client by studying the client's cumulative record before the interview. However, such study also can lead him to restrict his concern to only those problems which were noted and reported by adults. Sometimes these are not the problems which trouble a pupil. Although the counselor will want to become as well acquainted with his client as possible before the interview, he must be wary lest he let preparatory impressions interfere with his trying to understand the client's situation as the client perceives it.

Sometimes a pupil is faced with an emergency. He recognizes the need for assistance and he wants to talk with someone immediately; he cannot wait for the counselor to study his record. On other occasions the pupil stops by the counselor's office for specific facts, such as information about a scholarship examination, a graduation requirement, or an activity program, and ends up discussing a very important personal problem. In such cases the counselor should not postpone the interview in order to consult the cumulative record. Instead, he should work with the immediate situation, listening to the pupil and helping the pupil explore the problems that trouble him.

WHAT CAN THE COUNSELOR LEARN FROM THE INTERVIEW?

What the counselor can learn from the interview depends upon his counseling skills, his understanding of human behavior, and his ability to listen effectively. There is another factor: a counselor's own needs and unresolved problems may interfere with his ability to understand what his client tries to communicate to him.

As the counselor struggles to understand his client (or clients in group counseling), he takes cognizance of emotionally loaded words, changes in speech patterns, facial expressions, and body movements. He is constantly aware that things may not be what they seem—that the client may communicate (and may even wish to convey) something very different from what he puts into words. Clients mask their real feelings for a number of reasons, such as these: they are ashamed of what they have done or how they feel; they find it difficult to admit such feelings or actions even to themselves; or they are not certain that they can trust the counselor. Whatever the reasons for it, the fact that persons often try to mask their real feelings and reactions is a commonplace—even children realize it—and most persons have developed some skills in detecting the phenomenon. The effective counselor uses this common knowledge, but has additional knowledge of human behavior from professional reading and graduate study. For example, he has learned that hair-pulling, scratching, and excessive body movement often mean that the client is anxious or disturbed; that crossing arms suggests client rejection of, or active resistance to, or suspicion of what is being said and done; and that arms open, especially with palms up, suggests acceptance of what is being said or done. He also has learned that clients express both positive and negative feelings in different ways. Some express positive feelings spontaneously; others act embarrassed. When some clients feel hostile they attack; others act bored or indifferent or defensive. Sometimes what appears to be affection is really hostility, and vice versa. Finally, the counselor recognizes that everything he observes about a client must be interpreted *in terms of all that he knows about that client;* though general principles of interpretation are useful in understanding most clients, they also may mislead a counselor. Every client has his own style of life, his own ways of behaving.

WHAT CAN PARENT CONFERENCES CONTRIBUTE?

Providing that the student realizes the purpose of the conference and understands that the counselor will not betray the youngster's confidences to the parents, parent conferences can contribute much to the school counselor's understanding of a client. On the other hand, failure to communicate the purpose of the conference and failure to keep confidences can destroy a counseling relationship. Because some counselors have assumed they have the right to share with the family what their clients have revealed to them, many students, especially secondary-school students, tend to be suspicious of such conferences. (The rare instance when a counselor must break confidence with a client in order to protect the client's or another's best interest is discussed at the end of the chapter.)

From parents the counselor can obtain their perception of the pupils' strengths, weaknesses, problems, and adjustment within the family. In such conferences the counselor also is able to identify family conflicts and to assess their seriousness.

WHAT CAN CASE CONFERENCES CONTRIBUTE?

In a case conference a counselor can learn from his colleagues how a client relates to peers and to authority figures, how well he uses his potentialities, how he responds to limits, and how he accepts responsibility. Of course, colleagues also obtain information from the counselor that enables them to understand the pupil better. The presence of several persons tends to sharpen the descriptions and to clarify discrepancies in perception. Furthermore, even with severe discipline cases, usually at least one of those attending the conference has learned to relate to the child well and can help others, including the counselor, to reach him.

WHAT CAN THE CUMULATIVE RECORD CONTRIBUTE?

If the cumulative record is well planned and organized, a counselor can learn much from it which will help him to understand a client: his family's status and role in community life, his personal, educational, and health histories, his extra-class activity record, his work experiences, and his plans for the future.

Building the Relationship

WHEN a pupil comes to a counselor seeking help, the counselor may assume that the pupil recognizes he needs help, that he wants to talk, and that he is motivated to do something about those problems which are bothering him. Under these circumstances he usually will assume more responsibility for solving his problems than do those pupils who are not sure why they are seeing a counselor. However, this does not necessarily mean that he will find it easy to talk about his difficulties.

Other pupils seek the counselor's assistance on the advice of teachers, parents, or classmates. Still others are called into the counselor's office by the counselor. Until such pupils recognize that they need help and believe that the counselor can aid them, counseling is not likely to help them.

As teachers improve their understanding of the counseling process and their ability to identify pupils who need counseling, they will be able to make better referrals. Then pupils will come to the counselor with a more accurate perception of what is expected from them and what they may expect from the counselor. If they are permitted to refuse help when referred, those who seek counseling also will come with greater readiness to discuss their problems. Those who refer pupils for counseling should, whenever possible, communicate to the counselor their reasons for making the referral and the pupil's reaction to it. This information helps the counselor to understand the pupil and to encourage him to talk about himself.

How can the counselor help the pupil who, even when identified and properly referred, does not accept the need for help? If the staff agrees that something must be done, the counselor calls the pupil in, explains why there is concern about him, outlines what counseling is and how it may help him, and then lets him decide whether he should seek counseling. Many such pupils at first refuse counseling, and then seek it later—after they have had a chance to think about what the counselor said, and to recognize that the choice is really theirs. If, however, such a pupil does not seek counseling, and the need for help persists, the counselor can enlist the assistance of colleagues and parents to plan appropriate action. If he has reason to believe that the client might seriously hurt himself or others, then the counselor is obligated to discuss the pupil's case with his supervisor. If the latter concurs, the two have a responsibility to discuss the case with the pupil's parents. Such a pupil should be referred to a psychiatrist for diagnosis and possible treatment.

Though the pupil, before he can be helped by counseling, must be willing to examine ways in which he must change to improve his school adjustment, school officials must recognize that others should be willing to change too. Often a pupil's poor adjustment is as much the fault of other people as it is that of the pupil. To expect him to do all the adjusting is not only unfair to the youngster, it may make it impossible for him to achieve better adjustment. Furthermore, he needs the assistance of important other persons for putting into practice the changes he recognizes and accepts.

The point also should be made that counseling is not the only way to help pupils. For example, an antisocial, nonconforming pupil may best be helped by better definition and enforcement of appropriate limits. This responsibility must be shared by the discipline officer, the teachers, and the parents.

What problems does the counselor face in trying to help the reluctant client? He may have difficulty communicating with him. Usually he has even more difficulty accepting the client's decision not to seek counseling. Forcing counseling upon such a client can create serious problems for the counselor too: success is unlikely, time is unnecessarily wasted, and the client may quite properly conclude that the counselor is invading his private life—a type of complaint that damages the counselor's relationship with other pupils.

Even when a pupil comes to the counselor of his own accord, it will not always be immediately clear to the counselor why the pupil has come to see him. Sometimes the pupil presents superficial problems as an excuse. In other instances he moves right into a discussion of the problem worrying him. While it helps the counselor to know why the pupil came, he should not press the pupil for an answer. Instead, he should help the pupil talk about the things he wants to talk about and listen to what the pupil has to say. Through listening he frequently learns the answers to the questions stated below; these answers help the counselor understand the pupil and also his own relationship with the pupil.

—With what problems does the pupil want help?
—With whom has he already discussed these problems?
—How did he learn about me? Did he come because some friends told him that I had helped them? Did he learn about me from one of his teachers? Was he referred to me by one of the staff members?
—What does he expect from me?

FIRST FEW MINUTES

When the pupil appears for his appointment or stops the counselor in the hall to say he would like to talk with him, the counselor is confronted immediately with the problem of building the best possible relationship for counseling. In Chapter 3 the point was made that the discussion following the pupil's request for a conference will include some of the elements of a friendly social conversation. Making the pupil feel welcome and, if the surroundings permit, helping him get comfortably seated, are two of these common elements. Though a counselor must adapt counseling techniques to his own natural way of relating to others, he can learn much about developing the counseling relationship by studying professional literature and by observing an effective counselor working with a client. To be effective the counselor must be sincere in showing a genuine interest in the client and conveying to the client some of the unique features of their relationship. For example, it is important that the pupil recognize early how the counselor-pupil relationship differs from other adult-child relationships, such as parent-child or teacher-pupil relationships.

Since the pupil comes to the counselor to talk about some specific question, he usually will start talking after exchanging greetings with the counselor. Of course, he may not start talking about what is bothering him most. He may try the counselor out first before sharing his most important problem. As he comes to feel that he can trust the counselor and that the counselor is trying to understand him, he will sense that it is all right to talk about anything that is important to him.

Should the pupil not start talking, then the counselor may help him start with such a comment as "What's on your mind?" or "What would you like to talk about today?" Through such remarks the counselor indicates that he believes the pupil knows better than anyone else what they should talk about.

Naturally, it makes a difference *how* the counselor says what he says. Even though he uses the right words, his tone may make the pupil feel threatened to the extent that he will find it difficult to talk. Or a different sort of pupil may fight what he believes to be a harsh comment by the counselor. Neither situation helps create a friendly and permissive atmosphere in which the pupil feels he can talk freely about his problems.

Occasionally, though the pupil wants to talk about something specific, and though he trusts the counselor, he still has difficulty discussing the matter. Too often the beginning counselor is willing to blame himself in such a situation, when the difficulty resides within the client. The client may have difficulty discussing the topic because he has never discussed it with anyone; perhaps he is not sure that he knows how to share it, or even that he wishes to.

SMALL TALK

When a pupil has difficulty talking, some school counselors use "small talk," especially during the first interview, to put the pupil at ease. These counselors assume that a friendly social conversation about school activities and the pupil's interests helps to prepare him to talk about his problems. But a counselor's use of this technique may lead the pupil away from the problem which he just barely had developed the courage to face. It also may give him an inaccurate picture of counseling. When effective, counseling helps a client to face and to deal with problems. Small talk can easily become a means of running away from them. Therefore, when a pupil comes for help, the counselor should help him to talk about his *problems* rather than encourage social conversation. If the pupil cannot face his problems, the counselor should help him tell why he cannot face them— why it is difficult to discuss the material involved. Occasionally, the pupil will turn to "small talk" at such times. This usually means that the topic is too threatening for the pupil to cope with at the moment. While the counselor may allow the pupil to use "small talk," he should not use it himself to find a secure role in the relationship: if he does so, he is putting his own needs ahead of the client's. When initiated by the counselor, "small talk" wastes both the client's and the counselor's time. Worse still, it may postpone the time when the client faces his problems.

If the beginning counselor could really believe that clients come in to talk about something, he would devote all his attention to trying to understand each client and to helping him talk. Failure to believe that the client wants to talk about something important to him causes the beginner to become anxious at the very time when he needs to be functioning at his best, when he needs to establish the groundwork of the counseling relationship. Sometimes it is necessary for the counselor to explain in layman's language what counseling is, what a client can do to help himself, what the counselor can do to help, and how counseling is of use to clients.[1] On such occasions the counselor should add that clients profit most when they talk to the counselor about matters that worry and disturb them.

PAUSES

The function of periods of silence in counseling is another topic usually dealt with in structuring—preferably when the first uncom-

---

1 This is called structuring. Though structuring is necessary on some occasions, best counseling services are provided in schools where the nature of the service is generally understood by pupils and staff. Counselors may promote such an understanding by describing counseling to pupils (use of examples

fortable pause occurs. Awkward pauses are difficult in social conversation; they are also difficult in counseling. Badly handled pauses are frustrating for both the pupil and the counselor. If the pupil does not understand the significance of the pause, he may be distracted from the problem with which he is struggling. If the counselor is bothered about the period of silence, his uneasiness may distract the pupil from the issues facing him. Yet during these pauses something very worthwhile may be going on within the pupil. He may be gaining some new insight or possibly organizing what he has to say.

During early interviews, pauses of only fifteen or twenty seconds may seem long, and embarrass the pupil because he does not know what to do and say in this situation. Rather than break the pauses with probing questions, the counselor should help the pupil realize that it is all right to take time to think about what he is saying.

Periods of silence are awkward because counselors make them awkward. In both academic and social settings there are times when persons engaged in conversation anticipate and accept periods of silence. When pupils are struggling with a difficult problem in a classroom, and everyone knows it will take time to turn up the first clue for a solution, no one is bothered by periods of silence. Similarly, no one is bothered by anticipated periods of silence during social activities. It is all a part of the game. So too in counseling, pauses are not disturbing when the counselor and the pupil know that it is normal for them to occur.

If the counselor understands the significance of a pause and feels comfortable, he remains silent, concerned only with the problem of understanding and sensing what the pupil is feeling. The counselor must learn to sense the unsaid if he is to help the pupil. Struggling to capture the pupil's feelings, the counselor may detect uneasiness in the pupil. Perhaps the pupil is having trouble talking about the issues before him; perhaps the pupil is disturbed about the pause. The counselor should respond to the pupil's discomfort.

The counselor must be watchful, however, not to break into the pupil's personal struggle unnecessarily. Interrupting the pupil's thinking when he is making satisfactory progress from his own point of view may lead the pupil away from some important issue which he is almost ready to examine.

Sometimes unproductive pauses may be explained by counselor

and case materials increases the effectiveness of such experiences) and answering their questions.

involvement. Since the dangers of counselor involvement were discussed in Chapter 3, only its effect on pauses will be considered here. When the counselor becomes so engrossed in his own needs and his ambitions for the pupil that he fails to respond to what the pupil has said, unproductive pauses result. At such times the pupil feels that the counselor is not "with" him. He cannot seem to make his statements meaningful to the counselor. Eventually he becomes so confused that he does not know how to explain again what he means. If, at such a point, the counselor will admit involvement, as Mr. Tiederman did in the examples cited in Chapter 3, then he probably can reestablish an effective relationship. Unfortunately, the counselor does not always recognize his own involvement. If, when he becomes aware of an unproductive pause, he investigates his own feelings prior to the pause, he may detect involvement. Then he can admit it, as was suggested above, or he can remain silent and try to capture the pupil's feelings and respond to them. When the pupil is so confused by the counselor's involvement that he cannot pick up the loose ends and proceed, then a response like, "I guess I have pulled you away from what you wanted to talk about. What would you like to talk about now?" gives the responsibility back to the pupil, with another chance to attack his problems in his own way.

Pauses are productive when their value is understood by the pupil and when the pupil uses them to decide how he feels, what he wants to say, and how he wants to say it. They are uncomfortable, confusing, and unproductive when they are not understood and when they result from the counselor's involvement.

Usually the pupil merely needs a chance to talk. But most pupils will not fight for that chance. Counselors should be alert continually to the possibility that they are talking too much or talking at the wrong time. Sometimes a counselor does not follow what the pupil says because he has already made his diagnosis and fails to listen. Quite sure that he sees what is bothering the pupil, he is anxious to know whether he guessed correctly, and he is so intent on his own thinking that he loses his client. Instead, the counselor should try to be another self for the pupil. He should try to stay out of the pupil's way. He should listen attentively. He should allow time for the pupil to finish saying what he has to say. Through use of such expressions as "M-hm-," he can let the pupil know that he is following him and that he understands what the pupil means. If he is not sure whether or not he understands what the pupil means, he can check himself through use of comments like: "You mean . . ." or "You feel that they do not . . ."

Periodic recording of interviews enables counselors to listen to their own performances in order to improve them. As the counselor listens to his own recordings, he should seek the answers to questions like these:

—Did I help the pupil say what he wanted to say?

—Was I trying to follow what the pupil was saying, or was I trying to get him to discuss those subjects about which I wanted to talk?

—How often did I interrupt the pupil?

—Did I give him a chance to say later what he wanted to say when I interrupted him?

—Did he try to interrupt me and fail? What did he try to say? Did he ever try to say it again?

—What did I do to help him clarify how he felt?

—Was I able to detect the subtle points that he tried to convey?

As the counselor listens to his own recorded interviews, he can detect changes he should make, and then work to improve his practices. At times he requires the assistance of a trusted professional friend who will detect errors which the counselor fails to note. Recordings may be employed also by teachers to improve their methods of teaching as well as their guidance techniques. Making recordings and listening to playbacks can lead to improvement in any relationship that involves talking.

DEVELOPING THE CLIENT'S CONFIDENCE IN THE COUNSELOR

The client's reason for seeking counseling, the extent to which he feels he needs counseling, the way the counselor receives him, and the counselor's success in helping the client talk are all important in developing the client's confidence in the counselor. The counselor's reputation outside the office is also important: what he does in extra-class activities makes a difference; if he teaches, the impression he makes as a teacher counts. Spending extra time helping his pupils with their work attracts pupils' attention. If a counselor wishes to be trusted, he cannot be an all-accepting person in his office, and something very different outside of it. *Wherever* youngsters meet him and work with him, they should find in him the personal qualities which lead them to accept him and believe in him.

The following example presents still another aspect of establishing a good counseling atmosphere. Jane's father, who meant much to her, had recently died. Almost as soon as Jane began talking to the counselor about her father, she started to cry. She would talk and then cry, talk some more and then cry again. While she talked out and cried out her problem, the counselor did not even hint that he felt sorry for her; yet he did try to see how she felt and to help her tell him about it. During one fairly long period, she just wept while he sat saying nothing. Finally, she stopped crying and said, "Thanks for letting me cry it out. I feel better now. You understand, don't you? You know why I had to cry it out, and you don't make me feel a bit ashamed. Why do people have to spoil a cry by making you ashamed because you cried?" Jane's comment suggests that simple acceptance of the pupil and his feelings helps more in creating a counseling relationship than reassurance does.

The counselor's reputation for keeping confidence is also important to a pupil. Mr. Black's experience with one of his pupils, for example, might have gotten him into trouble with a less understanding principal, but it won him the pupil's trust. Early in his first year at a new junior high school, one of his eighth-grade mathematics pupils asked to see him after class. Once they were alone, the pupil went right to the point and told how he had stolen fifty dollars from the athletic fund. The counselor helped the boy tell his story, discuss the motivations for the theft, and consider its possible consequences. Eventually, he made sure that the boy put the money in a safe place.

Immediately after their conference, Black went to a faculty meeting. There he heard the principal describe the theft and request the assistance of everyone in apprehending the thief. Black was faced with an ethical problem. Should he go to the principal and report the boy or should he keep the confidence? He said nothing.

Four days passed before the boy returned to see Black. Apparently, no one knew who had stolen the money except Black and the boy. After a few minutes, the boy asked Black why he had not been called into the principal's office or arrested. This led to a discussion of what counselors do with confidential information. Black also explained why he made sure that the money was in a safe place.

Then the boy asked Black to return the money to the principal. Black responded to the boy's feeling of inadequacy in facing the angry principal, and they discussed these feelings in some detail. Eventually the boy concluded that he would have to "face the music" and return the money himself. Black offered to role-play the scene with the boy and play the principal's part. They went through the scene several times and discussed the problems involved in talking to the principal and returning the money. Finally, while the boy went for the money, Black arranged for the principal to see the boy. He told the principal only that an emergency demanded his attention immediately, and that he thought the principal would appreciate the importance of the event when he talked to the person who was coming to see him. The principal never revealed exactly what happened when the boy returned the money, and Black never learned what the boy told his peers, but their subsequent reactions to Black as a counselor indicated that the boy certainly must have said something that caused them to trust Black with their problems.

The next day Black requested a conference with the principal in which he described his role in the case, the ethical issues involved, and his reasons for acting as he did. Black felt tense and defensive at the beginning of the conference, but as he tried to see the principal's side of the case he grew less defensive. The principal helped, too, by discussing freely his own negative and positive feelings about Black's action. While he had always believed it was the counselor's job to keep him informed on such school problems, he said that he was now willing to help Black try his way. They agreed that Black should break confidence and discuss cases with the principal only when someone could be *seriously hurt* through failure to take steps of prevention. They concluded that this theft was not such a case.

These agreements helped Black. From that point on he found it easier to build a counseling relationship with his clients in this school. First, he was aided by knowing what to expect from his principal. It also helped to have so many pupils come to him at least partly prepared to believe in him.

Nevertheless, Black still had to build a counseling relationship with each pupil who sought his help, and he had to be aware of the dangers growing out of counselor involvement. He knew that he always had to be conscious of his feelings toward the client in building a counseling relationship, and that sincerity was important. He knew that when he rejected a youngster or was not truly interested in someone's problem, he would be adversely affecting the counseling relationship.

The counselor can try to override feelings of distaste or discomfort, he can try to be friendly and want to accept a pupil for what he is

—but until he understands why he feels about the pupil as he does, he will not be able to accept him. When he really accepts the pupil and tries to understand what he is saying and feeling, then he can establish the most effective relationship.

Sometimes when the counselor is successful in establishing a good counseling relationship, he is dismayed to find he has become a target for aggression. Although the pupil may not be attacking the counselor as an individual, he may attack him either because he sees the counselor as a symbol of authority, or because the counselor does not do what he wants him to do. He also may only seem to be attacking the counselor when in reality he is trying to determine whether or not the counselor is really accepting him. If the counselor recognizes this situation for what it is, he will find that he can more easily accept the pupil's aggressive attitudes. It is important that he accept the pupil's need to test limits and to release hostile feelings, and that he help the pupil tell how he feels rather than scold him for feeling aggressive. This understanding attitude helps to build an effective counseling relationship.

Helping the Client Talk

WHEN a good relationship has been developed and the client understands and trusts the relationship, he will discuss the topics with which he believes he is ready to cope. With respect to other relevant subjects which the client avoids, the counselor helps to prepare him to face the threatening content involved. Some of the common problems the counselor faces in achieving this end are discussed here.

STRUCTURING

Effective structuring helps the client talk. During the process of structuring the school counselor is often confronted with several communication problems: he may fail to state in the pupil's language what is expected from the pupil and what counseling may do for him; or he may use appropriate language, but fail to communicate with the pupil because of the pupil's previous experiences with adults who have tried to help him. Some clients fail to understand or to accept limits. Some doubt the counselor's sincerity when he refuses to do what they want him to do. In every one of these instances the counselor must be alert to the danger that he is talking over the head of a client or failing to communicate the unique features of the counseling relationship. (Of course he must first have a clear perception of these features himself.) The counselor also must communicate to his client that he is trying to understand why the client assumes the counselor will treat him as other adults have treated him.

But the above suggestions deal only with the definition of the relationships, including setting limits. What can the counselor do about the client who refuses to accept limits or the one who tries to manipulate the counselor? Here too the best answer is to try to understand how the client feels and to reflect these feelings to him —e.g., "You are angry with me because I insist on stopping on time," or "You are trying to get me to fix things up with your English teacher. Perhaps this is your way of trying to find out whether I really want to help you. Probably you wonder why I try to help you do things for yourself rather than do things for you." When spoken in an understanding way such comments help the client deal with the motivations behind the behavior, and at the same time convey the counselor's genuine desire to understand the client.

REFLECTING FEELINGS

In attempting to reflect his client's feelings, a counselor faces at least five problems: (1) developing a relationship that will enable the client to express his real feelings; (2) understanding the client (and identifying the feelings to which he should respond); (3) helping the client to recognize feelings of which he is not fully aware or those which he has difficulty accepting; (4) determining when to reflect these feelings; and (5) trying to reflect the client's feelings without suggesting either agreement or disagreement with them.

The first two problems were discussed in previous sections of this chapter. The third and fourth involve consequences similar to those associated with probing. When the counselor detects feelings of which the client is not fully aware or which he would find threatening, he must try to assess whether the client is ready to cope with the material. Forcing the client to look at these feelings can be debilitating as well as helpful. Though pupils profit most from counseling when they discuss the topics that worry and upset them most, they can cope with only a limited amount of anxiety. This is especially true of adolescents.

With reference to the fifth problem listed above, the counselor should, when structuring, make clear that he will reflect the client's feelings and not express his own feelings. When the pupil says, "My history teacher is the meanest person I ever met," or "My father is the most low-down, no-good man in town," he should realize that the counselor's response indicates his efforts to understand how the pupil feels rather than his personal agreement or disagreement with the feelings expressed. While trying to see situations through the pupil's eyes, the counselor also wants the pupil to realize that the views expressed are the pupil's, not his own.

When, for example, Michael came to the counselor to discuss his vocational plans, he launched into a discussion about his dad. What he said went as follows: "You know, Mr. Robinson, my dad is a great guy, but I am pretty disgusted with him. We have always done a lot of things together—swimming, fishing, playing ball and the like—but now he takes it for granted that I will go into business with him when I finish high school. I have enjoyed his companionship so much that probably I would have decided to go in with him had he talked it over with me and invited me. I think I would like the work, and that I would do well, too. But I just can't stomach his smooth way of trying to finagle me into doing it. Why do you suppose he would do a thing like that?"

The counselor's response, "Your dad is a swell guy, you like him a lot, and now he has done something that bothers you and you wonder why," made Michael feel that the counselor understood how he felt, and it also let him know that he could tell the counselor more about his feelings. This response did not indicate, however, that the counselor agreed with Michael.

Many young people who, like Michael, feel anger or hatred for loved ones, have learned to repress these feelings. Before such a person can talk freely to a counselor about his feelings, he must be convinced that he can trust the counselor, and he must believe that it is all right for him to talk frankly about any person or topic. With the assistance of an accepting and understanding counselor, the youngster learns to express both the positive and negative feelings that he needs to explore. As the pupil is able to make these feelings meaningful to the counselor, he also comes to understand himself and is able to decide what he should do.

Neither giving Michael a lecture on respect for parents nor taking Michael's side would have helped the boy—who needed to examine and clarify his feelings toward his father. And though the release of feelings is important in counseling, there is a good deal more to the counseling process than that. Either by himself or with the help of the counselor the client must discover why he feels as he does, and learn what he can do to achieve the positive adjustment and happiness he seeks.

THE DEPENDENT CLIENT

The rationale for discouraging dependency was presented in Chapter 3. Although most teachers and counselors recognize the inherent dangers in encouraging dependency, the dependent client does make the adult feel important: he makes the adult feel needed and appreciated. Thus, the temptation to satisfy his own needs is a problem for the counselor in working with a dependent client. The counselor must achieve his personal satisfactions from observing his clients learn to make independent decisions and to act upon them. When this happens, his clients genuinely appreciate the counselor for trying to understand them and for helping them learn to make decisions. They tend not to feel grateful for his help in solving their problems because they feel that they have solved their own problems.

Another difficulty for the counselor in dealing with the dependent client is the danger of being manipulated. When confronted with a counselor who will not tell him what to do or run interference for him, the dependent client often tries to manipulate the counselor: he gives the impression that he is so weak that he cannot be expected to act independently, or he appeals to the counselor's ego. As was suggested under the sub-topic "Structuring," the counselor's best approach is to use reflection of feeling to let the client know that he understands why the client wants to manipulate him. If, on the other hand, the client really is too weak to act independently, the counselor must teach him to do so gradually—giving him increasingly greater responsibility for his decisions.

What may at first appear to be a clear-cut request for information may actually be a request for advice. The client may want to be told what to do in order to avoid responsibility for his behavior. In such cases the counselor who is eager to help may fail to discriminate between giving advice and giving information.

When the counselor assists the pupil in finding the best factual answers to his questions and in determining what these facts mean without projecting his own personal needs into the analysis and interpretation of the facts, he is giving information. During this process he tries to respond to the pupil's needs, helps the pupil to make the information meaningful to himself, and allows the pupil to use or ignore the information as he chooses.

Whenever the counselor makes judgments for the pupil or projects his own values and needs into his suggestions, he is giving advice; in most cases, an observer would have difficulty discriminating between a counselor's suggestions to pupils and his advice to pupils. In defending what they have labeled a suggestion, some counselors will make such a comment as, "But I was merely suggesting the obvious. This pupil overlooked an obvious alternative." But there are no obvious solutions: if a solution were obvious, the pupil would have seen it without the counselor's pointing it out. Sometimes, indeed, that "obvious" solution is the choice which the counselor likes, the one he wishes he could have made.

Because the counselor never fully understands the person across the desk, it is difficult for him to follow the pupil's attack on his problem. At times the pupil eliminates the alternative which from the counselor's viewpoint appears to be best. The pupil may do this because of some perfectly good reason which is known only to him. On the other hand, he may see the alternatives differently because he and the counselor hold different values. When the counselor advises reconsideration of an alternative that the pupil has eliminated, he forces the pupil to give that alternative special status. The pupil can no longer weigh it equally with the other choices, for the counselor's prestige forces the pupil to give it a special priority. Whether the pupil fully realizes it or not, he no longer has a completely independent choice of alternatives.

With the giving of advice, also, the counselor assumes a certain responsibility for his pupil. Should the advice turn out to be bad, then the counselor shares at least part of the blame for the consequences.

Directly related to the problem of information and advice is the problem of decisions. Pupils seek help, after all, because they are faced with problems that appear too difficult for them to solve alone. Sometimes they need to release the tensions that prevent them from using their own resources to solve their own problems. At other times, they need facts about themselves and the conditions in their environment, facts that they can use to achieve the insight necessary for choice. Though the counselor should help the pupil achieve all of these goals of counseling, the pupil must feel responsible for making the decision he feels is best for him.

Pupils learn to make independent decisions gradually, through solving problems that are important to them. They need the help of both teachers and counselors to achieve this maturity. When, for example, Ernest had difficulty choosing between geometry and world history, his adviser became impatient and suggested that he take world history: by telling Ernest what to do, the adviser missed an opportunity to teach him how to make such a decision himself. The adviser should have responded to Ernest's conflict; he should have helped the boy talk about why he was having difficulty making the choice, what he needed to know before he could decide, and how he could find the information which would help him decide.

Dorothy's adviser, in contrast, helped her work her own way to the solution of a similar problem. When Dorothy asked her adviser whether she should take senior science or chemistry, he said, "You want me to decide what you should take when you are the only one who can really make the choice. Since you seem to understand what each of these courses offers, you must make the choice in terms of your educational and vocational plans. You should also take into account what each course will contribute to your life now. I can help you think through these plans, but you, better than anyone else, can decide what you should do." After Dorothy had studied her abilities, aptitudes, and interests, she found that she was able to formulate for herself tentative educational and vocational plans and, consequently, that she could make the choice between the two courses.

Sometimes a pupil seeks a counselor's help, even defines alternatives, and then never reaches a decision as far as the counselor knows. At least the pupil stops coming for help before reaching the decision. The counselor should be able to accept such behavior, though he often finds it hard to do so. Sometimes conditions change so that what previously was a serious problem for a pupil no longer seems important to him; hence, he need not make a decision. At other times the pupil concludes, perhaps, that he has achieved all he can from counseling, or perhaps that he has reached the point where he can proceed on his own. These are appropriate choices even though they may disturb some counselors.

THE HOSTILE CLIENT

There are a number of reasons why a client appears to be or is hostile. Suppose a client shows hostility when he is trying to decide whether he really wants help. Rank [2] described this condition within the client as the conflict between wanting help and at the same time resisting it. There are several other related reasons for hostility on the part of clients: (1) some cannot believe that anyone would care enough to try to understand them and to help them, and so they are angry at what seems to them the insincerity of the counselor's interest; (2) others do not feel that adults *can* understand them; and (3) still others act and feel hostile because they believe that counseling is being forced upon them, that the counselor is invading their private world against their will. This usually happens when the counselor calls a pupil in, offers him counseling, and expects him to accept it. Sidney Berman [3] reports that adolescents often are brought into counseling against their will. He also notes that adolescents are made to feel that they are the ones who are expected to change. Therefore, they tend to be suspicious, defensive, and anxious. N. W. Ackerman reaches a similar conclusion concerning adolescents:

. . . one observes their extra-ordinary sensitiveness to other persons' judgments of their worth, their constant concern with proving adequacy, their profound sense of vulnerability to criticism and attack from without. They are caught between the two horns of conformity and defiance. It is small wonder that they show such triggered-edge irritability.[4]

Finally, a client often acts hostile when he approaches a topic that he finds too threatening. This reaction is resistance.

It is always essential to remember that resistance has a strong protective value. The patient will usually reject any insight that is too traumatic, or he will toy with it for a while, then forget it. However, through careful handling, he may gain insight as to how and why the resistance is operating. First of all he must be made aware of the resistance. Merely calling

2 Otto Rank, *Will Therapy and Truth and Reality* (New York: Alfred A. Knopf, Inc., 1950), p. 16.
3 Sidney Berman, "Psychotherapeutic Techniques with Adolescents," *American Journal of Orthopsychiatry*, XXIV (1954), 238–44.
4 N. W. Ackerman, "Group Psychotherapy with Mixed Group of Adolescents," *International Journal of Group Psychotherapy*, V (1955), 249.

his attention to it makes him concentrate on a specific task. It prevents him from burning up all his energy in maintaining the resistance; it enables him to use some of his energy in tracing down its meaning.[5]

These mechanisms must be understood by every counselor. Even normal people exhibit resistance when they approach threatening topics before they are ready to deal with them. Every counselor also should recognize various kinds of behavior which indicate resistance: such recognition should signal him to be cautious lest he uncover too much and should help him to locate problem areas with which the client needs help.

When the client acts hostile, the best course of action for the counselor is to try to understand what is happening. Even the layman can understand this as the most effective method for reaching people in less extreme conditions; it is also the best way to reach the angry, suspicious client. When such a client attacks another, he expects to be attacked. If, instead, the counselor tries to understand the client and to help him express his hostility, this behavior often will catch the client off guard and break through his resistance. It also will convey genuine acceptance. Nevertheless, many beginning counselors find such a response difficult because they resent the hostile client's lack of respect for his elders, and his criticism of his teachers and the school's practices. Though it is easy to understand why counselors want to defend these persons and practices, they must learn to curb this tendency and to direct all of their psychic energy toward understanding the client.

RESISTANCE

The problem of coping with the hostile client and with resistance was discussed above. This section will focus attention on behavior that suggests resistance. Obviously, this topic cannot be dealt with adequately in such a limited space; but even a brief discussion can alert those planning a career in public school counseling to some of the problems they will face and help them to see that they can learn to cope with these problems. This discussion may also help those teachers and administrators who are taking a beginning course in guidance to understand why some clients behave as they do with counselors. When, for example, during counseling a pupil criticizes

---

5 Lewis R. Wolberg, *The Technique of Psychotherapy* (New York: Grune and Stratton, Inc., 1954), p. 479.

his counselor, it can mean that the counselor is so effective that the client is becoming aware of the need for certain changes which are so threatening or difficult to accept that he resists them.

How does the client behave when he tries to avoid discussion of hurtful experiences or when he defends himself against change? Ways in which these behaviors have been exhibited by clients are described below.

1. Resistance against improved understanding of self. Two clients, both of whom had asked to have tests interpreted, exhibited this behavior for very different reasons. One was a college freshman who was on probation. Soon after he married a professional man's daughter, he decided to leave his cabinet-making trade in order to prepare for a high school teaching position. When he got into college he found his courses so difficult that he soon became discouraged; furthermore, it was a real struggle for him to examine his chances for college success. Most students like this, for whom a college education means a great deal, find it difficult to face the fact that their chances for success are poor. But for this young man the problem was especially difficult: he was afraid that failure to earn a college degree would also mean loss of his wife's and father-in-law's respect. He also felt guilty about blaming them for getting him into this hurtful situation.

People sometimes resist understanding their strengths as well as understanding their limitations. The other client was an eleventh-grader who was convinced by his father that he lacked the academic aptitude for college. When, in interpreting a mental test (he registered an I.Q. of 124—only five points below that of his brother, for whom the father had great hopes for academic success), his school counselor explained that he had unusual academic promise, he rejected the test scores. He had chosen an occupation, a girl friend, and a way of life based upon one perception of himself; hence, he tried to ignore the new information, which he feared might force him to reevaluate his present plans. Fortunately, the counselor did not try to defend the test; neither did he try to force the boy to reexamine his plans. However, he did detect and reflect the boy's feelings accurately. This seemed to help the boy explore his attitudes toward himself and his plans, and eventually to accept a more accurate image of himself.

2. Self-devaluation. This term describes the response of the second client cited above. It also characterizes the behavior of the

gifted underachiever. He tries to convince those who try to help him that he cannot be expected to do any better.

3. Flight to health. This kind of resistance, through denial of difficulties, often emerges when a client is referred or when he explores the value of counseling with a counselor. For example, the author recently explored the possibility of group counseling with a prominent physician and his wife. Their daughter's teacher had referred them because the girl was underachieving and they were concerned about her. When the father realized that the group counseling method of helping his daughter would expose his own feelings of inadequacy, his first inclinations were to play down his daughter's need for help.

When a client approaches problem areas that are too threatening or disturbing, he tries to convince the counselor, and himself, that he has solved his problems and has no further need for counseling. He may even begin to behave in a manner that confirms this notion —e.g., a pupil who was referred for poor grades may temporarily improve his grades. Sometimes he works so hard to prove that he does not need counseling that he maintains the improved academic work.

4. Nonparticipation and blocking. The type of client who expresses resistance this way comes late, breaks appointments, relapses into silences, has difficulty remembering what he wanted to talk about, or reports that he has nothing else to talk about.

5. Superficial talk. Many clients exhibit resistance by "small talk" or by preoccupations with side issues. This protective talking also may take the form of talk about symptoms; or it may take the form of intellectualizing. Intellectualization tends to mislead the counselor because the client does talk about himself—but he talks with little or no affect. He discusses himself in such an impersonal manner that the content is no longer threatening. For example, a graduate student in clinical psychology tried to avoid discussing his need to change by talking about his case history. He understood how he had come to be what he was, but he was afraid to try to change.

6. Direct attack. Clients make their assaults in a variety of ways. When the counselor interpreted the psychology student's resistance, described above, the student became very hostile and criticized the counselor for failing to obtain an adequate history. Some will criticize the counselor in their relations with others outside of counseling. If the counselor can accept the client's criticism of him, the

client may go on to question the value of counseling—using this as a means of putting the counselor on the spot. Some also try to seduce the counselor as a means of putting him on the spot.

7. Dependency. Another kind of client, when threatened, resorts to a demonstration of dependency and self-pity. When this method fails, some clients will criticize the counselor on the grounds that he does not care enough to try to help.

"SPILLING TOO MUCH"

Since much attention has been given here to ways of freeing a client to speak, it should be said that merely helping the client talk is not a goal in itself. The counselor must help the client talk about topics and issues that will help him improve his adjustment or solve his problems, and "spilling too much" does not help him achieve these objectives. In fact, it can even damage the relationship with the counselor. Talking too freely in counseling also may cause the client to spill too much outside of counseling. When he wonders whether he has talked too much or to the wrong persons, he is threatened, and the counseling relationship may be damaged. If the counselor suspects that a client may talk too freely outside of counseling, he is obligated to help the client see the difference between talking freely with a counselor and talking freely with a friend— another example of structuring. If he feels that the client, in the counseling situation itself, is exposing more material than he is prepared to deal with at the moment, the counselor should slow him down. For example, he could say,

I am having difficulty keeping up with you—in really understanding all you are telling me. I am wondering whether it would help if you slow down a bit and talk about fewer topics to make it easier for me to follow what you are trying to share with me.

Or he could use this approach:

There are several things that seem to be bothering you. Obviously, we won't be able to talk about all of them today. I wonder if it would help to stop and think for a moment about the ones that are most important for you to discuss now. Perhaps we should select one or two and then have you discuss them a little more slowly and carefully in order to help me understand what is bothering you. Usually this helps the person on your side of the desk too—for as you struggle to make sense to me, things tend to make more sense to you too.

Giving Clients Information

WHENEVER possible, the counselor should be thoroughly familiar with information in the pupil's cumulative record. He should also review his interview notes prior to an interview so that he can follow better what the pupil says and understand how the pupil relates this to what he said previously. At the same time he must not let these notes so influence him that he tries to see life through the eyes of the pupil as he was during the last interview, and thus fails to empathize with the pupil as he is today.

Although the counselor needs information on pupils, he must guard against spending so much time gathering facts that he does not have time for pupils and teachers. He should also guard against reading too much into what he learns. Information is most useful to the counselor when it helps him see things with the pupil's eyes and helps him find answers for the pupil's questions. When the counselor forces information into the client's deliberations, or when information causes the counselor to respond to only part of what the pupil says, information is a handicap.

Whether or not there is a cumulative folder on the desk where the pupil can see it and whether or not the counselor uses it in the pupil's presence really is not very important. In the event that he is called upon to interpret data which he cannot interpret without further study, the counselor should feel sufficiently secure to admit that he is not prepared, and that special study of the data will be required before he can interpret them for the pupil.

Showing the pupil the contents of the folder is a very different matter, and very undesirable. Such a practice often provides the pupil with test scores which have no meaning for him. Furthermore, such action could result in the counselor's violating the confidence of people who provided confidential reports on the pupil's behavior.

ANSWERING A CLIENT'S QUESTIONS

A client has many different reasons for asking a counselor questions. These include his need for information about himself, his situation, and his expectations in counseling; his need for reassurance; his way of expressing feelings of dependency and inadequacy; and his way of putting the counselor on the spot. When a client asks a question, the counselor should try to assess what the client's real need is. If a pupil is expressing feelings of inadequacy, then the pupil must examine these feelings before he can incorporate facts into his thinking for solving his problems. The high school senior who has made a poor record and is now attempting to enter the state university needs more than an interpretation of the university test scores when he waits anxiously for the counselor to whom he has been referred for the interpretation. Until he can talk freely about his feelings of inadequacy, accept those inadequacies which he cannot change, discover some of his strong points, and be grateful for these strengths, he will not be able to accept the test results, nor himself for that matter. Once he has accomplished these goals, it is quite likely that he will no longer need to ask questions and may in fact be able to predict approximately how well he did on the tests.

In contrast, a bright, gregarious farm boy who has had much success in his high school work could be confused on a large university campus not because of lack of faith in his ability to get along there, but because the environment is considerably more complicated than anything he has known. Answers to his questions may be all that he needs.

There are still other reasons for pupils' questions. Most pupils have some preconceived notion about the way they wish others to perceive them. If a pupil has ambitions that require abilities and aptitudes he is not sure he possesses, he may search constantly for assurances that he possesses the desired traits. He may want to learn this so much that he hears only that part of the conference which indicates he will be able to achieve his goals. Occasionally, a pupil is so deeply committed to a particular goal that he will ignore weaknesses of his which suggest that success is unlikely. He may even twist the facts that he secures in order to create the picture of himself which he wants to see. If the counselor fails to take cognizance of the pupil's perception of himself and his readiness for information, he may find the pupil either ignoring or misinterpreting the information given him. Sometimes the youngster may even appear to accept new goals but fail to do those things that true acceptance of the information would have motivated him to do.

As the pupil talks in a permissive atmosphere about his goals, his picture of himself, and the meaning of the information he has received, he is able to express his doubts about himself. He can also tell why he does not want to find and use certain strengths that he might have. In this kind of emotional climate the pupil can request information with a minimum of personal threat and can use it with greatest effectiveness. Here, the counselor can give information when he has it. If the information is not readily available, the counselor and the client can decide together how to obtain it.

DECIDING WHAT IS NEEDED

Once the counselor decides that the client sees the need for information and that he is ready to use it, he should help the client state and clarify his questions. This in itself is difficult. Perhaps it is even more difficult to help a client decide what is adequate information. For example, how can one be sure that a high school student who is trying to select a vocation knows enough about his preferred occupation, about the institutions offering preparation, and about his own abilities, aptitudes, and interests? Moreover, because the client often minimizes his desire for information in areas in which he feels no information exists, the counselor may overlook his need—e.g., an adolescent may want information that would enable him to better understand and get along with his peers or his family, but because he thinks such material does not exist, he does not inquire further. Or he may wish information about sex but be reluctant or embarrased to request it. Discovering what the client wants or needs requires patience, careful listening, and considerable understanding of the client. (Under the topic "Understanding of Physical and Emotional Changes" in Chapter 2, a number of additional suggestions were made for helping pupils answer their questions about themselves.)

The more the client participates in the process of deciding what information he needs, the greater the odds are that he will obtain that information and use it in solving his problems. Bordin and Bixler [6] make an excellent case for this point of view with respect to test selection. It applies equally well to other kinds of choices and problems.

HELPING A CLIENT ACCEPT AND USE INFORMATION

Helping a client obtain the information he recognizes he needs is, however, still just one part of the guidance procedure. The next problem is what the client will do with the information he now has. As suggested earlier, a client is often unable to accept information

6 Edward S. Bordin and Ray H. Bixler, "Test Selection: A Process of Counseling," *Educational and Psychological Measurement,* VI (1946), 361–73.

that disagrees with his perception of himself. He also may have difficulty understanding some of the information he obtains. Frequently, he needs assistance in integrating the new information with his previous information. Participation in the selection process makes all of this easier. Bordin and Bixler [7] concluded that client participation in selection of tests made the testing experience itself more meaningful to clients and altered their attitudes toward themselves. The author's own experience suggests that it also increases clients' readiness for test data. Dressel and Matteson [8] found that counselors who encouraged most client participation in test interpretations tended to help their clients achieve greatest increase in self-understanding.

Clients also have difficulty understanding and accepting other information. Whenever a client is given information or referred to a source, he should feel free to seek the counselor's assistance in understanding it and in discussing his reactions to it. For example, high school students often have difficulty accepting what they learn about requirements for their preferred occupation or for entrance to their chosen college. On such occasions, they must realize that it is appropriate to discuss their difficulty with a counselor.

Termination Problems

THE interview is over whenever the pupil has finished talking about whatever he wishes to say, or when he has used up the time assigned to him for that session. The counselor should hold to the time limits out of consideration not only for other pupils who may be waiting to see him, but also for the best interest of the pupil with whom he is talking. Holding to time limits teaches the pupil to use the counselor's time efficiently and helps the pupil learn to accept limits.

There are times, however, when the counselor should either extend the period or arrange to see the pupil again very soon—possibly later in the same day. The youngster who has found it very difficult to talk about his problem is just beginning to express his feelings on specific issues when his scheduled time is up. He may waste time in warming up to the problem even so soon as the next day. In such a case, flexibility in scheduling is highly desirable. This holds true also for the pupil who needs to release intense feel-

7 *Ibid.*, p. 372
8 P. L. Dressel and R. W. Matteson, "The Effect of Client Participation in Test Interpretation," *Educational and Psychological Measurement,* X (1950), 693–706.

ings. He may be faced with a real emergency and may badly need at least temporary relief. However, even these two kinds of clients usually profit more from a second appointment during the same day than from lengthening of a single session.

But such pupils are not the ones who usually have trouble with time limits. A more common type is the pupil who does not like to face the disturbing issues which caused him to seek the counselor's assistance. He uses most of the period for "small talk," but then, during the last few minutes, he moves into a serious discussion of his problems. Pleading for more time, he claims that there are just a few things about which he must talk. The counselor should warn this type of pupil of the amount of time left and thus help him reach crucial issues earlier in the session: "I don't want to hurry you, but you have only fifteen minutes left. You suggested that there was something special you wanted to talk about when you came in," reminds the pupil of his time limits. While the pupil should not be forced to abandon small talk, he should be helped to see the value of using counseling time more profitably. By giving extra time to the resisting client, the counselor may actually interfere with the client's growth rather than stimulate it.

When pupils know how much time has been allotted to them and realize how fast they are using it up, they usually accept these limits. Most pupils have other commitments and prefer to operate on a businesslike basis. Occasionally, the counselor has to remind the client of time limits in order to allow himself adequate time between interviews to make notes and prepare for the next interview.

LOOKING AHEAD TO OTHER INTERVIEWS

While the pupil should know that he can continue counseling if he chooses to, and that the close of one session is a good time to arrange with the counselor the time of their next session, he should also know that he can discontinue counseling whenever he wants to. The counselor should help the pupil with this decision by making it easy for him to clarify the counseling relationship and to evaluate his counseling experiences. Both the clarification and evaluation should arise, however, only if the pupil desires such discussions. From them the pupil should obtain the information that he needs to decide whether to schedule another appointment.

Making the next appointment near the close of a counseling session prevents the pupil from leaving with uncertainties about future sessions. Scheduling has the obvious advantage of avoiding waiting lines for the pupil and slack periods for the counselor. Scheduling may also prevent interruptions during an interview. Mr. Sampson's experience is pertinent here. He was a well-trained counselor who taught general psychology part-time in a junior college. He did counseling in his classroom and had no secretary to schedule appointments. Naturally Mr. Sampson found it very disturbing to have a student break into the room when he was counseling another. He also found that his clients were reluctant to discuss personal matters readily when they feared that someone else might come into the room. He discussed the situation with the dean, who suggested that he set up a student-maintained scheduling chart like those used on tennis courts and in recreation rooms. Using this idea, he drew up a weekly schedule showing his counseling periods in half-hour intervals. He posted schedules covering a two-week period with the following directions for their use:

If this door is closed, please do not open it. Either I am gone or I am talking to someone who probably wouldn't appreciate having you break in. Select a free period on my schedule which is convenient for you and cross off that time. Then write your name and the time you have chosen on one of the slips of paper provided, and slip it under the door. If I am in and I am not talking to someone, my door will be open. Thanks much. You know how you would feel if someone broke into some of our conferences. R. SAMPSON.

A client's growth toward better adjustment occurs between interviews as well as during interviews; the counselor should keep that in mind when scheduling appointments. More is accomplished when appointments are not scheduled too close together. One appointment (with some pupils two) per week is usually very satisfactory.

In deciding how much time to set aside for an interview, the counselor should take into account the time normally used by the pupil and the number of pupils who want his help. Four well-spaced fifteen-minute interviews probably will result in more pupil growth than will a single one-hour interview. The counselor should avoid interviews of less than fifteen minutes each. On the other hand, he usually gains little by extending an interview with a pupil beyond one hour.

In the process of arranging appointments, the counselor should make it easy for the pupil to raise questions about activities that are to be carried out between sessions. Sometimes, for instance, either the counselor or the student assumes responsibility for getting certain information between sessions. Occasionally, the pupil is to do specific reading, which the pupil selects after hearing the counselor describe books that might answer some of his questions.

Suggestions for reading should grow out of the pupil's expressed need for information; the counselor should then discuss with the pupil what material is available and how each reference can answer some of the pupil's questions, so that the pupil can choose from among the best sources the ones most appropriate for him. Of course, the pupil may elect to use or ignore any of the references recommended.

Because pupils' problems involve a variety of situations, a counselor may recommend books from many fields. For example, secondary-school and college counselors often recommend books and pamphlets dealing with adolescence, boy-girl relations, occupations, choosing an occupation, choosing a college, family living, job-hunting, improvement of study skills, scholarships, and mental health.[9] Whatever reading materials the counselor suggests should fit the special needs of the pupil. In describing the materials from which the pupil may choose, the counselor should be aware of the pupil's reading level, his emotional maturity, and the seriousness of his problem. The pupil's use of carefully chosen literature between interviews can enrich the counseling sessions: its effectiveness is increased by self-initiated action and the fact that the insights obtained by him grow out of independent self-examination.

REFERRALS

Every professional worker should realize what services he is qualified to provide for clients; he should also realize when his clients need the services of other professional workers. But this is a special problem for the counselor and all others who help clients with personal problems, because those who provide such help cannot agree on the professional limits for each group.

Whenever a pupil seeks help from a counselor, the counselor

9 Teachers and counselors who desire the names of books, short stories, and other reading materials which young people can use to achieve insight into their own problems will find the following reference to be very helpful: John J. DeBoer, Paul B. Hale, and Esther Landin, *Reading for Living, An Index to Reading Materials*, Illinois Curriculum Program Bulletin No. 18 (Springfield, Ill.: Office of Superintendent of Public Instruction, 1953).

should ask himself whether he has the professional competencies to provide the help that the pupil needs. The teacher should ask himself the same question when he talks with a pupil who comes to him with a problem. Rarely is anyone hurt by simply telling his story: besides, the worker involved often cannot decide whether he is prepared to provide the needed assistance until he has heard what the troubled one has to say. Beyond this initial stage, however, there is danger. While the pupil usually has within himself the power to solve his problems once he has freed himself of the emotional blocks that prevent him from using his assets, the unskilled person may probe for material that forces the pupil to look at problems before he is ready to handle them.

To determine whether he understands the personality dynamics in a case, the counselor should ask himself whether he would know what to do if he felt as the client does. If there is the slightest doubt about his ability to handle the case, he should consult with someone better qualified than he is, such as a counseling psychologist or psychiatrist. From such a conference he not only learns whether he should make a referral, but he also learns to whom he should refer the case and how it should be done.

Failure to recognize the need for referral can result in a counselor's further confusing a pupil who was badly confused when he sought help. Such failure can also cause a pupil to lose some of his drive to resolve the conflict. Still other pupils conclude from unsuccessful attempts of counselors that they cannot be helped with their problems.

Deciding when to make a referral is not easy, and the school counselor certainly must avoid the two extremes: being so cautious that he never attempts to help anyone, and being so insensitive to his own professional limitations that he hurts clients. Some counselors who do not want to accept their professional limitations often justify working beyond their level on the grounds either that previous referrals have not been helped or that adequate referral resources are not available. Neither reason justifies a counselor's efforts to help someone he is not qualified to help. Admittedly both reasons may be correct, but often they merely reflect the worker's inability to admit even to himself that he is not competent to help the client. Occasionally, it also is a matter of counselor involvement. He wants so much to help the client or to prove to the client that he can help him that he cannot make a referral.

Once a counselor (or teacher) accepts the need for a referral, he must decide what type of service would be most appropriate and describe that service to his client. In order to do this adequately, the counselor must himself understand the services provided by the various referral agencies, he must himself see the advantages of the referral for the client, and finally he must be able to convey what he knows so as to help the client discover how the services could help him.

But the most difficult problem a counselor faces in making a referral is to find adequate referral resources or to obtain help for a client within a reasonable period of time. In spite of the fact that there has been a steady increase in the number of community mental health clinics, most of them still have long waiting lists. If this problem is to be solved, the school staff must take an active part in encouraging the establishment and enlargement of these services. More promising young people also must be encouraged to prepare for this work. One referral source that is often overlooked is the college or university which offers systematic preparation in counselor-education, including supervised practice in counseling. Information on the mental hygiene clinics that serve an area may be obtained from the State Psychological Association, the State Association for Mental Health, and the State Commission on Mental Hygiene.

When the counselor, recognizing the need for a referral, finds that no referral agency is available or that the pupil must wait for service, he must decide whether his continuing to see the pupil will be useful or damaging. In attempting to answer this question, he usually does well to enlist the assistance of his colleagues in a case conference. Besides serving to obtain added information, this approach gains support for the counselor and wins the staff's cooperation in planning activities for the pupil to minimize the chances of hurting him while he waits for treatment. Additional considerations are discussed under the question of the counselor's ethics at the end of this chapter.

The Interview Record

MAKING NOTES

Some authorities on counseling believe that taking notes during the interview interferes with building a good counseling relationship; others believe that if the counselor is to obtain an accurate record he must take notes during the interview. Both groups agree on the importance of the counselor's keeping an accurate record of the interview; they disagree simply as to when he should take notes.

Each counselor must examine his own attitudes on the question of taking notes during interviews. Some counselors find that they cannot follow the discussion and take notes at the same time. Other counselors feel guilty about taking notes; they recognize that they need the information but do not feel that they can justify their notes to the pupil. If taking notes interferes with a counselor's ability to follow the conversation, he should not take notes during the interview. If he does not feel right about doing so, the pupil will detect those feelings. The pupil may not know what the counselor is concerned about, but still may sense something wrong; consequently, it becomes difficult for the pupil to discuss his problems his own way.

The counselor often seems more concerned than the pupil is about note-taking during the interview. Once the counselor has developed note-taking techniques in harmony with his feelings, he probably will not run into much difficulty with the pupil. This does not mean, though, that all of his pupils will be unconcerned over his note-taking. When the counselor senses a pupil's disturbance about his making notes during an interview, he should try to assess how the pupil feels and respond to these feelings; usually the pupil wonders why the counselor needs to take notes and how he will use them.

These last questions are closely related to worry over the subject of protecting confidential information. When pupils realize that the counselor simply makes notes so that he can bring himself up to date before the next interview and thus help start the new interview where the previous one left off, usually they will accept the procedure. A few may continue to be disturbed by note-taking. In these cases the counselor will have to make the notes after the interview.

How should notes be kept? As we pointed out earlier, it is often desirable for the counselor to make a tape recording of the interview. This not only provides him with a complete report of what was said, but also helps him detect some of the errors he made during the interview.

When it is not feasible for the counselor to record the whole interview and study it later, his next best procedure is to keep a running account of the main points made by the pupil and by himself. These notes should of course describe the pupil's and counselor's behavior as accurately as possible, not reflect merely what the counselor thought was happening.

Most counselors need to develop some shortcut that will enable them to keep a running account of the conversation. Key ideas in incomplete sentences is one such technique. With a few minutes between interviews, the counselor can put these brief notes into shape for future use. Few counselors, if any, can wait until the end of the day to record their notes. When they postpone making notes, they tend to introduce errors.

The counselor can save considerable time by using some of the recently available dictation equipment: instead of writing out a complete report, he can dictate from his notes. The belt and the flat-record types of machine are very efficient, enabling the counselor to dictate notes quickly and then place the record in a folder, ready to be played back before the next interview. At the end of each interview the counselor can add more dictation. Such records do not have to be transcribed; they are cheap and convenient. Even when he has a complete recording of events, the counselor usually wants this running account of highlights because it takes too long to listen to the complete recording in preparing for each interview.

Should the counselor want to supplement the running account with a diagnostic summary, he would do well to include such material as the pupil's reason for seeking the counselor's help, the pupil's own statement of his problem or problems, the important topics discussed, strong negative feelings, strong positive feelings, requests for information, insights gained, conclusions reached, tasks to be carried on between interviews, a description of responsibilities assumed by each person during the interview, evidence of client growth (or lack of it), and the counselor's appraisal of his ability to help the client.

If the counselor supplements the running account with the type of summary described above, he should keep this summary separate from the running account for two reasons: (1) the running account should describe behavior, not interpret it; otherwise, in using the material later, the counselor will fail to distinguish between what happened and what he thought about what happened; (2) if the pupil asks to read interview notes, and the counselor permits him to read them, the pupil can follow the running account and profit from it. He can see where he and the counselor have gone, he is brought up to date, and he may even achieve new insights from this reading. Interpretations and diagnostic summaries, on the other hand, can be threatening and often misleading to the pupil.

Complete notes serve an additional function for those counselors who worry about their clients and carry their clients' problems around with them. Knowing that they have a good record of what happened helps these counselors leave their cases in the office; they know that they can return to each case when the time comes to prepare for the next session.

KEEPING CONFIDENCES

The pupil who seeks the counselor's help hopes that the counselor will hold in confidence what he says, for he is uneasy lest others, especially some of the persons most directly involved, learn how he feels. Until he is certain that he can trust the counselor, he hesitates to talk frankly about his problems. The counselor's reputation for keeping confidences helps most pupils develop faith in his integrity and reliability in other matters as well.

Some pupils develop faith in the counselor only very slowly, some never trust at all. Such students may have told intimate secrets to others, at some previous time, only to have the persons whom they trusted betray them. After being disappointed once, they are very cautious lest they be disappointed again.

A counselor can allay suspicions by being careful not only about what he says but where and when he says it. Some perfectly reasonable acts on the counselor's part may create or extend suspicion in the pupil if the counselor times them poorly. If, for example, the counselor, immediately following the interview, were to do any of these three things, he would make the pupil suspicious: (1) confer with the person who was the target of the pupil's aggressive feelings, (2) mention the pupil's name in a conversation that the pupil can hear, (3) seek the parents' help without first discussing the matter with the pupil.

It is difficult for the counselor to decide exactly what he can say and where he can say it. His first guide is to think what is best for the pupil. He must also try to determine what the pupil considers to be information for the counselor and for no one else. Of course, with the pupil's permission, the counselor can release any information to specified people. But there are other important and difficult questions. Does keeping confidences mean that a counselor seeking assistance cannot take a case to a fellow professional worker? If the answer is "yes," then to whom may he ethically go for help? Is he at liberty to break confidence with the pupil when someone may be hurt through his failure to break confidences? [10] We can examine these questions under three headings: the definition of confidential information, the ethical issues involved in turning to others for help, and the question of protecting society.

First, what is confidential information? *Everything* discussed in a private conference is confidential information; none of it should be shared with anyone other than professional workers assisting with the case, and some of it not even with those workers unless the pupil gives his permission. Obviously, this situation involves the judgment of the counselor. He must define principles which determine what information he can share with others. He must also recognize the need for discussing the question of confidences with colleagues to whom he would give information. Should the counselor be unsure whether the pupil would want certain information divulged, he should discuss the issues with the pupil.

Second, what are the ethical issues involved in a counselor's securing help from others? Earlier we pointed out that teachers and counselors should make referrals to other professional workers. One cannot expect a consultant to assist a counselor or a teacher without having been told at least something of what is known about the case. Neither is it wholesome for the consultant or the person seeking help from him to feel that the other believes him unworthy of trust. However, everyone should accept the fact that it is appropriate for a staff member to withhold certain information that he believes a pupil considers confidential.

Suppose that two teachers and a counselor were involved in a case conference and that one of the teachers asked the counselor a specific question about the pupil's family life. In the event that the counselor felt he could not answer the question, he might say,

Your question involves some detailed information which I don't feel I can share with you without obtaining Ralph's permission. When Ralph

10 C. Gilbert Wrenn, "The Ethics of Counseling," *Educational and Psychological Measurement,* XII (1952), 161–77. All counselors and teachers should read this paper, which discusses the counselor's legal status and the importance of a code of ethics for counselors. The writer also presents ethical principles with reference to the counselor's responsibility to his client, to his colleagues, to his employing institution, to his profession, and to society.

talked about this, I concluded that he was telling me something that he did not want me to repeat to anyone. You know how you would feel if you revealed a guarded secret to me and then I let you down by telling it to another person. All I can say is that he has some family problems that worry him very much.

Though the teachers are worthy of trust, the counselor must keep faith with the pupil who shared something special with him. To prevent situations like this from causing difficulties, the workers must examine their relationships again and again as they work together on individual cases. They can usually establish mutual understanding best through open examination of the feelings of each of them.

Third, what is the counselor's responsibility to society? Persons professionally interested in counseling are generally agreed that the counselor should take steps to protect individuals or groups in the event that the client discusses actions in which someone could be hurt. However, counselors differ on the degree of seriousness that would justify violating confidences concerning a client's previous actions or his anticipated actions. In contemplating a violation of confidence, counselors must consider not only the effect on the one client, but also the effect on relationships with other clients if "the word gets around." Earlier, in the case of Mr. Black and the junior high school boy, we saw how a counselor's behavior in a single situation can shape his reception by an entire community. Although Mr. Black kept information confidential for the purpose of helping the boy, his action also made it easier for him to establish a good working relationship with other pupils.

Before taking action in cases like this, most counselors prefer to discuss with the pupil the implications of their planned action for the pupil and for the others involved. When, to protect others, the counselor breaks confidence without the pupil's permission, the pupil-counselor relationship is usually damaged. Rather than try to re-build a counseling relationship with the pupil, it usually is better, whenever possible, for the counselor who broke confidence to refer the pupil to another counselor.

What the counselor can do to protect others depends upon the state laws and the attitude of the local authorities. While there is no legal machinery in many states for protecting society against emotionally sick people, often cooperative local officials will use the information provided by the counselor to protect the citizens involved.

What a counselor can do to protect others against future events is one matter, but it is a very different matter to deal with events that have already happened and that do not seem to involve future danger. In such cases it is *not* the responsibility of the counselor to make sure that society's "justice is done." His first responsibility is to the person who seeks his help for finding a better way to deal with life.

THE COUNSELOR'S RECORDS

For whom does the counselor make a record of interviews with clients? Where should these records be kept? What should be recorded in the cumulative folder? The counselor keeps a record of the events that occur during counseling to help him understand his client and to assess his client's progress. This confidential information must be kept in a private, locked file to which only the counselor has access. In the cumulative folder the counselor notes that he has seen or is seeing a client and, after the counseling sessions have been terminated, he tries to write, without breaking confidences, a summary of what was accomplished in order to help others better to understand the client. Here is an example of such a summary:

Bill B. saw me ten times during the spring semester of his freshman year in high school. He is a very bright boy who has never applied himself. Now I believe he is genuinely interested in improving his ways. There is some evidence to support this belief: he has been getting home on time, he has not been absent from school, nor tardy, for five weeks, and he has turned in his homework regularly. In spite of these changes, most of his classmates and teachers still see him as he was. Obviously, he is always faced with the temptation to return to his old habit pattern, and the failure of others to see and accept the new self makes this temptation even greater. His teachers could help a great deal by looking for and rewarding his improved behavior. 5–2–62. M. M. O.

(While placing this report in the folder is good, the counselor could accomplish more in this particular instance by holding a case conference, giving this information to the client's teachers personally, and then discussing it with them.)

The Counselor's Ethics

BEFORE a code of ethics can be developed for the school counselor, it is necessary to determine the counselor's primary responsibilities and to identify the primary organizations with which he is expected to affiliate. Since the counselor usually begins his career as a teacher, one would expect him to be affiliated with the National Education Association and, consequently, to be influenced by the code of ethics of that group.[11] That code describes the teacher's obligations to his students, students' parents, community, employer, and fellow teachers. Both teachers and counselors should reread this code periodically. The counselor should take special note of the statements concerning fair treatment of all students, consideration of individual differences and needs, development of individual goals that encourage self-actualization, keeping confidences, and respect for the parents' responsibility for their children.

When the teacher becomes a counselor he should affiliate with the American Personnel and Guidance Association. This organization has its own set of standards, recently published by its Committee on Ethics. It deals with the counselor's responsibilities to clients, colleagues, and society.[12]

Further, since the school counselor is expected to help teachers understand their pupils as well as to counsel pupils, he should be a student of human behavior; therefore, increasingly greater numbers of school counselors also should become members of the American Psychological Association. *Ethical Standards of Psychologists* [13] represents an effort on the part of psychologists to define ethical values for themselves; these values certainly apply to counselors, too. The code cites specific problems, describes incidents, and establishes principles to guide the behavior of psychologists. The committee that formulated these ethical standards received suggestions from over two thousand members, and encourages members to continue to submit suggestions for improving the standards.

Since space will not permit a complete review of ethical principles for school counselors, the following is a selection of common ethical problems that a counselor faces, and principles to guide his behavior.

1. Today there is a very serious shortage of qualified school counselors. Moreover, some school administrators still question the

11 *Code of Ethics* (Washington, D.C.: National Education Association, 1952).

12 "Ethical Standards for American Personnel and Guidance Association," *Personnel and Guidance Journal*, XL (1961), 206–09.

13 *Ethical Standards of Psychologists* (Washington, D.C.: American Psychological Association, 1953).

necessity for special professional preparation for school counselors. These two conditions have resulted in schools employing inadequately prepared counselors and expecting them to provide services that they are not qualified to give. *It is unethical for a school counselor to even imply professional qualifications which exceed those which he has attained.*[14] Not only should he limit himself to those services that he is qualified to provide, but before accepting a contract for a counseling position, he should ask for a job description that clearly defines his responsibilities. His acceptance of a contract implies that the job definition and the school's general policies are satisfactory.[15]

2. A counselor must try to understand himself and to discover how any of his own needs, values, and problems may interfere with his success in helping his clients.

A psychologist . . . should be aware of the inadequacies in his own personality which may bias his appraisal of others or distort his relationship with them, and should refrain from undertaking any activity where his personal limitations are likely to result in inferior professional services.[16]

A counselor's professional preparation should provide increased self-understanding as well as knowledge and skills.[17]

3. Whenever a counselor discovers that a client has a problem with which the counselor is not competent to cope, he should make a referral.

In cases involving referral, the responsibility of the psychologist for the welfare of the client continues until this responsibility is assumed by the professional person to whom the client is referred or until the relationship with the psychologist making the referral has been terminated by mutual agreement.[18]

In situations where referral is indicated and the client refuses referral, the psychologist must carefully weigh the possible harm to the client, and to himself and his profession, that might ensue from continuing the relationship. If the client is in clear and imminent danger, the psychologist should in general insist on referral or refuse to continue the relationship.

14 *Ethical Standards of Psychologists* (Washington, D.C.: American Psychological Association, 1953).
15 APGA Standards, *op. cit.*, pp. 206–07.
16 APA Standards (1952), *op. cit.*, p. 3.
17 APGA Standards, *op. cit.*, p. 209.
18 APA Standards (1953), *op. cit.*, p. 79.

Due consideration should be given to the possibility of assisting the client through therapy to avail himself of the professional assistance needed.[19]

4. A counselor should respect a pupil's right to make his own decisions, and when the pupil is not competent to make his own decision, the counselor should show similar respect in consulting parents or a legal guardian. To fulfill this general objective of client autonomy, a counselor must be able to accept client's decisions that are based upon values different from his own. This also suggests that a counselor not impose his services upon a client.[20]

5. Since the importance of keeping confidences has already been discussed, only APA's basic principle concerning this matter is quoted here:

The psychologist should guard professional confidences as a trust and reveal such confidences only after most careful deliberation and when there is a clear and imminent danger to an individual or to society.[21]

To realize this principle, teachers and counselors must not only respect confidences, but also insure privacy while discussing confidential matters with colleagues as well as with pupils.

6. When a counselor has established effective working relationships with his colleagues, he often finds that some of them will seek his professional assistance in solving their own problems. This situation raises an ethical question:

Psychologists should not enter into clinical relationships with members of their own family, with intimate friends, or with persons so close that their welfare might be jeopardized by the dual relationship.

(1) In the case of associates, students, and acquaintances, the psychologist has the responsibility of assessing the difficulties which ensue in establishing a clinical relationship and to refuse assistance if there is a possibility of harm to the client.

(2) If there is a tentative decision to work with a person with whom the psychologist has other relationships, the nature of the situation and the possible difficulties should be carefully explained and the decision left to the person involved.

19 *Ibid.,* p. 79
20 APA Standards (1952), *op. cit.,* p. 4.
21 APA Standards (1953), *op. cit.,* p. 55, and APGA Standards, p. 207.

(3) This principle does not bear upon supervising relationships in the training of therapists.[22]

Because most people try to build a favorable image of themselves for the members of their family, friends, colleagues, and employers, clients usually have difficulty talking with a counselor who falls into any one of these categories about any topic that puts them in an unfavorable light. Since a client must be able to talk about whatever bothers him, and since this often involves negative self-references, the counseling relationship is necessarily impaired. Even when the counselor is able to help a client discuss relevant material, such a client will often decide that he divulged too much, and perhaps even that his inadequacies were unnecessarily exposed. Consequently, he attacks and/or embarrasses the counselor outside of the counseling relationship.

For a counseling relationship to be truly effective, a client must learn to trust his counselor completely, to be himself, and to talk about whatever worries or bothers him without fear of rejection or reprisals. This is what is unique about the counseling relationship. A client can examine his most foreboding thoughts and desires, he can relive hurtful moments in his past, and, in the accepting atmosphere, the unbearable becomes bearable, and a solution seems possible for the most difficult problems. This relationship cannot be achieved when the client is trying to impress someone.

SUGGESTED READINGS

1. BORDIN, EDWARD S. *Psychological Counseling*. New York: Appleton-Century-Crofts, 1955. Part III.

    a] What are some of the critical points for the counselor to remember in building the counseling relationship?
    b] How did the college counselor help Miss Tir?
    c] Why involve the client in test interpretation?
    d] How can a counselor deal with resistance?

2. BRAMMER, LAWRENCE M., and EVERETT L. SHOSTROM. *Therapeutic Psychology*. Englewood Cliffs, New Jersey: Prentice-Hall, Inc., 1960.

    The authors draw upon psychological theory and research in describing methods that may be used in personal counseling. Chapters 7–10 deal with

22 APA Standards (1953), p. 52.

such practical problems as developing the counseling relationship, dealing with transference, interpreting behavior, and giving advice.

a] What makes reflection of feeling an effective technique?

b] What significant contributions does transference make to a client's growth?

c] What common types of interpretation are made by counselors?

3. CRONBACH, LEE J. "The Counselor's Problems from the Perspective of Communications Theory," *Guidance Readings for Counselors*, ed. Farwell and Peters. Chicago: Rand McNally & Co., 1959, pp. 177–92.

a] What are the implications of communication systems for test selection?

b] What can information theory contribute to helping counselors resolve some of their common communication problems?

4. McKINNEY, FRED. *Counseling for Personal Adjustment in Schools and Colleges*. Boston: Houghton Mifflin Company, 1958.

Writing for the counselor who works in an educational setting, the author uses case material very effectively to illustrate how the counselor can deal with the situations he meets. Chapters 8, 10, and 11.

a] What can counselors do to reduce resistance?

b] What produces insight?

5. MOUSTAKAS, CLARK E. *Psychotherapy With Children*. New York: Harper & Row, Publishers, 1959.

Chapters 3 and 4.

a] How does the normal child's behavior in therapy differ from the disturbed child's behavior in therapy?

6. PATTERSON, C. H. *Counseling and Psychotherapy: Theory and Practice*. New York: Harper & Row, Publishers, 1959.

This book deals effectively with many of the problems the beginning counselor meets. The approach is based upon phenomenological psychology and the client-centered approach. Chapters 3, 4, and 5.

a] To what extent can the counselor control the ways in which his values influence his clients?

7. ROGERS, CARL R. *Counseling and Psychotherapy*. Boston: Houghton Mifflin Company, 1942.

This book made such a significant impact upon guidance practices in American schools that those who expect to make a career in counseling should read the entire book. Chapter 9 is recommended here because it deals with many practical problems that a counselor must face.

a] How frequently should interviews be scheduled?

b] How much time should be set aside for an interview?

c] What should the counselor do about broken appointments?

d] Does nondirective counseling actually require more time than directive counseling?

8. WOLBERG, LEWIS R. *The Technique of Psychotherapy.* New York: Grune & Stratton, Inc., 1954.

This comprehensive and helpful volume is written for the practitioners. Though written by a psychiatrist for psychotherapists, it presents many suggestions that can be helpful to school counselors. Part II.

a] What are some of the basic guide lines for the initial contact?

b] How can the counselor assess his client's general condition?

c] What can a counselor do to establish a good relationship?

SUGGESTED FILMS

1. *Angry Boy,* 33 minutes, sponsored by the Mental Health Film Board and produced by Affiliated Film Producers, Inc., 1951.

The problem of this film is initiated when a teacher sees a boy stealing from her purse. The film reveals the basic causes of this act by showing the psychiatrist's work with the child.

a] How would you have reacted had you been in the teacher's place?

b] What did the principal do to help the mother accept psychiatric care for the boy?

c] What were the basic causes of the boy's stealing?

2. *Counseling Adolescents,* New York: McGraw-Hill, 1954. This series of three films, (1) *A Counselor's Day,* 12 minutes; (2) *Using Analytical Tools,* 15 minutes; and (3) *Diagnosis and Planning Adjustment in Counseling,* 18 minutes, is correlated with the book by E. G. Williamson, *Counseling Adolescents,* 1950.

The first film gives a picture of the counselor's work, as the title suggests. The last two demonstrate how Williamson uses information in diagnosing the student's problems and in planning counseling.

a] Which guidance duties should the counselor delegate to others?

b] Evaluate the counselor's use of information in counseling.

3. *Emotional Health,* 20 minutes, New York: McGraw-Hill, 1947.

This film presents the problems of a high school boy who appears to have heart trouble. His experiences with the psychiatrist reveal psychological causes for what first appeared to be a physical health problem.

a] What were the boy's responsibilities in this therapy experience?

b] What responsibilities did the psychiatrist assume?

c] How did this psychiatrist use the facts that he obtained from the boy?

d] Explain why the boy reacted as he did to the suggestion of referral to a psychiatrist.

Counseling Individuals Within the Group Setting

SCHOOL counselors have become increasingly interested in group counseling, partly because of the serious shortage of qualified counselors. An estimate by the American Personnel and Guidance Association and the United States Office of Education indicates that the schools need twice as many counselors as they now have.[1] Even though more persons enter the profession, obviously it will take time properly to educate such a large number. Appropriate use of group counseling, along with the improvement or discarding of guidance procedures that fail to help young people, makes more efficient use of the counselor's time.

Some educators hope that, because of its seemingly more efficient use of the staff, group counseling will supplant individual counsel-

1 *Identification and Guidance of Able Students* (Washington, D.C.: American Association for the Advancement of Science, 1958).

ing. But although group counseling can accomplish a great deal, it is not a substitute for individual counseling. Some pupils respond best in groups; others profit most from individual counseling. Still others seem to need both. Time and cost should not be the basis for deciding which method to use; educators must be primarily concerned with the best service for each individual. The eventual cost to society of a maladjusted person far exceeds any financial saving that could accrue to a school district from hiring fewer counselors.

Group counseling seems particularly appropriate for adolescents, whose special needs include conformity with and acceptance by their peer group, opportunity to share ideas and to obtain reactions from their peers, occasion to participate in worthwhile activities, help in understanding themselves, opportunity to define meaningful life roles, and independence from adults, especially from parents. These needs can be satisfied within an effective counseling group. With varying degrees of depth each client discovers: (1) that his peers have problems too; (2) that, in spite of his faults, which his peers want to help him correct, they accept him; (3) that at least one adult, the counselor, can understand and accept him; (4) that he is capable of understanding, accepting, and helping his peers; (5) that he can trust others; and (6) that expressing his own real feelings about himself, about others, and about what he believes helps him to understand and accept himself.

Further support for counseling adolescents in groups appears in the work of Berman [2] and Ackerman,[3] both of whom found that the group situation alleviates the strong resistance to therapy on the part of adolescents. Berman reports that adolescents are brought to psychotherapy against their will (in many high schools they are called in for periodic counseling interviews whether they want help or not), and made to feel that they are the culprits, and that whatever the difficulty is, the responsibility for doing something about it rests solely with them. Ackerman finds that adolescents are very sensitive to others' criticism and judgments of their worth. For all these reasons adolescents, whether they are passive and seemingly compliant, or openly hostile, enter counseling and psychotherapy with misgiv-

---

2 Sidney Berman, "Psychotherapeutic Techniques with Adolescents," *American Journal of Orthopsychiatry*, XXIV (1954), 238–44.

3 N. W. Ackerman, "Group Psychotherapy with a Mixed Group of Adolescents," *International Journal of Group Psychotherapy*, V (1955), 249–60.

ings. Group counseling helps adolescents satisfy their special needs and also enlists their cooperation in developing a climate conducive to their growth; therefore, it should help alleviate their doubts about the counseling process. Ackerman also found that within the group situation his efforts to reach beyond mere talk to reflect his adolescent clients' genuine feelings were contagious, and motivated the clients to push for honest self-evaluation.

Group counseling also appears to be an effective technique for helping prospective counselors resolve their own problems or learn how to keep their problems from interfering with their success in counseling. It enables prospective counselors (1) to discover that others like themselves have problems, that they can be helped by counseling, that they too can learn to live more richly; (2) to extend their knowledge of human behavior and to apply this knowledge in understanding fellow clients; (3) to observe how a qualified counselor assists various clients; and (4) to serve as co-therapist and apply their knowledge of counseling in helping fellow clients.

Hulse says,

> Man is a group animal. He operates primarily in group settings. He has learned to curb his egocentricity and replaces it by cooperative behavior. His participation within the group gains for him a sense of belonging and of security which is essential to his well being.[4]

To the extent that an individual's major source of conflict involves— as it usually does—his relationships with others, and to the extent that he feels secure enough to talk, counseling within a group setting is appropriate for him. If proper use is made of role playing and of such materials as clay, finger paints, and dolls to help clients communicate their feelings, even primary-school-age children may be counseled effectively in groups. Unfortunately, there is little research evidence to help us determine who best can be counseled in groups and who should be counseled on an individual basis.

Group Counseling Defined

WHEN this writer reviewed the literature on group guidance procedures he was appalled at the frequency with which various authors used the same terms to describe very different processes and

4 W. C. Hulse, "The Therapeutic Management of Group Tension," *American Journal of Orthopsychiatry*, XX (1950), 834–38.

used different terms to describe what appeared to be identical processes. Chapter 3 defined the term "counseling" and reviewed some of the ways in which it helps youth. Individual counseling is to individual psychotherapy what group counseling is to group psychotherapy, and the clients' level of adjustment rather than the process determines whether it is counseling or psychotherapy. Both processes require special, though somewhat different, professional preparation. Ohlsen and Proff [5] chose the term "group counseling" to indicate that they were working with normal youth in a nonmedical setting.

If a sophisticated observer were to listen in on a group counseling session, he would note that the topics of conversation are not the topics of an ordinary social group. The members of this counseling group talk about themselves, about the things that disturb them, and about what they can do in order to improve their adjustment. Such problems are not group problems, but personal matters; the conversants are working together to help one another face individual conflicts that are too difficult for any one of them to solve alone.

In reliving tense and disturbing moments, some members become defensive. Others discuss quite freely both their hurtful experiences and their bitterness toward others. Still others will treat a member of the group as though he were the adversary in the conflict. At first, some members of the group find these reactions difficult to accept. Eventually, all members learn to tolerate such behavior; most learn to understand and accept it. The individual who wants to express negative as well as positive feelings then finds that he can do so with the knowledge that others will be able to accept these feelings. Indeed, group members learn to go further: they learn to help one another express their feelings.

But mere release of feelings, since it gives only temporary relief, is not sufficient. Each group member also must try to understand why he feels as he does, develop the will to act, and obtain the facts or skills needed to solve his problem. An effective group helps its members accomplish these ends. Its members help each person to discover and use his own resources with increasing success.

In his foreword to Slavson's book, *The Practice of Group Therapy*,

5 Merle M. Ohlsen and Fred C. Proff, *The Extent to Which Group Counseling Improves the Academic and Personal Adjustment of Underachieving Gifted Adolescents,* Cooperative Research Project No. 623 (Urbana: University of Illinois, 1960).

N. D. C. Lewis wrote as follows of the relationship between individual and group treatment:

> Group psychotherapy is basically a special application of the principles of individual treatment to two or more persons simultaneously, which brings also into the situation the phenomena and problems of interpersonal relationships.
>
> . . . The underlying aim of group therapy is to introduce therapeutic activity designed to direct the individual's efforts toward useful undertakings and to clarify the psychological conflicts so that they may be transformed into a normal way of living.[6]

The counselor's responsibilities to his clients are similar in individual and group counseling, but the task is more complicated in the latter. While trying to capture the speaker's feelings and trying to help him discuss the topics relevant for him, the counselor also must observe how the speaker's comments, as well as the various clients' nonverbal behavior,[7] influence each of the other clients. The counselor also sets an example which clients use in trying to understand and to help each other. The counselor's behavior gradually conveys to each and every one in the group his warmth, understanding, and acceptance of them and his genuine desire to help them.

Group counseling differs from individual counseling in other respects. Each member is given a chance to discuss and appraise his perceptions of himself, of his situation, and of various methods of attacking his problems, and he is also given an opportunity to accept groups of peers and to obtain from them simultaneous multiple reactions, prior to taking action. Frequently, a client uses role playing to convey more clearly how he feels, what his situation is like, and what he proposes to do about it. He also may use role playing to develop the confidence he needs for facing a difficult situation, to try out various methods for handling a specific situation, and to get his peers' reactions and suggestions concerning these methods before he tries to apply them in a real-life situation.

Robert Hinckley and Lydia Hermann say that the group therapy process may be identified by:

6 S. R. Slavson, ed., *The Practice of Group Therapy* (New York: International Universities Press, 1947), p. 9.

7 Evelyn W. Katz, M. M. Ohlsen, and F. C. Proff, "An Analysis Through Use of Kinescopes of the Interpersonal Behavior of Adolescents in Group Counseling," *Journal of College Student Personnel*, I (1959), 2–10.

(1) the therapeutic aim of the unit, with lack of group goal; (2) the alleviation of emotional tensions by sharing experiences—a process involving catharsis, the partial reliving of old experiences, and increasing self-awareness; (3) the permissive and supportive role of the therapist; (4) the direct interest in and attack on personal problems in order to foster attitudinal modifications.[8]

With respect to the first point, Hinckley and Hermann are in one sense right: the group does not have a problem that all of its members are trying to solve, and in that sense they have no common goal. In another sense, the members do have common objectives: to try to understand each other, and to help each solve his own problem in his own way.

The leader of guidance groups provides information on educational, vocational, and social problems, and encourages the members of the group to discuss this information. What Hinckley and Hermann have called social group work can be readily applied to group guidance activities. They say that this type of group activity may be characterized by a leader who provides information or leads a discussion designed to socialize members or to help them achieve some group objectives.

Informing Pupils About Group Counseling

WHENEVER a counselor introduces a new guidance service he must describe it accurately to pupils and teachers. One of the best ways to do this is to talk to pupils in classes, preferably in required courses where the counselor can reach everyone and avoid duplication from class to class. The counselor may use such opportunities to talk about the entire guidance program and answer questions about it, or to describe a new service, such as group counseling. Listed below are some of the questions that secondary-school pupils have asked about group counseling and the author's answers to these questions:

—Why would a pupil elect to join a counseling group? To discuss with pupils whom he trusts the things that bother him.
—Who will be in the group? Others like himself who want to discuss their problems.

8 Robert G. Hinckley and Lydia Hermann, *Group Treatment in Psychotherapy* (Minneapolis: Universtiy of Minnesota Press, 1952), pp. 19–20.

—Who decides which pupils will be in each group? From those who volunteer for group counseling the counselor selects pupils who are ready to talk about their problems, who have similar problems with which they want help, and who appear to fit in with others who have similar problems. Prior to selecting anyone for a group, the counselor holds an individual conference with each prospective client to assess whether he really wants to join a group, to explain how counseling may help him, to answer any further questions he may have about group counseling, to tell him what would be expected of him, and to let him know what he may expect from the group.

—How does the counselor know which pupils have common problems? Some of them discuss their problems with him in private conferences. Others have indicated on a problem check-list the matters they would like to discuss. (If no one asks this question the author distributes a problem check-list at the end of the discussion to give pupils some idea of the kinds of problem pupils discuss in group counseling. He tells them that although such a check-list is used to identify pupils with common problems, the check-list cannot reveal anything about a pupil that the pupil does not choose to reveal about himself. Therefore no one is asked to fill it out until he is ready to talk to the counselor about joining a counseling group.)

—What does the counselor expect the pupils to do in the group? He expects them to talk about matters that bother them and to try to figure out what they can do about them. He expects each to help create a friendly and understanding feeling within the group, and to try to understand the others and help them talk about their problems.

—What does the counselor do in the group? He tries to understand how each pupil feels, to help each tell how he feels, and to help each discover what he can do to realize his potential and to live more richly. The counselor also tries to sense how each person affects the others, and to help them all help one another. He helps the group decide how they can work together. Sometimes he helps them decide what they should try to do. When necessary, he may also see individual pupils between group meetings.

—What can pupils say in the group? It is the privilege of each person to talk about anything or anybody.

—What do the rest of the members do while one person is talking? They try to help him talk, to help him clarify what he says, and to help him understand himself. They try to see what they can learn from him that will help them. And they consider what they want to say about their own problems when they have a chance to talk.

—Will pupils worry about discussing personal problems in the group? Although some members of the group may hesitate to discuss certain topics, and even wonder afterwards whether they should have discussed a particular topic, most pupils will find out that they can learn to trust the rest of the group. If there is anyone whom a prospective member would not want included in his group, he should report this fact to the counselor before the groups are organized. Very close personal friends, relatives, and those with whom the pupil is not friendly fall into this category. In any case, each pupil should know that he can always talk about why he finds it difficult to discuss certain topics. By the time he has finished explaining why he has difficulty discussing a subject, he usually finds he can discuss it.

—Why not include a pupil's close friends, relatives, and unfriendly acquaintances in his group? Since these people are often involved in the pupil's problem, he may be unable, in their presence, to say frankly what he must say in order to solve his problems.

—Can a pupil really trust the other members of the group with his personal problems? The issue of keeping confidences is a crucial one. The group must think this question through and make a decision about it, before starting to discuss problems. Usually, the members feel more secure when they agree not to discuss anything mentioned in the group with anyone except the counselor.

—How do the members of the group decide how they will work together? First, the pupils decide what they can expect from one another and from the counselor. They also decide when they will meet, how long each meeting will be, and what they will talk about.

—Where does the group meet? They should meet in a room that is reserved for them, in which they will be neither interrupted nor overheard.

—When should the group meet? How long should they meet? How often should they meet? The group must decide these questions. If they meet during the school day, the best arrangement usually is to meet for a school period. Since most school periods are slightly less than an hour long, two meetings a week, well-spaced, are usually effective.

To further the development of good working relationships with the teachers, the counselor would do well not to take the pupils out of class for counseling. But he should be allowed to take students out of study hall.

—Should members be expected to attend counseling sessions regularly? This again is something groups must decide for themselves. Usually, it is best to start on time whether everyone is there or not. The pupils who profit most from the group tend to put the meetings ahead of everything else. Therefore, failure to attend regularly or a tendency to arrive late may be an indication of pupil indifference. However, such behavior is more apt to result from a pupil's inability to face his problems.

After the counselor has discussed with the group the nature of the group experience, and has answered questions (of which the above are typical), the pupils should have a chance to examine the checklist and decide whether they want to become involved to the extent of filling it out. By this time, the class period may be drawing to an end. To avoid putting pressure on pupils to join a group, the counselor should simply tell them where they can leave their names or where they may report if they wish to take the next step toward affiliating with a counseling group. It is very important that pupils realize that participants join counseling groups only on a voluntary basis, and that each group will define its own working rules. The counselor should remind those who fill out the checklist that at any point prior to starting group counseling they may elect not to proceed with it.

Selecting Clients

THE first step in forming a group is to define a basis for selecting group members. Unfortunately, there is no single criterion that the counselor can use. He is guided in his choice of group members by his own professional competence, by full study of all available information about each pupil, and by his goal—the selection of compatible working teams, each of which may differ from any other.

How will the group affect each individual? How will each individual affect other individuals in the group and the group process itself? Once the pupil decides he would like to join a counseling group, the counselor assigns him to a group in which he can help others as well as receive help for himself. This means, of course, that the pupil will not be assigned to a group until he can be placed in one that is appropriate.

Very aggressive, extremely shy, and seriously disturbed persons tend not to fit well in most groups of normal pupils. Before the counselor classifies anyone in any of these three categories, he should study all the information available. He should also keep in mind that an individual who is a poor risk for one counseling group may well fit into another one where personalities are more nearly compatible with his. It is interesting to note, for example, that the aggressive child and the child who is socially ahead of his age group often fit well into a counseling group with children somewhat older than themselves. Their opposites, the shy child and the child who is socially immature, tend to adjust better to groups with children younger than themselves.

Should the counselor try to select a relatively homogeneous group? Even though he may prefer a homogeneous group, the best the counselor can hope to do is to select pupils whose scores on some measurable traits fall within certain limits. First, however, he should ask whether he wants homogeneity; and if he concludes that he does, then he must decide for which traits he needs homogeneity. Different kinds of people, and people with different types of difficulty, often enrich the counseling experiences for the group. But on the other side, the more heterogeneous group faces communication problems. Successful untangling of communication problems can in itself contribute to growth, but while adults may be able to overcome such problems, it is usually very difficult for young pupils, even senior high school students, to do so.

If the counselor decides to select a relatively homogeneous group, the guides stated below will help him in this selection:

—Has sufficient consideration been given to the social maturity of the individual? The counselor usually decides this issue on the basis of chronological age. Children tend to adjust best to a group if they are within a year of the median age of the group. However, the issue is *social* maturity; therefore, the counselor should not think only of chronological age.

—What weight should the counselor give to the intellectual maturity of the individual? While the question of intellectual level is not crucial, a youngster has difficulty participating in a group when several members talk over his head. If, on the other hand, he finds himself talking down to the rest of the group, he may reject, and be rejected by, the other members. Of course, the student's verbal proficiency need not become a problem unless he makes it one by continuing to talk in terms that are not understood by the rest of the group.

—Should both sexes be represented in the group? Usually a mixed group is desirable, particularly when the group is considering boy-girl relationships. In considering these relationships, pupils frequently seek reactions of group members of the opposite sex. Moreover, they usually can discuss issues on a higher plane and with greater frankness in a mixed group than in a segregated group.

—Should the pupils have some problems in common? Having problems in common with others helps the individual feel that he belongs and that he is understood. This is especially reassuring to the adolescent, who wants so very much to be like his peers. In working with prospective secondary school clients, the author generally uses problem check-lists to identify students with common problems—or at least to identify problems to which they have assigned the same labels. Several of the problem check-lists described in Chapter 8 may be used for this purpose.

Although it is useful to identify adolescents with similar problems, it is unwise to include in any one group too many students who may find it very difficult to discuss a given topic. Unless there is at least one strong member who is able to discuss the troublesome topic—and highly motivated to do so—the clients will reinforce each other's defenses and avoid the subject entirely. M. B. Freedman and Blanche Sweet, who also encourage homogeneity with reference to certain traits, similarly warn counselors about clients' reinforcing each other's defenses:

> Within broad limits attempts are made to arrive at relatively homogeneous group composition with respect to age, educational level, and socioeconomic background. On the other hand, it is considered desirable to avoid homogeneity with respect to diagnosis. It has been our experience that members of groups uniform with respect to personality structure tend to reinforce each other's defenses. . . .[9]

Although we have been discussing the dangers of homogeneity, we should also note that absolute sameness does not exist. Even though the young people in the group may appear to have a common problem, the counselor should realize that probably no two individuals in the group sense the same facets of that problem. Each member has arrived at his present state of maturity along his own peculiar route. While he may give his problem a name similar to the labels used by other members, each pupil sees his problem in a very special way.

The problem of making vocational plans, for example, may appear to be essentially the same for each youngster—discovering his interests, his strengths, and his weaknesses, and securing information about the occupations that seem to be appropriate for him. But other considerations, such as his family's financial ability to support any necessary training program, will also influence his choice. Indeed, a wide variety of pressures complicate the decision-making

9 M. B. Freedman and Blanche S. Sweet, "Some Specific Features of Group Psychotherapy and Their Implications for Selection of Patients," *International Journal of Group Psychotherapy*, IV (1954), 357.

process: for each group member there are different kinds of social pressure from family, friends, teachers, and acquaintances; into the choice flows a whole backlog of attitudes toward jobs and people in jobs. Even children of the same sex from the same family may approach such a problem with backgrounds of experience that cause them to see it quite differently. What seems to be the same general problem is never identical for any two persons.

Who are most apt to profit from group counseling? Normal pupils who volunteer to participate after they realize what the group will expect from them and what they may expect from the group are good prospects. They have some matters to talk about and they will try to talk about them in the group. They also possess another of the characteristics Allport attributes to an effective group member: [10] the ability to become ego-involved. They can invest in others and reap satisfaction from seeing a fellow member solve his problems.

William Ryan [11] finds that the degree of clients' involvement in group therapy is related to mutual dependence. He defines mutual dependence as (1) potential for giving (ability to empathize with others, to form relationships with others, to delay gratification of needs, and to derive satisfaction from gratifying needs of others) and (2) management of dependency wishes (extent to which an individual accepts or denies his wishes to have other persons gratify his needs for him).

Stranahan, Schwartzman, and Atkin [12] conclude that those who profit most from these group therapy experiences have some capacity for insight, a degree of flexibility, and a desire for change; and that early in their lives they had experience with authority figures who possessed some measure of steadiness, hopefulness, direction, and maturity.

For both individual and group therapy Nash, Frank, Gliedman, Imber, and Stone [13] note that those who rejected treatment tended

10 Gordon W. Allport, "The Psychology of Participation," *Psychological Review*, LII (1945), 117–32.

11 William Ryan, "Capacity for Mutual Dependence and Involvement in Group Psychotherapy," *Dissertation Abstracts*, XIX (1958), 1119.

12 M. Stranahan, C. Schwartzman, and E. Atkin, "Group Treatment for Emotionally Disturbed and Potentially Delinquent Boys and Girls," *American Journal of Orthopsychiatry*, XXVII (1957), 5–18.

13 E. H. Nash, J. D. Frank, L. H. Gliedman, S. D. Imber, and A. R. Stone, "Some Factors Related to Patients Remaining in Group Psychotherapy," *International Journal of Group Psychotherapy*, VII (1957), 264–74.

to be more irresponsible, withdrawn, and impulsive than those who accepted it. Most patients who rejected group therapy after a brief exposure to it indicated that their experience intensified their symptoms—probably it weakened their defenses and made them feel worse rather than better. These clients probably found it easier to deny their problems than to do something about them.

Early in this chapter it was pointed out that adolescents often have misgivings about counseling. Ohlsen and Oelke [14] found that though their adolescent clients were told why they were invited to participate in group counseling and though they were allowed to reject it, they still retreated to impersonal topics significantly more frequently than did adult clients who initiated group counseling. One explanation is that these adolescents did nothing to initiate counseling. The underdeveloped ego and superego functions of adolescents, as well as their low tolerance for anxiety, also may account in part for the observed difference. The difficulties of working with adolescents in group counseling are further increased by the fact that the climate of a group of young adolescents is very sensitive to changes in individual clients, and can be influenced markedly by the absences of either a client who wants to help develop and maintain a therapeutic climate or one who impedes its development. Therefore, it is very important that prior to selecting clients the counselor try to assess each prospective client's willingness to discuss his problems and accept responsibility for doing something about them. When counseling *is not initiated by the client it is especially important that he understand what will be expected from him, what he can expect from the other members, how counseling may help him, and that he can refuse counseling.*

A client who has received counseling on an individual basis and who is then referred for group counseling will usually want to speak with a counselor before deciding whether or not to join a counseling group. The pupil who has not been involved in counseling on an individual basis should also receive assistance in deciding whether he should join a group, and also needs answers to his personal questions about the nature of the group experience. Therefore, the counselor should provide an individual conference for each prospective client before assigning him to a group.

14 M. M. Ohlsen and M. C. Oelke, "An Evaluation of Discussion Topics in Group Counseling," *Journal of Clinical Psychology*, XVIII (1962), 317–22.

Developing the Counseling Relationship

THOUGH they have had a chance to ask their questions about group counseling in general, and about what will be expected from them, most pupils want to discuss certain questions within their group before they start talking about themselves and their problems. To show how such questions are handled by a counselor, parts of two recorded interviews are presented here. (The counselor's reasons for recording [15] the interviews were discussed with the pupils in their individual conferences prior to this first group session.)

C: Let us begin by introducing ourselves. I am Mr. Owens. Two years ago I was assigned to this high school as a counselor. Before I came here I taught math in Washington Junior High School. In this group I shall try to help you talk about the problems you want to discuss. As each of you introduces himself, it would help us if you would tell why you joined the group. (*Pause for about fifteen seconds.*)

RAY: I am Ray Stanley. Last August we moved here from California. When Mr. Owens visited my history class and talked about these groups, I told him I wanted to join one of them. I am having trouble making friends here.

JOE: I am Joe Murphy. I'd like to make more friends in this school. I ride the bus and don't have much time to meet school gangs. My folks won't let me have the car to come in to school parties. They are too strict.

So went the introductions for all seven students. Each one was concerned either about making school friends or learning how to get along with others. Several were having troubles with their parents.

C: While each of you states it differently, all of you would like to learn how to get along better with people.

SAM: But how can we do that by just talking about it?

C: You are not sure that you can get help here?

SAM: That's right. How are you going to help us?

C: To profit most from these sessions each of us should help the other students in the group to feel that he wants them here and try to make it easy for each of them to talk freely about the things which worry him.

15 Because he recorded this interview, it was possible for Mr. Owens to study his performance and discover ways of improving his methods.

Not only is each of you here to solve your own problems, but you also have a responsibility for helping the other fellow solve his problems. You can do this by trying to understand how the other fellow feels and by helping him talk about it. Discussing frankly how he feels about himself as well as others helps him solve his problems. (*Ten-second pause.*) Also you have a chance to try out your ideas in here—to learn how others feel about your way of meeting your problem. I'll try to help each of you do these things, and try to help each learn to help the others, too.

SAM: Will that help me?

C: You're still not sure whether this will help you? Have you ever tried to explain something to someone only to discover that you understood it better by the time you were able to make him see what you were talking about?

SAM: Yeah.

C: That's what happens here. By the time the rest of us understand how you feel and what you worry about, you'll probably understand it better, too. You will find that these other students in here will have some suggestions for you, too.

MARY: Sam, we went over all that when Mr. Owens visited our classes and when we had our individual conferences with him. Let's get started talking.

RAY: Don't you think that we should first make up our minds when and where we should meet?

JOE: This time is okay, isn't it? How many times a week should we meet?

MARY: Let's start meeting here once a week at this hour.

C: How do the rest of you feel about Mary's suggestion?

They agreed on the proposal.

RAY: Do we have to come to all the meetings?

C: You are uncertain about committing yourself?

RAY: No, that's not it; I want to come, but I'd feel better if I knew whether we all were really going to try to be here every time.

C: That is something we'll have to decide. You know we can't get much from anything if we don't give it an important place in our day. Our coming regularly is just one way of showing that this is important to us.

RAY: Then you think we should come every time. I suppose we could be absent if we had a good excuse.

C: I can see why you think that, but that isn't exactly what I meant. I meant to say that if you feel this is very important, you will do your darndest to be here every time.

RAY: If you don't want to say what you think, how can you help us? Won't you tell us what you think we should do to solve our problems?

C: You want me to listen to your problems and then tell you what to do? Do you think this would help you? Do you think that you would follow my advice?

JEAN: You know what we should do, don't you?

MARY: I didn't come here to have him tell me what to do. I know plenty of grownups who would like to do that and I am not taking my problem to them. Anyway, Mr. Owens said that we would get together to help one another. When I said he should count me in on this thing, I thought we would talk about the things which were upsetting us and try to figure out together what we could do. There are a lot of things I would like to talk about with you.

SAM: But how do we get started?

C: Ray, could you describe how we got started talking by ourselves?

Ray had been Mr. Owens' client for six weeks. Mr. Owens felt that Ray found it quite easy to talk.

RAY: Well—this is different. (*Thirty-second pause.*) Maybe these two things are alike in some ways. Normally, I just started talking, or you asked me what was on my mind and then I started telling you. Say, what were you doing, anyway?

C: I was trying to understand what you were feeling and saying, trying to see your problems with your eyes and trying to help you say what you wanted to say.

RAY: Oh (*pause*)—guess that must be right. Sometimes, I could talk on and on. At other times, I felt pretty mean about someone or something, and I hated to say those mean things. Sometimes I had a hard time talking because I didn't know how to say what I wanted to say.

C: And I helped you then, too?

RAY: I guess you just waited for me to think it out or you helped me tell why it was hard to talk.

C: Does that answer your question, Sam?

SAM: Yes and no. It helps me see how we could talk about my problems by ourselves, but I am not sure that those rules work here.

C: You are not sure that the thing which worked for Ray and me would work in this group?

SAM: No, but maybe we can start with what Ray described. You will help us keep going?

C: Yes, I'll try to help you tell about yourself. Of course, I hope that each of you will help others say what they want to say, too. Usually we can help him best by commenting on what he said only when we are not sure that we understand what he meant or when he is having trouble saying it because it is very personal.

MARY: We can try anyway.

RAY: Makes sense to me.

The others agreed.

C: Then it seems that we have reached one agreement as to how we can help each other. Earlier, we agreed on the meeting time and place. Maybe we should have someone write down our house rules so we can refer back to them whenever we want to do so. Of course, we can change them whenever we want to. Would someone volunteer to do this job for us? (*Sally volunteered.*) Thanks, Sally. Anytime you are not sure what we expect from one another, call on Sally for a review of the rules. Sally, if you are in doubt as to whether you have stated the rule correctly, read it back to us for corrections.

Are there other working guides which we need? (*Ten-second pause.*) When I talked to you in your classes and in our private conferences, several of you were worried about students' discussing outside of this room what we say here. If you are still concerned about this issue, you should make some decision on this point. Since our time is up now, maybe we could think about this question and any others for which you feel rules or working guides are required. We shall start with them next time.

At that point the meeting ended. At the next meeting, a week later, Jim Owens began as follows: "What do you want to talk about today?"

JEAN: If we are going to say what we think, I don't want anybody telling anybody what I say in here.

C: You feel that everyone should agree not to discuss anywhere what is said here? Does that mean students can't talk with me about what goes on in here?

This discussion continued until the group agreed on rules about keeping confidence, taking in new members, members dropping out of the group, and attendance at meetings.

BILL: I still don't see how I can get help from this deal. I don't see how I can help the rest of you kids and I don't see how you can help me.

MARY: Well, I do. Why don't you try it for a while? Then if you still don't think you are getting any help, you can drop out.

SALLY: I feel a little like Bill. Then, too, I am afraid that the rest of you will feel that the thing which is worrying me is pretty silly. I am different. My folks are different, too.

C: You're afraid of what we will think of you when you talk about your problem?

SALLY: That's right.

JEAN: I don't see how the rest of you can tell how I feel when I am mixed up about it myself.

MARY: We are getting right back to where we were. Let's quit stalling and get going. Say, how should we start?

C: Last week, Mary, you said that you wanted to talk about the things which worried you and get this going to help you figure out what you could do. Should we try that now? The rest of us will try to help you tell us how you feel. Someone may have suggestions for you.

Mary told about feeling lonely in school and believing she was expected to carry too heavy a load in her home. Joe and Jean commented about what Mary said or asked her questions. In addition to helping Mary tell about her feelings of loneliness, Ray told how he missed his old friends. This discussion took the remainder of the period.

Now let us examine together what happened. In general, these first two sessions were very well handled. Among the many good techniques the counselor used, these stand out: (1) he defined his role clearly and briefly; (2) he helped the clients introduce their problems in their initial remarks; (3) his response to the pupils' opening remarks attempted to reveal similarity between clients' problems; (4) he conveyed his sincere desire to understand and help them; (5) he showed patience in helping them get started talking about their problems; (6) he explained how talking helps clients; (7) he helped them develop their own house rules; and (8) he revealed his respect for clients by letting them struggle with house rules and by asking Ray to explain how clients get started talking in counseling.

The research of Florence Powdermaker and J. D. Frank [16] supports several of Mr. Owens' techniques. Though their research was concerned with hospitalized veterans, they discovered several effective devices that are relevant for a school counselor in working with adolescents: (1) generalize from one client's remarks in the hope that other clients will see the relevance of the discussion for themselves; (2) emphasize the similarity between the problems and emotions of two or more clients; (3) paraphrase a client's statements to

16 Florence B. Powdermaker and J. D. Frank, *Group Psychotherapy* (Cambridge: Harvard University Press, 1953).

clarify them for other members of the group; (4) encourage mutual respect by referring questions to another client or to the rest of the group; (5) emphasize the continuity of meetings by reviewing important events from the previous meeting at the beginning of the next; (6) apply general statements to immediate situations; and (7) help clients discuss the relationships developing among them.

Although Mr. Owens made no errors that seriously interfered with helping his clients develop a therapeutic climate for their work, he could have responded more effectively at times than he did. In his third response to Sam, for example, he should have merely reflected back Sam's doubts concerning the value of counseling and stopped there. If the counselor had waited a minute or two, Sam probably would have elaborated on the nature of his doubts and, by thinking the problem through, increased his readiness for counseling. After all, he had sought help after hearing Mr. Owens describe group counseling and answer the students' questions about it. Had Sam said nothing, another client probably would have attempted to answer Sam's question. As a matter of fact, a moment later Mary indicated that she knew what was expected. Had Mr. Owens said nothing and had Mary not attempted to answer Sam's question, Mary probably would have commented much as she did anyway, then Mr. Owens could have applied Powdermaker and Frank's fourth point by asking Mary to explain to Sam how group counseling might help him.

Mr. Owens also could have used Mary's reaction to Sam to speed up the group's workings. Instead of asking the group how they felt about Mary's suggestion, he might have responded to three feelings she expressed by offering a comment such as: "You know what is expected of you, you can see how counseling will help you, and you are impatient to get started." Such a statement would have encouraged Mary to begin talking immediately about herself and her problems, and the others could have learned how to talk from her. Of course, this would have taken time that was used to settle certain basic house rules, but a group does not define all of its working relationships during the first session anyway. These arrangements develop gradually as counseling progresses. Moreover, success in helping someone like Mary usually contributes more to the therapeutic climate than merely talking about the nature of the relationship.

When Ray raised his question about regular attendance, Mr. Owens made a good response to Ray's feelings about commitment, but backed off when he decided that he had made a bad guess. Instead of answering Ray's question he should have said, "This is so important to you that you know that you will come every time, and be here on time, but perhaps you are not certain that the other members of this group will do the same." Such a response would have provided members with the same information that Mr. Owens' other comment provided, but would have associated it with Ray's concern about helping the group succeed. This reply also might have encouraged several members, especially Mary and Ray, to begin talking about themselves and their feelings toward other members, and to review the expectations from clients which they recalled from previous contacts with Mr. Owens.

Usually someone will ask the question that was then raised by Ray: "If you don't say what you think, how can you help us?" When a client makes such a comment, a counselor is often tempted to say something like: "I can't solve your problems for you. My responsibility is to help you learn to solve your own problems, and I can't do that by telling you what to do. Anyway, most people don't want to be told what to do, and they don't follow other people's advice very well." However, best results are usually achieved, especially with adolescents, by responding to dependency feelings as Mr. Owens did in the first sentence of his response to Ray. This encourages the dependent client to examine his dependency needs, and encourages an independent client like Mary to express her feelings toward those who resist her efforts to achieve independence. Furthermore, it is difficult for a counselor to convince a dependent client that the counselor should not tell him what to do. Helping him discuss his dependency needs contributes more to his readiness for counseling than arguing with him about what is good for him.

Because Ray had responded well in individual counseling, Mr. Owens assumed that he would be able to answer Sam's question: "But how do we get started?" As it developed, however, he put Ray on the spot. Apparently Ray had not thought much about how he got started; perhaps he hoped to be more dependent upon the counselor in this new situation than he had been in individual counseling. He may have assumed that group counseling would be something like group instruction. In any case, Ray's effort to explain how one gets started talking helped his fellow clients, and it also probably helped clarify for Ray what would be expected of him in the group.

THE CLIENT'S RESPONSIBILITIES

Since each member elects to join a group only after careful study of the nature of group counseling, one should be able to assume his willingness to help build a relationship in which members can solve their problems. Obviously, the members of a counseling group must know why they are together and what each can expect from the others. Although the understanding of working relationships does not occur automatically and is never complete, most members early in the relationship accept their responsibility for creating and maintaining the permissive emotional climate. As they work together, others learn that they, too, can help build a permissive relationship.

The group also expects every individual to define his own goals. Each member should accept the idea that different individuals have different purposes in joining the group and that any individual can withdraw from the group whenever he recognizes that he cannot gain help from it, or whenever he has achieved his own goals. Usually each member comes to understand himself better as a consequence of observing how others learn to harness their resources for effective living.

As long as a pupil remains in a counseling group, the counselor and the other members expect him to be considerate of the needs of others, particularly the need of each individual to discover his own method for attacking his peculiar problem. They also expect him to share the counseling time with them: such sharing involves not only consideration of others but also recognition of one's responsibility for helping others learn to participate.

The role of the member of a counseling group, then, entails listening to the speaker, trying to understand every other member, and helping each to express his feelings, whatever they may be—feelings of guilt, fear, rejection, acceptance, sorrow, love, hate, ambivalence, confusion, or inadequacy. Sometimes the individual who happens to have the floor at the moment needs help in discussing these feelings. The other members are aware that they too may have difficulty, and that each one should help others say what they are trying to say.

THE COUNSELOR'S RESPONSIBILITIES

Early in a group session, an observer would recognize, if he were admitted to the group, that there is a special person present. This person is the counselor. He gives his full attention to helping others, to serving the group without expecting the other members to help him work out his problems. He is aware of his own needs and blind spots and tries not to let them interfere with his helping the members of the group. While he is conscious of all the members in the group, he usually concentrates his attention on the pupil who is speaking at any one time. He tries to capture the speaker's feelings and to help him unfold his story. At the same time, he observes the responses of others and helps them to become involved. He gradually conveys to each and every one in the group his warmth, his understanding, and his acceptance. From him, they learn to accept one another and to help one another talk about crucial problems.

Even though between six and eight pupils are receiving help at one time, each individual obtains help with the problems of greatest concern to him. However, the counselor-client relationship in group counseling is not the same as a counselor-client relationship in individual counseling. It cannot be the same because other people are present—not only present, but participating. In fact, the presence of other people makes group counseling the most desirable approach for some clients; for others, the group situation is undesirable, either because of the disturbing effect the group may have on these clients, or because of the disturbing effect these clients may have on the group.

The counselor tries to accept each pupil as he is, even though the pupil's point of view may differ widely from his own. This does not mean that the counselor has the same personal values that the pupils have, nor that he admires all of each pupil's behavior. It does mean that the counselor respects each pupil and the pupil's right to have or to develop values that differ from his own. As the counselor works in the group, he indicates to each pupil that the pupil need not see things as the counselor does; neither need the pupil feel that he must behave as the counselor would were he faced with the pupil's problems.

Not only must the counselor be able to help clients build a permissive relationship and help them talk freely (just as he does in individual counseling), but he must also sense the effect that pupils have upon one another. He responds to these relationships, helps the pupils define working relationships, assists pupils in changing the rules whenever they feel a need for such changes, and helps pupils learn to help one another. He helps them develop a real "we" feeling, which will in turn make it easier for individual pupils to share their feelings openly.

ADAPTING PROCEDURES FOR YOUNG CHILDREN

The author's own experience and research with groups indicate that though the same basic principles of counseling apply to all age groups, the counselor must adapt his techniques to his clients' social and emotional maturity, their previous experiences in groups, and their communication skills. Previously, he referred to Ohlsen and Proff's [17] work with ninth-graders. Since 1960 those involved in the group counseling research project at the University of Illinois—the author among them—have counseled bright underachieving fifth-, sixth-, seventh-, and eighth-graders in groups. They found that seventh- and eighth-graders responded to the techniques described above, but that the fifth- and sixth-graders did not; the younger student had difficulty becoming ego-involved in other clients' problems, and in setting and enforcing limits for themselves within this permissive climate.[18] From their analysis of these younger children's behavior, the researchers arrived at a number of modifications of their original procedures. They concluded that pupils must be screened more carefully to insure that both pupils and their parents understand what will be expected of the pupils in the groups, and that both see value in the group experience; that underachievers be placed in counseling groups in which there are other pupils who are genuinely concerned about improving their school achievement; that counselors must consult with the teachers regularly; that fewer clients should be treated in a group (perhaps four or five instead of eight); that clients need more limits, especially during the early stages of counseling; and that more attention must be given to selecting a room with the fewest possible distractions. They also decided that they should have made more use of role playing in working with these younger clients. Perhaps they also could have profited

17 *Op. cit.*
18 Merle M. Ohlsen, *Assessing Outcomes of Group Counseling for Under-achieving, Bright Fifth-graders and their Parents*, Quarterly Progress Report to Cooperative Research Branch of U.S. Office of Education, June 30, 1961.

from experiences like those described below for primary children.

The counselor who works with primary-school-age children must give special attention to the children's communication skills and previous experiences in groups. For example, the counselor cannot expect primary-school-age children to rely on verbal communication to tell how they feel about the important other people in their lives and the ways in which these important others have affected them. With modeling clay, finger paints, dolls, and the assistance of an understanding counselor who knows a great deal about primary-school-age children and their common problems, children of this age can learn to express these feelings and to cope better with the problems they associate with these feelings.

Perhaps a brief look at a counselor at work with five first- and second-graders would clarify how they can be helped in a group. Provision was made for the pupils to sit around a long table in a playroom. Before they entered the room, the counselor had laid out sheets of brown wrapping paper, finger paints, modeling clay, and dolls of various sizes. When they came into the room, each selected the materials of his choice and sat down to play. One of the girls and two of the boys chose to play with finger paints. The third boy played with clay and the remaining girl began her play with the dolls (primary-school-age children have less experience of, and perhaps less need for, group interaction than do older pupils). The counselor moved about, responding first to one child, then to another. He would watch a child at play and after he figured out what the child was trying to express, he responded to the child in the same medium—e.g., if the child was playing with finger paints, he responded with finger paints. The children also were permitted to help each other and to respond to each other. Occasionally, one of them wanted to tell the entire group something. When necessary the counselor helped him get everyone's attention. This often resulted in others wanting to tell the group something (a sort of show and tell). Although this talking can be very effective, Ginott warns against forcing a child to verbalize:

Many serious mistakes in child therapy are committed by adults who try to give verbal insight to children whose language is play. Forcing them to verbalize is like compelling them to converse in a foreign language.[19]

19 H. G. Ginott, "Play Group Therapy: A Theoretical Framework," *International Journal of Group Psychotherapy*, VIII (1958), 413.

Maintaining the Counseling Relationship

THE crucial elements in developing and maintaining a counseling relationship in individual counseling were discussed in Chapters 3 and 4. These elements apply to group counseling too. The previous sections of this chapter indicate how the basic principles of individual counseling can be adapted to creating a therapeutic climate in group counseling. Among those techniques that the counselor can use to develop and to maintain an effective working atmosphere within a counseling group, the following stand out: (1) communicate to clients that he is trying to understand them; (2) invest in clients without becoming unwholesomely involved in their private lives; (3) detect and respond to clients' feelings; (4) convey to clients how to detect and respond to fellow clients' feelings; and (5) develop in clients the feeling of responsibility for developing and maintaining a climate conducive to client growth. The counselor also must have an adequate understanding of human behavior and believe that his clients have something they want to talk about when they elect to join a group.

Obviously, the writer of an introductory guidance text cannot deal with all the critical incidents a school counselor meets within the group setting. Therefore, only a few of the typical problems will be discussed.

One of the questions that counselors often ask is "Do pupils really discuss their private thoughts in a group?" The answer is yes. Some find it easier to talk in a group. Hearing others talk frees them to talk; they also find it reassuring to be associated with an accepting group of persons of their own age who are struggling with problems similar to their own.

Those who are reticent about the things that bother them may be shy, or they may have learned to conceal their feelings about themselves and others. Hearing others discuss their problems usually encourages these pupils to talk too.

As was indicated at the beginning of this chapter, many adolescents approach counseling with suspicion. Frequently, they try to antagonize the counselor. Although he is often tempted to fight back, that is the worst response he can make because it would confirm all their suspicions. They just cannot believe what the counselor has told them about the relationship; too many adults have told them what to do, and blamed them for things for which the important adults in their lives were at least partially responsible. But when they discover that they can reject counseling if they choose, that they can really help define their own house rules for the group, that others can learn to trust them and the counselor, and that the counselor really tries to understand them, even they learn to talk.

As members realize that some find it difficult to talk, they learn to assume responsibility for bringing the nonparticipant into the discussion. Occasionally, the clients talk about how they could make it easier for the nonparticipant to become involved in the discussion. Usually, the counselor need only reflect the feeling of the pupil who cannot participate. Sometimes it involves nothing more than helping the client get the floor. When, for example, the counselor notices a client who is always interrupted before he can make his statement, the counselor could, at his earliest opportunity, say, "You were cut off again a few minutes ago just when you were about to speak. Perhaps you are wondering whether it's worth it to try again." Such a remark makes members aware of their responsibility for helping fellow clients participate. Otherwise those who have difficulty speaking go unnoticed in the general activity of the group. While spontaneity in a group decreases awkward pauses, it can result in the neglect of the shy or reticent client. Fortunately, pupils, once their attention has been directed to the problem, are quick to recognize this type of youngster and to help him work his way into the discussion. They note when he wants to talk and even help him break into a lively discussion among pupils who find it easy to talk.

With upper-elementary-school- and junior-high-school-age clients, the counselor is often frustrated by a different problem: several clients talking at once. The counselor is tempted to point out what is expected; he often does so, in a tone of voice that makes the clients feel they are being scolded, thus causing them to confuse the counseling and teaching roles. A more effective response is,

I should like to try to understand what each of you is saying, but I can't when several of you talk at once. I realize that you have something that you would like to say, and that it is difficult for you to wait your turn, but all of us must be able to hear what each of you is saying in order to help you.

The way in which the group explores its topics is another important aspect of group discussion. While there usually are conversational themes, with points of focus and a clear-cut beginning and cut-off point, the group does not explore all such themes completely. They frequently bring themes into the conversation only to drop them, sometimes returning to them later, sometimes not returning to them at all. This practice often bothers the counselor, but it is normal. The counselor should not force the group to follow a theme through to any "logical" conclusion. The group must be allowed to discuss whatever they wish and move the topic along at their own rate rather than at the counselor's rate. Ohlsen and Oelke [20] show that every contribution made to a discussion has its own special significance. From their content analysis of interactions in group counseling for two groups of adolescents and three groups of prospective counselors, they conclude that what a client discusses in a group is a function of his own peculiar needs, his sense of security within his group, and the other members' ability to communicate understanding and acceptance of him and his problems. It is important that the counselor does not disrupt the group's natural functioning with his personal views of what should be discussed and when.

In Chapter 4 the point was made that a counselor should give a client information only when the client is prepared to accept it and use it. In group counseling there is an additional restriction on giving information to a client: the counselor must be cautious lest he break confidence with the client. It is up to the client, not the counselor, to decide what information about himself he is willing to share with the group. The counselor should not, therefore, introduce any information about a client which the client himself has not first introduced.

Although there are good reasons for counseling adolescents in groups, this approach involves a number of problems. For example, although adolescents often need to talk about their problems in understanding and accepting adult roles, their struggle for independence, their domination by peers, and their defining and enforcing their house rules for their counseling group, they also can be very defensive about these topics. Whenever a counselor interprets behavior or reflects too deeply, he may find that not only does the client to whom he responded become defensive, but that several persons, or even the entire group, also become defensive. Furthermore, when the counselor notices that a client is interfering with the therapeutic experience for another or others, he should respond to the hurt or neglected one rather than to the disruptive one. Sometimes it is best to let the troublesome activity go on until a client notices it, and then help that client deal with the distracting or blocking client.

Gradually, the members learn to carry the discussion without leaning on the counselor. Clients increasingly learn to play the assistant counselor role. Ideally, every member should feel responsible for trying to understand the speaker and helping him express his feelings, for preventing a few from monopolizing the time, and for moving the discussion along. When members sense that the discussion really belongs to them, they learn to carry it; and when something interferes with productive discussion, they assume responsibility for doing something about the disruption.

Role Playing

ROLE playing is a technique for extending the effectiveness of group counseling; it provides pupils with an opportunity to act out as well as talk out their problems. Some writers discuss this topic under two other headings: psychodrama and sociodrama—thus distinguishing between role playing that touches very intimately on a pupil's private life, and role playing that involves the less personal problems. Since counseling is concerned with a pupil's private life, the literature on psychodrama has most relevance here. Role playing also can be used effectively for leadership training and for helping pupils cope with the common problems of social adjustment that they meet in daily school activities. In these latter instances, some of the most useful literature is published under titles concerning sociodrama.

Opportunities arise naturally for bringing role playing into the counseling process. When, for example, a group of senior high school students were discussing the problems of "going steady," Joe told about wanting to have a date with the new girl, Sally. He was troubled because he had been going steady with Dorothy for almost two years. (Neither girl was a member of the counseling group.) The exchange of comments brought out that he did not want to break up with Dorothy. One of the girls asked whether he had thought about how the two girls involved would feel when each learned of the other; with that, he turned to Nancy, another member, and asked how she thought they would feel. Nancy said she would have to know more about the girls to answer his question.

At this point, Joe described the two girls and then said,

> You pretend that you are Dorothy and that you just learned that I had had a date with Sally. After we act that out, pretend that you are Sally and you just learned that I have been going steady with Dorothy. I'd like to know what I should say when I meet one, then the other.

Nancy agreed to role-play these scenes. Several of the members of the group made suggestions as to how Nancy could "get in the mood" to play her parts. When they finished acting out these skits, Nancy and Joe decided to trade parts and play the scenes over again.

After the group had discussed this experience and helped Joe to see better what was involved, they turned to a discussion of the advantages of using this technique in the future. While considering the question, they reviewed Joe's and Nancy's performances in an effort to determine ways of improving what was done. Then they considered conditions that might suggest the use of the technique again. Finally, they talked about the responsibilities of the various people involved.

Joe's experience suggests how a counselor can help a client introduce role playing in group counseling. During structuring the counselor should introduce the notion of role playing and explain how the technique can be used by members during counseling.

When can role playing be used effectively in group counseling?

—When a client is having difficulty describing a situation or communicating his feelings about it to others.
—When a client wants to know how others perceive him and his situation.
—When a client wants to know how others react to his proposed actions.
—When a client feels that he needs practice with social skills or that he needs practice in dealing with a difficult situation in order to develop the confidence to act.

What basic principles should be followed in using role playing?

—Whenever the counselor identifies a situation for which he thinks role playing would be appropriate, he should review how the technique works and explain briefly why he thinks it would be appropriate in this instance. He also must try to communicate that it is effective only when the client involved sees value in using it, and when fellow clients volunteer for the roles needed.

—The scene to be acted out should be described by the member whose problem suggested it. As he describes the scene and the characters in it, there should be ample opportunity for questions and comments from the other members. To profit most from the act itself and the discussion growing out of it, every member of the group should obtain the best possible picture of the situation, as it is seen by the pupil who suggested role playing.

—Following the description of the scene, members of the group should be encouraged to volunteer for the various roles. (Even the reticent youngster will often be able to select a role he feels he can play.) When roles are left unfilled, clients should be encouraged to suggest persons for these roles. Usually it is best for the counselor not to play a role. The pupil who suggested role playing should perform much as a dramatic director in setting the stage for the scene and in preparing members for their parts. The counselor assists the director. Even here, he does not play the authoritarian role we usually associate with the drama teacher. Instead, he merely helps the student director clarify his perception of the situation and the players' role in it.

—The counselor should help the players look upon role playing as an impromptu play in which everyone makes up his own lines in an effort to portray his character's feelings. Each player should realize that once he believes he understands his role, he is on his own. He should do and say what he feels the person whose part he is playing would do and say in real life. Even though he may have been given actual sentences spoken by the character he is playing, he should not be concerned about remembering and repeating them. Instead, he should try to feel as he believes his character would feel and to express the character's feelings as best he can, using his own choice of words. The counselor also may wish to encourage a client to use soliloquy when his character says one thing and feels another (or when he has a reaction that he is not ready to express).

—Just before beginning the scene, the counselor should try to assess whether everyone understands his role. Anyone who feels unsure about his role should have an opportunity to ask questions. During the role playing the counselor remains inactive except when he feels he can help a player express feelings that he has difficulty expressing.

—Every actor should feel free to cut the scene whenever he feels unable to proceed or whenever he feels that the group has accomplished its objective. When the role playing is terminated by someone other than the

director, the one who terminated it should be given the first opportunity to express his feelings and/or to ask his questions about it. Next
the director, then the other actors, and finally the audience, should be
given a chance to speak.
—When it appears profitable to replay the roles, all the members should
have a chance to volunteer for the roles.

What can role playing contribute to the therapeutic process? The
following impressions stand out:

—Regardless of the role he plays, the pupil whose problem precipitated
the role playing achieves new insights as he directs and participates
in the scene. As he describes the situation and the people in it, tells
how he thinks they feel, acts out his part and listens to the reactions
of the group, he improves his understanding of himself and the situation.
—The audience asks questions and makes comments that help to identify
the major forces within the field, to clarify the feelings of various characters toward one another, and to show role players how they are perceived by others.
—When a pupil volunteers to play his own role, he usually finds that he
can express his feelings even more freely in a role-played scene than
he can when he talks about the same problem in the group.
—When a pupil deliberately tries to play another's role in order to see
the situation through this other person's eyes, he not only captures part
of the other person's picture of the conflict, but he sees himself in
action as he watches the other person trying to play his role. In addition to achieving a better understanding of the situation, he acquires
a picture of himself that he probably has never seen before—a picture
that he could not see clearly until he tried to look at himself through
another's eyes.

Most of these clinical impressions are supported by research. The
research evidence also suggests additional advantages of role playing.

—Edgar Borgotta [21] found that role playing stimulated greater participation of the silent members, and that clients' responses were closer to
real-life behavior than those obtained from written tests.

21 Edgar Borgotta, "An Analysis of Three Levels of Response: An Approach
to Some Relationships Among Dimensions of Personality," *Sociometry*, XIV
(1951), 267–315.

—In his work with training foremen, M. R. P. French [22] noted that role playing stimulated participation, involvement, and identification in such a way that it brought out the deeper emotional aspects of interpersonal relationships.

—Katz, Ohlsen, and Proff [23] found role playing to be highly effective in facilitating spontaneous expression of feelings.

—Charles Kean [24] used role playing in religious conferences and retreats to give teenagers from varied backgrounds a sense of togetherness; he discovered that it also enabled them to go more deeply into their problems.

—In a review of the literature on role-playing Rosemary Lippitt and Ann Hubbell [25] listed its contributions as follows: (1) it facilitates expression of feelings and attitudes; (2) it provides useful data for diagnosis of problems; (3) it enables clients to try out different ways of behaving; (4) it gives clients a chance to practice behavior skills in a permissive setting; and (5) it gives clients insight into their own behavior and how it affects others.

Terminating Group Counseling

DURING the first or second session, the group should agree on a starting and closing time for each session. Meetings held before and after school, as well as those held during school periods, should be scheduled and operated within defined limits. Pupils usually favor a regularly scheduled time and place.

Eventually, the pupils will have talked about all the problems that they care to discuss. They should terminate the counseling sessions at that point. However, a very strong "in-group" or "we" feeling develops. The members find strength and security in the group to such an extent that they sometimes resist terminating counseling. When the counselor believes this is occurring, he should respond to these feelings as he would to other feelings, helping pupils face the problem of breaking a satisfying personal relationship.

Only the individual member can know when he has achieved his

22 M. R. P. French, "Role Playing as a Method of Training Foremen," in *Group Psychotherapy*, ed. J. L. Moreno (New York: Beacon House, 1946), pp. 172–87.

23 *Op. cit.*

24 Charles Kean, "Some Role Playing Experiments With High School Students," *Group Psychotherapy*, VI (1954), 256–65.

25 Rosemary Lippitt and Ann Hubbell, "Role Playing for Personnel and Guidance Workers: A Review of the Literature with Suggestions for Application," *Group Psychotherapy*, IX (1956), 89–114.

goals in group counseling. Probably all members will not reach that point at the same time. Should the group decide to break up before all members feel they can go on alone, it is up to those who need more help to decide for themselves which of the other possibilities is best suited to their needs. They may seek help through individual counseling, they may join another group, or they may add members to their present group. In any case, the group terminates counseling whenever a majority of its members decide that the group has fulfilled their needs. However, members also are encouraged to consider the needs of those not ready to terminate.

The Interview Record

THE record of the counseling interview was discussed in the previous chapter. The basic principles outlined there apply here also, except that the multiplicity of the counselor's duties makes it more difficult to take notes in a group session than in an individual one. The acceptable procedure for recording both types of counseling is to make a running account of what participants say. Since each person's statement affects what others say, the account should try to identify who said what. The method of numbering all the persons in the circle and then recording numbers instead of names simplifies the recording process and makes it easier to review the nature of the participation pattern.

A description of each individual's progress, made after the session is finished, is also very useful. Group counseling stresses individual growth; therefore, it is reasonable to note evidence of such growth. For some, increased participation is in itself evidence of growth; for others, it is the nature of the participation that indicates growth. What the individual says and how he says it are important to the counselor in studying the individual's progress.

SUGGESTED READINGS

1. BACH, GEORGE R. *Intensive Group Psychotherapy*. New York: The Ronald Press, 1954.

> *Part I of this volume presents a practical discussion of problems encountered by a psychologist in private practice. He discusses such topics as orientation of clients, selection of clients for group treatment, management of resistance, use of role playing, and the therapist's role in the treat-*

ment process. Though the book was written for those who deal with disturbed patients, it offers many practical suggestions that the school counselor can use.

a] What does the counselor contribute to client growth?

b] What criteria should a counselor use in selecting clients?

c] How do clients help each other within the group setting?

2. HINCKLEY, ROBERT G. and LYDIA HERMANN. *Group Treatment in Psychotherapy.* Minneapolis: University of Minnesota Press, 1951.

Here a psychiatrist and a social worker describe, in nontechnical language, the nature of group therapy. To clarify theoretical principles, they have presented well-chosen case materials.

a] How do these two writers define the therapist's role?

b] How do they define the client's role in the therapy process?

3. HOBBS, NICHOLAS. "Group-Centered Psychotherapy," Chapter 7 in Roger's *Client-Centered Therapy.* Boston: Houghton Mifflin Company, 1951.

Hobbs uses case materials very effectively in discussing the nature of group psychotherapy and what it does for clients. He also examines the similarities and differences between individual and group therapy.

a] How does Hobbs decide who should be included in a therapy group?

b] Why do some clients talk more freely in group therapy than in individual therapy?

c] How does individual therapy differ from group therapy?

4. LIFTON, WALTER M. *Working with Groups: Group Process and Individual Growth.* New York: John Wiley & Sons, Inc., 1961.

This book describes how group procedures can be used in various types of groups. Two chapters are most relevant for our purposes: 3 and 5.

a] How may one member help another clarify what he is trying to say?

b] What can other members do to help the silent member participate?

c] How does the counselor cope with the monopolist?

5. MAHLER, CLARENCE A. and EDSON CALDWELL. *Group Counseling in Secondary Schools.* Chicago: Science Research Associates, 1961.

This pamphlet tells how to introduce and maintain a group counseling program in the secondary schools.

a] What is group counseling?

b] How does it fit into a good secondary-school guidance program?

c] How may it be introduced?

d] How may its worth be evaluated?

6. MORENO, J. L. "Psychodrama," McCary's and Sheer's *Six Approaches to Psychotherapy.* New York: Holt, Rinehart & Winston, Inc., 1955, pp. 287–340.

The foremost exponent of this technique traces its development as a group treatment method and explains how he uses it.
a] What is psychodrama?
b] What does psychodrama do for the patient?

7. SLAVSON, S. R. "Group Psychotherapies," McCary's and Sheer's *Six Approaches to Psychotherapy.* New York: Holt, Rinehart & Winston, Inc., 1955, pp. 127–78.

Here we learn from one of the foremost authorities on group therapy what he believes group therapy is and how it may be used to help patients, especially children.
a] What criteria may be used in selecting members for a therapy group?
b] What does Slavson believe group therapy does for patients?

SUGGESTED FILMS

1. *Activity Group Therapy,* 50 minutes, Columbia University Press, 1950.

   This film, produced by the Jewish Board of Guardians under the supervision of S. R. Slavson, shows how a therapist worked with emotionally disturbed ten- and eleven-year-old boys. Since the producers used hidden cameras in making this film over a two-year period, teachers and counselors can see the operation of a real group and the changes brought about in the individual members.
   a] How did the therapist in the film define his role? How is it like the counselor's role, as defined in this chapter? Cite at least one example of each similarity or dissimilarity.
   b] Which situations would you have found most difficult to handle?

2. *Role Playing in Human Relations Training,* 25 minutes, National Education Association, 1949.

   This excellent training film was sponsored by the National Training Laboratories in Group Development, and produced by Educational Film Productions. It shows when and how to use role playing, and reviews the skills needed by those playing roles.
   a] Make an outline of suggestions that the teacher may apply to sociodrama in the classroom.

6

Child Study: An Introduction

T HE CHILD study service is designed to help counselors understand their clients, to help pupils understand themselves and
their own capabilities, and to help teachers understand their
pupils so that they can plan appropriate learning experiences for
them. Effective child study also enables (1) a pupil and his teachers
to determine whether or not the pupil's progress in his school work
is satisfactory; (2) a pupil and his teachers to identify and to diagnose learning problems and to plan appropriate remedial work;
(3) a teacher to determine a pupil's readiness for a school experience or the next phase of the school program; (4) teachers and
counselors to identify pupils for special programs directed toward
exceptional children, whether gifted or handicapped; (5) a pupil
to discover what he must know about himself in order to make intelligent educational, vocational, and social plans; and (6) a pupil
to identify those forces within himself and his environment that
interfere with efficient learning and healthy living.

Child study is a cooperative enterprise: in an effort to understand a child and to help him understand himself, various people share what they have learned about him from observations and tests. The case conference is one of the best ways to encourage this cooperative undertaking. The following case illustrates how an effective elementary-school principal used the case conference to initiate action to help a child.

Late in the spring, Ruth's second-grade teacher, Miss Johnson, decided that Ruth was not reading as well as she should be. Ruth's cumulative record indicated that she had transferred to the school at the beginning of the first grade after having attended a kindergarten in a large city some fifty miles away. Attached to Ruth's record was a Stanford-Binet report revealing an intelligence quotient (I.Q.) of 124. On the report the examiner had noted that Ruth appeared to be working under tension during the testing session.

Recognizing that she needed more information in order to help Ruth, Miss Johnson turned to Mr. Armstrong, the principal. He, in turn, called in Miss Baxter, Ruth's first-grade teacher, who reported that she had never felt reading was a serious problem to Ruth in the first grade. The three decided to investigate the matter further.

On the surface, this seemed to be one problem that the three of them could reasonably expect to solve with the help of the resources available to them. Mr. Armstrong agreed to check the possibility of taking Ruth to a teacher-training institution for a reading diagnosis and some additional testing. Miss Baxter volunteered to go to Ruth's home with Miss Johnson to enlist the parents' help. Miss Baxter had been in Ruth's home several times during the preceding year, and had found that the family took time to do things as a group even though the father was a busy young doctor. Miss Baxter's and Miss Johnson's visit confirmed what Miss Baxter said about the home atmosphere; it revealed also that the parents had noticed Ruth was beginning to dislike school. Ruth's mother volunteered to take Ruth to the teacher-training institution.

Miss Johnson accompanied the child and her mother to the reading clinic. After making a thorough diagnosis, the reading clinician suggested the parents arrange for a medical eye examination. The clinician gave Miss Johnson specific suggestions for teaching Ruth and also said that if the results of the eye examination supported her hunch, Ruth should begin immediately on the eye exercises that the doctor would prescribe.

The clinician's hunch proved to be accurate, and Ruth did the exercises all summer. When the doctor checked Ruth's eyes again the next September, he found her vision much improved. However, she was not enthusiastic about returning to school.

Soon after the opening of school, Mr. Armstrong arranged for a meeting of Miss Roche (Ruth's new teacher), Miss Baxter, Miss Johnson, and himself to discuss how they might help Ruth get off to a good start. As a result of her better vision, the staff's planning, and appropriate remedial instruction, Ruth gradually improved her reading until her performance was on a par with her ability. As she achieved this success, she tried harder and learned to like school better.

What happened to Ruth and the people who tried to help her? It was too late in the school year to do much about improving Ruth's reading when Miss Johnson discovered the problem. Even so, the fact that Ruth's reading problem now meant something to her teacher probably made Ruth feel that she was better liked and understood.

From this situation, the three teachers and the principal had one of the many object lessons that teaching provides on the value of working together in studying pupils. They learned how to share information, how to work together, and how to involve parents in helping children. They became more aware of the out-of-school agencies that could be called upon to help with special problems, and they learned how to make use of such agencies.

There was no guidance specialist in Ruth's school. Still, Ruth's defective vision was corrected and remedial reading assistance was provided because the classroom teacher recognized a child with a problem and asked colleagues to help. And the next fall, the staff, sensing the value of a follow-up, helped Ruth's new teacher. These teachers reaped the definite satisfaction that results from helping a child improve his work; they were successful because they chose to help a pupil *who could be helped through use of the resources available to them.*

The Guidance Committee

To encourage the kind of cooperative child study described above, a small guidance committee whose primary responsibility is to conduct case conferences should be appointed for every school. Any member of the staff may suggest having such a committee, but it cannot succeed without the support of the principal and three or four of the teachers. If those who wish to try this approach wait until everyone accepts the idea, they may never use it—because there are usually some persons who are threatened or upset by any new proposal. But with patience, tact, and understanding even most of these people can be brought to accept the advantages of the guidance committee. Practical suggestions for introducing and using this committee are discussed in the next several pages.

PLANNING A CASE CONFERENCE

Once the cooperation of the principal and several colleagues is assured, the first step toward appointing a guidance committee is to organize a case conference. At a teachers' meeting, the purposes of the case conference should be outlined to the staff, as well as the role of each staff member, and *the importance of guarding confidences.* Then, with the help of the faculty, the names of a couple of pupils should be selected; these pupils would be discussed in case-conference fashion at another teachers' meeting for which attendance is voluntary. It is best for the staff to name pupils whom *they believe they can help.*

A FIRST CASE-CONFERENCE SESSION

At the case conference, the cases of specific pupils are discussed, as previously planned. During the discussion, the person who is trying to initiate this project should note teachers who exhibit an especially good understanding of children. After the members of the staff have discussed the pupils' cases, the staff should be asked to consider establishing a faculty group (a building guidance committee) responsible for such case conferences, and the functions of such a group should be discussed.

FORMING A BUILDING GUIDANCE COMMITTEE

After the case conference, the names of potential committee members should be discussed with the principal. Usually it is better to have a small committee—say, three teachers, the principal, and others who have special guidance duties. Once an acceptable committee has been selected by the principal, each person should be consulted to determine whether he wishes to serve. It is important that each member knows what he is getting into, and what will be expected from him. Those who agree to serve should be compensated by relief from some of their other special duties.

FORMAL APPOINTMENT OF
THE GUIDANCE COMMITTEE

The committee should be formally appointed by the principal. When announcing the committee's membership, the principal should formally outline its duties and describe the way in which it will operate. (This statement should be prepared with the help of the committee.) At one of its first meetings the committee should elect a chairman and a secretary. Since the principal has many other responsibilities, which might require him to miss some committee meetings, it might be well to elect one of the teachers as chairman.

When a teacher realizes that he needs assistance in working with a pupil, he goes to the guidance committee chairman. The chairman, in turn, prepares for a committee meeting by obtaining the child's guidance record and inviting the appropriate people to attend. Generally, it is a good idea to invite the guidance specialists and all teachers who know the pupil well. Although teachers are busy, most of those invited will attend if attendance is voluntary, and if they believe that their services *are really needed*. Of course, the committee should always make uninvited members of the staff feel welcome at any of these sessions.

During the actual meeting, the chairman should give everyone a chance to present his own picture of the child. The first speaker describes the child as he sees him. Other speakers note new information. Of course, each speaker offers points both of agreement and disagreement. Since the remarks of a specialist might unduly color the other reports, it is usually better for him to speak last. Committee members try to help teachers describe pupil behavior and clarify how they feel about the pupil.

As the group discusses the pupil and his problems, the secretary records the answers to the following questions: (1) What do we know about the pupil? (2) What are the positive elements upon which we can build? (3) What is each of us going to do to help the pupil? These deliberations lead each participant to feel that his help is needed, show him how he can help, and involve him directly in providing guidance services.

Too often teachers feel ignored when their pupils are referred to specialists: they feel that the services provided by the specialists involve some mysterious processes to which they are permitted to contribute only the simplest kind of information. But teachers really participate in the guidance committee. No individual or group takes cases out of the hands of the classroom teacher; instead, the teacher receives suggestions from others and makes suggestions to them. If the committee conclude that a specialist's help is needed, they cooperatively decide how to make the referral. When a pupil is referred to a specialist, either a member of the committee or the specialist himself keeps the teacher informed of the pupil's progress so that he can resume full responsibility for the pupil as soon as possible.

The chief value of the building guidance committee is its provision for continuous study of children. It is also valuable for providing in-service training for teachers through study of the children in their classes. The guidance committee can also insure better use of the resources available in the school and the community, and can provide for better coordination of the help given any particular child.

The Cumulative Record

PROBABLY most of us in the teaching profession have had the experience of seeking information about a pupil, only to find that the folder containing the needed information was stuffed with disorganized and irrelevant material. The bulging folder evoked the instant reaction, "Of course, this is just what one would expect; he has always been a problem." To find what we wanted to know in this confused mess was too much bother; more often than not, we stopped there. We proceeded to help the child, but only on the basis of faulty memory and personal bias.

Failure to use the facts available in the cumulative record means depriving a child of the best possible help. But if the record is to be used, it must be functional; the staff should collect only information that is pertinent, and then organize it so that it will be usable. The purpose of guidance is defeated when the staff spend so much time collecting information that they do not have sufficient time to help youngsters with their problems.

The cumulative record is an effort to provide the staff with an efficiently organized body of information which will help them answer their most common questions about pupils. Teachers as well as specialists should have a hand in planning the folder. With the aid of school guidance committees and the system-wide coordinating guidance council described in Chapter 16, the faculty can build a cumulative record system that will fill their own needs for data.

SELECTING INFORMATION

Every experience a child has affects in some way his growth toward maturity. A carefully designed and well-organized cumulative folder should help teachers and counselors study his development. It should help them identify the pupil's strengths and weaknesses as well as the sorts of experiences that seem either to have stimulated or thwarted the maximum development of his potentialities.

Listed below are some of the questions the members of a school faculty may want to consider in evaluating its cumulative record and in selecting new material for the record:

—What must we know about each of our pupils? Which of these questions are adequately answered in our present records?

—Are we collecting any material that we rarely, if ever, use? Does the record include any material that is used by only one person for a short period of time? If so, why does not he collect that data and dispose of them when he is through with them?

—For what questions are new data needed? How may these data be obtained?

—Are we using the best available techniques to obtain answers to our questions? What changes should be made?

—Is our staff qualified to use the data we now have? If not, what in-service education is needed? What additional in-service education may be needed to prepare the staff to use new techniques for collecting data?

—What changes in the organization and housing of records would make them used more?

—What staff members should be assigned responsibility for collecting information for the records? When should it be collected?

—Should we place any restrictions on use of this information? If confidential information cannot be treated with special consideration, should it be collected? When data are collected, what commitments to guard confidence should be made to pupils? How will failure to make such commitments affect pupils' answers?

—Can we afford to spend the time required for gathering these data?

—Are we giving the normal child sufficient consideration in selecting the items to be included in the cumulative record? Does our record system provide us with an adequate picture of the normal child as he progresses through school?

DESIGNING AND MAINTAINING THE FOLDER

What should the cumulative folder look like? Preferences vary among school faculty groups, but most staffs prefer either a manila folder, or a manila jacket sealed on three sides. In order to minimize the clerical work, very few items should be recorded on the folder itself. Space is usually provided on the folder for such facts as the following: the pupil's name, the parents' names, home address, home telephone number, the pupil's semiannual attendance record, the names and locations of the schools he has attended, his school grades, and his test results. Sometimes a space is provided for the activity record and the work record.

As the staff members add new data, they should be aware of what is already in the folder, they should eliminate useless information, and if necessary they should reorganize the folder for efficient use. Even though the staff does a good job of selecting and arranging information, the folder still may become too bulky for convenient use. This happens for a number of reasons. Sometimes, even after test results have been recorded, workers leave used test booklets and answer sheets in the folder, expecting to use the test responses later on to diagnose the pupil's learning difficulties and to plan appropriate remedial instruction. Once the remedial instruction has been given, and its effects have been evaluated, the answer sheets can be thrown away. If answer sheets are not used with standardized tests, the teacher may do well to prepare an item-analysis table like the one described in the appendix on statistics. With this one table and one copy of the test booklet the teacher has, for every pupil in the class, the information for remedial instruction revealed by the test.

Nevertheless, a few of the folders always become congested and unusable, since many persons contribute facts to them and work with them. Because only a small proportion of the pupils' folders fall into this category, a reasonable amount of time and work can improve the situation. The best method is to summarize the teachers' miscellaneous reports and anecdotes according to problem areas. Some one person, such as a homeroom teacher or counselor, should be made responsible for this job. First, he should study and define the pupil's major problem areas as they are described in the folder. Then he should cite the evidence presented on each problem and trace its development, taking particular care to note whether or not progress is being made in correcting the difficulty. Where problems are described but no information on follow-up contacts is in the folder, he should seek the additional evidence from those on the school staff who know the child best. As has been pointed out, the case conference is the most efficient way to obtain such necessary new information.

This process of summarizing the information by problem areas not only reduces the mass but also arranges the data in a more meaningful order. But it requires clinical skill and clerical time; and clerical help cannot always be secured easily. However, if the work is divided among several persons (such as the homeroom teachers) or if someone can be employed to transcribe the counselor's dictation, it need not become an unduly heavy burden.

Lack of clerical help is indeed one of the big problems in maintaining all school records. As teachers well know, they spend too much time doing clerical work when they should be working with pupils. To reduce clerical chores to a minimum, shortcuts should be sought. When, for example, teachers select a test, they should be encouraged to arrange for machine-scoring. In most states at least one of the colleges or universities provides a test-scoring service on a minimal cost basis. This service costs the school very little and frees teachers from hours of routine clerical work. Time-saving devices should be considered in selecting nontest, as well as test, techniques. As an important example, most information for the cumulative record—other than test scores, academic grades, and personal identification data—should not have to be copied into the cumulative folder. Instead, the staff, at the time when it decides to use a child study technique, should design proper forms for securing the information so that the data can be filed without being recopied.

Another way to alleviate the clerical problem is to draw on the supervised work programs that many schools have for their business education students. If business education teachers select these students carefully, and if the staff feels that the selected students can be trusted, the students can gain good work experience and provide excellent clerical help by recording test scores and transcribing counselors' and homeroom teachers' summaries from cumulative folders. However, folders should be carefully checked before such assignments, to save students the embarrassment or frustration of stumbling upon information about themselves, and to protect them from coercion to reveal information about relatives and friends. Some people contend that high school students cannot be trusted with such confidential information. But if they do not trust these carefully selected high school students, why should they trust these students' sisters and cousins, only a year or two older, who are serving as secretaries to businessmen, professional men, and school people? The fact is, of course, that some school secretaries, and even some teachers, violate confidences. On every level, from pupils to administration, violating confidence is a serious matter, and those who break confidence should be disciplined. And of course, students should not be used for such clerical work unless the administrator and the staff are convinced they can be trusted.

All students who are to be used should be told that they are working with confidential information, and that failure to keep confidence may hurt someone. Moreover, they should realize they were chosen for the job because they are prepared to do it well, and because they can be trusted. Under these circumstances it is unlikely that they will break confidences. These young people are learning to do a job, and they are aware that they must do it well.

RECORDING THE PUPIL'S PROGRESS

We have considered some of the problems of selecting information about a pupil and of maintaining the record. How may this record follow the child through school?

The first entry in the cumulative record should be made following a preschool conference involving parent, teacher, child, and sometimes a school nurse. At that time, pertinent facts from the child's infancy and early childhood should be recorded on the school's personal history questionnaire. In many school systems the results of preschool medical and dental examination are attached to this same form.

As the child progresses through school, appropriate information should be added as it is needed. Such information could be obtained by using child study techniques, as described in Chapters 7 through 9. The last entry on the record will probably be made when the student has been well placed on a job or in another educational institution.

Because information about the transfer pupil is not always sent with him and is sometimes hard to obtain, the principal in the new school should take action immediately to secure it. He should obtain from the new pupil (or his parents) the name and address of the principal of the child's former school, and he should then write a letter to the principal requesting the needed information. If there are many such cases, he may choose to send a form letter with the questionnaire; but better results are obtained when the request is typed as a personal letter. Either way, the letter should make the principal from the former school feel that the staff in the new school are sincerely interested in the new pupil, and that they need the information requested in order to do their job well.

Although the form for this questionnaire should be designed to collect as many as possible of those facts that the school has recorded for its other pupils, it should not be so long that it imposes an onerous chore upon the former school's principal. The pupil's personal history, health record, and school progress report are the minimum to be obtained. After the principal has assigned the new pupil to his homeroom teacher, the teacher should ask the pupil (or his parents) for information similar to that obtained from other pupils in that grade. Information quickly and reliably available from the pupil need not be requested in the questionnaire designed for transfer students.

FILING AND STORING RECORDS

Where should the records be kept? There is no single best answer for all schools. Since elementary-school children usually spend most of the school day with one teacher, this teacher may keep the records in his classroom. If a secondary school is organized so that a homeroom teacher has one group for a considerable part of the day, then the homeroom teacher may want the folder in his room. If the pupils do not have homerooms, or spend little time in homerooms, then the records may be kept in the central office. The decision will best be made by the staff members using the records.

Regardless of where the records are kept, the staff must make sure that the confidential information is accessible only to appropriate persons. The counselor's interview notes must not be accessible to anyone else without the pupil's permission. But the general body of information should be made available to all the professional staff.

While most information in the cumulative record is confidential in the sense that it has been collected for the staff's use, more and more employers, training institutions, and colleges are finding that they need the information too; and they request the school's help in reconstructing an individual's personal history. If the schools are going to be able to help these employers and educational institutions, the information must (with discretion) be shared; therefore, the cumulative folders should be maintained for efficient use after the student leaves school. Before the folders are placed in the inactive files, they should be screened for extraneous materials. After they are put in good shape, folders should be sent from all the schools in the system to one central place for filing.

Developing a Testing Program

A SUCCESSFUL testing program must be planned around the pupils' needs, the teachers' and counselors' questions about their pupils, and the professional competencies of the staff. As the guidance committee members help their colleagues study pupils, they learn what information the school needs about most pupils. The guidance committee also has an opportunity to cooperate with committees from other schools through the system-wide coordinating guidance council described in Chapter 16.

Every test that is used should be administered for a specific purpose which is clear to those administering and interpreting the test, and those taking it. Obviously, the more mature the pupil, the better he will understand the reasons for his taking the test, but even the least mature child should be helped, on his own level, to understand as best he can why he is being tested. Certain tests have value for only a small part of the school population; usually only the pupil and his counselor are involved in these cases, so others need not understand the reasons for testing. Other tests—those around which the basic testing program is built—help supply information that teachers and counselors feel they need for all pupils. These tests, which all youngsters must take, are of course intended to improve teachers' understanding of their pupils; but in order to achieve this objective teachers obviously must understand how to interpret the test scores, and how to relate them to other facts about their pupils. Unless the school staff contains people trained to use these data, the school should not give the test, for an incorrect interpretation of tests may hurt children.

Since teachers help the guidance committee members decide what questions they want answered through use of tests, some will become oriented to the use of a test before the school first gives it. Furthermore, increasing numbers of teachers are taking graduate work in tests and measurements. Nevertheless, there are usually staff members who do not know how to interpret test results and how to use them along with nontest data to better understand pupils. These people should be given in-service training in the use of these data. If the principal does not have a staff member who can provide the necessary in-service education, he should provide it himself; if necessary he may obtain assistance from other trained workers in the system, from nearby teacher-training institutions that offer counselor education, or from the office of the state superintendent of public instruction.

Once teachers and counselors have decided to give a certain general type of test, and the administration has provided for the inservice training of teachers who need it, the chairman of the guidance council for the entire school system should seek the help of an expert in selecting the specific test of that type which best meets the school's needs. While teachers can help decide what questions they want answered through tests, the selection of a specific test requires considerable professional preparation and experience. The school does best to employ a counselor well qualified in tests and measurements. If it chooses not to, it can usually obtain the assistance of a qualified person from a teacher-training institution recognized for its counselor-education program.

Before he can select an appropriate test, the counselor or outside consultant will need certain information from the school:

—What questions does the staff hope to answer with this test?
—What is the general socioeconomic background of the school population?
—What test scores are already a part of these pupils' cumulative record?
—What other information can the school make available to the staff to supplement these test scores? Is this information sufficient? Should the staff collect other data before using the test?
—How much time is the staff willing to have the pupils spend on this testing experience?
—For how long a period can these pupils work efficiently?
—How much money can the school spend on tests?
—What experience and training has the staff had in administering and

interpreting tests like this? What additional training, if any, will the staff need?

Guided by the answers to these questions, a qualified person should be able to study the research on the best test prospects for the school and make a recommendation. As part of the critical study of tests, a number of evaluative questions should be asked of any test reviewed.

—What characteristic does the test measure?
—How is this characteristic related to the question that the school staff hopes to answer?
—How do the results of this test compare with other measures of the same characteristic?
—How did the author of the test determine whether his test actually measures what he intended it to measure (validity)?

Often the author, to determine his test's validity, will correlate pupils' scores on his test with the scores that the same pupils earned on another test of the same type. Occasionally, the author of a test obtains a spuriously high coefficient of correlation through this method, by selecting pupils with a wide range of ages and thus increasing the coefficient of correlation through introducing the age factor which affects performance on both tests. But if he confines the tests to a given grade level, and then reports a high coefficient of correlation (.80 or better), this merely means that both tests tend to measure the same characteristic. Then the person who has responsibility for selecting the test must ask whether either of the two tests is appropriate for the school.

Sometimes an author will validate his test by correlating a pupil's scores with the youngster's performance on the job or in school programs. For example, an author of a mental test frequently will determine the relationship between scores on his tests and school grades. However, when such studies are applied to the better mental tests used in the high schools and colleges, they produce a coefficient of correlation of only about .50.

—Does this test measure consistently whatever it measures? How did the author of the test attack the problem of determining whether the test measured consistently what it was supposed to measure? What pupils did he use in the study? What statistical techniques did he use?

Theoretically a test should produce the same results upon repeated testing with the same pupils—providing, of course, that the pupils learned nothing new on the subject between testing periods. The proper use of appropriate statistical techniques produces reliability coefficients of nearly .90 on the better tests. A test must measure consistently whatever it measures before anyone can define with confidence what the test actually measures.

—How did the author of the test develop the norms for the test? What pupils took the test when the norms were developed? How are these pupils like the pupils in the school that will use the test? How are they different? It is important for the teacher to know with whom he is comparing his pupils when he uses the test norms. Unfortunately, many authors fail to include specific information on the norm group in the test manual.

—What assumptions did the author of the test make about the educational and cultural backgrounds of pupils taking his test?

—Are the printed directions for administering and scoring the test clear? What additional information should the test expert provide for the school staff?

—Has the staff considered the possibility of having the test machine-scored? If the staff decides to have the test machine-scored, what arrangements should it make for this before ordering test materials?

For most questions that a staff hopes to answer with tests, there are usually a number of tests from which to choose. Although each test may have certain advantages, all of them will not be equally well suited for a particular school's use. A wise choice demands careful study of the local situation by a person with theoretical training in evaluation theory, test construction, statistics, and research methods.

Using and Interpreting Tests

TESTS can be and are used by teachers and counselors to help them understand pupils, and by counselors to help pupils get the information they need about themselves in order to make certain decisions. But tests by themselves will not provide the answers to all the questions for which teachers and counselors seek information.

For example, when an elementary teacher selects teaching materials, he needs to know about the learning levels of his pupils. He should first study the scores from the mental test and achievement test (especially the reading test). But to obtain all the facts he needs for giving individual assistance, the teacher should supplement these data with information gained by observing the pupil at work, by examining his written work, by studying other teachers' anecdotes about him, by analyzing his academic record, and, when necessary, by having a case conference with colleagues.

In addition to questions about pupils' learning problems, teachers may ask other questions: What do his parents expect from this pupil? What are their goals for him? To what extent are his parents' goals consistent with his goals, interests, abilities, and aptitudes? How does he feel about his peers and the adults with whom he associates? How do they feel about him? In exploring such questions, the teacher gains insights that enable him to empathize with a pupil, to better communicate understanding and acceptance of him, and to help him win recognition and acceptance in his classes. In addition to improving classroom learning, these data may help a teacher understand and cope with discipline problems. High school teachers also can learn much from such nontest techniques as students' autobiographical themes, academic records, extra-class activity records, and work records—all of which will enable them to supplement the counselor's work in helping students discover their abilities, aptitudes, and interests. Obviously, then, test data must be supplemented with nontest data. When a teacher or counselor uses a test, he must know what nontest data are needed to supplement the test results.

The person in charge of the testing program also must know the test. If the recommendations made in the previous section are followed, he will know the test thoroughly before he selects it, and he will make every reasonable effort to insure that those who use the test know it first. The person who is assigned responsibility for the in-service education program should know the test manual and the major research studies on the test, and should review the pertinent information from each for the staff. As a very minimum, he should have studied the reviews of the test in such a standard reference as Buros.[1]

From this careful study of a test the person in charge of the test-

1 Oscar K. Buros, *The Fifth Mental Measurements Yearbook* (Highland Park, N.J.: The Gryphon Press, 1959). Other tests are reviewed in earlier editions.

ing program should get some idea of how accurate its scores are. In part, the degree of accuracy with which a given score describes a pupil depends upon the way he felt while taking the test and the conditions under which the test was administered. Inaccuracy in test scores also results from errors in measurement. The standard error of measurement [2] is the most common method for taking account of measurement errors in test interpretation.

Almost a quarter century ago H. E. Garrett [3] and J. P. Guilford [4] presented arguments for and against the use of the standard error of measurement as a method for dealing with measurement errors. The issue has been argued periodically since Garrett and Guilford originally presented their views. Those who have a basic knowledge of statistics could profit from C. H. Patterson's [5] careful review of the literature on this issue.

With the standard error of measurement (σ_M) a test interpreter can say that the observed scores for approximately two-thirds of the persons tested should fall within $1\sigma_M$ of their true scores (or if he wants to be more certain, that 95 percent of their observed scores should fall within $2\sigma_M$ of their true scores). Though there is, from the statistician's point of view, good reason for criticizing the use of an observed score as an estimated true score, the observed score is generally used this way; the practice is not a perfect solution, but it is a practical one and a marked improvement over accepting an observed score as an exact measure. If, for example, a test interpreter found that $\sigma_M = 6$, he would assume that for an observed score of 64, two-thirds of observed scores should fall between 58 and 70 (or that 95 percent of the observed scores should fall between 52 and 76). In other words, a test interpreter can use the standard error of measurement to define the width of a test-score band that is needed to allow for measurement errors.

2 The formula for the standard error of measurement is $\sigma_M = \sigma_N \sqrt{1-r}$. In this formula σ_N is the standard deviation of the group upon which the coefficient of reliability (r) was computed. If the test manual does not provide σ_N, σ_M can be obtained from the test publisher. For further help with these statistical concepts, the reader may consult the appendix on statistics.

3 H. E. Garrett, "An Interpretation of the Standard Error of Measurement," *American Journal of Psychology*, XLIX (1937), 679–80, and "A Rejoinder," *American Journal of Psychology*, XLIX (1937), 683–85.

4 J. P. Guilford, *Psychometric Methods* (New York: McGraw-Hill Book Co., Inc., 1936), and "More Concerning the Interpretation of the Standard Error of Measurement," *American Journal of Psychology*, XLIX (1937), 680–83.

5 C. H. Patterson, "The Interpretation of the Standard Error of Measurement," *Journal of Experimental Education*, XXXI (1955), 247–52.

Test publishers [6] have also used the standard error of measurement to define test-score bands for graphic devices that take account of measurement errors in test interpretations. This technique has the obvious advantage of giving a visual image of the relationship among test scores. It helps those who interpret the test to determine easily whether chance can account for the differences noted between any pair of scores.

Recently, test publishers have produced a number of graphic devices to help test users understand test data, and to help them interpret tests for pupils and their parents. Along with their graphic devices, some use the idea of test-score bands to help test interpreters note measurement errors. At least one publisher [7] has also developed a table from which test users can obtain standard errors of measurement for given values of reliability coefficients and standard deviation. A few have also included contingency tables, accompanied by graphic presentations of the data from the tables, to help users interpret tests more effectively. It is reasonable to assume that these various materials have helped test users to understand the test results and to provide the information in meaningful language. However, the success with which these devices are used should be evaluated by research.

Unfortunately, these graphic devices have often been accompanied by suggestions for self-interpretation of tests by pupils. This practice is not consistent with the recommendations made in the section on test interpretations in the bulletin on *Technical Recommendations for Psychological Tests and Diagnostic Techniques:*

> The problem of accuracy is not the only consideration related to test interpretation. An equally important concern is the examinee's reactions to interpretations of his test scores, if the interpretation is made to him. Many educational and clinical uses of tests require reporting the interpretations to the person tested. The teacher who interprets the results of an academic achievement test affects the student's self-concept and future learning. The clinician, in making interpretations which bear upon the client's areas of conflict, may unwittingly intensify those conflicts . . . B 3.11 The manual should not imply that the test is "self-interpreting" or that it may be interpreted by a person lacking proper

6 John E. Dobbins, "The Scores on SCAT and STEP" (Cooperative Test Service, Educational Testing Service, mimeographed, 1958).

7 "How Accurate Is a Test Score," *Test Service Bulletin* (New York: The Psychological Corporation, 1956), pp. 1–3.

training. B 3.12 The manual should point out the counseling responsibilities assumed when a tester communicates interpretations about ability or personality traits to the person tested.[8]

Another undesirable practice suggested by some test manuals is to give pupils either raw scores or percentile ranks and ask them to draw profiles. Although pupils are usually given very good instructions on how to draw their profiles, and frequently the pupils are encouraged to discuss the test results in groups, the test interpreter must not assume that pupils are able to accept and use the information about themselves. As a review of research evidence will show later, pupils do not readily accept information about themselves that disagrees with their self-image. Furthermore, even when they are told about test bands, and why they are used, the fact still remains that pupils have scores that they can use to compare themselves with their siblings and classmates. Consequently, they often treat differences that can be accounted for by chance as if they were real differences. Secondary-school students also resent receiving test scores where classmates can learn their scores or coerce them into revealing their scores. Such experiences cause them to question whether the staff can be trusted with confidential information.

Pupils and their parents have the right to know what schools learn about pupils through the use of tests, and pupils should be informed periodically of their progress. But while this means that pupils and their parents should expect to have tests interpreted for them, it does not mean they should be given a pupil's test scores. This is a matter not of withholding information, but rather of communicating what is known. The following statements were made by two of a group of six of the nation's leaders in tests and measurements who were asked to answer the question: "Under what circumstances should test scores be reported to students and parents?"

Test scores should be discussed with individual students and parents in a confidential conference or interview. The confidential nature of test scores should be stressed. In view of the fact that there are errors of measurement inherent in any test score, it is wise not to release the obtained specific score. It is better to indicate that the student has apti-

8 *Technical Recommendations for Psychological Tests and Diagnostic Techniques*, prepared by a joint committee of American Psychological Association, American Educational Research Association, and National Council on Measurements Used in Education (Washington, D.C.: American Psychological Association, 1954), pp. 10, 12.

tude or achievement that places him, for example, among the upper-fourth or upper-half of the students of his same age or grade; or to indicate that he is reading at fourth grade, fifth grade or sixth grade level.—Wrightstone [9]

Pupils and parents will derive maximal benefit from the tests when a trained counselor gives them information about the results in the context of other data and observation.—North [10]

There are two graphic devices which, though they have weaknesses, seem to make sense for conveying test scores to students. The first, a profile which uses the test band idea, makes it easy for the test interpreter to take account of measurement errors and to help a pupil see the relationship between various scores. It also makes it relatively easy for him to communicate which differences between scores are significant. When the profile sheet includes both achievement-test scores and intelligence-test scores, the interpreter can easily help the pupil make these comparisons and relate both to school grades. The only real weakness of this device is the fact that the profile sheets usually provide pupils and their parents with scores; some persons use these figures to make unjustified comparisons with other individuals.

The other graphic device provides a five-point rating scale for each score, at the same time including several types of test data on a single sheet, e.g., achievement-test scores and intelligence-test scores (and relevant school grades, which the counselor will find space to record if he feels they help in making comparisons). Both devices are used most effectively in individual conferences, with the pupil encouraged to participate in the test interpretation and to provide additional personal data to supplement test data.

For the rating scale, all scores are divided into five categories, e.g., (1) bottom 10 percent, (2) next 15 percent, (3) middle 50 percent, (4) the 15 percent just above the middle, and (5) top 10 percent. Each of these is then defined in terms that are appropriate for the students and the tests. In interpreting intelligence scores to junior high school students, the test interpreter might say,

This test was developed to help students like you discover how easily you learn. I would like you to estimate about where you would fall, in comparison with others your own age, as I describe five groups of students: (1) learns with considerably greater difficulty than most (with

9 "Reporting Test Results," *Education*, LXXXI (1960), 86.
10 *Ibid.*, p. 87.

great difficulty); (2) learns with greater difficulty than most (with difficulty); (3) learns as easily as most (like most); (4) learns more easily than most (easily); and (5) learns much, much more easily than most (very easily). (The words in parentheses appear on the scale.) Now you check where you think you would score on this test, and I will indicate whether the test describes you as you described yourself.

Most pupils seem to understand these descriptions better than they do test bands. With test data from several tests recorded on a single sheet, it also is relatively easy to compare the various scores and to compare each with school grades. Moreover, pupils are not given test scores with which they can make invidious comparisons. On the other hand, when one uses this technique it is more difficult to determine whether differences between scores are significant than is the case when one uses profiles with test bands. But since there is a method for coping with this problem, the author prefers the rating scale over the profile with test bands.

Test publishers who provide profiles with test-score bands use the standard error of measurement to lay off a percentile band on either side of specific scores. Such bands can also be computed by a test interpreter who uses the rating scale. He follows these steps: (1) he obtains either the standard error of measurement or data for computing it from the publisher (computed on the basis of raw scores), and (2) he converts this figure into percentile bands for each of the following parts of the scale: one for the middle 50 percent; another for the two 15 percent parts on either side of the middle; and still another for the top and bottom 10 percent. Since the raw score differences between percentiles gradually increase as one moves away from the mean in either direction, one must take account of this fact in computing estimated percentile bands for each of the five parts of the scale. Using this method the author found that for one test the percentile bands that were roughly equivalent to the standard error of measurement for the various parts of the scale were 15 (middle), 9, and 4 (extremes). Therefore, a percentile rank of 46 had a band of roughly 31–61, but a percentile rank of 81 had a band of only about 72–90. Consequently, a percentile rank of 81 for this test is significantly different from one of 46, but not different from one of 70 (61–79). When the bands for two percentile ranks overlap, chance can account for the observed difference between the two scores involved.

Increasingly, tests are used to improve pupils' self-knowledge. Staff members should therefore not only understand the test results but also be able to communicate to pupils what the test results mean. When pupils seek information about themselves they often fail to learn from the conference what the teacher or counselor tried to communicate. Even when the staff member tries to understand how a pupil reacts to the information and encourages him to discuss it, the pupil often distorts or rejects that information not congruent with his present self-image. The chances for helping a pupil to improve the accuracy of his self-image are even poorer when someone tries to provide him with test information that is not solicited *by him.* Under these circumstances he usually does not understand why the tests were given and how the results are relevant for him. Sometimes he resents being given information about himself—either because he sees no need for such information or because he is afraid that he will discover that he lacks the abilities or aptitudes to achieve some goal that is very important to him or to someone whose love and respect he needs.

The fact is that all too often conscientious workers interpret test scores, but fail to improve pupils' understanding of themselves. Though some studies clearly indicate that careful interpretation of tests does improve pupils' self-knowledge, more studies show that knowledge of test results failed to produce growth in self-understanding. We will consider these research results next, reviewing first those studies that used elementary-school pupils as subjects, then those that used secondary-school students as subjects, and finally those that used college students as subjects.

Except for work in progress, the author located only one study that used elementary-school pupils as subjects to investigate the extent to which interpreting test scores improved self-understanding. James Lister and Merle Ohlsen [11] used fifth-, seventh-, ninth-, and eleventh-graders as subjects to investigate the effects of pre-testing orientation on: (1) pupils' motivation for learning test results and (2) increased accuracy of self-estimates following test interpretation. They found that (1) the accuracy of pupils' self-estimates at all four grade levels increased significantly following test interpretation, and that pupils maintained significantly more accurate

11 James L. Lister and Merle M. Ohlsen, *The Effects of Orientation to Testing on Motivation for and Outcomes of Test Interpretation,* Cooperative Research Project No. 1344 (Urbana: University of Illinois, 1962).

self-estimates over a two-month follow-up period; (2) the orientation resulted in greater motivation for learning test results within grades seven and nine (and in spite of the fact that almost nine out of ten of all eleventh-graders asked to have their tests interpreted, the difference between the experimental and control groups for grade eleven was very nearly significant); (3) however, no evidence indicated a relationship between orientation and improved accuracy of self-estimates following test interpretation; (4) only limited support was found for the hypothesis that motivation for test interpretation increases accuracy of self-estimates following test interpretation; (5) a significant positive correlation (though relatively low) was found between measured intelligence and accuracy of self-estimates of achievement and intelligence, but a negative one was found between measured intelligence and pupils' ability accurately to estimate their interests; and (6) pupils' satisfaction with self-estimates and perceived accuracy of self-estimates increased over the four self ratings (pre-testing, post-testing, post-test interpretation, and follow-up). This last point was interpreted to mean increased acceptance of the self information provided. Lister and Ohlsen suggested two reasons for pupils' increased self-understanding: (1) counselors involved pupils in the test interpretation process and (2) counselors tried to detect and to help pupils discuss their feelings toward test estimates of their mental ability, school achievement, and interests.

Edward Adamek [12] compared the changes in perceptions of interests, mental abilities, and problem areas for two experimental groups and one control group of ninth-graders. The testing program included Kuder Preference Record-Vocational, Chicago Primary Mental Abilities, and the SRA Youth Inventory. For Experimental Group A the tests were interpreted by a well-qualified counselor in an individual interview, with emphasis placed upon communicating information and no effort made to deal with affect. For Group B the same counselor used the publisher's suggested technique for self-interpretation in small groups. Neither method of test interpretation improved significantly the congruency between test-estimates and self-estimates.

12 Edward G. Adamek, "The Effects of Testing and Test Interpretation on Selected Self Perceptions" (unpublished dissertation, University of Illinois, 1961).

Froehlich and Moser [13] also used ninth-graders as subjects. They administered the DAT, had pupils draw their own test profiles during the test interpretation, and permitted them to keep their profiles. Pupils also were encouraged to request further assistance. In a fifteen-month follow-up the pupils were asked to redraw their profiles. Most did not report their scores accurately in the follow-up, and errors were made by both high and low ranking pupils. Though the level of accuracy varied from test to test, more pupils reported their highest score accurately than even their second highest score.

John Lallas [14] used eleventh-grade students to compare three methods of test interpretation: individual interview, group interpretation, and group interpretation plus individual interview. He found that after test interpretation all three experimental groups were superior to the control group in ability to estimate their ability and to identify areas of greatest and least ability. He concluded that all three procedures improved a student's ability to make self-estimates that can be measured by a self-rating scale.

Belovsky, McMasters, Shorr, and Singer [15] used twelfth-graders as subjects. Though they labeled what they did as counseling, their treatment consisted primarily of testing and individual interpretations of tests for one group, and of testing and group interpretations of tests for the other. Using realism of vocational choice as a criterion of success, they found that chance could account for the slight differences noted between the two groups (58 percent vs. 57 percent made a realistic choice).

David Lane [16] compared the effectiveness of "traditional" and "permissive" techniques for interpreting test results to eleventh- and twelfth-grade clients. He interpreted the tests for both groups himself. Then a week later he administered a multiple-choice check-list and an essay question, both designed to measure memory of test scores. Three weeks later the check-list and the essay question

13 C. P. Froehlich and W. E. Moser, "Do Counselees Remember Test Scores?" *Journal of Counseling Psychology,* I (1954), 149–52.

14 John E. Lallas, "A Comparison of Three Methods of Interpretation of Results of Achievement Tests to Pupils," *Dissertation Abstracts,* XVI (1958), 1842.

15 David Belovsky, William McMasters, Joseph Shorr, and S. L. Singer, "Individual and Group Counseling," *Personnel and Guidance Journal,* XXXI (1953), 363–65.

16 David Lane, "A Comparison of Two Techniques of Interpreting Test Results to Clients in Vocational Counseling," *Dissertation Abstracts,* XII (1952), 591–92.

were readministered, showing a correlation between the two scores of .764. Lane also checked to determine whether he actually played different roles in the two experimental treatments and found that he did. Since he found almost identical scores for the two groups he concluded that the methods were equally effective.

In a study of the interests of high school students Stanley Singer and Buford Stefflre [17] obtained self-estimates of interests first prior to testing and counseling, and then three months following test interpretations. They found some significant differences between both means and standard deviations, differences that suggested increased congruency between test-estimates and self-estimates. They concluded that use of correlational approaches and tests of significance between means in these and similar studies were not adequate. They suggested that investigators who use self-rating techniques should examine the direction of discrepancies between test-estimates and self-estimates, as well as the mere size of these discrepancies.

Seth Arsenian [18] investigated the extent to which taking tests increased college freshmen's estimates of their scholastic aptitude, achievement, adjustment, and interests. He also compared over-estimators and underestimators. Post-testing ratings agreed better with test scores than pre-testing ratings. However, the variability in estimates continued to be large. Those who grossly overestimated and underestimated their abilities, knowledge, and adjustment were somewhat less intelligent and less well-adjusted than the rest of the group.

Kathryn Biersdorf [19] recruited, from introductory psychology and speech courses, male college students who were interested in receiving assistance with vocational plans. By random methods the students were divided into three sections: (1) a section receiving limited group treatment, (2) a section receiving extended group treatment, and (3) a control section. The limited treatment group received group interpretation of the vocationally relevant tests they had taken. The extended treatment group experienced, in addition to the test interpretation, a discussion of factors relevant for

17 Stanley L. Singer and Buford Stefflre, "Analysis of the Self-Estimate in the Evaluation of Counseling," *Journal of Counseling Psychology*, I (1954), 252–55.

18 Seth Arsenian, "Own Estimates and Objective Measurement," *Journal of Educational Psychology*, XXXIII (1942), 291–302.

19 Kathryn R. Biersdorf, "The Effectiveness of Two Group Vocational Guidance Treatments," *Dissertation Abstracts*, XIX (1958), 162–64.

making vocational plans. The researcher concluded that neither was more effective than no treatment.

From discussion with their counseling staff, Paul Dressel and Ross Matteson [20] concluded that there were wide variations in the procedures used by their counselors in interpreting tests. These procedures differed largely in the amount of client participation involved. For the purposes of their study they developed a test of self-understanding in order to determine the actual increase in the client's self-knowledge of characteristics tested, and they also constructed a reliable rating scale which was used by judges to assess the degree of client participation in test interpretation. They found that counselors varied greatly among themselves in the amount of participation elicited from clients (university freshmen) and that the mean gains in self-understanding made by clients appeared to be closely related to the mean client-participation index. These findings suggest that high client-participation counselors were more successful in stimulating self-understanding than were the other counselors.

John Gustad and A. H. Tuma [21] investigated the effects of three methods of test introduction (with the counselor assuming varying degrees of responsibility for introducing the idea of testing) and four methods of test interpretation (with the counselor assuming varying degrees of responsibility for pointing out discrepancies between students' self-estimates and test-estimates). Neither the methods of introducing tests nor the methods of interpreting tests showed any differential effects on client learning. Client learning was positively related to initial accuracy of self-ratings, but not to scholastic aptitude. In another paper the two researchers [22] also investigated the effects of client and counselor personality on client learning. Counselors who used essentially the same method with similar clients produced different effects. From their analysis of these findings, the investigators concluded that there was a positive

20 Paul L. Dressel and Ross W. Matteson, "The Effects of Client Participation in Test Interpretation," *Educational and Psychological Measurement,* X (1950), 693–706.

21 John W. Gustad and A. H. Tuma, "The Effects of Different Methods of Test Introduction and Interpretation on Client Learning in Counseling," *Journal of Counseling Psychology,* IV (1957), 313–17.

22 A. H. Tuma and John W. Gustad, "The Effects of Client and Counselor Personality on Client Learning," *Journal of Counseling Psychology,* IV (1957), 136–43.

relationship between amount of client learning and amount of client-counselor similarity.

June Holmes [23] compared four methods (varying in amount of student participation encouraged) of presenting test information to freshmen students in teacher education. The students were matched in age, sex, and residence. She concluded that all four methods tended to increase self-understanding. Furthermore, the extent to which student participation was encouraged did not seem to influence students' attitudes toward their counselor.

D. G. Johnson [24] used volunteer male clients to study effects of vocational counseling on increased accuracy and certainty of self-knowledge. He concluded that significant growth was achieved for both. A follow-up a month later indicated that these gains were maintained. Gains in self-understanding were greatest with respect to measurement of intelligence, followed by interests and personality, respectively.

Robert Kamm and C. Gilbert Wrenn [25] appraised clients' acceptance of self-information for forty educational-vocational planning interviews with General College freshmen at the University of Minnesota. They reported that a client was most apt to accept information when both the client and the counselor were relaxed, when the client was expressing positive attitudes, when the information given was directly related to the client's immediate problem, and when the information was not in opposition to the client's self-concept. Moreover, information that made the client appear to be like others was better accepted than information that made him appear to be different from others. They concluded that a counselor would do well to pay less attention to the content of what the client says and to devote more attention to how the client seems to feel about what he is learning about himself.

L. B. Rogers [26] compared two kinds of test interpretation: (1) test-centered method, which allowed little client involvement, and

23 June E. Holmes, "The Comparison of Four Techniques Used in Presenting Test Information to Freshmen Students," *Dissertation Abstracts,* XXI (1961), 3379.

24 D. G. Johnson, "Effects of Vocational Counseling on Self-Knowledge," *Educational and Psychological Measurement,* XIII (1953), 330–38.

25 Robert B. Kamm and C. Gilbert Wrenn, "Client Acceptance of Self-Information in Counseling," *Educational and Psychological Measurement,* X (1950), 32–42.

26 L. B. Rogers, "A Comparison of Two Kinds of Test Interpretation Interview," *Journal of Counseling Psychology,* I (1954), 224–31.

(2) self-evaluation method, which emphasized self-study and use of nontest as well as test data. Both methods seemed to contribute to improved self-understanding of college students with respect to abilities and interests. No statistically significant differences in effectiveness were noted between methods.

E. Paul Torrance [27] used college freshmen as subjects for his study. Like Arsenian, he found little relationship between self-estimates and test-estimates. For example, in the original estimate, over 65 percent of the total group placed themselves in the upper fourth of their class in scholastic ability, and 95 percent placed themselves in the upper half. When the students were given a chance to reevaluate themselves after conferences with counselors and academic advisers, there was a general revision downward in the direction of more realistic self-evaluation. Women evaluated themselves much more accurately than did men, but also more frequently underevaluated themselves. Clinical judgments suggested that those who made the greatest errors in describing themselves were plagued by a sense of vulnerability.

E. Wayne Wright [28] compared two groups, used to show the effects of two methods of interpreting tests, with a control group. Both groups were invited by letter to have their freshmen guidance tests interpreted. Students assigned to Group A had their tests interpreted in individual interviews while those assigned to Group B had their tests interpreted in groups of from five to ten. For both groups, self-estimates became significantly more congruent with test-estimates of aptitude and achievement profiles, but for only Group A did self-ratings on interest tests become more congruent with test-estimates. While very few differences were obtained between the two counseled groups, both improved significantly more than the control group.

Although many of the studies reviewed above compared various methods of interpreting tests to students, they were also concerned with the extent to which test interpretation increased self-understanding. For only the mature students was increased self-understanding usually achieved. Let us now consider those factors that seem to influence self-understanding.

27 E. Paul Torrance, "Practical Uses of Knowledge About Self-Concept," *Educational and Psychological Measurement*, XIV (1954), 120–27.
28 E. Wayne Wright, "A Comparison of Individual and Multiple Counseling for Test Interpretation Interviews" (unpublished dissertation, University of California, Berkeley, 1957).

Except for Lister and Ohlsen's [29] study, the students' maturity seems an important factor in determining whether they profited from having their tests interpreted for them. O'Hara and Tiedeman's [30] study supports this notion: these workers investigated ninth- and twelfth-grade boys' estimates of their aptitudes, interests, social class, general values, and social values. Except for the area of social class, self-estimates of twelfth-graders were more congruent with test-estimates than were self-estimates of ninth-graders. At grade nine, self-estimates correlated with test-estimates as follows: interest .70, work values .69, general values .56, and aptitudes .44. However, at grade twelve they correlated as follows: interest .83, work values .84, general values .63, and aptitudes .69. The investigators concluded that self-concepts are clarified as boys pass through grades nine to twelve.

In many of the studies just cited, a self-rating device was used to appraise the effectiveness of test interpretations. Ralph Berdie,[31] though he states that these devices are useful for such purposes, feels that the distinction between learning and accepting has to be taken into account. Learning, he points out, refers to the ability to reproduce verbally, while accepting refers to changes in the total pattern of behavior. His point is a good one. Until these changes in self-images that clients reproduce verbally are integrated and translated into improved behavior, little is accomplished by improving congruency between self-estimates and test-estimates. Very likely more accurate self-ratings precede improved behavior.

The extent of student participation also seemed a factor in increasing congruence between self-estimates and test-estimates. (This point may have relevance for Berdie's notion of acceptance too.) Championing the cause of student involvement, Carl Rogers for some time has attacked the idea of a counselor's using tests to evaluate a client. He has argued that if real growth is to be achieved, the focus of evaluation must remain within the client. He sums up his case as follows:

In sum, it is my concern that this major trend in clinical work leads gradually and subtly to some loss of confidence in the ability of the

29 Op. cit.

30 R. P. O'Hara and D. V. Tiedeman, "The Vocational Self-Concept in Adolescents," Journal of Counseling Psychology, VI (1959), 292–301.

31 Ralph F. Berdie, "Changes in Self-Ratings as a Method of Evaluating Counseling," Journal of Counseling Psychology, I (1954), 49–54.

self to evaluate, to a basic dependence growing out of loss of self-confidence, to a lesser degree of personhood, to a subtle and sincerely well-meaning control of persons by a group which, without realizing it, has selected itself to exercise that control.[32]

Torrance [33] concluded that the use of self-evaluation procedures contributed to college freshmen's understanding of themselves:

The self-evaluation procedures built into the testing program itself contribute to the development of more realistic self concepts. The initial estimates produce a set for self evaluation. Having this set, the freshmen may be expected to view the test-taking from the standpoint of self evaluations.[34]

He also went on to suggest how this method encouraged students to continue self-evaluations by discussions with peers and by conferences with counselors and academic advisers.

This concern about readiness for testing is not new. For many years clinical psychologists have been concerned about those extraneous factors that influence test scores, and about developing rapport with pupils in individual testing in order to obtain accurate test scores. What is relatively new is the idea of preparing students for group testing and for interpretation of test scores. In 1946 Bordin and Bixler [35] suggested that counselors encourage client participation in selecting appropriate tests for vocational counseling. From their experience they concluded that client participation in the selection of tests made the testing experience itself more meaningful to the client and altered his attitudes toward himself. Seeman [36] appraised Bordin and Bixler's technique. His results indicated that clients selected from tests available the appropriate ones for prediction 93.2 percent of the time. Seeman also concluded that the manner in which an individual approaches vocational choice is a function of his total prevailing level of adjustment. Ambivalence and conflict in selecting tests offer the same opportunities for counseling

32 Carl R. Rogers, "Divergent Trends in Methods of Improving Adjustment," *Harvard Educational Review*, XVIII (1948), 209–19.

33 *Op. cit.*   34 *Ibid.*, p. 127.

35 Edward S. Bordin and Ray H. Bixler, "Test Selection: A Counseling Process," *Educational and Psychological Measurement*, VI (1946), 361–73.

36 Julius Seeman, "A Study of Client Self-Selection of Tests in Vocational Counseling," *Educational and Psychological Measurement*, VIII (1948), 327–46.

as any other problem does. Perhaps many of the advantages cited for client participation in test selection can be achieved by careful orientation of students for group testing. The writer's own experience suggests that these experiences increase students' readiness for test interpretation.

Leo Goldman said that when a client participates in reaching conclusions about himself from test results, as well as from other data, it is very likely that he:

(1) is more accepting and less defensive about the interpretations, since they are in part his; (2) learns about himself more effectively and will remember better and longer what he has learned, because he was an active participant in the learning process; (3) brings in more new relevant data about himself and family, his experiences, and so on, so that the interpretations finally arrived at are more valid than would be true otherwise.[37]

As Goldman sees it, taking the client's frame of reference involves more than trying to understand the client. One who attempts interpretation of test scores also must try to sense the client's perception of his abilities, e.g., what it means to him to have average college aptitude.

Though he is discussing the use of tests in vocational planning, and though he takes more of an external frame of reference than most of the authors cited above, Cronbach also stresses the importance of helping the client accept as well as understand test results:

One reason is that vocational choice is not a single final throw of the dice. As a person goes through school and into his first jobs, he has many occasions to narrow his field of concentration or even to transfer in a new area. High-school courses and introductory college courses provide opportunities for him to explore and develop aptitudes and interests. In an expanding economy, workers change positions or change responsibilities within the same establishment. The engineer in the technical firm, for example, may become a manager, a salesman, a creative designer, or an expert on detailed specifications. Wise choice requires self-understanding; no "prescription" filled out by a tenth grade or freshman year counselor can anticipate these subsequent decisions. Test interpretation is only one step in a long process of self-discovery.

37 Leo Goldman, *Using Tests in Counseling* (New York: Appleton-Century-Crofts, 1961), p. 365.

Secondly, the client is more likely to accept recommendations which he understands. The counselor may be convinced that a freshman should get out of engineering and into advertising. Even though advertising is consistent with the boy's talents and interests, he may resist or ignore the recommendation. If he has been visualizing himself as an engineer for years, such a change of program requires him to alter his entire self-concept and may seem like an admission of defeat. To accept the new goal requires that he understand the facts the counselor considers significant. Acquiring a new self-image requires both factual and emotional learning.[38]

From a review of the literature, the author has developed the following principles for test interpretation:

1. Orientation of pupils for acceptance and use of test results should precede testing.

2. Until someone is qualified to use and interpret a test, that test should not be given.

3. Test scores should be released only to those staff members who are qualified to use and interpret them.

4. Test scores should be interpreted only for appropriate persons (e.g., pupils and their parents or legal guardian), and such interpretations should be offered in a setting in which unauthorized persons cannot hear or see the results.

5. Since the release of test scores fails to take account of measurement errors and often results in invidious comparisons, test results should not be released but rather interpreted for pupils and their parents.

6. Before interpreting a test, a teacher or counselor should familiarize himself with the nontest data available on the pupil. During the test interpretation he also should encourage the pupil and/or the parents to supplement the test results with nontest data.

7. A test interpreter should encourage pupil participation in interpreting test scores. To help a pupil recall what a test, or a part of a battery, was like and to estimate how well he did on it, the counselor should describe it in nontechnical language; showing the pupil sample items from the test is often helpful.

8. The test interpreter must be very sensitive to cues that suggest that the pupil does not comprehend the information being given him. If the counselor is to pick up these cues successfully, he ob-

38 FROM *Essentials of Psychological Testing* by Lee J. Cronbach, pp. 284, 285. Copyright © 1960 by Lee J. Cronbach. Reprinted with permission of Harper & Row, Publishers, Incorporated.

viously must know the pupil, or at least be familiar with this type of pupil, and he must be equally familiar with the tests.

9. The pupil should be encouraged to react to the test results—to raise questions or to comment on how he feels about the way the test or tests describe him. When he feels free to comment, a pupil will often respond to data quite spontaneously—telling how pleased he is with some scores or how he does not like or cannot accept others. The test interpreter, by detecting these feelings, responding to them, and helping a pupil examine them, increases the chances for helping the youngster understand and accept himself as he is.

10. Obviously, there is no justification for arguing with a pupil about his test scores. Moreover, little can be accomplished by either defending a test or criticizing it. What the test interpreter should do is explain to the pupil how he may use the results to understand himself and to make certain predictions, and with what certainty he can do so.

These principles can also be applied to interpreting tests for parents. Like pupils, parents do not always learn from a conference what the teacher or counselor tries to communicate. Most parents not only have preconceived notions about their child but also usually have aspirations for him. While their image may not be accurate, they frequently are so committed to the goals they envision that they cannot accept test data that suggest these goals are unrealistic for their child. There also are occasions when parents cannot accept test scores that are higher than they anticipated. If, for example, poorly educated parents feel that having a bright child means that they should send him to college, they may not be able to accept a high scholastic aptitude test score because either consciously or unconsciously they believe that educating him may cause him to reject them. The use of technical terms may interfere with the communication of test information to parents too. Consequently, those who interpret tests for parents must be aware of many of the same human needs that they consider in interpreting tests to children.

Ethics of Testing

A NUMBER of professional groups have given serious study to the problem of ethical behavior for those who use test results. For our purposes here, the most relevant publications are the *NEA Code of Ethics, APGA Ethical Standards, Ethical Standards of Psychologists,* and *Technical Recommendations for Psychological Tests and Diagnostic Techniques.* Every one of the principles reviewed here is stated in at least one of these four sources.

1. A test should be selected with care and should be administered under the conditions specified in the test manual. Since prior knowledge of test items invalidates test results, those who have responsibility for testing must assume responsibility for security of tests.[39]

2. Tests and test scores should be released only to those professional persons who are professionally qualified to use and interpret the tests.[40]

3. Test scores should be interpreted only for appropriate individuals, e.g., students and their parents or legal guardian.[41]

4. It is unethical for a supervisor to assign a staff member responsibility for interpreting a test when he lacks adequate professional preparation for the task.[42] Even when the test involved is one for which the staff member might be expected to have adequate professional preparation, the supervisor should provide supervision and appropriate in-service education.

5. Self-interpretation of test scores should be discouraged.[43] However, a qualified person might well encourage a pupil and/or his parent to participate in the interpretation of tests.

6. The student's welfare should be the test interpreter's first concern.[44] To achieve this objective the test interpreter must be qualified to recognize and cope with emotional reactions to test data.[45] Consequently, test scores should be interpreted instead of merely being released or distributed.

7. The test interpreter should understand test scores sufficiently well to communicate information on test results in a meaningful way for a pupil or his parents, and be able to answer questions about

39 "APGA Ethical Standards," *Personnel and Guidance Journal,* XL (1961), 206–09.

40 *Ethical Standards of Psychologists* (Washington, D.C.: American Psychological Association, 1953), pp. 146, 148, and 150.

41 *Ibid.,* p. 65.

42 *Ibid.,* pp. 146, 148, 150, and "APGA Ethical Standards," p. 208.

43 *Technical Recommendations for Psychological Tests and Diagnostic Techniques* (Washington, D.C.: American Psychological Association, 1954), p. 12, and *Ethical Standards of Psychologists,* p. 150.

44 *Ethical Standards of Psychologists,* p. 164.

45 *Technical Recommendations,* p. 10.

the results.[46] This means that the test interpreter must understand the limitations of the test as well as the ways in which its results can be used by the pupil and his parents.

8. The test interpreter should know the relevant nontest data that he needs in order to supplement test data and to evaluate accuracy of test data.[47]

9. The entire school staff should guard confidences.[48] When a school staff member leaves test scores in an unsafe place, or discusses test results where unauthorized persons can obtain test results, or releases test scores to unauthorized persons, he is breaking confidence with students.

SUGGESTED READINGS

1. CRONBACH, LEE J. *Essentials of Psychological Testing.* New York: Harper & Row, Publishers, 1960.

This is the second edition of a widely accepted text. It discusses principles of testing and the use of tests in a variety of situations but especially in schools. Chapters 5 and 6.
  a] Why isn't wide acceptance of a test a good criterion to use in selecting a test?
  b] What elements seem to determine validity for a test?
  c] What temporary factors may account for variations in an individual's test scores?

2. FINDLEY, WARREN G. (ed.) *The Impact and Improvement of School Testing Programs,* The Sixty-Second Yearbook of National Society for Study of Education (Chicago: University of Chicago Press, 1963).

This publication was designed to help school personnel use tests.
  a] How may testing programs influence curriculum development?
  b] How may school counselors use tests to help clients make crucial decisions?
  c] What does a staff member need most to know in order to interpret the various types of tests used in the schools today?
  d] How stable are test scores?
  e] Why do current testing practices often fail to increase congruency between students' self-estimates and test-estimates?

46 *Ibid.,* p. 10.
47 *Ibid.,* p. 11, and "APGA Ethical Standards," p. 208.
48 *Ethical Standards of Psychologists,* pp. 63 and 65, and "APGA Ethical Standards," p. 207.

$$y = \mathcal{Y} e^{-\frac{z^2}{2}}$$
$$y = r_{xy} \frac{\sigma_y}{\sigma_x} (X - M_x) + M_y$$

Child Study: Appraisal of School Achievement and Mental Growth

EFFECTIVE teachers realize that they must know what they can expect from each pupil in order to provide him with meaningful and challenging learning experiences. They also realize that it is important for the pupil to know what he can expect from himself, and for him to obtain feedback periodically on how well he is doing. From time to time teachers must try to assess whether a pupil is ready for the next phase of his school work. When he does not make satisfactory school progress, his teachers may require additional data from a remedial teacher, a school psychologist, or a school counselor, to identify and diagnose learning problems. Teachers usually need both mental-test and achievement-test data to solve these teaching problems, and the test data must be supplemented with relevant nontest data. School counselors also use these test data to help clients obtain the information they require in order to make educational and vocational choices.

This chapter discusses the purposes of achievement and mental tests, and some of the difficulties encountered by teachers and counselors in using scores obtained from the tests. It also suggests how nontest data may be used to supplement these test scores in studying pupils.

Teacher-constructed Tests

MOST teachers try to determine the extent to which pupils have mastered the skills, concepts, and knowledge presented; and good teachers use a variety of both verbal and nonverbal cues to determine whether their pupils have profited from assigned readings, lectures, and class discussions. Except for the oral examination (or class recitation), perhaps the most often used device is the teacher-constructed test. When carefully constructed, such tests can help the teacher identify and diagnose learning problems and provide periodic feedback to pupils on their school progress.

Most teacher-constructed tests are paper-and-pencil tests, but many teachers must design performance tests. For example, teachers of art, music, and vocational subjects use primarily performance tests; others, such as chemistry and physic teachers, should develop performance tests to appraise laboratory skills. Though performance tests are quite different from paper-and-pencil tests, they should be developed with the same care. Listed below are some questions that teachers can use as guides in developing their own tests:

What are my pupils doing that I want them to do better as a result of this learning experience? Before the teacher can build a test, he must define clearly the skills, concepts, and knowledge he wants to measure. Then he must be able to organize these elements into an orderly outline.

How can I evaluate the elements that are to be measured by the test? Can I measure them through use of paper-and-pencil tests? If so, what kinds of item would be most appropriate to appraise mastery of each skill, concept, or body of knowledge? If some or all of these elements cannot be measured with paper-and-pencil

tests, what special equipment and materials will I need for performance tests? How should I use them? What pupil behavior should I
observe while I am using them? How will I know whether the performance is acceptable? What behavior will reveal the pupils' need
for remedial instruction?

*How can I insure that the test will sample the elements ade-
quately?* The teacher must certainly begin by deciding the relative
importance of each element. While he is assigning values to the
element, he should also note particular ideas around which to build
test items. He should supplement these points with good test-item
ideas which he collects while studying the text, reading references,
and participating in class activities. Finally, after writing the items,
he should tabulate them according to the element dealt with and he
should decide whether he has given adequate coverage to each element.

How do I decide what types of item to use? After studying ideas
for test items sketched out under each element, the teacher should
select for each idea the most appropriate type of test item and write
its first draft. Each item should be written on a separate card so that
items can be easily filed and located for future use.

In building the typical fifty-minute test, the teacher should avoid
too many types of item, for otherwise pupils lose too much time in
reading new directions and deciding what to do.

How will I know when an item is a good one? In evaluating each
item, the teacher should try to determine whether it measures what
he set out to measure with it.

The words used in good items will be meaningful to the pupils.
If the teacher wishes to measure understanding of special vocabulary, he should prepare special items for this purpose so that he may
evaluate understanding of vocabulary independently of ability to
use and interpret subject matter. Further, the teacher should use
simple, straightforward sentences.

A good item requires more of a pupil than ability to recall facts.
It should force him to use knowledge, skills, and concepts in carrying
out an assignment.

A good item does not contain clues for the "test-wise" pupil, nor
does it contain textbook phraseology or unnecessary information. If
it is a multiple-choice item, every choice must appear plausible to
someone. After the teacher has set down his question, he should
follow every common error in logic through to its conclusion, then

list the answers resulting from these errors, along with the right answer. Through this approach the teacher produces tests that can be used in diagnosing difficulties. Finally, he should arrange choices in the item through some chance technique, such as alphabetical arrangement by the first letter in the first word.

A good item should discriminate between the best and poorest students. As he writes the item—and before he has an opportunity to test it through use—all the teacher can do is keep this point in mind. But after he has used the item, he should note what percentage of the best pupils (top 25 percent) and the poorest (bottom 25 percent) obtained the correct answer. Only those items on which best pupils did definitely better than poorest pupils should be re-used.

How should I arrange the items in the test? Some writers recommend that the teacher arrange items in order of their difficulty. Others feel that the teacher so frequently misjudges the difficulty of items when he first uses them that chance arrangement is probably satisfactory. If the teacher encourages pupils to move through the test trying first all the items that are easiest for them, it makes little difference how the items are arranged.

What about directions? In simple, straightforward sentences, the directions should state exactly what the teacher expects the pupils to do. While the teacher cannot take anything for granted, he should make the directions as brief as possible.

When reading the test the last time before duplicating it or putting it on the blackboard, what should I watch for?

—Are the items accurately and clearly worded?
—How difficult is each of the items? Before testing, the teacher can only guess, but after testing he can record on the card, for future use, the percentage of the pupils that obtained the correct answer.
—Do these items emphasize the important features of the unit that I hoped to cover by the test?
—Are the directions clear?
—Are the time limits reasonable? Since most teachers are interested in developing power tests rather than speed tests, they should allow adequate time for the test. At first, inexperienced teachers have difficulty estimating time required, but after some experience with their pupils and after timing several tests, they learn to estimate the time quite accurately, even for a test composed largely of new items.
—Is the answer sheet appropriate for this test? Does it provide space for

recording the types of answer produced by the test? Is adequate work space provided? Are answers arranged so that they can be easily scored?

Once the test has been scored, its real usefulness in teaching begins. First, the teacher analyzes the responses in order to identify material frequently missed on the test; then he reteaches this material. He also enlists the pupils' assistance in identifying test items that were not written clearly. Finally, he gives special individual help to those who missed items that were not missed by many of the group.

From the test the teacher selects promising items that he may use in building another test on the same material. Some items will be reusable without change. Class discussion will show that others need revision. On the card for each item retained or revised, the following information should be recorded: (1) the percentage of the class that obtained the correct answer (the *difficulty level* of the item); (2) the percentage of the best students (those earning total scores in the top 25 percent) obtaining the correct answer; (3) the percentage of the poorest students (those earning total scores in the bottom 25 percent) obtaining the correct answer. The data for (2) and (3) can best be recorded as the ratio best/poorest, which is called the *ratio of discrimination.* Through this procedure, the teacher gradually develops a stockpile of good items for repeated use. Nevertheless, the teacher should continue to include some new items in every test.

Standardized Achievement Tests

As a consequence of recent attacks on the schools, increasing numbers of parents are asking teachers such questions as "How much is my child learning?" "Why does he spell or write poorly?" "Why doesn't he know his multiplication tables?" "Why was he encouraged to take general mathematics rather than ninth-grade algebra?" "Will he be eligible for college?" "What are his chances of getting into college?" Since ours is a mobile population, since our children may have to attend school in another part of the country next year, it is not sufficient to know how well they are doing within the local situation. It is only natural for parents to want to know how their children are doing in terms of some national norms. School grades and the results of teacher-constructed tests must be supplemented by standardized achievement tests in order to provide adequate answers for parents. Often even these data must be further supplemented by appropriate mental-test data.

When achievement tests are administered at the beginning of the fall term, the teacher also obtains estimates of "take-home pay" —what the pupils learned and retained from one fall to the next. Fall testing also helps a teacher determine the present level of pupils' work, so he can adapt his plans to meet the pupils' instructional needs. Though some achievement-test batteries are better than others for this purpose, most provide useful data for identifying and diagnosing learning problems. For best results the pupil should be encouraged to help the teacher pick from the items missed the types of difficulty he feels he could correct within a reasonable period of time. This approach conveys respect for the pupil's judgment and suggests that all of his deficiencies do not have to be corrected at once. Such experiences usually increase the pupil's readiness for remedial instruction.

Even though the staff selects achievement tests with great care, the individual classroom teacher will have to supplement test results with other information. He may, for example, discover why a pupil has trouble with certain work by analyzing his written assignments. By observing a pupil at work, and by having him demonstrate how he does his homework, a teacher may discover additional causes for his difficulty. As was suggested earlier, teacher-made achievement tests provide other valuable clues.

Finally, there is yet another way that achievement tests serve as a corrective device for class grading. Certain types of pupils tend to be over-graded while others are under-graded. Whenever a pupil's achievement-test scores are significantly higher, or lower, than his school grades in the same school subjects, his teachers should try to determine why this situation exists. Is he graded fairly in the classroom? Has he been given the benefit of a doubt because he conformed? Was he graded on the basis of some criterion other than school achievement? Did the standardized test stress skills and concepts different from those stressed in class?

SELECTING AND SCHEDULING TESTS

It is purposeless to test pupils on concepts, skills, or types of knowledge that have not been taught, or that the school may not even intend to teach. Sometimes teachers fail to recognize that their school has one set of objectives while their achievement-testing program stresses another. Under these circumstances, teachers tend to teach that which their achievement tests stress. To reach the school's true objectives, teachers must first decide what they want to do for their pupils and then select the particular standardized test battery that will evaluate pupils' progress in terms of these objectives.

A careful examination of the items within a test battery should help a teacher decide whether that particular test covers the content he includes in his course, and whether it measures the other qualities that he wants to measure. To evaluate the test fully, the teacher must also have specific information about the norm group. The teacher who lacks this information can use his pupils' test results for diagnosing learning problems, and can establish school norms for his own purposes, but he cannot make any generalizations about the general proficiency level of his class.

Fortunately, most teachers recognize that certain basic skills play an important part in determining whether a child makes normal school progress. This category usually includes work study skills, a pupil's ability to communicate his ideas (speaking and writing), ability to understand and interpret the ideas of others (listening and reading), and ability to use basic mathematical skills, concepts, and knowledge. Annually, *beginning in grade 4,* a school should evaluate pupil growth in these skills. If budgetary or other limitations prohibit annual testing, the school should test these skills in alternate grades.

Unfortunately, in practice, not every teacher fully accepts the idea that he should be expected to diagnose learning problems and provide remedial instruction. Little, if anything, will be accomplished by forcing such teachers to administer achievement tests. Until the teacher sees value in achievement testing and understands how to use the results obtained, it is unlikely that he will use the test results to diagnose learning problems and to plan remedial instruction.

Finally, comparing a pupil's performances on different tests of the same subject matter is difficult. The reason for the difficulty is that authors usually sample different areas of content and select pupils for establishing norms on somewhat different bases. Teachers should keep this fact in mind when they try to compare a pupil's performance on one test with his performance on another.

In summary, then, when choosing standardized achievement tests, workers should ask themselves questions like these:

—What may I learn from this test that I could not learn from my own tests?
—What basic subject matter does the test cover? How does this subject matter compare with what I teach?
—What does the test do other than determine which facts my pupils memorized?
—How does it attempt to measure pupils' ability to use subject matter?
—With whom am I comparing my pupils?
—When was the test written? Is the subject matter up-to-date?
—Who wrote the test? Is the author qualified for this responsibility?
—Shall I be able to use the test results in helping my pupils diagnose their own strengths and weaknesses?
—Did the author understand and apply good principles of measurement in constructing the test?

STABILITY AND ACCURACY OF TEST SCORES

Chapter 6 discussed some of the reasons that test scores are not precise measures and suggested how the test interpreter could define a band that would enable him to take account of measurement errors. Though there is little research evidence on the stability of standardized achievement-test scores, they are probably at least as stable as mental-test scores. Errors in measurement, the conditions under which the tests were administered, the pupil's attitude toward himself and the test, and the quality of his learning skills all influence his achievement-test scores. If, for example, a pupil is handicapped by poor reading skills, he may do poorly even in mathematics where he is very competent. Upon repeated testing following successful remedial reading instruction, his mathematics scores may be improved markedly without any further instruction in mathematics. Changes in the school curriculum or use of a new achievement-test battery also may change achievement-test scores markedly. When the knowledge, concepts, and skills stressed by the test are very similar to those taught in the school, the pupils will obviously do better than when the emphasis differs. Furthermore, some achievement-test batteries evaluate primarily the mastery of knowledge, whereas others evaluate the ability to apply knowledge. Warren Findley [1] believes that these two different emphases in

1 Warren G. Findley, "The Problem of Prediction: Two Views" (a paper

achievement testing could account for the variations in scores noted for one type of gifted underachiever. This type of pupil is too indifferent and nonconforming to master the details; yet he pays enough attention to absorb the central ideas, and he is bright enough to apply what he has learned. In the newer type of achievement-test item, with the emphasis on the ability to apply knowledge, and with much of the information needed being provided, this type of underachiever is only slightly dependent on his organized fund of knowledge. When, on the other hand, he is called upon to recall facts, he is caught short. No one should be surprised when this pupil's score varies markedly on these two different types of achievement test.

INTERPRETING TEST SCORES

As the first step in interpreting an achievement test, the test interpreter should review the notes that he made on the test during the in-service education session. Among other matters he should try to determine which of the test's sub-scores are valid and reliable enough for intelligent use. Some achievement tests still provide subtest scores that are based upon too few items to be reliable. Next he should review the test's manual, looking especially for ideas that he can use to diagnose learning problems and to describe the test in a meaningful way for a pupil or his parents. Whenever he interprets a test for the first time, a test user would do well to write out, before he begins, what he expects to say about each score, and to obtain reactions from someone who knows the test better than he. (This advice applies to other types of test too.) Prior to interpreting the test to a pupil, he also should review relevant nontest data and try to assess where these agree and disagree with the test data.

If, for example, a test user were called upon to interpret an achievement test (five scores: vocabulary, reading, language skills, work study skills, and arithmetic skills) for a seventh-grader, he might say:

About a month ago you took an achievement test. Perhaps you remember that it had five main parts. The first part was called a vocabulary test; if your score is compared with those of others in your grade, you get some idea of how well you understand the words you read and hear others use. The second part gives you some idea of how well

read at the American Personnel and Guidance Association Convention in Denver, 1961).

you understand what you read. The third part tells how well you know and can use your language skills, e.g., spelling, punctuation, use of verbs, etc. The fourth part can help you find out how well you can use maps, graphs, and tables, and such reference books as dictionaries and encyclopedias. Finally, the last part helps you discover how well you understand the main ideas in arithmetic and can use them in doing arithmetic problems. [*It is helpful for the test interpreters to show the pupil the various parts of the test as he describes each.*] Here is a line on which parts are marked off to indicate how well you did on each test. There is a line here for each of the five parts of this achievement test, and one to indicate how well you did on the entire test. After I tell you what each part of this line means, I want you to put a check on that part of each line which describes how well you think you did.

VOCABULARY

DID VERY POORLY	DIDN'T DO AS WELL AS MOST	DID AS WELL AS MOST	DID BETTER THAN MOST	DID VERY WELL

——|————|————————————————————|————|——

Reading

——|————|————————————————————|————|——

Language Skills

——|————|————————————————————|————|——

Work Study Skills

——|————|————————————————————|————|——

Arithmetic Skills

——|————|————————————————————|————|——

TOTAL

——|————|————————————————————|————|——

This big space in the middle is the part where most pupils' scores fall, and if you think that you did about as well as most on the vocabulary test, you should put your check mark there. If you feel that you did better than most seventh-graders, you should put your check mark in this part just to the right of the middle, or if you feel you did not do as well as most seventh-graders, you should put your check mark in this part on the left side of the middle. This part over here [*Point.*] to the extreme right describes those pupils who did a lot better than most seventh-graders and the one on the other side [*Point.*] describes those who did a lot less well than most seventh-graders. Do you have any questions? [*Pause for questions.*] Now you put your check marks where you think you fall on each of these six lines. As you put your check marks I wish you would tell me whatever you would like to say about the test and how you felt when you were taking it. After you have finished putting in your check marks I will tell you what the test said about you. Here, too, I hope that you will feel you can tell me how you feel about the results. When, for example, you like what you learn about yourself, or don't like what you learn, say so. Whenever you disagree with what the test says about you, tell me about it. All of this will help me to understand you and will help you make sense out of what we learn about you from these tests.

When a pupil's self-estimate agrees with the test-estimate, the test interpreter notes that they agree; then he can be reasonably certain that the pupil knows where he stands. If the pupil makes no negative comments about the results, or exhibits no negative nonverbal behavior, the interpreter may assume that the pupil has accepted himself as pictured by the test. When, however, either the nontest data from the cumulative folder or material provided by the pupil suggests that the test-estimate may be incorrect, the discrepancy should be discussed further with the pupil (or the parent), and the test interpreter may wish to arrange for further testing or for counseling.

When a pupil's self-estimate disagrees with the test-estimate, the test interpreter indicates where the test-estimate places the pupil and watches for any reactions that suggest the pupil is having difficulty accepting the results. A common error that the test interpreter makes is to assume that a pupil will accept better scores than he expected, but not poorer ones. Some pupils have great difficulty accepting better scores than they expected. Whenever a pupil exhibits dissatisfaction with a test-estimate, the test interpreter should try to understand how the pupil feels and encourage him to talk about these feelings. Within this permissive relationship the pupil can more easily reevaluate his picture of himself, and even change his self-estimate. This is especially true for adolescents, who are very sensitive to others' criticisms and judgments of their worth.[2]

2 N. W. Ackerman, "Group Psychotherapy With a Mixed Group of Adolescents," *International Journal of Group Psychotherapy*, V (1955), 249–60.

Perhaps some readers, at this point, are posing various questions about disagreement of self-estimates and test-estimates. For example, "Does this *occur only* when the two estimates fall within different parts of the five-point scale?" or, "Does falling within different parts of the same segment of the scale necessarily indicate that there is no significant difference in the estimate?" To answer these questions, the test interpreter must ask the pupil what was intended whenever he puts his check mark at the top or bottom part of the scale. Usually when a pupil does this he is trying to indicate that he is at the very top or bottom of that part of the scale. If that is not what was intended, the test interpreter uses the median percentile rank for that part of the scale to determine whether the pupil's estimate is significantly different from the percentile rank for the test-estimate. (See the section on "Use of Graphic Devices" in Chapter 6 to determine how to compute these differences.) When a pupil places himself at the top of one part of the scale and the test places him at the bottom of the scale above it (or vice versa), the test interpreter does not suggest that there is disagreement; instead he merely notes that the pupil's score falls at about the dividing line between the two parts of the scale.

The frame of reference for most elementary-school pupils is their present classmates. When, therefore, their local reference group differs from national norms, the test interpreter should interpret the test first in terms of their local reference group, then in terms of national norms. For elementary-school pupils, the test user also may wish to supplement the rating scale information with grade equivalent scores. Where it seems appropriate to use achievement-test data to predict future behavior (e.g., high school students' chances for success in college), the test interpreter should supplement the data on the rating scale with data from contingency tables provided by publishers. He also should seriously consider developing such tables on the basis of local needs.

Even when matters have gone well up to this point in the test interpretation, pupils and parents will often ask whether the student's scores were satisfactory, and they should be encouraged to do so. To determine whether a child's scores are satisfactory one must have adequate data to answer three additional questions: (1) How easily does he learn? (2) Does he have any serious learning handicaps that interfered with his school progress? and (3) What progress has he made during the past year? The grade equivalents of those who do as well as most in a typical school (the middle 50 percent or average group) usually vary from approximately one grade below their grade placement to one grade above. Of course, the range for those who fall within the middle 50 percent of the norm group varies from one achievement test to another. Hence, the teacher must consult the manual for the test that he is using to identify the width of this part of the scale for the middle group.

Finally, what happens to the rating scale after the test has been interpreted? It should be filed in the student's folder; furthermore, the test interpreter should have recorded on it such information as pertinent nontest data, the pupil's and parents' reactions to the test results, suggestions for using results to improve learning, and, when necessary, the interpreter's suggestions for further testing or counseling. The interpreter also should note on the rating scale the name and form of the test, the norms used, the pupil's age and grade, the date administered, the date interpreted, and for whom it was interpreted.

Mental Tests

FORMAL mental testing in the schools began in Paris:

Paris school officials (1904) became concerned about their many non-learners and decided to remove the hopelessly feeble-minded to schools where they could be taught a simplified curriculum. The officials could not trust teachers to pick out the feeble-minded. They did not want to segregate the child of good potentiality who was making no effort and the trouble-making child the teacher wished to get rid of. Moreover, they wanted to identify all the dull from good families whom teachers might hesitate to rate low, and the dull with pleasant personalities who would be favored by the teacher. . . .[3]

A year later Binet completed the first edition of his famous test with the assistance of his colleague Simon.

Ever since Binet developed his test to identify feeble-minded children in the Paris schools, most authors of mental tests have assumed there are certain mental tasks which children at each age level can do; they also have assumed that mental ability gradually increases

3 FROM *Essentials of Psychological Testing* by Lee J. Cronbach, p. 160. Copyright © 1960 by Lee J. Cronbach. Reprinted with permission of Harper & Row, Publishers, Incorporated.

with age up to mental maturity. Consequently, they try to construct problems that will discriminate between children of different ages.

Prior to constructing a test, authors try to determine what knowledge, concepts, and skills the children whom they expect to test will have had equal opportunity to learn. Then they construct problems that are appropriate for each of the ages to be tested and try these test items with children to determine whether the items actually discriminate between children of different ages. After the authors have developed an adequate number of discriminating items, they combine them into a test, arrange for a carefully selected group of pupils to take the test, and use those pupils' scores to develop norms for the test.

Although most authors of tests select with great care the children who participate in the program for establishing these norms, some few do not. In any case, staff members who use such norms on the test should have the facts about the norm group and the way in which authors established the norms. They cannot understand the full significance of the test results unless they know with whom they are comparing their pupils.

Even though the typical group mental test is a satisfactory measure of mental ability for most pupils, it usually fails to identify the real learning potentialities of some children. Pupils growing up in homes with limited cultural background often have missed many of the educational opportunities that test builders assumed to be common background for all children. Also children handicapped by poor reading skills cannot answer even those questions for which they have mastered the knowledge. More and more teachers recognize that both of these groups of children tend to earn lower scores on group mental tests than their ability to solve problems in a nonverbal setting indicates. Teachers can obtain a more accurate picture of the mental ability of such children by referring them to a school psychologist or counselor for individual testing. Poor verbal skills tend not to be as great a handicap in individual testing as in group testing; furthermore, the specialist can give all of his attention to the study of one child at a time, and the specialist has the professional skill to interpret the child's responses.

Since the results obtained from most mental tests provide teachers and counselors with nothing more than an approximate measure of mental ability, pupils should be tested several times while they are attending elementary and secondary schools. The school system should obtain the first estimate prior to the child's admission to first grade. In deciding whether or not the child is ready for first grade, the staff should supplement the test results with an analysis of the child's behavior during the testing experience, and an es'imate of his physical and social maturity. A careful study of school readiness can prevent early school failures for many children.

From the time a child enters first grade his teachers should have some idea of what they can expect from him. Teachers also are expected to identify pupils for special programs for exceptional children, including the gifted and talented as well as the mentally handicapped, and to make recommendations concerning each pupil's readiness for the various phases of the school program. A pupil also should know what quality of work he can expect from himself, and what his strengths and weaknesses are, so that he can make intelligent choices of a high school curriculum, develop post-high school educational plans, and select an occupation. In addition to certain information on school achievement, mental-test data are required for these decisions.

The school system, having tested the child prior to first grade, should obtain *at least* one other estimate of his mental ability while he is enrolled in elementary school. If it administers *only* one other mental test, the best time is in either the fourth or fifth grade, for by this time, most children will have the verbal skills necessary in group testing. Here, as always, the teacher must be on the watch for pupils who are handicapped by poor verbal skills. Obviously, he cannot expect a poor reader, even if he is a bright child, to do well on most group tests: such a pupil usually earns a score that is lower than that of his real problem-solving level.

While a pupil is attending junior high school, he should be given at least one mental test; he should be given another while he is in senior high school. If the school system begins group testing in the fourth or fifth grade and administers group mental tests in alternate grades, it can obtain a good picture of mental growth for all pupils except those who should be referred to specialists for individual tests.

STABILITY AND ACCURACY OF TEST SCORES

Anyone who has examined intelligence-test scores for school children is aware of the wide variations in scores for certain individuals. Even the scores obtained from the same intelligence test administered at different times vary considerably. The scores obtained on preschool and primary-school age levels are particularly unstable. With reference to this point Cronbach says:

> Scores of emotionally disturbed or uncooperative children are especially unstable. If maladjustment is continuous, the child's test score and his general performance may be constant, at an impaired level. But, if the causes of emotional disturbance are remedial, drastic changes in I.Q. occur. Long-range planning on the basis of the I.Q. is justified so long as two precautions are observed: Interpretation must consider the elements in the child's background which tend to raise or lower scores, and all judgments must be made tentatively, leaving the way open for a change of plans when change in development appears. . . . Test scores are unstable when behavior patterns are being acquired, and we would expect a pencil-and-paper test score to be unstable in the earliest school years. . . . Despite this stability [at age 17], the tester should not rely on an old mental-test score when a critical decision is being made. Some young people make substantial changes in mental performance over a three-year period.[4]

Scores are also affected by the pupil's attitudes toward himself and his school work. When, for example, a child who developed a serious reading problem in the third grade was tested on the Stanford-Binet at age 5, she earned an I.Q. of 115. When she was retested on the Stanford-Binet by the same psychologist in the third grade, she scored an I.Q. of 98. Following remedial reading and a year of academic success she was again retested on the Stanford-Binet by the same psychologist in the sixth grade, and her I.Q. this time was 123. Findley makes a similar point:

> Since 1920, we have learned that mental ability measured by tests is not stable under all conditions. A learning climate that challenges and stimulates, but does not frustrate a child tends to increase I.Q., while a cold, forbidding educational climate operates in reverse for many children.[5]

Mildred Allen found:

> Coefficients of correlation between Kuhlman-Anderson measures in grade 1 and educational achievement in grade 3 range from .32 to .53, and between the same test (Kuhlman-Anderson Intelligence Test, grade

4 *Ibid.*, pp. 179, 223.
5 Findley, *op. cit.*

1) and educational achievement in grade 4 from .30 to .56. These low correlations indicate that long-range predictions of educational achievement based upon only one group intelligence test in the first grade are highly questionable.[6]

May Seagoe [7] reported the following correlations for repeated measurements:

Detroit First Grade at 6–4 with Detroit Primary at 8–8	.64
Detroit First Grade at 6–3 with Haggerty Delta at 8–8	.66
Detroit Primary at 8–9 with National Form B at 10–8	.73
National Form A at 10–4 with Terman at 12–5	.80
National Form B at 10–7 with Terman at 12–6	.87

T. F. Renick,[8] studying those who earned doctorates in the various disciplines, found that among these successful advanced graduate students many appeared to have only average mental ability as high school students. Lindsey Harmon [9] and Samuel Strauss [10] obtained similar results in their studies of successful doctoral candidates. From his study Renick concluded that mental-test scores are useful in making immediate decisions but these scores should be used with caution in making long-term predictions. Cronbach comes to a similar conclusion:

Predictions of intellectual performance over short intervals of time can be made with substantial accuracy, but mental test permits only approximate long-range predictions in lower grades of school. . . . The rather large number of "late bloomers" . . . warns against making a definite and final separation between students with high and low ability at the start of high school. . . . Many potentially able students, though, will not be recognized in the ninth grade. Any grouping plan must make provision for the student whose ability is discovered midway through high school.

6 Mildred M. Allen, "The Relationship Between Kuhlman-Anderson Tests Grade 1 and Achievement in Grades 3 and 4," *Educational and Psychological Measurement*, IV (1944), 161–68.

7 May U. Seagoe, "An Evaluation of Certain Intelligence Tests," *Journal of Applied Psychology*, XVIII (1934), 432–36.

8 T. F. Renick, *Early Identification of Potentially Successful Graduate Students* (unpublished dissertation, University of Illinois, 1961).

9 Lindsey R. Harmon, "High School Backgrounds of Science Doctorates," *Science*, CXXXIII (1961), 679–88.

10 Samuel Strauss, "High School Backgrounds of Ph.D.'s," *Science Education*, XLIV (1960), 45–51.

He must be able to fulfill college requirements without too much loss of time; otherwise much of his talent will be wasted.[11]

INTERPRETING TEST SCORES

At best a test score is nothing more than an estimate of ability, but because a test does provide a number, we accept this measure at face value, discounting other estimates of the same trait or characteristic. Most group mental tests give us merely a rough estimate of how easily our pupils learn from books (verbal ability). Thus guidance workers must always interpret mental-test scores in terms of all other known facts about a child. To supplement mental tests, a worker should observe a child in a variety of situations. He should note how the child presents his ideas. The pupil's knowledge of words, the effectiveness with which he uses them in writing, reading, and speaking—how well he interprets other people's written ideas, and how well he can make his own ideas meaningful to others—all this reflects his verbal ability. In particular, the worker should try to determine how quickly the child "catches on"; with what speed and skill he solves problems when he must use verbal symbols, as in taking objective tests in such areas as social studies. A teacher should also note how easily a child handles problems that involve little use of verbal symbols, how quickly he solves a puzzle or works out an arithmetic problem that is read to the group. As the teacher observes the child in these activities, he should compare the child's performance in each of the two types of problem setting with the performances of two other pupils for whom the school has measures of verbal ability. Then he may compare mental-test scores of the three, and thus obtain an estimate of the child's learning ability in both verbal and nonverbal settings. In such fashion a teacher often discovers a child who "catches on" as quickly as one of the brightest children when the problems require little use of verbal symbols, but who performs like one of the slower children when he solves problems involving verbal symbols.

Even though a child appears to have more ability than he manages to exhibit on tests, the same factors that interfered with his test performance will probably influence his school success. Some pupils know more subject matter than their verbal skills permit them to exhibit on achievement tests, but until they receive the necessary

11 *Op. cit.,* pp. 223, 228.

remedial instruction, they will function below their best level in classrooms as well.

Most authors of tests provide some method for assigning a mental age (M.A.) to the results obtained from a mental test. Usually the manual provides a table for converting raw scores into M.A.'s and I.Q.'s (intelligence quotients). In effect what one does when he refers to these tables is to compare each pupil's performance with the performance of the children who were given the test to establish the test norms. Of the two scores the M.A. tends to be more useful and more easily understood than the I.Q. The M.A. is an estimate of the level at which the child functions in solving problems, while the I.Q. is a ratio of the mental age to the chronological age (C.A.) multiplied by 100 (M.A. $\div$ C.A. $\times$ 100). If, for example, an M.A. of 15-0 (an I.Q. of 107 for a pupil 14-0) were required to succeed in ninth-grade algebra, most mathematics teachers would not hesitate to admit a sophomore with an M.A. of 15-2, but they would probably hesitate to admit him if they saw only an I.Q. of 101. In other words, the M.A. is more meaningful in making educational placements.

There is another important advantage to recording M.A.'s: it helps the teacher study mental-growth patterns. If, for example, we compare three children all with the chronological age (C.A.) of 8, and M.A.'s of 6, 8, and 10, the range in M.A.'s is 4 (and the I.Q.'s are 75, 100, and 125). But assuming that I.Q.'s remain constant, when these children reach age 12, their M.A.'s will be 9, 12, and 15—a difference of 6 between the brightest and dullest child. Teachers should know whether a child is slowly gaining on his classmates or slowly falling behind them. These facts should be considered in selecting teaching materials and in screening students for remedial instruction.

Today more and more secondary schools are recording percentile ranks instead of I.Q.'s. Because I.Q.'s are difficult to translate into meaningful descriptions, this trend should be encouraged. An even better approach is the use of a five-point scale which was described in Chapter 6. Since many schools still record I.Q.'s, two tables that were developed by Cronbach (see TABLES 1 and 2, pp. 236 and 237) are included here to give meaning to I.Q.'s. The first was based upon the research of Seemans, Haly, and Dunnigan [12] and Plant [13]

12 H. H. Seemans, T. C. Haly, and L. H. Dunnigan, "A Study of the June 1955 Graduates of Public High Schools in Certain California Counties," *California Schools*, XXVII (1956), 417–30.

13 Walter T. Plant, "Mental Ability Scores of Freshmen in California State College," *California Journal of Educational Research*, IX (1958), 72–73.

TABLE 1   Percentage of Distribution of I.Q.'s

I.Q.	H.S. GRADUATES (N 21,597)	COLLEGE GRADUATES (N 1,093)
120 & above	9.7%	31.7%
110–119	22.8	46.1
100–109	29.9	18.1
90– 99	23.2	4.0
89 & below	14.3	0.1

and the second was based upon studies by Beckman,[14] Havighurst and Janke,[15] Plant and Richardson,[16] and Wolfle.[17] Cronbach also drew upon data which were reported in the *Guide to Use of GATB.*[18]

What was said in the section on Interpreting Achievement Tests concerning preparation for test interpretation applies to intelligence tests and interests tests too. Perhaps the precautions on using sub-test scores are even more relevant here. Before accepting the verbal and quantitative (or language and nonlanguage) scores at face value, test users should study with care the test reviews and the research literature on the test he is using. Increasingly during the last three decades, intelligence tests have tended to provide users with separate scores for verbal and quantitative abilities, and the use of factor analysis in the study of intelligence has tended to support this trend. Recently, however, some of the measurement specialists have challenged this approach to intelligence testing and presented a case for a single measure of general intelligence. Obviously, space cannot be provided in this chapter to review all the elements in this debate, but users of tests that provide these sub-scores should be thor-

14 A. A. Beckman, "A Minimal Intelligence Level for Several Occupations," *Personnel Journal*, IX (1930), 309–13.

15 R. J. Havighurst and Lesta L. Janke, "Relations Between Ability and Social Status in a Midwestern Community," *Journal of Educational Psychology*, XXXV (1944), 357–68 and XXXVI (1948), 499–509.

16 Walter T. Plant and Harold Richardson, "The I.Q. of the Average College Student," *Journal of Counseling Psychology*, V (1958), 229–31.

17 Dale Wolfle, *America's Resources of Specialized Talent* (New York: Harper & Row, Publishers, 1954).

18 *Guide to Use of the General Aptitude Test Battery* (Washington, D.C.: Government Printing Office, 1958).

TABLE 2   Expectancies at Various Levels of Mental Ability

I.Q.

130	mean of persons receiving Ph.D.
120	mean of college graduates
115	mean of freshmen in typical four-year college
	mean of children from white-collar and skilled-labor homes
110	mean of high school graduates
	has 50–50 chance of graduating from college
105	has 50–50 chance of passing in academic high school curriculum
100	average for total population
90	mean for children from low-income city homes or rural homes
	adult can perform jobs requiring some judgment, e.g., operating sewing machine or assembling parts
75	about 50–50 chance of reaching high school
	adult can operate small store, perform in orchestra
60	adult can repair furniture, harvest vegetables, assist electrician
50	adult can do simple carpentry, domestic work
40	adult can mow lawns, do simple laundry

oughly familiar with the research evidence on the test. They cannot take for granted that the scores predict the behavior that common sense tells them the scores should predict.

Reported below are a twelfth-grader's scores on an intelligence test that provides two sub-scores. The boy is a farmer's son. Neither of his parents graduated from high school. Throughout elementary school he did satisfactory work in all subjects, and exceptionally well in arithmetic. Early in the seventh grade his general science teacher took special note of his work and encouraged him to study science. For the first 3½ years of high school he made almost all A's in mathematics and science, but mostly C's in English and social studies. The one exception in social studies was an "A" he earned in economics. He wanted to go to college, but was not sure he could measure up to the demands of college rhetoric.

When the boy asked the counselor about his test results, the counselor encouraged him to estimate how well he did on the test. The sub-scores and the parts of the scale were defined for the boy as follows:

This test was designed to help students like you discover how easily you learn. The verbal score tells how well you understand words and can use them to solve problems. The quantitative score tells how well you use numbers and can deal with ideas that are expressed in numerical terms. The last score combines the two into a total score. The parts of this line have the following meaning: (1) if you put a check mark here in the middle, you are indicating that you learn *as easily as most* students your age; (2) put your check mark in the part to the right of the middle when you wish to indicate that it is *easier for you* to learn than it is for most students; (3) a check mark in this part to the left of middle indicates that it is *more difficult for you* to learn than it is for most students; (4) a check in this part to your extreme right indicates it is *a lot easier for you* to learn than it is for most students; and (5) a check mark in this part to your extreme left indicates that it is *a lot more difficult for you* to learn than it is for most students. After you have made your estimates, I shall indicate how the test described you. I hope you will feel free to talk about how you feel about the way the test describes you.

In each instance the "√" is the boy's self-estimate and the "X" is the test-estimate that was added by the counselor after the boy had made all three of his self-estimates.

A LOT MORE DIFFICULT	MORE DIFFICULT	AS EASILY AS MOST	EASIER	A LOT EASIER

Verbal

|———|———|————————— √ —————— X —|———|———|

Quantitative

|———|———|—————————————— √ —— X —|———|

TOTAL

|———|———|———————— √ —— X ——————|———|

How did this boy react to the discrepancies between his self-estimates and the test-estimates? When the counselor indicated that the boy had underrated himself, the boy said he was pleased to learn that his scores were higher than he thought they were, but he did not seem pleased. The counselor responded to the boy's inability to accept the new image of himself: "You say you are pleased because the scores are higher than you expected, but you don't seem to be convinced. Perhaps you like the idea, but you just cannot believe it." This helped the boy discuss his doubts about his chances for success in college. When he realized that the counselor could understand why he doubted his ability, he was able to examine his doubts more completely than he ever had before. He also discovered how these doubts had affected his school work—why he gave up too easily in some courses when perhaps he could have done better if he had had more confidence in himself. Moreover, he was encouraged when the counselor made suggestions about how he could correct certain deficiencies.

THE UNDERACHIEVER

The above case was selected to illustrate how the differences between these sub-scores can be meaningful. Achievement-test scores, grades, and the boy's personal history not only supported, but also tended to account for, the scores. Whenever a test user discovers such differences in verbal and quantitative scores, he should investigate the possibility of a reading problem. In this case the investigation revealed that the boy read as well as most seniors, but that was not good enough if this boy were to realize his full potential. Remedial reading instruction and a semester's work in vocabulary instruction improved his achievement-test scores significantly in both reading and vocabulary. These experiences also improved his confidence in his ability to succeed in college.

Often teachers discover another type of underachievement—pupils who are either educationally or culturally so deprived that they cannot exhibit their real ability on either sub-score. Whenever a teacher discovers a pupil who seems to have *much* better ability than he is able to exhibit on tests, the teacher should refer the pupil to a psychologist for an individual intelligence test and a diagnosis of learning skills. Even when a child knows more subject matter than his verbal skills permit him to exhibit on achievement tests, he cannot be expected to perform well in school until he receives the needed remedial instruction. Those factors which interfere with test performance also interfere with school success.

There also are underachievers who possess the learning skills to do well but lack the will to achieve. On the type of rating scale described above, their intelligence-test scores usually fall in a part of the scale that is one or more steps above their grades. Their grades usually fall below their standardized achievement-test scores too. Those in the top 5 percent of the group may even earn mostly A's and still be underachievers. Teachers usually recognize that in spite of superior performance these students are not doing what they are capable of.

Some experts believe that such underachievers' failure to achieve merely reflects their antisocial attitudes. Another explanation that deserves careful study was developed by John Gilmore.[19] He claimed that underachievement satisfies some of these students' unconscious needs, e.g., expression of hostility toward their parents, acceptance by their peers, and the belief that they are no good and that they do not deserve to do well.

Much has been written recently about the gifted underachiever and about methods that could be employed to salvage this needed manpower. Those who would like to achieve a better understanding of the gifted underachiever and to obtain suggestions for helping him would do well to examine the new U.S. Office of Education bulletin,[20] Karnes' research report,[21] Pierce's research report,[22] and Shaw's research report.[23] The intellectual capacity of those selected for study varies from the top 5 percent to the top 25 percent of the population. Of this group Shaw said,

It has been a typical research experience to find that students classified as underachievers on the basis of grades, characteristically are achieving at, or near, their true level of potential as indicated by the results of standardized achievement tests. The converse situation is not always true. Typically, if a high ability student has received high grades, his

19 John V. Gilmore, "Clinical Counseling and Academic Achievement" (a paper read at American Personnel and Guidance Association Convention in Chicago, March 30, 1953).

20 Leonard M. Miller (ed.), *Guidance for the Underachiever with Superior Ability* (Washington, D.C.: U.S. Office of Education, Department of Health, Education, and Welfare, 1961).

21 Merle B. Karnes, *Factors Associated with Underachievement and Over-achievement of Intellectually Gifted Children* (Champaign Public Schools, Ill.: mimeographed, 1961).

22 James V. Pierce, *The Educational Motivation Patterns of Superior Students Who Do and Do not Achieve in High School* (University of Chicago: mimeographed, 1960).

23 Merville C. Shaw, *The Interrelationship of Selected Personality Factors in High Ability Underachieving School Children* (Chico State College: mimeographed, 1961).

achievement-test scores will reflect this. Only occasionally do high ability students who have received high grades fall below their expected level of performance on standardized achievement tests.[24]

These gifted underachievers have certain characteristics that may help school personnel to identify them. Shaw concludes that underachievement is predominantly a male problem. His review of the studies reveals that approximately half of all males with above average ability were underachievers whereas only approximately a fourth of such girls were underachievers. Shaw and McCuen[25] found that chronic male underachievers displayed underachieving behavior in primary grades whereas most girls did not tend to exhibit this behavior until late elementary school or junior high school grades. Shaw and Grubb[26] described underachievers as hostile, as did Gowan.[27] Gowan also described them as self-sufficient, indifferent to their responsibilities, and hard to reach. Pierce[28] found that, compared with gifted achievers, underachievers were less responsible and independent, were less active in extracurricular activities, exhibited less leadership, and saw their fathers as less important to them. Karnes[29] reported that the following factors appeared to be associated with academic underachievement:

(1) a perceived lack of emotional support from parents; (2) poor peer relationships; (3) guardedness and lack of spontaneity in interpersonal relationships; (4) superficial self-reliance and independence used to mask feelings of inferiority; (5) unrealistic goals; (6) a high level of anxiety, latent or manifest; (7) withdrawal tendencies in competitive areas; (8) difficulty in personal integration; and (9) lack of persistence in attaining goals.

For grades four through ten, Shaw and Grubb[30] found that underachievers had a more negative outlook than achievers of the same

24 Merville C. Shaw, "Definition and Identification of Academic Underachievers," Chapter II in *Guidance for the Underachiever With Superior Ability* (Washington, D.C.: U.S. Office of Education, Department of Health, Education, and Welfare, 1961).

25 M. C. Shaw and J. T. McCuen, "The Onset of Academic Under-Achievement in Bright Children," *Journal of Educational Psychology*, LI (1960), 103–08.

26 M. C. Shaw and J. Grubb, "Hostility and Able High School Underachievers," *Journal of Counseling Psychology*, V (1958), 263–66.

27 John Gowan, "The Underachieving Gifted Child—A Problem for Everyone," *Journal of Exceptional Children*, XXI (1955), 247–49.

28 *Op. cit.*   29 *Op. cit.*   30 *Op. cit.*

sex and grade level; underachievers also had negative self-attitudes, and though they seemed to be conforming, they displayed their hostile feelings rather than suppressing them. Broedel, Ohlsen, Proff, and Southard [31] used a four-man observer team to analyze gifted, underachieving ninth-graders' behavior during counseling. These observer teams noted that the adolescents were hostile, difficult to reach, and self-rejecting; they also noted that the underachievers questioned whether they were gifted. This tendency of underachievers to reject their good learning aptitude may explain why their intelligence-test scores sometimes drop significantly between lower elementary grades and high school.

THE EXCEPTIONAL CHILD

When educators speak of exceptional children they usually define four groups: (1) the mentally deviant, (2) the educationally handicapped, (3) the emotionally disturbed, and (4) the physically handicapped. The underachiever can fall into either (2) or (3) or both. Perhaps the best way to cope with underachievement is to prevent its development. Early identification appears necessary in order to help the gifted child understand and accept his unusual intellectual potential, to help his parents understand his ability and assume responsibility for its development, and to help his teachers understand him and plan challenging school experiences for him.

Who is a gifted child? How does he differ from other children? How can he be identified early? These and many other questions concerning the identification and education of gifted children are discussed in *Education for the Gifted Child*.[32] For example, in Chapter 3 Witty says that their superiority may be readily observed in most gifted children early, through such evidence as

1. The early use of a large vocabulary, accurately employed.
2. Language proficiency—the use of phrases and entire sentences at a very early age, and ability to tell or reproduce a story at an early age.
3. Keen observation and retention of information about things observed.

31 J. Broedel, M. Ohlsen, F. Proff, and C. Southard, "The Effects of Group Counseling on Gifted Underachieving Adolescents," *Journal of Counseling Psychology*, VII (1960), 163–70.

32 Robert J. Havighurst (ed.), *Education for the Gifted Child*, The Fifty-Seventh Yearbook of the National Society for the Study of Education (Chicago: University of Chicago Press, 1958).

4. Interest in or liking for books—later enjoyment of atlasses, dictionaries, and encyclopedias.
5. Early interest in calendars and in clocks.
6. Ability to attend or concentrate for a longer period than is typical of most children.
7. Demonstrations of proficiency in drawing, music, and other art forms.
8. Early discovery of cause-and-effect relationships.
9. The development of ability to read.
10. The development of varied interests.[33]

The same writer continues:

It is desirable to recognize that the use of an intelligence test offers a valuable means of locating one type of gifted child—the child of high abstract intelligence. We should recognize, however, that the use of intelligence tests will not enable us to locate all types of gifted children. Nor will the intelligence test provide an accurate measure of the ability of some children whose backgrounds or whose homes are impoverished or underprivileged. In spite of these and other limitations, the intelligence test is undoubtedly the most effective single instrument to be employed in identifying children of high abstract intelligence.[34]

Group mental tests can be used for preliminary screening, but they must be supplemented by individual intelligence-test scores and careful observation by teachers. Additional suggestions of characteristics for which elementary-school teachers should look in order to identify talented as well as intellectually gifted youth are outlined in the *Roster Workbook* by Jack Kough and Robert DeHahn.[35] The intellectual level to be selected for programs for intellectually gifted varies from the top 25 percent (I.Q. 110–112 or above), to the top 2 or 3 percent (130 I.Q. or above), depending upon the school's curriculum, its facilities, and its faculty. Group mental tests can be used for the mental deviates who fall into the mentally handicapped category, but only for the preliminary screening. To determine what type of program is most appropriate for such a student, he must be given an individual intelligence test. When he reaches upper elementary school and is referred for appraisal as a possible prospect for some phase of the program for the mentally handicapped, he should also be given a good diagnostic achievement test. Oliver

33 *Ibid.*, p. 49.   34 *Ibid.*, p. 49.
35 Jack Kough and Robert F. DeHahn, *Roster Workbook for Identifying Children with Special Needs* (Chicago: Science Research Associates, 1955).

Kolstoe [36] recommends that the slow learner (I.Q. of 75–90) be educated in a regular classroom in which the teacher allows him extra time to master the subject matter and, when necessary, gives him extra help with tasks that cause him difficulty. He also recommends that teachers give more attention to a pupil's mental age in deciding whether he should be promoted. He feels that social promotions often put this type of child in the impossible position of being expected to learn materials hopelessly beyond his ability to comprehend. Usually those who possess less mental ability (I.Q. of 75 or less) must be placed in special classes. A number of factors—mental ability, educational achievement, previous school experiences, age, ability to care for themselves, and social maturity—must be considered in determining (1) whether these children are educable and (2) which one of the classes available is most appropriate for each child.

Common Test-Interpretation Errors

THE most serious errors made in interpreting achievement and mental tests are:

1. Indiscriminate distribution of test scores. As a consequence of this error, pupils and/or parents obtain scores which they do not understand and often use to make invidious comparisons.

2. Failure to recognize and take cognizance of emotional reactions to test scores.

3. Failure to communicate what the test scores mean and to help the pupil and parent accept and use test data in making decisions.

4. Treating scores as more precise measures than they are.

5. Failure to consider relevant nontest data.

6. Either making unwarranted predictions or failing to use the test data to make reasonable predictions.

7. Making educational placements on the basis of only a single mental-test score, e.g., selecting gifted students for advanced placement in a secondary-school subject on the basis of scores from a single group test. For such decisions, group test data should be supplemented by scores from an individual intelligence test, by achievement-test scores in the subject area, by previous grades in the sub-

36 Oliver P. Kolstoe, "Teaching Exceptional Children," Chapter 18 in *Modern Methods in Elementary Education,* ed. M. M. Ohlsen (New York: Holt, Rinehart & Winston, Inc., 1959).

ject, by recommendations from former teachers in that subject, and by a statement from the student on how relevant he feels the special course is for him. During the process of developing his case for admission to such a course, the student often clarifies his own goals and makes the commitments that he needs in order to succeed in the course. When a bright underachiever makes a good case for admission, and the person or committee responsible for selecting students demonstrates respect for his judgment by admitting him to the course, even if only on a trial basis, he tends to accept the challenge and to do well.

Achievement vs. Mental Tests

THERE was a time when the difference between an achievement test and a mental or intelligence test was quite clear: the achievement test was designed to measure the relative excellence achieved in some phase of a child's learning while the mental test was designed to measure his learning potential, or at least to appraise his repertory of problem-solving skills. With the shift in emphasis in teaching away from the memorization of facts and toward understanding and developing ability to apply knowledge, there came a similar shift in emphasis in achievement testing. Consequently, achievement tests have stressed appraisal of a pupil's ability to interpret and use information in solving problems, and have come to use a type of item that is often very similar to those used in mental tests. However, some differences still exist. The nature of these differences is described by Tom Hastings and Gordon Rummel:

The achievement test differs from the intelligence test in that it is focused more precisely on the learnings that have taken place in the classroom. Naturally, there is a rather high positive relationship between intelligence tests and achievement tests, since we really are saying that, in general, learning in the classroom situation parallels learning in the total social situation, which includes the classroom.—Hastings [37]

The typical achievement test usually deals with a narrower range of academic knowledge than the typical intelligence test and includes more items for a comprehensive measurement of that range. On the other hand, many parts of the typical intelligence test involve novel situations not usually found in the typical achievement test. Thus the intelligence

37 "The Role of Intelligence Testing," *Education*, LXXXI (1960), 76.

test's novelty and apparent unrelatedness to ordinary school subjects may create greater interest and better testing morale on the part of the students who have antipathies toward one or more subjects than will the achievement test . . . —Rummel [38]

SUGGESTED STANDARDIZED ACHIEVEMENT TESTS

1. California Achievement-Test Batteries (E. W. Tiegs and W. W. Clark), California Test Bureau, 1934–58.

   This general achievement-test battery provides comparable scores in reading, language, and arithmetic for grades 1–14. Though the battery also provides ten sub-scores, each is based upon too few items to be reliable. At the 9–14 grade level, changes in scores on even a few items can have a marked effect on a student's grade placement. For the 1957 edition several of the sub-tests were improved, and the new norms were developed with care. Its manual provides an excellent description of the construction of the test and its new norms.

2. Iowa Tests of Basic Skills (E. F. Lindquist and A. N. Hieronymus), Houghton Mifflin Company, 1955–56.

   This elementary-school battery provides fifteen scores in five areas: vocabulary, reading comprehension, language skills, work study skills, and arithmetic skills for grades 3–9. The battery appraises the development of learning skills rather than the mastery of subject matter, and its excellent manual offers many useful suggestions to teachers for diagnosing learning problems and for planning remedial instruction. Finally, the test was very carefully constructed and standardized.

3. Iowa Tests of Educational Development (prepared under the direction of E. F. Lindquist), Science Research Associates, 1942–58.

   This high school battery appraises students' understanding of basic social concepts, general background in the natural sciences, correctness and appropriateness of expression, ability to do quantitative thinking, ability to interpret reading materials in social studies, ability to interpret reading materials in natural sciences, ability to interpret literary materials, general vocabulary, subtotal, and use of sources of information. In addition to appraising a student's general educational development, its manual suggests how the test can be used to predict success in college and in certain occupations.

4. Sequential Tests of Educational Progress (STEP), Cooperative Test Division, Educational Testing Service, 1956–58.

   This test was designed to appraise both formal and informal learning experiences for grades 4–14 (four grade levels of tests: 4–6, 7–9, 10–12,

[38] *Ibid.*, p. 79.

13–14). It includes seven tests: reading, writing, mathematics, science, social studies, listening, and essay tests. Though it emphasizes the utilization of knowledge and skills, the mastery of certain basic knowledge should certainly increase a pupil's chances for success on the test. Its content was selected with care, but the battery was released for general use before adequate norms were developed.

5. Stanford Achievement Test (T. L. Kelley, R. Madden, E. F. Gardner, L. M. Terman, and G. M. Ruch), Harcourt, Brace & World, Inc., 1923–56.

In this comprehensive battery there are tests for four grade levels: 1.9–3.5, 3–4, 5–6, and 7–9. In addition to the total score, five scores are provided in the first-level test: paragraph meaning, word meaning, spelling, arithmetic reasoning, and arithmetic computation; an additional score in language is provided in the second-level test; and in the two upper-level tests three additional scores are provided: social studies, science, and study skills. Its content was selected on the basis of a careful analysis of contemporary textbooks, courses of study, and the professional literature in the various subject areas. It is a good conservative test battery that stresses the mastery of subject matter rather than the ability to apply knowledge and skills in solving problems.

SUGGESTED GROUP MENTAL TESTS

Although the mental tests described below are group tests, there are many instances in which an individual intelligence test *is required*. At such times, the Stanford-Binet and the Wechsler Intelligence Scales are usually administered. Although everyone who uses mental tests should have special professional preparation, those who give individual tests require more theoretical preparation in the behavioral sciences as well as supervised practice in the administration and scoring of these tests. From careful administration of these tests a skilled administrator obtains more than an estimate of mental ability; he also learns how the child attacks various problems during testing, and how the child reacts under stress. He also gets some notion of the kinds of situation in which the child feels secure and of others in which he is unsure of himself.

1. California Test of Mental Maturity (E. T. Sullivan, W. W. Clark, and E. W. Tiegs), California Test Bureau, 1957 edition.

Tests are provided for seven grade levels: K–1, 1–3, 4–8, 7–9, 9–13, 10–16, and adult. Eight scores are provided, but only three have demonstrated validity: language, nonlanguage, and total. In addition to its nonlanguage feature, the test contains a wide variety of items. Included among the improvements for the 1957 edition were better norms, helpful information for comparing pupils' achievement with ability level, and additional information on reliability and validity. The short form appears to be less reliable than the full test.

2. College Qualification Tests (G. K. Bennett, M. G. Bennett, W. L. Wallace, and A. G. Wesman), Psychological Corporation, 1955–58.

The CQT was designed for college admission officers, but high school counselors also should find it to be useful in helping juniors and seniors assess their chances for success in college. It provides six scores: verbal skills, numerical skills, science information, social science information, total information, and total. The test was carefully constructed, and it does predict general college success reasonably well, but has only very limited value in predicting success in specific courses.

3. Cooperative School and College Ability Tests, Cooperative Test Division, Educational Testing Service, 1955–57.

This (SCAT) is the replacement for the ACE—one of the most well-accepted tests for college freshmen. The new tests serve five grade levels: 4–6, 6–8, 8–10, 10–12, and 12–14. Like the CQT, the SCAT attempts to measure school-learned abilities and to use them to predict academic success in the future. Three scores are provided: verbal, quantitative, and total. From the research data available at this time it appears that the verbal score is a better predictor of academic success than the quantitative score, but some recent experience and unpublished findings suggest that the quantitative score may be useful in predicting success in mathematics and engineering courses, and in identifying one type of underachiever. For this latter purpose the use of the test-score band idea and the profiles obtained from scores for both this test and the STEP should be valuable. This appears to be a promising test, but more research evidence is needed on its validity.

4. Henmon-Nelson Tests of Mental Ability (T. A. Lamke and M. J. Nelson), Houghton Mifflin Company, Revised edition, 1957.

This is a carefully designed short test of general mental ability for grades 3–6, 6–9, and 9–12. By use of the Clapp-Young self-marking device, the test can be easily and quickly scored. Its authors claim that a single score will predict academic success as well as a test which provides several scores, and they support their claim with relatively high correlation coefficients with both teachers' grades and achievement-test scores.

5. Kuhlman-Finch Tests (F. H. Finch), American Guidance Service, Inc., 1951–57.

This series of mental tests includes eight group tests, with no duplication of content. There is one test for each of the elementary grades, one for junior high school level, and one for senior high school level. With the exception of one verbal sub-test for grade 3, the content of the test booklets for the first three grades is wholly nonverbal. One of its unique features is the use of the median sub-test score on the scale to determine M.A. and I.Q. By using this score instead of the total raw score, the user avoids giving undue weight to extreme sub-test scores. A good rationale is presented for the validity of the tests, and the development of items on the basis of their ability to discriminate between levels of mental ability at successive ages was based upon extensive item analysis; however, additional evidence is needed on the validity of the tests. The art work and the general appearance of the booklets also should be improved.

6. Lorge-Thorndike Intelligence Tests (Irving Lorge and R. L. Thorndike), Houghton Mifflin Company, 1954–57.

According to its authors, this test measures abstract intelligence. For grades K–1 and 2–3 only nonverbal content is used. The tests for the other three grade levels (4–6, 7–9, 10–12) include both verbal and nonverbal content, and provide both verbal and nonverbal scores. This test was well designed and carefully constructed, and its manual makes good suggestions for its use.

SUGGESTED READINGS

1. ANASTASI, ANNE. *Psychological Testing.* New York: The Macmillan Company, 1961.

This book presents principles of psychological testing and introduces the reader to the major types of test used today, and it does these things well. Occasionally, its author assumes a background in psychology which some students enrolled in their first course in tests and measurement do not have. However, those enrolled in Introduction to Guidance will find the following chapters very useful at this point in their study: 1, 9, and 10.

    a] What is the primary function of psychological tests?
    b] How did the early interest in the welfare of the feeble-minded influence mental testing?
    c] What is the unique contribution of aptitude-test batteries?
    d] For what purposes would one elect to use a nonlanguage test?

2. CRONBACH, LEE J. *Essentials of Psychological Testing.* New York: Harper & Row, Publishers, 1960.

Chapters 7 and 8.

    a] In what ways did the forces which motivated Binet to develop an intelligence test influence the nature of his first test?
    b] What are the chief differences between Binet and Wechsler's test for children?
    c] Why are performance tests usually unreliable?
    d] What are the chief weaknesses of most group mental tests?

3. FROEHLICH, C. P., and K. B. HOYT. *Guidance Testing.* Chicago: Science Research Associates, Inc., 1959.

This is the third edition of a successful handbook designed for teachers and counselors. Two chapters are especially relevant here: 5 and 7.

    a] What does one know when he knows a child's I.Q.?

b] How may a counselor use data obtained from an achievement test to help clients?

4. LINDQUIST, E. F., ed. *Educational Measurement*. Washington, D.C.: American Council on Education, 1951.

From this reference source, teachers can obtain many helpful suggestions for improving their own examinations. They will probably find the most valuable part of this book to be Part II: "The Construction of Achievement Tests."

a] What should be the teacher's fundamental goal in constructing achievement tests?

b] What crucial elements must the teacher consider in writing a good test item?

c] Why must the teacher give careful attention to the way in which he administers and scores tests?

5. REMMERS, H. H., and N. L. GAGE. *Educational Measurement and Evaluation*. New York: Harper & Row, Publishers, 1955.

This is the second edition of another successful measurement text. Classroom teachers find the suggestions for the use and construction of achievement tests especially helpful: Chapters 2, 3, 4, and 5.

a] For what purpose would teachers elect to use essay questions?

b] What basic steps should a teacher follow in constructing an examination?

c] What are some of the common weaknesses of achievement-test batteries?

d] What factors should a teacher consider in interpreting a pupil's mental-test scores?

Child Study: Appraisal of Personal Adjustment

T HIS CHAPTER is concerned with helping teachers and prospective counselors understand each pupil so that they can help him to understand himself and to identify those forces within himself and within his environment that interfere *with his learning.* Teachers and counselors must try to identify early those children who are not making normal progress toward self-actualization—both the well-adjusted ones who are confronted with temporary problems that require their special attention, and the emotionally disturbed, who may require referral for extensive treatment.

In order to appraise a pupil's growth toward self-actualization, teachers and counselors must try to obtain the answers to such questions as:

—What is this pupil's attitude toward life?

—What kind of person does he perceive himself to be? Is this a reasonably accurate perception?

—Is his perception of reality similar to that of most pupils of his age?

—Is he gradually becoming better acquainted with himself, with what he wants to become, and with what he must do to achieve his goals?

—Is he developing increasingly greater self-acceptance, self-respect, and self-confidence?

—Is he learning to take increasingly greater responsibility for himself? Can he make the decisions that a person of his age should be expected to make? Can he act on his decisions after he has made them?

—Can he give and accept love?

—Is he adequate in his interpersonal relations?

—Can he enjoy and perform adequately in work and play?

—How does he react to important other people? What does he expect from them? Is he responsive to them and to their needs?

—To what extent are his basic needs being met?

—What are his problems? Can he cope with them? How do his problems affect his school success? Does he have problems that his school experiences aggravate? If his problems are caused by school experiences, what may be done to alleviate the sources of the difficulty?

If those pupils who require special attention are to be identified early, teachers and counselors must recognize behavior that suggests poor adjustment. They may suspect adjustment problems if the student

Has a physical handicap to which he cannot readily adjust (it may or may not be perceived as serious by others).

Has failed one or more grades.

Works hard yet does poor school work.

Gives up easily when things do not go well—lacks confidence in himself.

Does poorer (or much better) work than one would expect from a child with his ability.

Has great difficulty in adjusting to changes in routine.

Tends to be overdependent on adults.

Hesitates to try new things.

Does not seem to know how to earn recognition from his classmates.

Tends to be chosen last—to be left out of things.

Usually works and plays by himself.

Hesitates to participate in the group's activities—is seclusive, reticent, and extremely quiet.

Is afraid to stand up for his own rights.

Is extremely sensitive or "thin-skinned"—frequently has his feelings hurt.

Carries a chip on his shoulder—tends to be defensive and quarrelsome.

Tends to be uncooperative—to want to do as he pleases regardless of what his classmates wish to do.

Is so sure of himself that he cannot see and accept deficiencies in himself which others see readily.

Is resentful of criticism.

Tends to be cruel, malicious, or destructive.

Tends to bully other children.

Lies frequently.

Steals frequently.

Is often truant.

Does an excessive amount of daydreaming.

Is easily excited.

Is tense and easily upset.

Is restless and hyperactive.

Exhibits nervous behavior, such as fidgeting, biting fingernails, and crying easily; also may have tic such as an eye twitch.

Frequently talks about fears and guilt feelings.

Is extremely jealous of other pupils.

Is often sullen or moody.

Is usually suspicious of others.

Has unusually pessimistic outlook on life.[1]

To obtain a label for a child is not an end in itself, and can even be harmful. Although the above descriptions may help to identify youth who need assistance, they must be used with care lest a child be labeled as maladjusted and then nothing be done to help him. The guidance worker's purpose is to understand and to help youth.

Techniques which teachers and prospective counselors may use for these purposes have been divided into four discussion topics: (1) personality tests and inventories, (2) self-reporting techniques, (3) sociometric methods, and (4) staff reports.

Personality Tests and Inventories

PERSONALITY tests and inventories are used for various purposes: (1) to identify the emotionally disturbed; (2) to identify leaders; (3) to identify persons with characteristics believed to be relevant for success in certain positions and professions; (4) to help youth identify problems that they can discuss with counselors; (5) to re-

1 Merle M. Ohlsen, ed., *Modern Methods in Elementary Education* (New York: Holt, Rinehart & Winston, Inc., 1959), pp. 50–51.

duce resistance in counseling; (6) to diagnose clients' problems and to plan appropriate treatment; (7) to predict chances for success in counseling; and (8) to help clients better understand themselves. Sometimes a single test is expected to provide the basic data for all of these purposes, even when its author had only one or two of the purposes in mind when he constructed it and standardized it. Obviously, no single test can be expected to satisfy all of these various needs of personnel people.

In personality assessment, perhaps the most difficult problem concerns criteria.

A special problem that arises in personality assessment is the frequent unreliability of the criteria which so often represent subjective judgments that vary from one criterion rater to another. This unreliability imposes a serious limitation on the potential validity of personality assessments, and it makes it difficult to evaluate some of the low validity coefficients reported.[2]

If therefore an unusually valid test were developed, even it may not look good when compared with the inadequate criteria commonly used to validate personality tests.

Before measures of adjustment can be validated, adequate criteria must be defined. Stern, Stein, and Bloom [3] suggest beginning with an analysis of the specific situation in which the individual will function, in order to identify the elements related to success in the situation. Then the inquirers are ready to search for measurement devices that will enable them to assess these characteristics and competencies of persons prior to placing them in the situation—to predict behavior in a situation on the basis of relevant data. The researchers described personality assessment as a three-fold process: (1) study of the environment in which the individual to be assessed is to act; (2) study of the individual; and (3) study of the congruence between the two.

Obviously pupils are expected to function in many and varied situations. Since failure in any one situation tends to affect his behavior in other situations, no facet of a child's life can be ignored. If, however, adjustment is to be appraised, specific but limited cri-

2 Ronald Taft, "Multiple Methods of Personality Assessment," *Psychological Bulletin*, LVI (1959), pp. 336–37.
3 George G. Stern, Morris I. Stein, and Benjamin S. Bloom, *Methods in Personality Assessment* (Glencoe, Ill.: The Free Press, 1956).

teria like those discussed in Chapter 1 and at the beginning of this chapter must be defined. Instead, personality questionnaires and inventories are often selected that are supposed to do the job. Unfortunately most personality tests have not been standardized with the same care that most achievement and intelligence tests have been. Since they are rarely used in schools, little space will be devoted to projective tests. However, it should be noted that they are justly criticized because the results obtained from them are colored by the personality of the person who administers and scores them. As will be shown later, results of personality questionnaires and inventories are also influenced by the person who administers and uses them. Personality questionnaires and inventories are also criticized because they can be easily faked and because their items are often ambiguous.

One does not have to be a tests and measurements expert to discover why most personality questionnaires used in the schools fail to identify children needing special help. If one takes his favorite personality questionnaire, reads the directions, and responds to the items, he will discover that he is able to present whatever picture of himself he wishes to present. This is true for pupils, too. What a pupil tells a staff member about himself through use of the questionnaire will depend on his awareness of his problems, his ability to see the similarity between his problems and those presented in the questionnaire, his ability to understand the statements made, and his willingness to report his problems to those who will see the test results. Whether pupils can, or are willing to, trust those who will see their responses, and whether they can face their problems, will also determine how they respond to the test.

All in all, other sources of information prove more helpful than personality questionnaires.

In detecting the presence and estimating the severity of a neurosis, tests of mental functioning proved useful as did certain of the more sophisticated questionnaires, among which the Minnesota Multiphasic appears to be most valuable. Even more pertinent were autobiographical data obtained in interviews or from written records.[4]

From his study of personality assessment Sines[5] concluded that the diagnostic interview was consistently observed to contribute

4 Henry Murray, Foreword in *Methods in Personality Assessment*, p. 11.
5 Lloyd K. Sines, "The Relative Contribution of Four Kinds of Data to

greater accuracy of judgment than the Minnesota Multiphasic, the Rorschach, or biographical data.

In order to obtain the best predictive value from life-history data, Paul Meehl [6] recommended that data obtained from personal histories be recorded on a standard form so that they can be treated statistically. From his analysis it would appear that the use of a Q-sort by an interviewer or observer would improve reporting.

Somewhat earlier Albert Ellis [7] summarized the validation studies on personality questionnaires. He concluded that most of them are of dubious value in helping anyone distinguish between the adjusted and maladjusted. He also indicated that they were of even less value in helping a counselor discover the source of a pupil's problems. When he reviewed the literature seven years later [8] he again raised certain questions about their value but was less critical than he had been in the earlier report. But even in this later paper, he reported that in most instances paper-and-pencil tests of personality do not measure the independent traits they are supposed to measure.

What may one conclude from the literature cited above? Guidance workers should take special note of personal histories. Perhaps even better appraisals of adjustment will be obtained from them and from the cumulative record when clinicians, interviewers, and observers are required to record their impressions of a pupil on a behavior inventory or to describe him with a Q-sort. Moreover, few schools employ personnel qualified to administer and interpret those personality tests that identify pupils requiring special assistance. Used under appropriate conditions by counselors and qualified group leaders, some personality inventories and problem checklists *may* be of use to identify pupils who want help and to help pupils identify the problems they would like to discuss with someone whom they can trust. However, most teachers and prospective counselors will have to rely primarily on nontest data in appraising the personal adjustment of pupils.

Accuracy in Personality Assessment," *Journal of Consulting Psychology,* XXIII (1959), 483–92.

6 Paul E. Meehl, "Some Ruminations on the Validation of Clinical Procedures," *Canadian Journal of Psychology,* XIII (1959), 102–28.

7 Albert Ellis, "The Validity of Personality Questionnaires," *Psychological Bulletin,* XLIII (1946), 385–440.

8 Albert Ellis, "Recent Research With Personality Inventories," *Journal of Consulting Psychology,* XVII (1953), 45–49.

Self-reporting Techniques

OBVIOUSLY, most personality tests and inventories used in the schools are self-reporting devices. Since these devices have been discussed, this space will be devoted to such child study techniques as private conferences, personal history questionnaires, autobiographical themes, and picture stories.

PRIVATE CONFERENCES

What can be learned about a pupil from conferences with either the pupil or his parents depends upon the interviewer's ability to develop a good relationship with the pupil or his parents and the interviewer's ability to listen, to try to understand, and to comprehend nonverbal as well as verbal behavior. (See Chapter 4.) When a good relationship has been established, a competent interviewer can obtain from a pupil his perception of himself, of his relationship to his family, of his relationship with classmates and other peers, of his school successes and failures, of those situations in which he has been happiest and unhappiest, and of his problems.

Although it is highly important to distinguish fact from fiction, the teacher must realize that feelings are facts. A child's feeling that his mother is disappointed in him or that his home is old-fashioned is a significant part of the information needed to help him, even though the child's concept does not agree with the facts as seen by a more objective observer.[9]

The interviewer must help the child describe situations as he sees them, and thus learn how the child perceives things. Only by understanding the child's perception of things can he understand the child and his behavior. Therefore, the interviewer must be cautious in pointing out discrepancies in the pupil's perceptions lest he convey doubts and suspicions; a child shares his perceptions with only those persons who seem to accept him and try to understand him. On the other hand, the interviewer should note where the child's perceptions seem to disagree with others' perceptions of the same situations.

9 T. L. Torgerson and G. S. Adams, *Measurement and Evaluation for the Elementary School Teacher* (New York: Holt, Rinehart & Winston, Inc., 1954), p. 168.

Applying these same principles to conferences with parents, a competent interviewer can obtain the parents' perceptions of the pupil's strengths and weaknesses, his primary interests, goals, and hobbies, his problems, and his adjustment within the family. An interviewer also may be able to identify family conflicts and assess their effect upon the child.

PERSONAL HISTORY QUESTIONNAIRE

A common source of information on all the pupils is the personal history questionnaire. Usually it provides the school staff with some information on the child's home life, his family background, his special abilities, his special interests and hobbies, and the way in which he spends his time outside of school. The administration should obtain this information from the parents when the child enters the school system in the lowest grade, and from parents or the pupil himself when the child transfers to the school.

From time to time, as the child matures, the staff will need other new information. Since teachers secure the information for their own use, they should decide what should be included in the original questionnaire, and when to supplement it with additional information. The questionnaire should provide space for new information; some schools provide short supplements for each grade level and use them in connection with registration. To retain all of the supplements, while avoiding unnecessary clerical work, each supplement may be stapled to the original questionnaire.

After the staff have decided what they want to know about their pupils, they must decide which of their questions they can answer by the questionnaire technique. Because the staff will use these questionnaires as a mass approach, they cannot request personal data that parents and pupils will reveal only to a trusted counselor. Some questions will not be answered by a pupil if he feels that they probe too deeply into his personal life. Other questions may be resented by parents. Many pupils and parents, for example, resent questions pertaining to family income, parent-parent relationships, and parent-child relationships. On the other hand, the wording of a question is often as important as the information requested. Teachers should scrutinize the wording of every item from the parents' and the child's point of view: the questionnaire should include only those items to which the respondent would feel he could reply truthfully with a minimum of personal threat. When this principle is ignored in the construction of questionnaires, pupils often give inaccurate answers or leave questions unanswered.

THE AUTOBIOGRAPHY

There is a direct relationship between the personal history questionnaire and the autobiography. As a matter of fact, some personal history questionnaires merely present a series of questions through which the staff hopes to obtain the crucial parts of the autobiography. The extent to which accurate information is obtained from a pupil on either a personal history questionnaire or autobiography is determined by the accuracy with which he perceives himself and by the degree to which he trusts the staff member involved.

Some who use the autobiography attempt to secure specific facts about each pupil by giving detailed directions. At the other extreme are teachers and counselors who feel that detailed directions produce little useful information, and who recommend giving the pupil complete freedom in writing his life story. In any case, the pupil must know what the staff member expects from him and what the staff member will do with the autobiography once it is written. To get meaningful results, teachers and counselors must allow adequate time for the pupils to discuss questions like these, which are examples of questions pupils have asked when given the chance to discuss writing an autobiography:

—What should I include in my autobiography?
—How should I write it?
—Who will read it?
—How can members of the staff use these themes to help me?

During the discussion of such questions, it is usually profitable to comment on the following questions as well: What methods will help a pupil remember the important events in his life? Why does an occasional pupil omit certain parts of his life story or write the story as he wishes it had been lived?

Obviously, it is not easy to build an emotional climate in which all the pupils will come to feel that they can tell their real-life stories. If the pupils already trust those collecting and using the data, they well find it easier to express their doubts and raise their own questions. Both doubts and questions, expressed, help create the classroom climate required to produce revealing themes.

The following directions for writing an autobiography are an example of an approach that may be used by a secondary-school teacher to begin discussion of the assignment:

I should like to know each of you better than I do now. As I come to know you better, I believe that I will be able to work with each of you more effectively. Each of you can help me do this by writing the story of your life for me. No one other than myself will see what you have written unless you give your permission.

Start with your early childhood and make an outline of the important events in your life. Try to remember the whole story. I also hope you will include in your life story a description of your happiest moments and your unhappiest moments. After you have prepared the outline and arranged all the events in the order in which they occurred, forget about this assignment for several days.

Then review the outline, adding other events that you forgot to include the first time. As you add these events, note details on all events so that you will remember to include them in your story.

Finally, build your story around your outline of events. Concentrate on making your story clear to me; do not worry about grammatical errors while you are writing it. If you feel you would like assistance in polishing the style and in correcting the grammar, I will help you when you have completed a rough copy. Do not feel, however, that you must see me. Remember, the important thing is to tell the story of your life as accurately and clearly as possible.

Since primary-school children have not developed the writing skills to write their life stories, some primary teachers have used "show and tell" time for this activity at the beginning of the school term. This method helps the teacher become better acquainted with the pupils and helps them to become acquainted with each other. In addition to the suggestions made above for creating a climate for these stories, the teacher's structuring must take account of what would be appropriate for pupils to share with the entire class.

A teacher should not attempt to replace discussion with a set of directions for writing. However, he can use a set of directions to initiate discussion on the assignment. Discussion clarifies the purpose of the assignment and helps to build the proper emotional climate.

Even after such discussion, some youngsters cannot bear to examine certain of their experiences that were either too unhappy or too embarrassing. Many pupils reconstruct their past to make it more like the life they wish they could have lived: they are not able to describe life as they actually lived it. Becoming aware, through discussion, that they have such attitudes may help some youngsters, though not all, to write an accurate story. Still others do not have sufficient trust in the staff member involved to unveil the full story as they know it. Nevertheless, as an important by-product, the experience of writing a life story does help each pupil clarify relationships among events in his life. As he tries to make his life story make sense to someone else, he comes to understand himself better.

THE BIOGRAPHY OF AN IDEAL

This theme is an interesting variation of the autobiography. It can produce effective results when the teacher assigns it after the pupils have completed their autobiographies. In making the assignment, the teacher should suggest that each pupil first decide what person is his ideal, then collect the information for a biography of this ideal, following the same outline used in writing his autobiography. He need not reveal the ideal's real name. Neither should he feel compelled to obtain details corresponding to every fact included in his autobiography. The purpose of this assignment is to help the pupil and his teacher or counselor become acquainted with the ideal the pupil sets for himself. Through a study of these themes, the guidance worker frequently discovers the discrepancies between what the pupil conceives himself to be and what he wishes he were.

AN AUTOBIOGRAPHY OF THE FUTURE

While an autobiography of the future is only an extension of the autobiography, it provides a different type of information, for the pupil has an opportunity to project himself into the future, to discuss his ambitions. Because he feels less inhibited than he would in discussing his more formal plans for the future, he reveals more readily what he values most highly.

Either of the following sets of directions may be used to initiate class discussion of this theme:

—Imagine yourself ten years in the future and have a big daydream about it. Describe a day in this life ten years in the future. Visualize the sort of person you would like to be, the sort of life you would like to be living, and the sort of things you would like to be doing. Start at the time you get up and describe your activities until you go to bed at the end of the day.

—Imagine yourself fifty years in the future and write what should be added to the autobiography that you just completed. Describe the important things you would like to have accomplished and the people who helped you accomplish them.

Both sets of directions, used in the proper emotional climate, produce valuable information about the secondary-school student's important goals in life. Most students discuss family plans, social aspirations, and vocational plans more freely here than in their autobiographies. If the church is important, the student will bring this into the discussion. Generally he reveals how self-centered or other-centered he is. The first set of directions above provides information about the youngster as he moves into his most productive years, while the second tends to reveal what he hopes to accomplish during his whole lifetime.

THEMES ON THE PUPIL'S PERSONAL LIFE

The considerations that help obtain the best possible data from the autobiography apply also to other self-revelatory themes. Used in the appropriate emotional climate, themes can help teachers understand their pupils. The following are but a few examples of topics that reflect the pupil's feelings about his family, his classmates and other acquaintances, his outlook on life, his special needs, his special abilities, his hobbies, interests, and ambitions:

Friends—Who Are They?
Friends—Where Do You Find Them?
High Spots in My School Life
Leaving Home for College
Leaving Home for Work
Living in My Home
Spending Leisure Time in Our Town
The Person I Admire Most
The Person I Pity Most
What I Want Most from Life
How I Expect to Earn a Living (the reasonable goal)
How I Would Like to Earn a Living (the dream goal)

Similar information may be obtained by having pupils select pictures about which they write stories. The teacher should encourage the pupil to use any picture he may wish, but since some pupils will not have other sources to draw from, the teacher should have a collection of newspaper and magazine pictures—each of which includes children of his pupils' age group. The collection should stimulate pupils to express a wide range of moods and feelings, and therefore ought to include scenes ranging from the happiest to the unhappiest. Preferably, the material in the pictures should be as unstructured or as ambiguous as possible so as to make it easy for the pupils to project themselves into the scene.[10]

To use this story technique most effectively, pupils should be given specific directions for telling or writing their stories. Their teacher should tell them to select a picture and write as dramatic a story as they can. In his story each pupil should relate what he thinks led up to the event shown in the picture, describe what is happening at that moment, and give what he thinks will be the outcome. The pupil should be encouraged to give special attention to the characters' feelings. When the pupils are ready to submit their stories, it may be worthwhile for the teacher to ask each pupil to add a note in which he tells why he happened to choose that particular picture for his story. However, the teacher should put no pressure on the pupil to give a "logical" answer. Wherever possible, the pupil should attach the picture to his theme.

The teacher or counselor will find these stories very useful if he reads in order to understand a pupil's perception of the world around him without attempting a diagnosis which only a qualified clinician could make. Another important point for the teacher to remember is that a pupil's stories are colored by temporary conditions in his life; a teacher should hear or read at least five or six such stories over a period of several months before formulating any conclusions about the child.

Pupils tend to express their real feelings more readily in a picture story than in an autobiography. Typically a pupil identifies with one person in the picture and expresses his feelings about himself, about important other people, and about life in general, through this character. Usually this identification figure is either the person

10 The supporting psychological theory and directions for using this technique were developed by Henry A. Murray, in *Thematic Apperception Test Manual* (Cambridge: Harvard University Press, 1943).

mentioned first in the story or the one who does most of the acting. Frequently, these two are the same person. Through a careful examination of what the identification figure says and does, a teacher or counselor may obtain the answer to such questions as: To what extent does the pupil accept himself? How does he try to solve his problems? How does he feel toward important other people in his life? How does he believe these important other people feel toward him? What are some of the problems with which he is faced? What are some of his important needs and ambitions? Do things usually work out all right? (Do his stories usually have happy endings?)

THE DIARY AND DAILY LOG

Another technique that counselors can use to help pupils discover and reveal their problems is the diary. Many preadolescents and adolescents keep diaries, but most of them consider their diaries to be private property. The private diary helps them express their own deep feelings about life—both pleasant feelings and unpleasant.

Occasionally, a pupil will permit a trusted counselor to read his diary. Through study of this personal document, the confidant, in conference with the pupil, can learn much about the pupil's problems, needs, and life goals. Many times the counselor discovers deep feelings of guilt and fear which the pupil unconsciously associates with his pleasant experiences. A counselor also may find among the diary entries comments that reveal the reasons for the unpleasant associations and the basis for the pupil's problems. Counselors have, for example, asked pupils to keep a record of their happiest and unhappiest moments, and the incidents that led up to each. These entries often help the pupil identify recurring elements that have been associated with the happy and unhappy parts of his life.

Less jealously guarded, but also less deeply revealing than the diary, is the pupil's daily log of activities. To gain a real understanding of how he spends his time, the pupil must want to reveal the facts, and he must keep a log of his activities for at least one week. Even then the daily log will not be meaningful if the week happens to be unusual. This log of his activities helps the pupil see how he uses his time; in a sense it shows him what he puts first in life. It also helps others to understand him and his behavior.

The teacher can use the log of activities to help a pupil learn to use time more efficiently. Since, however, the log reflects what the pupil puts first in life, the pupil must be ready to examine his values in order to improve his work habits. Many teachers and counselors have been disappointed by pupils who were able to formulate good study schedules but were unable to apply the schedules in their daily lives; of course it is much easier to develop an efficient-looking schedule than to change the motivations that maintain inefficient work patterns.

Sociometric Methods

ADEQUACY in interpersonal relations is one of the characteristics of a well-adjusted person. He accepts his peers and they accept him. The degree to which a person is accepted by others also may reflect his ability to accept others; and his ability to accept others is often an indication of the extent to which he accepts himself.

A teacher may use sociometric methods to identify pupils who are accepted, rejected, and not known (isolates) in the group. He also may use these methods to identify leaders for specific tasks and even early school drop-outs.[11] These data also may be used in organizing work and play groups. Before a teacher can help his pupils improve their human relations skills, he must know how they really feel about each other.

But some teachers argue that they do not need sociometric test data to assess peers' reactions to a pupil. Usually teachers of primary-school-age children can assess accurately how a pupil's classmates react to him, but the task becomes more complex as children mature. Increasingly, pupils learn to conceal how they really feel toward each other. Consequently, a teacher's ability to assess pupils' attitudes toward each other becomes less accurate. These inaccurate impressions may mislead the teacher in his efforts to improve pupils' skills in living and working in groups and in helping individuals find their way into a group.

Whenever a teacher uses sociometric methods he must satisfy certain basic conditions to obtain reliable results: (1) he must convey to the pupils why he wants the information and how he will attempt to use it to help them make friends in school and improve their skills for working with peers; (2) he must assure them that no

11 Raymond G. Kuhlen and E. Gordon Collister, "Sociometric Status of Sixth-Graders and Ninth-Graders Who Fail to Finish High School," *Educational and Psychological Measurement*, XII (1952), 631–37.

one except himself will see their responses; (3) he should prepare a large seating chart and place it where everyone can see it to recall and spell names; (4) he should arrange for each pupil to be seated so that no other pupil will see his responses; (5) both the questions and the directions must be understood by the pupils; and (6) he should watch for pupils who need assistance in answering the questions.

SOCIOMETRIC TEST

The following sociometric test was developed by an eleventh-grade English teacher (who taught a unit on occupations) with the assistance of his pupils. A dittoed copy of the test, including the directions, was given to each pupil.

DIRECTIONS: Most people agree that the teacher should understand his pupils to work with them most effectively. Knowing how they feel about one another is an important part of the teacher's understanding.

You are to answer seven questions. After reading each question, write in the space provided on this sheet the names which you think of first. Please note that questions 1 through 6 provide space for two names. In answering question number 7, use as many names as you wish; you may also answer it with the word "none."

Please remember that you do not have to say that you dislike anyone—neither do you have to say that you like anyone in this class. You are to name the person whom you would choose first if you had to select someone from the class for a particular purpose. Then you are to name the person whom you would invite last in the event that you could not invite them all. Remember that no one except your teacher will see what you write.

Write your name in the space provided, now, before you forget it.

_____

YOUR NAME

1. If you were going to have a birthday party, which two pupils would you invite first? _____; _____

2. If you were going to have a birthday party and could include all but two, which two pupils would you leave out? _____; _____

3. If you could select someone to help you with your project on choice of occupation, which two pupils would you choose first? _____; _____

4. If you could invite all but two pupils to help you with your project on choice of occupation, which two pupils would you leave out?
   _____ ; _____

5. If I said that you could select someone to help you polish up your themes, which two pupils would you select first? _____
   _____ ; _____

6. If I said that you could seek assistance from all but two pupils to help you polish up your themes, which two pupils would you leave out?
   _____ ; _____

7. With which pupils do you feel you are not well enough acquainted to know whether or not you should use their names? _____

Perhaps some readers will wonder why questions 2, 4, 6, and 7 were included in the test. If one uses only the positive questions one cannot differentiate among three very different types of pupil: [12] (1) the well accepted who are rarely chosen first by anyone; (2) the rejected; and (3) the isolate (the unknown person—question 7).

Questions can be put in two ways: (1) "Whom would you like most (least) to have as your lab partner?" and (2) "If you had to select a lab partner from this group, whom would you choose first (last)?" Pupils tend to select the same names but appear to be less threatened by the second form; therefore, it would be well for the teachers to use the latter form. Those pupils who like everyone do not feel that they are forced into a position of rejecting anyone. Neither are those who reject the group made to feel that they must say that they like some members.

The teacher, having obtained pupils' responses to the sociometric test items, must then summarize pupils' responses in some manner which encourages careful analysis of the material. He should direct attention to the relationship among the responses to various questions as well as the responses to individual questions. The sociogram has proven to be a very effective method for studying pupils' reactions to each other on a single question. FIGURE 1 illustrates how the sociogram can be used to study the relationship of only first choices made in response to item number 1. The sociometric test used here was administered to teachers and prospective

12 M. M. Ohlsen and C. E. Dennis, "Factors Associated with Education Students' Choice of Classmates," *Educational Administration and Supervision,* XXXVII (1951), 277–90.

FIGURE 1   Sociogram for Guidance Class First Choices in Question 1

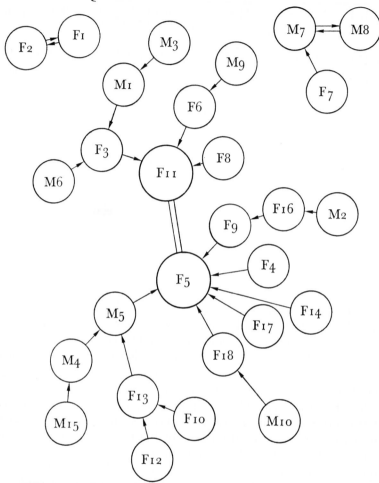

counselors enrolled in one section (34 students) of the graduate course for which this book was designed as a text. (The directions and items are copied below.)

With only the first choices on item 1, F5 is the star. What FIGURE 1 does not reveal is the mutual choices that show up in second and third choices. FIGURE 2 indicates these, in addition to the cumulative effect of the choices. Obviously, it would be difficult to super-

FIGURE 2 Matrix Table for Guidance Class

CHOOSERS

	F1	F2	F3	M1	M2	F4	M3	M4	M5	F5	F6	M6	F7	F8	F9	F10	F11	F12	M7	F13	F14	F15	F16	M8	F17	M9	F18	M10
F1	1_3	5	1	3	4	5	5	5	5	5	5	5	1	5	$^2 5$	5	5	5	5	3	5	5	2	5	4	2	5	4
F2	1_3		1	3			3	2		4	5	2	2	5		1	5	4	5	4	5	5						5
F3	5	1		4					$^2 4$							1	3	3	1_3	2	2	5			4			5
M1	5		1_3		2		1		$^2 4$						2	5				1			5	4	4	5	3	3
M2									1_3									3	$^2 4$	$^2 4$		1		1_3				$^2 4$
F4		1	1		5		4				1_3		5	2	2			3		4	2	4	3					5
M3	5	5	1		5		3	2	$^2 4$						1	4	5	3	3	2		1						$^2 4$
M4			1		3				1_3				$^2 4$	$^2 4$				1_3										$^2 4$
M5	1_3	3	5	3	2	$^2 4$	$^2 4$		1	5	5		4				1									5	5	5
F5	5	5				1_3	$^2 4$	5	2		5	5				1_3		1		4	3							$^2 4$
F6		3		2	4			3		1		5	5	$^2 4$		1	1	5		3	4	2				5		
M6	5	1	1	3	2			1	4							5	3	3					2	4	2	5		
F7	3	3	1		2	4	2		4					5			4	1			2	1			5	3		
F8	3		1	1					2	2		4	1				4	3	4			2	3	5	5			
F9		4		3			3	4	1								1			1	3							
F10		3	3		2		$^2 4$									1										3	$^2 4$	
F11		5		1	3			1	1_3	5	5					5										3	4	$^2 4$
F12		1_3				4			2	2						$^2 4$	1_3	4	1_3	5							5	5
M7	5	5	5	5	3		5	1		1		5	$^2 4$	$^2 4$			3	2							1_3	4		
F13	5	1			5	3		1				5								3				3	1_3	5		
F14	5		5	2	5	3		5	1		5												1	3	4	1_3		
F15		5	4		3	4	5	1		4	1		2	2	3					2	3	5		1_3	4	5	5	
F16	5	5	4	2	3			3	4			2	5		1	5	5	1		4			1	2	3	5	5	
M8	5	5			1_3				$^2 4$						5			1_3		5					1	5		
F17	3					4			1			4							3	1	4			1				
M8		5		5	3	2	2		$^2 4$		1		4						3	1				1			3	4
F18		5							1		4	2	1_3	3						2				1_3				5
M10		5	5			4		5	5	5		4	$^4 2$						3	1	2		5	1_3		3	1	
Σ1-2	1	4	9	4	2	2	3	0	3	8	2	2	8	10	1	4	5	1	3	6	4	1	1	7	1	1	0	4
Σ3-4	4	4	1	1	10	2	3	3	6	1	1	1	7	5	1	0	4	0	5	8	6	4	1	4	4	4	1	5
Σ1-4	5	8	10	5	8	4	6	3	9	7	1	3	15	15	0	4	9	1	8	14	10	5	2	11	3	3	1	9
Σ5	6	13	4	4	1	3	3	2	3	2	3	9	3	2	4	2	3	6	1	1	2	2	7	1	0	5	7	9

impose even the second choices for question 1 on the sociogram in FIGURE 1.

DIRECTIONS: Though I should like to avoid it, I am required to give you a grade at the termination of the course, and this is a reasonable expectation of me. Through the years I have noted from both research evidence and informal observations that the students' impression of each other helped me assign grades more accurately and fairly. Usually, they had information about each other which I did not have that enabled me to assign grades more fairly and to describe them more accurately for the Office of Teacher Placement. Therefore, I solicit your assistance. For questions 1 through 4, please list three names for each question. For question 5 you may list as many names as you wish; you may also answer it with the word "none."

1. If you felt that you needed assistance in preparing for the final examination, whom would you choose first to help you? ———————————; ——————————; ——————————

2. If you wanted to invite the entire class to help you, but were unable to arrange a place for the entire group, which three would you leave out? ————————; ————————; ————————

3. If you had a problem with which you felt you had to get help and were forced to select someone from this class, to whom would you turn first? ————————; ————————; ————————

4. If you had a problem with which you felt you had to get help and were forced to go through the entire class in order to obtain help, to whom you turn last? ————————; ————————;

5. Perhaps there are some in this class whom you do not know well enough to know how you really feel about them. Who falls into this category? ——————————————————————

In contrast, FIGURE 2 analyzes the relationship among all the choices for all five items for this guidance class, through the use of a matrix. Since many teachers do not know how to construct a matrix table, directions are listed below:

1. Find a piece of graph paper with at least as many rows and columns as there are pupils involved.

2. Arrange the pupils' names in some order that makes sense to you—e.g., the order in which they appear in your roll book.

3. Copy the names along the left margin and across the top of the paper—moving from top to bottom along the left margin and from left to right across the top of the page.

4. Let the vertical column be the choosers and record the choices for each pupil in the row to the right of his name.

In FIGURE 2, letters were used in place of names, in order to keep confidences; they merely identify the sex of the students. Let us use F3 (the third female in the list) as an example. She chose F2, F11, and F13 on question 1; M4, F14, and F15 on question 2; F12, M7, and F13 on question 3; M1, M4, and M9 on question 4, and F1, F16, and M10 on question 5. For the work copy, the instructor recorded the responses to questions 1 and 3 in black, 2 and 4 in red, and 5 in green. Here the positive items are recorded in roman type, the negative are recorded in bold face type, and the "5's" are recorded in italic type.

From the summary at the bottom of FIGURE 2 we can see that the stars were F3, M2, F13, and M8. F3 and M8, who received most of the positive choices on question 1, both did very well on the midterm examination. (The sociometric choices were made just before the final.) M8 also did very well on the final examination, but F3 did not do so well on it. F2 did better on both examinations than either F3 or M8. F13 was frequently chosen on both questions 1 and 3, and she did very well on both examinations.

The most rejected were F7 and F8. The fact that they received the lowest grades on both examinations suggests that fellow students accurately assessed their mastery of the subject matter. The instructor also reported that one of the two found it very difficult to relate to the other students. Though the members of this class were generally friendly, the instructor described five of the six most often named on question 4 as either shy or indifferent to classmates. One (M10) of the five was frequently named as an isolate. The person most often named as an isolate was F2; she was the top student on both examinations, but she participated in the class discussion only once.

WHO'S WHO TEST

Though this technique, sometimes called the "guess who" test, differs from the sociometric test, the same general principles apply to its development and use. Instead of choosing a classmate with some particular activity in mind, pupils are asked to name classmates with particular characteristics. Listed below are some sample questions:

Who tries to please everyone?
Who is a good storyteller?
Who works hard but still makes poor grades?
Who gets along well with everyone?
Who learns a lot more easily than most?
Who does well in school without trying very hard?
Who gives up easily when things do not go well?
Who learns mathematics very easily?
Who finds mathematics very difficult?
Who usually works and plays by himself?
Who gets his feelings hurt easily?
Who doesn't like school?
Who stands up for his own rights without becoming rude?
Who is good at planning things?
Who is good at helping you with your homework in arithmetic?
Who is always showing off?
Who can be trusted with a secret?
Who is always friendly and considerate?
Who is always cheerful and happy?
Who is often unhappy?

Kuhlen and Collister used this sociometric method in their study of pupils who failed to finish high school. They said,

> The eventual drop-outs represent a group of children who are physically unattractive, poorly groomed, lacking in social know-how, shy, withdrawing and unhappy; in short, they are personally and socially maladjusted individuals.[13]

Pupils often have information about each other that the teacher doesn't know, and they are willing to share it with their teacher when they feel that he will use it to help the pupils. For example, at the beginning of the year it is helpful for an elementary teacher to know what subjects pupils find difficult or for a high school teacher to identify those pupils who find his subject difficult. Even pupils who do well on achievement tests may feel that they are not good in certain subjects. Knowing this, the teacher can take account of this fact and try to provide experiences to change the self-image.

13 *Op. cit.*, p. 646.

Finally, the technique can be used to identify leaders, pupils with special interests and hobbies, and those who can serve as teacher's assistants in pupil-centered teaching.

Some teachers ask pupils to write one or two names beside every question in the test; others permit each pupil to record as many names as he wishes—or "none" when he cannot think of anybody who fits a particular description. When the teacher involves the pupils in developing items for the test, only those items that describe some pupils are usually included in the test. Under such circumstances it is quite appropriate to encourage pupils to write at least one name beside every question.

THE SOCIAL ACCEPTANCE SCALE

This technique was developed by the Evaluation Division of the Bureau of Educational Research at Ohio State University [14] with the cooperation of a group of elementary teachers in Ohio. After the teacher has explained his reason for collecting the information and has answered the pupils' questions, he provides each youngster with the class roll and asks him to follow these directions:

1. Write 1 in front of your own name.

2. Write 2 in front of the name of every pupil whom you would like to have as a very close friend.

3. Write 3 in front of the name of every pupil whom you would like to have as a good friend.

4. Write 4 in front of the name of every pupil who is not a friend, but who you feel is all right.

5. Write 5 in front of the name of every pupil whom you do not know.

6. Finally, write 6 in front of all the names that are left.

As with other sociometric methods, the data obtained by use of the social acceptance scale can be plotted on a matrix table, with choosers listed along the left side as usual, and each pupil's ratings of his classmates entered along his row. From numbers 2, 3, and 4 the teacher learns the degree of acceptance of one pupil for another; the prevalence of 5's identifies isolates, and 6's identify the rejected.

For both the sociometric test and the who's who test, a teacher can give each question a positive or negative sign and compute an algebraic score for each pupil, as was suggested for the data in

14 Louis Raths, "Evidence Relating to the Validity of Social Acceptance Tests," *Educational Research Bulletin*, XXVI (1947), 141–60.

FIGURE 2. Although he also can obtain an algebraic score for each pupil on the social acceptance scale, he will have to assign some value to each item to do so: e.g., 3 points for each "2"; 2 points for each "3"; 1 for each "4"; and -3 for each "6." When such weights are assigned, item "5" is usually used only for identifying isolates, as it was in constructing Figure 2. Since item "5" does not seem to fit on the acceptance-rejection continuum, this seems quite proper.

Staff Reports

THREE techniques that teachers often use in describing personality development are the anecdotal record, the case-conference summary, and the pupil-rating sheet. Two factors determine the worth of such reports: the staff member's ability to observe accurately, and his ability to communicate what he observes.

ANECDOTAL RECORD

While a teacher is willing, in special cases, to write a complete case study of a child, he usually does not have time to write such reports for every pupil. The anecdotal record, therefore, is the most effective technique for obtaining a teacher's observations of a pupil's behavior in specific situations. The 3″ × 5″ card is a convenient form for a teacher to use to report these observations. He can record the pupil's name and a description of the pupil's behavior on one side of the card and, on the other side, his interpretation of the pupil's behavior, his own name, and the date. Such a report enables others to analyze both the description of the behavior and the interpretation of it, and then to make their own independent judgments using both. With little effort the teacher can file the card in the pupil's cumulative folder, preferably in a special pocket for these anecdotes inside the folder. The cards are best arranged in chronological order so that one may trace the development of behavior patterns in studying the anecdotes.

Teachers may find the following suggestions useful in writing anecdotes about a child over a period of time:

—The observer should try to know himself, to understand how his own personal needs and biases influence what he notices and records as significant behavior.
—He should describe the setting in which he observed the child.

—He should record what the child does and says in as much detail as possible, relating especially those events that reflect how the child sees himself and his problems. He should try to keep a running account of the events in the order in which they occur. Whenever possible, the observer should also note the actions of others that seem to be related to the child's behavior.

—He should observe the child in many different situations—in the classroom, in the lunchroom, in the halls, on the playground, at school parties, in the community, and in the home. He should observe the child at work and at play, with peers, subordinates, and superiors. He should observe the child during different periods of the day.

—The observer should describe typical behavior as well as unusual behavior. It is important to know what the child does in a familiar setting as well as what he does in a problem scene.

—Most observers find that they need to make some notes while they are observing. Teachers who are carrying on another activity while they observe must make very sketchy notes. However, even sketchy notes help eliminate errors.

—Observers should remember that the record of a single incident tells little about the child, but that a collection of reports kept over a period of time by several good observers reveals a significant pattern in the child's development.

When Mrs. Barker (a high school counselor) introduced the use of anecdotal records in her school, she left a pack of 3″ × 5″ cards on every teacher's desk and explained how they should be used. Because she kept the cumulative records in her office, which was convenient for faculty members to pass on leaving the building, she suggested that they leave anecdotes there. Nevertheless, she found that she still had to go to the teachers for information when following up certain cases. For example, Mrs. Barker requested the assistance of the high school guidance committee in studying Ralph. Following that meeting she received progress reports from all of the boy's teachers except Harold Wilson. Mrs. Barker's conversation with Mr. Wilson shows how she used the opportunity to teach him how to write anecdotal reports.

Stopping by his classroom before the students entered the building one morning, Mrs. Barker asked, "Harold, how is Ralph doing in social studies?"

Mr. Wilson replied briefly, "Better."

Mrs. Barker waited, but seeing that his mind was on other things, she asked again, "In what ways is he doing better?"

"He says he is able to keep up with his assignments now. He read a historical novel this semester, and that's something for him. He got a B on his last examination," said Mr. Wilson more fully. After a moment Mr. Wilson added, "He told me he had never had a B in any high school course outside of his mathematics before that examination."

Mrs. Barker was pleased. "That's real progress for Ralph." Then she added, "You know, that last remark of yours would make a good anecdote for the cumulative folder. Could you put it on this card? Then it can be shared with others who are trying to help Ralph." Mr. Wilson agreed. As Mrs. Barker left him at his class door, she added, "If you think of some special help he needs, it would be a good idea to write that on the card too."

Through such individual contacts Mrs. Barker helped the teachers learn how to observe students and write reports that other colleagues could use.

Both counselors and teachers find it difficult to record what the child does and says in a particular setting, without also relating how they felt about the behavior. Staff members have become so accustomed to evaluating child behavior that only with great effort can they separate the descriptions from the evaluations; sometimes, indeed, it seems that they record only their interpretations. In such cases, those who read the reports cannot possibly know the basis for the judgments.

Teachers' and counselors' own personal values, needs, and interests influence their selection and perception of the events they describe; hence, they may describe the same child very differently. Sometimes these differences can be accounted for by the fact that the child was observed in quite different settings. It is important, therefore, that the report describe precisely what the pupil did in a given situation, and that the description of the behavior be separated from the interpretation of it.

The writing of a good report is complicated by another matter: the observer is usually doing something else while he is observing the child. He may be teaching a class, or at least part of a class, while he observes one pupil. He may be administering a test, or he may be conducting an interview. It takes special effort, under such circumstances, to record accurately what the child says and does; it takes even more skill to detect how the child feels about himself, his problems, and the people around him. Nevertheless, many teachers and counselors have found that they can do this complicated job.

To report child behavior well, the observer must know what to look for, where to look for it, and how to recognize it. Practice with real cases and assistance from others are required to improve observations and to report them with greater accuracy. Cooperative effort on the part of the entire school staff is the best approach to this problem. Since everyone on the staff will not be interested in improving the quality of his reports, small faculty discussion groups can be organized by the principal or the counselor, or such groups may spring from the building guidance committee's need for more useful reports.

Teachers in such discussion groups read one another's reports, trying to determine whether interpretations are kept separate from the facts. When necessary, the readers suggest to the writer how the report may be rewritten so as to separate facts from opinions. Whenever the readers discover an interpretation not supported by observed facts, they ask what the writer saw or heard that led him to make that judgment. Then the writer adds these facts to his report, subordinating the interpretations to the data.

The faculty discussion groups, always helpful, can be especially so when the teachers in one group all know and report on one child; such an arrangement allows them to help the child, in a concerted manner, at the same time that they work to improve their reports. Also, the differences in their reporting of one child highlight strongly the problems of good report-writing.

Early in their study the members of these groups learn that they all need help. As a matter of fact, members of the staff must recognize their need for help, want help, and trust one another before they will discuss frankly each other's reporting errors. Voluntary participation and the leader's acceptance of members' errors without harsh judgments are important in creating the necessary permissive climate.

A counselor may invite prospective members of groups that are being organized to improve observation reports to attend a meeting in which he uses one functioning group for demonstration purposes. The demonstration group takes the first ten or fifteen minutes to analyze one or two of their reports,[15] and then the counselor involves

15 In such meetings, of course, the reports studied would be duplicated, projected on a screen, or copied on the blackboard.

the entire audience in evaluating the demonstration group's procedures. He then divides the entire group into study groups, each of which works on the same report with the help of the counselor and the members of the demonstration group. Finally, after ten or fifteen minutes of such work, the entire group reassembles to discuss the report and to raise further questions on the procedure. Thus, the counselor may initiate a number of these study groups at a single staff meeting.

The following two reports are brief examples of those that might be used by a counselor in initiating study groups:

Case 1 was written by a sixth-grade teacher:

Jane is a very bright girl. She figures out how to do her problems very quickly. She is usually the first one to finish her work. Just the same there are too many computational errors on her arithmetic paper for someone with her ability. Instead of checking her work for errors, she talks to her neighbors and reads mystery stories. All she wants to do is finish her work so she can play.

Case 2 was written by a fifth-grade teacher:

I watched Jimmy for the fifteen minutes just prior to the morning recess. He read from his geography book for about ten minutes. During this period he looked at the clock several times. Twice I saw him looking at Carol, who ignored him. The last few minutes he looked at his spelling words. He didn't do anything wrong, but he didn't accomplish anything either. And he needs to do so much work on his spelling.

First, how can the sixth-grade teacher's report be improved? In what ways did he fail to discriminate between what he observed and what he thought about his observations? Group discussion might reveal that the following questions would need answers before this report could be rewritten:

—How did he know that Jane was a bright girl?
—How many pupils finished their work ahead of Jane?
—On what evidence did he conclude that she made too many errors?
—How does he know that she wants to finish quickly so that she can play?

As a result of questions like these, the sixth-grade teacher's revised report reads as follows:

Jane was the first one to complete her assignment again today. In checking her work, I found seven errors. While she frowned when I asked her to redo these seven problems, she did the problems over and corrected her mistakes.

When we studied the sample problem in our new work, she was one of four who volunteered to demonstrate how to do the new work. According to our test scores she is one of the two or three brightest children in the class: Binet I.Q. is 129; California Test of Mental Maturity I.Q. is 134. When I came around to check her work, she was reading a mystery. (This happens frequently.)

Several times during the hour I noted that she spoke to both Jack and Sally.

Interpretation: My own feeling is that she is a very bright girl who would rather play than do her work as well as she can. She needs to improve her work habits.

In the second version of this report we find the data that justify the teacher's original judgments. We also have the facts so that we can make our own judgments.

Similarly, the following questions would have to be answered before Case 2, above, could be revised:

—What made the teacher think that Carol ignored Jimmy?
—What caused Jimmy's teacher to conclude that Jimmy did not accomplish anything?
—What proportion of the words does Jimmy usually spell correctly?
—What is the most efficient way for Jimmy to study his spelling?
—Why does the teacher think that this method is most efficient for the boy?

With the answers to these questions at hand, the teacher could substitute facts for opinions and rewrite the report. If the teacher did not know the answers to certain of these questions, then he would list them as questions to be answered through further study of the child. Finally, he should list his opinions and interpretations as a separate part of the report.

In addition to improving the anecdotes, these in-service education experiences increase staff awareness of individual differences among pupils, help the staff better to understand themselves, and improve their working relationships with colleagues.

CASE-CONFERENCE SUMMARY

Even where a school has a guidance committee whose members provide leadership for child study groups, the groups do not always record for future use what they learn. Reports of the case conferences should become a part of the child's cumulative record. Every guidance committee should elect a secretary to be responsible for making a record of the following:

—What did we learn about the child?
—What were the positive factors around which we might build a remedial program?
—What responsibilities did we assign to staff members selected to help the child?

Where we find the type of guidance organization described in Chapter 6, the guidance committee is responsible for conducting child study sessions. In other schools faculty members conduct child study sessions less systematically. In the latter situations, either the principal or the counselor usually arranges for case conferences whenever a staff member wants assistance in helping a pupil. Here, too, someone should be assigned responsibility for recording answers to the questions above.

PUPIL-RATING SHEETS

Although anecdotal records and case-conference summaries produce very important evidence for appraising personal adjustment, other evidence is needed from the staff to procure periodic assessment for all of the pupils. A carefully constructed pupil-rating sheet may be used for this purpose.

Where rating sheets have been used most effectively for preserving and communicating information about pupils, the persons who use the rating sheets have cooperated in designing them. If, for example, a rating sheet is to be used to evaluate pupil growth for parents, and at the same time to preserve a record of growth for the cumulative folder, then both parents and teachers should participate in the development of the rating sheet. This participation may be achieved by (1) asking all parents what questions they would like to have answered concerning the children's growth in school; (2) asking teachers what evidence of growth should be evaluated periodically for the cumulative folder; and (3) asking both groups to suggest names for an advisory committee to help develop the rating sheet.

After a parent-teacher committee has been appointed by the

principal, the committee should make a list of the questions for which parents and teachers would like answers. Upon careful examination of this list, they often discover that they have too many questions, and unnecessary duplication among questions. Though the members of the committee should try to keep every question, and in so far as possible keep the original wording, so that parents realize the staff is trying to provide answers to their questions, the committee should also consider whether the teachers can complete the rating sheets with reasonable effort. If a teacher can obtain the information he needs to complete the rating sheet by careful observation of his pupils in everyday contacts in school, then expectations have been reasonable.

When the committee has agreed on the final list of questions, they should prepare multiple-choice responses for each question. One way to do this is to have the teacher write brief answers to each question for each pupil for the first report, and then select, from all the answers for each question for all the pupils, the common responses; these can be used as the multiple-choice responses. Since this method tends to be too time-consuming for a high school staff, common responses have been obtained from them by two other methods: (1) having only homeroom teachers prepare these brief descriptions for pupils in their homerooms or (2) having each teacher describe only certain pupils who are selected by random methods. In either case it is essential that all who write descriptions focus their attention on *describing* behavior rather than on judging it. In other words they should avoid the use of terms like "excellent," "good," "average," and "poor" in describing a pupil's behavior. These general terms mean different things to different people; consequently, more precise language must be used to convey the intended meaning of the observer. In the final analysis, every multiple-choice response to every question should be evaluated in terms of whether its answer has a direct bearing on the question and whether it was stated in behavioral terms. Two such items are included here:

1. How effectively does this pupil work with his classmates?
   a. He assumes leadership when he is sure of himself.
   b. He avoids leadership when the work involves new tasks.
   c. He expects others to do things his way.
   d. He likes to help others.
   e. His assistance is often sought by others.

    f. He prefers to work alone.

    g. He stands up for his own rights without being rude.

    h. He tends to be pushed around by others.

    i. He tends to get angry when things don't go his way.

    j. He tends to lean on others.

    k. He tries to please everyone.

    l. (Others) _____

_____

_____

2. To what extent does this pupil assume responsibility for doing his schoolwork?

    a. Even when he is closely supervised, he often fails to complete his assignments.

    b. He completes assignments when closely supervised.

    c. He completes his assignments without supervision.

    d. Occasionally he will do special projects when he has completed his assignments.

    e. Though he must be carefully supervised in most of his work, he will complete his assignments in _____ without supervision, and will even do special projects in that subject.

    f. Usually he does more than what is expected.

    g. (Others) _____

_____

_____

To avoid a ranking of responses from good to bad, the responses should be arranged alphabetically for each question. Teachers may write in their own answers after "others" whenever the responses fail adequately to describe the child as they see him. Whenever a response appears regularly in the "other" category, it should be added as a new response.

If the school is using letter grades—and most high schools and many elementary schools do use them—teachers must of course continue to report letter grades, but may use the rating sheet to supplement them. If teachers are giving letter grades on character traits, they may be able to substitute the rating sheet for that part of the report card.

One carefully prepared rating each semester should be sufficient. More frequent reports tend to require so much time that teachers are forced to make superficial evaluations. Where an administrator asks the teachers to make one report each semester, he should let them do the reports at a leisurely pace throughout the last half of the semester. With the forms before them and the questions in mind, they can pencil in notes throughout this nine-week period.

Elementary-school teachers should prepare the original and one carbon copy. Since secondary-school teachers see so many pupils, only an original should be required from them, and someone, preferably a clerk, should be assigned the responsibility for transposing all the secondary-school teachers' evaluations to an original and a carbon, mailing the original to parents and filing the carbon in the cumulative folder. By retaining a carbon copy of each pupil's periodic appraisal, the staff acquires a periodic assessment of growth for every pupil.

Rating sheets of this type encourage the staff to record their observations on a standard form that lends itself to statistical analysis. When carefully constructed, a rating sheet also can suggest significant behavior that should be observed and reported.

The behavior inventory is another similar technique that can be used for this purpose. Heretofore the behavior inventory has been used primarily for research, but recently it has been used to obtain descriptions of pupil behavior in appraising self-actualization in school. Listed below are some items from an instrument used in research on group counseling of gifted underachievers.

—He gives up easily when he is not sure he can do the work.
—He is not interested in others and what they think.
—He is very patient with others.
—Usually he believes that things will turn out all right.

Important other people, such as parents, teachers, classmates, and friends, are asked to indicate the extent to which each statement describes a given pupil at a given time. The observer is required to select one of five responses on every item; the choices vary from (1) "This statement describes him very well. This is just the way he is," to (5) "This statement does not describe him. He rarely or never acts this way."

Appraising personal adjustment is very difficult. Even the best methods available to teachers and counselors are not very satisfactory. Nevertheless, teachers and counselors must try to understand their pupils and help their pupils understand themselves. To accomplish these objectives they must choose with care the techniques that they elect to use.

SUGGESTED INVENTORIES AND CHECK-LISTS

1. Minnesota Counseling Inventory (R. F. Berdie and W. L. Layton), The Psychological Corporation, 1957.

This was an effort to adapt the Minnesota Multiphasic Inventory for use with normal students. It consists of 413 self-descriptive statements to which high school and college freshmen are required to make a true-false response. Seven scores are provided: family relationships, social relationships, emotional stability, conformity, adjustment to reality, mood, leadership, and validity. Intelligent use and interpretation require some psychological sophistication.

2. Mooney Problem Check-List (R. L. Mooney; L. V. Gordon, co-author on college and adult forms), The Psychological Corporation, 1950.

There also are forms for junior high and senior high school students. Anastasi described this check-list as follows: "One of the clearest examples of content validation is provided by the Mooney Problem Check-List. Designed chiefly to identify problems for group discussion or individual counseling, this check-list drew its items from written statements of problems submitted by about 4000 high school students, as well as from case records, counseling interviews, and similar sources." [16]

3. SRA Youth Inventory (H. H. Remmers, B. Shimberg, and A. J. Drucker), grades 7–12, 1949–56, and SRA Junior Inventory (H. H. Remmers and R. H. Bauernfiend), grades 4–8, 1951, Science Research Associates.

Except for the use of different sized boxes that pupils are required to check to indicate the magnitude of their problems, this instrument is very similar to the Mooney.

SUGGESTED READINGS

1. ANASTASI, ANNE. *Psychological Testing.* New York: The Macmillan Company, 1961.

Chapter 18.

a] What are some of the unique features of the Minnesota Multiphasic Inventory?

16 Anne Anastasi, *Psychological Testing* (New York: The Macmillan Company, 1961), p. 494.

b] How may tests be constructed to minimize man's tendency to describe himself in a socially desirable way?

c] What are some of the common deficiencies of personality tests and inventories?

2. CRONBACH, LEE J. *Essentials of Psychological Testing.* New York: Harper & Row, Publishers, 1960.

Chapters 15, 16, 17.

a] What are the chief weaknesses of self-reporting devices?

b] What is meant by a dynamic picture of an individual?

c] How can one overcome the weaknesses of self-reporting devices?

d] For what purposes may a counselor use adjustment inventories?

e] Why are rating sheets often used in preference to written descriptions of behavior?

3. GRONLUND, NORMAN E. *Sociometry in the Classroom.* New York: Harper & Row, Publishers, 1959.

This book provides teachers with the principles of sociometric testing and suggests ways of using sociometric test data to understand interpersonal relationships within the classroom. Chapters 1, 2, and 3.

a] What can a teacher learn from a sociometric test?

b] What basic limitations are inherent in sociometric testing?

c] What are the advantages of using a matrix table?

Studying Interests and Aptitudes

THIS CHAPTER will introduce the prospective counselor to his future responsibilities for using interest inventories and special aptitude tests to help students make vocational choices, and will acquaint the rest of the staff with what they should expect from their counselors in this respect. Those who become counselors will augment the necessarily brief treatment of this topic here with further graduate work in tests and measurement.

Most counselors try to help a student assess his interests and aptitudes when they are asked to assist him with vocational and educational plans. Some look upon vocational counseling as primarily information-giving; others believe that every problem is a personal one for which the counselor must take cognizance of the student's underlying feelings. To be most effective, the counselor must recognize and deal with feelings as well as provide information.

Typically a high school student cannot remember when he first said what he would like to be when he grows up. Even in his play he assumed occupational roles. Sometimes he was a cowboy, at other times a policeman, a fireman, a doctor, a storekeeper, an actor, a teacher, a carpenter, a mechanic, or a mailman. Whom he impersonated was determined by the breadth of his experience and the attitudes he had toward people in specific jobs. Long before he was ready to choose an occupation, he speculated about success and recognition in adult jobs.

Many of today's youth will earn a living in occupations that are unknown to us now. Technological changes will force other workers to learn new skills even though they remain in the same job. Therefore, a young person must not only select an occupation with care, but he must also learn how to analyze his job skills so that he may readily adapt himself to new responsibilities.

Increasingly, school counselors are coming to realize that choice of occupation is not just one decision but a series of decisions that an individual makes as he matures and adjusts to a changing society. Thus it is imperative that the student understand himself and his aspirations, and gradually improve his ability to assess available opportunities so that he may use these insights to make the best choices for himself and society.

Far too many adults failed to make satisfactory educational and vocational plans while they were still in school; later they discovered that they lacked the training required for the positions to which they aspired. Often they found that they could not afford to quit a job to seek more appropriate employment or to train for another position, especially if they were married and had families. Many who have fallen into this trap left high school before graduating. Others graduated but, instead of studying themselves and the jobs most appropriate for them, they took the first job they were able to secure. Some eventually quit their jobs to seek more appropriate employment, but even they did not find satisfying jobs because they lacked an understanding of themselves and a knowledge of occupations.

Self-Appraisal

WHEN a student seeks a counselor's assistance in developing vocational and educational plans, the counselor should realize that the student probably has some impressions of what his own interests, abilities, and aptitudes are. Whether these impressions are accurate or not, the counselor must take account of them. One way he can do so is to encourage student participation in test interpretation, as suggested in Chapter 6. Another is to encourage the student to make a careful self-appraisal. Such an appraisal can stimulate the study of interests as well as the study of occupational skills. Listed below are some examples of questions for which a student should be encouraged to seek answers:

A. How do I feel about the various school subjects which I have studied?
   1. Which subjects have I liked best?
      a. In which of these have I done my best work? In which have I done my poorest work?
      b. Which of these subjects were easiest for me? Which were most difficult for me?
      c. How good was my best work and how poor was my poorest work?
   2. Which subjects have I liked least?
      a. In which of these have I done my best work? In which have I done my poorest work?
      b. Which of these subjects were easiest for me? Which of these subjects were most difficult for me?
      c. How good was my best work and how poor was my poorest work?
   3. For the subjects in which I did my poorest work, in which could I have done substantially better work?
   4. Were there any subjects which I never tried because I was convinced that I would do poorly in them?
B. How do I feel about my work-experiences?
   1. Which jobs, or parts of jobs, did I like best? In which of these did I do my best work? In which did I do my poorest work?
   2. Which jobs, or parts of jobs, did I like least? In which of these did I do my best work? In which of these did I do my poorest work?
   3. Which jobs, or parts of jobs, were most difficult for me?
   4. While working, did I learn about other jobs that appealed to me? What made these other jobs attractive to me?

5. While working, did I learn about other jobs that did *not* appeal to me? Why were these jobs not attractive to me?
6. Were there any jobs that I know about that I would not want to try because I am certain that I would do them poorly?
C. In what extra-class activities did I meet with unusual success? In what vocation could I use these abilities?
D. What do I believe to be my strongest traits? What do I believe to be my weakest traits?

There is one primary reason that such a self-appraisal should precede the study of preferred occupations: some students see themselves as having the interests, abilities, and aptitudes required for success in these occupations whether they really have them or not. Success in the preferred occupations can mean so much to a student that he will deny certain weaknesses. Before he realizes that certain weaknesses may influence his chances for success in preferred occupations, he can describe himself more accurately and accept these weaknesses.

Another important point to convey to a student is that he may change. New interests and job skills develop out of new school- and work-experiences. Certain academic weaknesses can be corrected with remedial instruction. Other characteristics are changed by counseling. Though a self-appraisal is useful in helping a student see himself as he is today, he should expect to reappraise his interests, abilities, and aptitudes when he is called upon to make new decisions in the future.

As young people study themselves, most of them discover abilities and aptitudes of which they were not fully aware. At the least, they discover new relationships among various abilities, aptitudes and interests, and frequently they also discover limitations. Everyone can understand why students find it difficult to accept limitations or weaknesses which conflict with their perceptions of themselves, but sometimes students also have difficulty in accepting strengths which conflict with their perceptions of themselves.

The latter was Steve's problem. He had always pictured himself as a good athlete, and he was. He had assumed that musical activities were for boys who were not athletes. Then the music teacher heard him singing in the locker room after football practice. Needing another good first tenor in the boys' glee club, he asked Steve to try out. Steve had had no formal training in music in the rural school from which he came and did not wish to expose his ignorance in music. Anyway, there certainly were no football players singing tenor in that glee club. He wondered what the other fellows would think about his singing. Had the music teacher not accepted Steve's negative reactions, encouraged him to meet the glee club before making a decision, and finally given him special help, Steve's singing talent would never have been developed.

Gilbert had difficulty accepting the fact that he had good mental ability. Although both of his parents were college graduates, his father was a very successful farmer, and Gilbert wanted to farm with him. While his father never discouraged the boy from farming, neither had he encouraged him. He always stressed the advantages of a college education, and said that Gilbert should find what work he liked best and prepare for it in college. So Gilbert went to college, and, during his second semester, elected to major in electrical engineering. He worked hard but did only mediocre work. This disappointed him, especially since he had ranked second in his high school class. Eventually, he heard about the college counseling center and went there for assistance. There he learned that all his scholastic-aptitude and achievement-test scores were high. Because he questioned the mental-test scores, he was given an opportunity to take another mental test. When he learned that he also ranked high on this test, he said, "This makes me unhappy. I don't even have a good excuse for doing poorly." With the aid of a counselor over a period of several months, he discovered that he had unconsciously done poorly in order that he might drop out of college to farm. Once he understood this, he changed his major from engineering to agriculture, and was able to accept his ability and do good college work.

During the process of self-appraisal, or as they seek information on specific occupations, students often discover the need for additional information about themselves. Much of this information can be obtained from tests, but its usefulness depends on the counselor's skill and the student's receptivity. A counselor's patient efforts to understand a student, including his feelings, conveys acceptance of him and respect for his integrity and judgment. Even when a student seeks information about himself he may not accept it. The counselor's task is to help him obtain the information which he recognizes he needs, help him examine what it means to him, and help him accept it. A student can be helped to understand himself only to the extent that he will permit himself to be helped; he will use only that information which he accepts and integrates.

Interest Inventories

BY THE time most students are sixteen, interest inventories can be used to classify their responses into patterns that help predict *job satisfaction*. These instruments help students reveal their feelings about people, activities, and occupations. Then the individual's responses can be compared with those of persons who are successful in specific occupations. The discovery of the relationship between interests and specific occupations also can be used to motivate the study of occupations as well as further self-appraisal.

Cronbach believes that interest inventories are peculiarly well adapted to vocational counseling:

The student expects his interests to be considered, and he is not threatened by the questionnaire as he might be by personality or ability tests. The interpretation, when given, carries considerable force, because the student can see that he is looking at himself in a mirror, that he is only receiving an analysis of what he himself has said.[1]

Measured interests may be supplemented by interests manifested in an individual's hobbies, his out-of-school activities, his academic record, his extra-class activity record, and his employment record. Special themes, such as picture stories and the autobiography of the future, also may reveal interests and commitments to values which have relevance for vocational choice.

If we accept the idea that the counselor must try to understand the client as the client sees himself, then the counselor must accept the client's stated as well as measured interests. Berdie found that:

Expressed interests and measured interests are far from identical. In terms of common elements, perhaps no more than between 25 and 50 percent of the factors associated with one are associated with the other . . . In no occupational area, however, was there close enough agreement between measured interest and self-estimated interests to suggest that coun-

1 FROM *Essentials of Psychological Testing* by Lee J. Cronbach, p. 432. Copyright © 1960 by Lee J. Cronbach. Reprinted with permission of Harper & Row, Publishers, Incorporated.

seling can be done on the basis of one or the other. As long as measured interests have a relevance for vocational satisfaction and as long as self-estimated interests play an important role in vocational deliberations of individuals, both types of interests must be considered.[2]

In using interest inventories, there is first the problem of when to introduce them in the development of vocational plans. Then there is the question of how to interpret them: some users believe that the counselor should call the client's attention to specific occupations from which he should achieve job satisfaction; others contend that the counselor should focus attention on the client's broad areas of interests.

Most school counselors favor the early assessment of vocational interests (after initial self-appraisal and exploration of stated interests) in the development of vocational and educational plans. As noted above, such assessment can be used to stimulate further self-appraisal and the study of occupations. Darley and Hagenah's summary of the research offers another justification for this procedure:

> The evidence points to the relatively early development of interest patterns—by age fifteen or sixteen—and comparative stability patterns thereafter . . . the evidence also indicates clearer differentiation of interests among the more able and more mature young people in our high schools and colleges.[3]

On the other hand, it should be noted that Darley and Hagenah [4] are two of the leaders in the field who are opposed to early use of data obtained from interest inventories. Their arguments against the early use of these data, and against relating the results to specific occupations, can be summarized briefly as follows: (1) without work-experience and knowledge of the occupations, students often have difficulty accepting the interest-test results; (2) students may get the impression that the counselor is ignoring their claimed interests; (3) it is difficult to translate the vocabulary of the world of work into the students' language; (4) when a student accepts the

2 Ralph F. Berdie, "Scores on Strong Vocational Interest Blanks and the Kuder Preference Record in Relation to Self Rating," *Journal of Applied Psychology,* XXXIV (1950), 49.

3 John G. Darley and Theda Hagenah, *Vocational Interest Measurement: Theory and Practice* (Minneapolis: University of Minnesota Press, 1955), pp. 195–97.

4 *Ibid.*

measured interests, he often assumes his ability to do the work in which he is interested; (5) at the expense of more important considerations, such practices encourage the student to consider such topics as opportunities, salaries, and training requirements too early in vocational planning; and (6) such practices fail to take account of faking in tests, changes in interests, and the fact that scoring keys are based on occupations as they were some time ago. As an alternative, these leaders recommend that

no reference be made to interest measurement until relatively late in the counseling process. Suppose, further, that the counselor permits the student to work through and verbalize the reasons for claimed choices. It may be that the student has done only superficial thinking about jobs, and that this fact itself is important to know. But the counselor may also discover the specific factors leading to the choices: information (or misinformation) regarding salary scales and "overcrowded" or "undercrowded" fields and job duties; satisfactions expected from work; self-estimates of strengths and weaknesses; evidences of family pressures or traditions dictating certain choices; self-estimates of the aspirations and motives that are operative in the choices; and evidence about life experiences to this date that have shaped the choices.[5]

Through their discussion of the use of interest inventories, Darley and Hagenah develop a good case for taking account of a client's feelings in interpreting interest inventories; they also recognize the need for helping clients obtain appropriate information. However, a counselor can note the problems they cite and still find interest inventories useful for helping a client identify groups of activities in which he has interests. Kuder Preference Record scores lend themselves best to this type of interpretation. The occupational grouping of interests developed for the Strong Vocational Interest Blank also contributes to this type of interpretation in terms of broad areas of interests. Although more research is needed to relate effectively these broad areas of interests to job families, these data can be used to stimulate students' thinking about choice of occupations and future vocational adjustment.

Important as it is for students to be aware of the implications of their broad areas of interests, many students will have to make a specific vocational choice when they drop out of high school or when they seek employment immediately after graduation. The

5 *Ibid.*, p. 197.

counselor must try to help these students identify jobs which will provide personal satisfaction, and at the same time make maximum use of their abilities and aptitudes. After allowing adequate time for discussion of their stated interests and of those personal problems that seem to be related to their choice of occupation, the counselor may use interest inventories to identify occupations for study and to stimulate further study of abilities and aptitudes.

The evidence on the relevance of measured interest for job satisfaction is summarized below by Donald Super and Anne Anastasi:

Inventoried interests are related to vocational development, for there is a strong tendency for people to enter and to remain in fields of work which provide outlets for their interests, and to leave inappropriate fields for more appropriate ones. Interest is related to success in occupations only under special conditions, when the congeniality of the activity is crucial to application; when, as in most occupations, motivation from other sources such as status or income needs can suffice, interest in the activity itself is not related to success. Vocational interest is important largely in determining direction and persistence of effort but not, apparently, the amount of effort.[6]

There is also extensive evidence to show that at higher levels of the occupational hierarchy (professional, managerial, etc.) job satisfaction is derived chiefly from intrinsic liking for work, while at lower levels there is increasing reliance on such extrinsic factors as pay, security, social contacts, and recognition as a person. The measurement of vocational interest patterns thus become less relevant as we go down the occupational hierarchy.[7]

STABILITY OF MEASURED INTERESTS

Super[8] found that interests begin to manifest themselves in adult vocational form in early adolescence, and that though they change in ways which are systematic for groups, they are still unpredictable for individuals during high school years. Ninth-grade boys are ready to consider problems of prevocational and vocational choice, but they lack readiness to make a vocational choice. Super also noted

6 Donald E. Super, *The Psychology of Careers* (New York: Harper & Row, Publishers, 1957), p. 224.

7 Anne Anastasi, *Psychological Testing* (New York: The Macmillan Company, 1961), p. 531.

8 Donald E. Super, "The Ninth Grade: Vocational Choice or Vocational Explanation," *Personnel and Guidance Journal*, XXXIX (1960), 106–09.

that Kuder scores changed more during high school years than did Strong scores.

George Mallison and William Crumbine [9] investigated the stability of Kuder scores between grades 9 and 12, and found considerable stability in the scores. For 80 percent of the students the highest area of interest at the ninth grade (70 percent for second highest and 52 percent for third highest) remained among the three highest at twelfth grade. However, because of the individual fluctuations, the researchers warn against making long-range plans on the basis of scores obtained from the Kuder in grade 9.

Frederick Herzberg and Arthur Bouton [10] investigated the stability of Kuder scores for high school students who attended college. Correlations for various scales ranged from .50 to .75. The mechanical scale was especially stable for boys. The social service scale tended to be the least stable, and the art scale the most stable.

E. L. Kelly [11] administered certain questionnaires (personality, value, attitude, and interest) to engaged couples between 1935 and 1938, and then readministered the questionnaire to the same couples in 1954. The Strong scores were the most stable.

Taken together, these findings suggest the possibility that for some men, there occurs an early (and perhaps premature) development of vocational interests characteristic of professional persons who work with and try to help people; this may lead to later disillusionment and a tendency to develop interest patterns more characteristic of persons who prefer to work with ideas and things rather than directly with other human beings.[12]

A pupil's interest-inventory scores may be unstable for a number of reasons. One is lack of maturity. The young person has not lived long enough and has not had varied enough experiences to crystallize his interests. Another is that the student may not be able to communicate his feelings through his responses to test items.

9 George G. Mallison and William M. Crumbine, "An Investigation of the Stability of Interests of High School Students," *Journal of Educational Research*, XLV (1952), 369–83.

10 Frederick Herzberg and Arthur Bouton, "A Further Study of the Stability of the Kuder Preference Record," *Educational and Psychological Measurement*, XIV (1954), 326–31.

11 E. L. Kelly, "Consistency of Adult Personality," *American Psychologist*, X (1955), 659–81.

12 *Ibid.*, p. 679.

Or he may assume different roles upon repeated administration of the inventory. This usually happens when a youngster has selected the occupation of an admired person, or an occupation with which he has associated prestige. Frequently he will develop a deep commitment to his model's occupation though he lacks awareness of the demands of the occupation. If during one administration of the test he responds to the items as he feels his model or a man in his chosen occupation would, and then, on a later administration, is able to respond as he really feels, significantly different scores may result. Where interest inventories are administered to the entire class with little or no orientation, variations in scores may be accounted for by sheer indifference and carelessness. Ability to comprehend the ideas in test items also may influence scores. Finally, differences between tests can account for differences in measured interests. For example, E. Robert Sinnett [13] concluded that Kuder scores may be largely a function of perception of self, while Strong scores may be largely a measure of identification with a job role. He believes that the Strong provides more information for the more complex jobs that are understood relatively late in life than it does for simple jobs understood early in life.

INTERPRETING INTEREST SCORES

Even when a student makes an appointment to have his interest-inventory scores interpreted, a counselor should not rush into the interpretation. Instead, the counselor should encourage the student to discuss his claimed interests, to estimate how he feels the interest inventory describes him, and to express his feelings about the interest inventory. Student participation is just as important here as it is for interpreting achievement- and mental-test scores.

When a counselor encourages student participation in test interpretation, he often discovers that the student did not understand the significance of the test results for himself while he was completing the interest inventory. (Better orientation to testing can prevent this problem for many.) A student also may react negatively to the forced choice feature of the Kuder, and need to discuss the rationale for this idea before he can accept the results. Interpretation of interest scores presents another problem: a student's failure

13 E. Robert Sinnett, "Some Determinants of Agreement Between Measured and Expressed Interests," *Educational and Psychological Measurements,* XVI (1956), 110–18.

to differentiate between interest in and aptitude for a vocation or avocation. This too can be detected by encouraging student participation in test interpretation. As the student discusses what the scores mean to him and how he feels about what he has learned about himself, the counselor can clarify what the test results mean.

Since the Kuder Preference Record is the most widely used interest test at the high school level, an eleventh-grade girl's scores on the Vocational-Form C have been selected for discussion here. Prior to interpreting the test the counselor examined the girl's cumulative folder. From it he learned that she is well liked, unusually mature, and responsible, that she learns as easily as most, that she did as well as most on an achievement-test battery which was given in September along with a mental test (all scores fell within the middle 50 percent of the national norm for high school juniors) and that her marks were mostly C, with occasional B's in English. Her percentile ranks for the ten Kuder scales were: 0–71, 1–2, 2–23, 3–78, 4–85, 5–12, 6–87, 7–18, 8–98, and 9–28. Prior to interpreting her test, the counselor checked her "V" score and used a table to convert her raw scores into stanines. (These were compared with the occupational families provided in the manual.)

Though he had no reason to question the validity of her scores (V = 43), he reviewed ways in which her scores could have been influenced by the conditions described above and gave her a chance to comment on them, and also encouraged her to discuss her plans. Among other things, she said that she hoped to marry early, but also had given some thought to the idea of becoming an elementary-school teacher. When she inquired about her interest scores, he said:

These scores will help you discover how much more you seem to like some things than other things. Frequently, this kind of study of interests can help you become acquainted with broad areas of interests and job families; it may also help you discover occupations which you could enjoy, but it will not help you decide whether you have the ability to do the work. Now I shall define each of the scale scores for you. If for any reason my definition doesn't make sense, please feel free to ask questions. [To the definitions provided in the manual he added several illustrations.] After I define each I would like you to indicate, with a check mark, where you think your score for the scale falls on the five parts of this line. When you have estimated your scores for all ten scales, then I will go back over them and tell you where the test-estimate agrees with your estimate and where it disagrees with your estimate.

Where the test agrees with your estimate I will merely report that fact, but where it disagrees I will add an "x" to indicate how the test describes you.

Listed below is an example:

OUTDOOR INTEREST

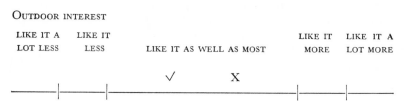

Obviously, her estimated scores agreed with the test-estimate on this scale. As a matter of fact, all of her estimates except those for scales 3 and 4 agreed with the test-estimates. In each of these instances she thought that she "liked it as well as most," whereas the test indicated that she "liked it more than most."

After they discussed her areas of most and least interest and the implications of these interests for her as she saw them, the counselor helped her compare her stanine scores for her entire profile with the profiles for the occupational families in the manual. In order to identify occupations from which she felt she could achieve job satisfaction, they selected the scales for which she felt she had most (4, 6, and 8) and least (1 and 5) interest and examined the lists of occupations included in the manual for these combinations of interests. From these lists she selected only "bookstore salesman" and "telephone operator." She also decided to keep "elementary-school teacher" on her list of preferred occupations. Before terminating the session, they discussed sources of information on these occupations, and scheduled the next interview.

Aptitude Tests

WHEN a person formulates or reevaluates his vocational and educational goals, he often raises questions about his chances for success in achieving these goals. The results of aptitude tests, along with nontest data obtained in a self-appraisal, can help him answer these questions.

Authors of tests have developed instruments to screen students who are seeking admission to the fields of art, music, law, medicine, and engineering, and to appraise applicants for clerical, assembly line, mechanical, and a variety of other industrial jobs. Some of these instruments have proven useful, and have been improved over the last quarter century. Others contribute so little to prediction that their use cannot be justified. Even high scores on the better instruments do not insure success; low scores, on the other hand, are fairly reliable in identifying poor risks for jobs and training programs.

Before deciding to offer a test to any student, the counselor should answer these questions to his own satisfaction:

Will this test help this particular student answer his questions? In addition to studying research findings and the claims made in the test manual, the counselor might do well to read and analyze the test items to discover for himself the relationship between the test data and job success, and also to become acquainted with the test so that he can prepare the student for the actual testing experience. Sometimes it is difficult for the counselor to obtain any conclusive research evidence on the reliability and validity of such tests. Frequently, the statements on validity fail to describe the work done by the employees whose job performances and test performances were correlated in obtaining the validity coefficient. A good description of the setting in which the test was validated is essential in order to assess the test's relevance for predicting a particular student's vocational success.

Are the tasks which are presented in the test appropriate for this student? A careful analysis of the actual test items may reveal that too many of the tasks require job experience, educational background, or maturity which the student does not have.

What subjects did the author use in establishing norms? National norms for a test have little meaning for the counselor unless he knows what subjects the author of that test used in building these norms. If the manual fails to describe the norm group, the counselor cannot interpret aptitude test scores intelligently; he must be able to compare the student's test performance with that of some carefully defined group of people whose job responsibilities have some relevance for the student.

Will I be able to interpret the test results in a meaningful way to the student? If the counselor is not trained to use the test, he may confuse, rather than help, the student. For the test data to be worthwhile, the student must integrate the test results with other known information about himself and his plans. To help the student do this, the counselor must understand the test thoroughly and know how to interpret it to the student.

Super states precisely what is needed in this connection:

> Tests for use in counseling should describe a person so that we can see him as he is at the time of testing; they should predict what he will be like and what he will do at some future date; they should be relatively timeless; and they should, like the people they test, be multipotential . . . They should tell what curricular and occupational groups he resembles, and how closely he resembles them. One of the purposes of testing is to get a picture of the person with whom one is dealing, to see to what degree he has a variety of psychological characteristics, where his relative strengths and weaknesses are, and how he compares in each of these characteristics with others who have had comparable experiences and have reached a comparable stage of development, or who are engaged in activities in which he might engage . . .[14]

Realizing what is needed, one could easily become discouraged with the instruments which we have to help youth assess their salable or potentially salable occupational assets. On the other hand, several promising aptitude batteries have been developed since World War II. Though we still need better validation of these instruments, they do represent a step forward. Business, industrial, and educational leaders have been doing an increasingly better job of defining the situation in which success is to be predicted and of using a combination of data to select persons for positions and training programs. Because intelligence is usually one of the important factors used in predicting success, it is fortunate that a number of promising new intelligence tests have been developed recently, and that new and better ones may soon be constructed. Readers also should take special note of the recent research and efforts to develop tests of creativity. Anastasi believes that this research is promising and that some of the forthcoming tests may even help identify research talent:

> It is too early to know what will be the final outcome of current research on the nature of creativity. One point appears to be fairly clear at this

14 Donald E. Super (ed.), *The Use of Multifactor Test Batteries in Guidance.* (Washington, D.C.: American Personnel and Guidance Association, 1958), p. 3.

time, however. Investigations of scientific talent are becoming increasingly concerned with creative abilities. Interest has shifted from the individual who is merely cautious, accurate and a critical thinker to one who also displays ingenuity, originality, and inventiveness. Thus creativity, long regarded as the prime quality in artistic production, is coming more and more to be recognized as a basis for scientific achievement as well. It is also likely that in the years ahead we shall see many new kinds of tests. The traditional emphasis on understanding and recall that has characterized intelligence and aptitude tests will probably give way to a more comprehensive approach with greater concentration on productive thinking.[15]

SUGGESTED INTEREST INVENTORIES

1. Kuder Preference Record—Vocational (G. F. Kuder), Science Research Associates, 1934–56 (grades 9–16 and adults).

   The Kuder Preference Record is one of the leading interest inventories. Originally Kuder began with a factor analysis of items in order to identify clusters of interests; these, in turn, were organized first into nine scales, and more recently into eleven scales—a verification scale and ten broad interest areas: outdoor, mechanical, computational, scientific, persuasive, artistic, literary, musical, social service, clerical. A masculinity-femininity score is also provided. This form is useful in helping students identify broad fields of work from which they may obtain job satisfaction. More recently, a new form (Kuder Preference Record—Vocational, 1956–58) was developed with occupational keys similar to the Strong.

2. Strong Vocational Interest Blank for Men (E. K. Strong), Consulting Psychologists Press, 1927–59 (age 17 and over).

   There is also another form of the test for women. This very successful test was developed on the assumption that those who have an interest pattern similar to successful men in a specific occupation will achieve job satisfaction from that occupation. Recently, occupational groupings of interests were developed in order to identify broad interest areas similar to those originally measured by the Kuder.

SUGGESTED GENERAL APTITUDE BATTERIES

1. Differential Aptitude Tests (G. K. Bennett, H. G. Seashore, and A. G. Wesman), Psychological Corporation, 1947–58.

   This battery was designed primarily for the counselor's use in helping high school students develop educational and vocational plans. It provides

15 Anne Anastasi, *Psychological Testing* (New York: The Macmillan Company, 1961), p. 420.

eight scores (verbal reasoning, numerical ability, abstract reasoning, space relations, mechanical reasoning, clerical speed and accuracy, spelling, and sentence structure) to measure abilities which seem to be related to job families and curricula. Though its authors have provided leadership for research on this battery and have developed an excellent manual for it, there is still need for much research in validating it against educational achievement and performance in jobs.

2. General Aptitude Test Battery, United States Employment Service, 1946–58.

The battery was developed by the staff of the United States Employment Service for vocational counseling of persons seeking employment. School officials may arrange for a representative from local offices of the State Employment Service to test students without cost to either the school or the students. From the twelve tests, a counselor can obtain nine scores: intelligence, verbal, numerical, spatial, form perception, clerical perception, motor coordination, finger dexterity, and manual dexterity. The objective was to develop special tests for every job family. Though this battery has been a very useful one, much research is still needed to validate it for the purposes for which it was designed. Users are cautioned against one danger: some users are inclined to encourage students to make firm decisions on only these test results. Obviously, other data must also be considered.

SUGGESTED READINGS

1. ANASTASI, ANNE. *Psychological Testing.* New York: The Macmillan Company, 1961.

   Chapters 14, 15, and 19.
   a] What stimulated the development of special aptitude tests?
   b] To what extent do special aptitude tests actually improve the prediction of success in an occupation?
   c] For what purposes would a counselor administer interest tests?
   d] How may research on creativity influence aptitude testing?

2. CRONBACH, LEE J. *Essentials of Psychological Testing.* New York: Harper & Row, Publishers, 1960.

   Chapters 10, 11, 12, and 14.
   a] What may counselors learn from aptitude-test batteries that they can use in vocational counseling?
   b] How can you account for the decreasing use of tests designed to predict success in specific school subjects?
   c] Why is it that job analysis is so important in predicting success on the job?
   d] To what extent are interest inventories useful in vocational counseling?

3. SUPER, DONALD E. *The Psychology of Careers: An Introduction to Vocational Development.* New York: Harper & Row, Publishers, 1957.

This book reviews the research and theory on vocational development. Chapters 13, 14, and 15 are especially relevant here.
   a] What criteria have been used in assessing vocational success? What is the primary weakness of each?
   b] What does choice of a vocation require of an individual?
   c] To what extent is vocational counseling merely information-giving?
   d] How does intelligence affect job satisfaction?
   e] How may a counselor use interest-test results in vocational counseling?
   f] When do interests affect success in an occupation?

4. SUPER, DONALD E. (ed.) *The Use of Multifactor Test Batteries in Guidance.* Washington, D.C.: American Personnel and Guidance Association, 1958.

This pamphlet includes a series of reprints published in the Personnel and Guidance Journal. *The series presents a description of all the multifactor batteries published in the United States except one for which its author declined an invitation to submit a paper.*

Information Service

THE INFORMATION service is a cooperative effort of teachers, counselors, and librarians to obtain appropriate informational materials, to organize these for pupils' most efficient use, and to help pupils understand the significance of the information for them.

During the process of growing up, children ask many and varied questions. Those who attempt to answer these questions should try to differentiate between a child's request for information and his efforts to communicate feelings of inadequacy (see pp. 126–28). They also should try to look at a child's questions from his point of view and to answer each question in a way meaningful for him (see pp. 35–37).

Patience and understanding are required to answer children's questions. Some questions are difficult to answer, either because they involve complex concepts that cannot be easily explained in the child's language, or because they involve those beliefs and ideals for which man continues to search for answers throughout his life. Moreover, the child often asks questions when the adult is busy with some other responsibility and is tempted to put him off or ignore him. Difficult as it is, adults must try to resist this temptation, for natural curiosity must be fostered, not squelched. Scholarship is built upon healthy curiosity. Parents, teachers, and counselors who feed this curiosity, and at the same time encourage the independent search for knowledge, help children to understand themselves and their environment, and to develop scholarly attitudes.

Some of the literature on guidance may lead one to conclude that the information service is primarily for secondary-school students. But elementary-school pupils also need a variety of information about themselves and their environment. Though only a limited amount of the occupational, educational, and social information available today is appropriate for elementary-school children, more is being written for them.

Norris, Zeran, and Hatch describe these three types of information as follows:

Occupational information is valid and usable data about positions, jobs, and occupations, including duties, requirements for entrance, conditions of work, rewards offered, advancement patterns, existing and predicted supply of and demand for workers, and sources for further information . . .

Educational information is valid and usable data about all types of present and probably future educational or training opportunities and requirements, including curricular and co-curricular offerings, requirements for entrance, and conditions and problems of student life . . .

Social information is valid and usable data about the opportunities of the human and physical environment which bear on personal and interpersonal relations. It is that information about human beings which will help a student to understand himself better and to improve his relations with others. Included, but not constituting the whole, are such broad areas of information as "understanding self" and "getting along with others," as well as such specific areas as boy-girl relations, manners and etiquette, leisure-time activities, personal appearance, social skills, home and family relationships, financial planning, and healthful living.[1]

1 Willa Norris, Franklin R. Zeran, and Raymond N. Hatch, *The Information Service in Guidance* (Chicago: Rand McNally & Co., 1960), pp. 22–23.

Since a number of good texts (see Suggested Readings) are concerned with the selection, evaluation, and use of educational, occupational, and social information, these topics will be discussed briefly here. Primary attention will be focused upon methods of disseminating the information to pupils.

Selecting Appropriate Materials

WHAT a given child wants or needs to know depends upon his age and his own personal situation. For example, one ninth-grader needs information on dating. His best pal has little need for such information, but needs to know how to study for tests. Senior high school pupils need occupational information on job entrance requirements, entry jobs, advancement patterns, and the supply of workers in specific occupations, but few elementary-school pupils are interested in these facts; they are primarily interested in what various workers do and the kinds of place they work in. Both junior and senior high school students are interested in what others their own age are like —what they think about certain issues, what their parents expect from them, what worries them, how they solve their problems, and what they do for fun.

Most schools already possess some books, pamphlets, catalogues, and audio-visual aids on occupational, educational, and social information. But no matter how good the library may be, the staff must constantly assess whether they have the material their pupils need. Periodically, they should inventory their materials to identify gaps, and to discover and eliminate outdated materials. Whenever new materials are purchased these should be carefully evaluated by the staff members best qualified to evaluate them. Questions that may be used as guidelines in screening these materials are listed below:

1. Who published the material? Are they reputable publishers?

2. Who wrote the material? Is the author qualified in this field?

3. What was his motive in preparing the material? Was he obligated in any way to present a point of view or to recruit for his sponsoring organization?

4. When was the material published? Is it still up-to-date?

5. Is the material well written? Is it on the reading level of those who should read it?

6. Is the material well illustrated? Will it appeal to pupils who should read it?

For more detailed discussion of criteria that may be used to evaluate occupational information, readers should consult the National Vocational Guidance Association's [2] standards for use and preparation of occupational literature. Additional information on criteria and their use in selecting materials may be obtained from the suggested readings.

Organizing Information for Student Use

OCCUPATIONAL information must be not only carefully selected and screened, but also organized so that students can readily find what they seek.

If the librarian were concerned only with unbound pamphlets in a small library, organization would be a relatively simple problem. The fact is that even in a small library there is a great variety of material: charts, pictures, posters, films, film strips, catalogues, biographies, pamphlets, monographs, books dealing with entire industries, and current information that is selected from magazines and newspapers for use on bulletin boards and in scrapbooks. Therefore, a systematic plan must be developed, preferably with the help of a student-faculty committee, for organizing materials for efficient use by students. All materials can be stored in accordance with the librarian's system, and listed on cross-reference cards that are filed with the unbound materials. Finally, time should be provided for the librarian to instruct students in the use and maintenance of these materials. Even then a set of directions for students' use of these materials should be placed in conspicuous places.

Most secondary schools use some kind of an alphabetical system for filing unbound occupational information. While filing such materials alphabetically by the job title requires little student instruction, it does create problems because many occupations bear more than one title. Moreover, the student tends not to detect readily the relationships among occupations. Both of these problems can be corrected through teaching the student to use the *Dictionary of Occupational Titles*.[3] From Part I he can obtain a brief description of

2 Occupational Research Division, National Vocational Guidance Association, "Standards for Use in Preparing and Evaluating Occupational Literature," *Occupations*, XXVIII (1950), 319–24.

3 U.S. Department of Labor, War Manpower Commission (Washington, D.C.: Government Printing Office, 1944).

occupations in terms of job duties and a job code number. With the job code number he can turn to Part II and identify related jobs. Finally, from Part IV he can obtain the names of entry jobs.

Several commercial plans have been developed that make it relatively easy for students to find material and also to detect the relationship between a specific occupation and other related occupations. Two examples of such plans are the SRA *Career Information Kit* [4] and the *Michigan Plan for Filing and Indexing Occupational Information:* [5]

1. The materials in the SRA Kit are organized in a coded file and cover more than 650 of the major employment areas described by the United States Bureau of Labor Statistics.

2. The *Michigan Plan for Filing and Indexing Occupational Information* was built around major job areas defined in the *Dictionary of Occupational Titles*. The plan provides for alphabetical filing of all unbound material within 165 folders.

Another variation of alphabetical filing has been developed around the particular interest test used in a school. If, for example, a school used the Kuder Preference Record—Vocational, then all unbound material and cross-reference cards would be filed alphabetically within that test's ten interest areas. This plan has the obvious advantage of helping students find easily the occupations related to their interest. Moreover, related occupations from several occupational levels tend to be grouped together.

With another method, all unbound materials are filed according to subject matter areas; [6] this approach is very convenient for teachers who present the vocational implications of their subject. Pupils also find this plan useful because it enables them to attack the study of occupations by beginning with favorite school subjects and those subjects in which they do their best work. However, it is difficult to classify all occupations according to this system, and many occupations are directly related to several subject matter areas.

Finally, other schools develop their filing system around either job

4 A. H. Edgerton, *Your Career Information Kit* (Chicago: Science Research Associates, 1961), and L. L. Belanger and W. M. Lifton, SRA Occupational Exploration Kit (Chicago: Science Research Associates, 1961).

5 Wilma Bennett, *Michigan Plan for Filing and Indexing Occupational Information* (Sturgis, Michigan: Sturgis Printing Co., 1950). Filing instructions and necessary materials may be purchased from the publisher.

6 Edward C. Roeber, *Missouri Plan for Filing Unbound Materials on Occupations* (Columbia, Mo.: University of Missouri, 1950).

families or major industries. When they use the major industries for classifying material, they usually try to build the system around the industries which usually employ the school's graduates. Often this system is supplemented by a special section on the major professions. Some schools try to increase the advantages of this system by organizing all unbound material into the occupational classifications defined by either the United States Bureau of the Census or the *Dictionary of Occupational Titles.* While the use of a number coding system simplifies the maintenance of files, it requires more careful instruction of students. The *New York State Department of Education Plan* [7] is an example of a commercial plan which uses code numbers for filing, based on the *Dictionary of Occupational Titles.*

Staffing the Information Service

PUPILS can answer many of their questions *by themselves* through reading. Some information, however, is best provided in individual counseling. The qualifications of counselors and the conditions under which such information is best provided were discussed in Chapters 3 and 4. Techniques for obtaining some of the information which the pupils want about themselves were discussed in Chapters 6–9. Certain questions can be answered most effectively in discussion groups. The leader of these guidance groups provides occupational, educational, and social information, and encourages pupils to ask questions and to discuss the relevance of the information for them. Most of the kinds of discussion group described here can be conducted by teachers. In fact, the information is sometimes provided in special classes, such as occupations or study skills courses. Best results are usually obtained in groups for which pupils volunteer for the sessions and participate in the selection of the discussion topics.

The last section in Chapter 3 described minimum professional qualifications for the school counselor. If he is doing group counseling, he should also have special course work in group counseling methods, and supervised practice in group counseling. This specialized training is desirable for group guidance leaders too, but it is not essential. Effective teachers who are familiar with the literature in child growth and development, mental hygiene, group guidance

7 *New York State Department of Education Plan* (Moravia, N.Y.: Chronicle Press, 1950).

techniques, group dynamics, and principles of guidance may provide excellent leadership in such groups. Obviously, a knowledge of the world of work and an understanding of techniques for using occupational information would be essential background for leaders of secondary-school groups. In selecting such leaders, the principal and guidance director also should look for teachers who are interested in their pupils and who have demonstrated that they are good discussion leaders.

If group guidance can be carried on by good teachers who possess the competencies outlined in the last paragraph, how does this guidance differ from good teaching? It is not substantially different from pupil-centered teaching. The leader must use good teaching techniques and, like the teacher, he must present his ideas clearly and also show a personal interest in his pupils. He must be able to create the good personal relationships described in Chapter 3 and demonstrate an understanding of children and their needs, as described in Chapter 2.

On the other hand, the discussions in group guidance differ from those of the typical classroom in a number of ways. In addition to providing information by lectures, suggested readings, films, and film strips, and encouraging pupils to ask questions, the discussion leader must help each pupil to evaluate the information, to examine what it means for him, and to integrate the new information into his perception of himself and his situation. These discussions emphasize understanding information and adapting it for one's personal use rather than the mastery of knowledge and concepts. Eventually, after they have participated in several of these sessions, pupils assume increasingly greater responsibility for gathering and presenting the information and for helping each other achieve the goals described above.

The leader should be conscious of his professional limitations. To avoid becoming too deeply involved in pupils' personal problems, he should try to limit himself to helping pupils clarify what they want to say and define what they need to know. Though it is appropriate for the leader to help the pupil discuss the personal implications of the information, he should not probe for information about the pupil's personal problems. Instead, the leader should simply help the pupil tell what he wants to tell, and help him clarify what he has difficulty saying. Even though the group guidance techniques described in this chapter do not ordinarily result in the examination of the pupils' personal problems, each member should leave the session feeling that the members, and especially the leader, are interested in him as a person. He should feel that he can use the ideas he believes apply to him and that he can ignore the others.

Faculty-planned Groups

WHEN educational, occupational, and social information is provided in organized groups, these are usually faculty planned groups. Elementary-school teachers provide this information to pupils in private conferences and in classroom discussions. At the secondary-school level such information is provided in homerooms, in orientation or guidance courses, in occupations courses, and in special units in such required school subjects as English or social studies. More often than not, the faculty decides what information pupils need and plans a series of discussions to provide it.

Although voluntary discussion groups produce better learning than faculty planned activities do, especially for adolescents, the faculty is obligated to try to provide pupils with information they feel the pupils need. When they limit such presentations to giving certain educational and occupational information, students seem to accept it. Though students also recognize the need for, and actually want, more personal information, they seem to accept that best when it is provided in the type of group described in the next section (see Voluntary Discussion Groups).

Adolescents usually resent being required to take a course which deals with personal topics. Sometimes such an experience causes them to be suspicious of all the guidance personnel, even to wonder why counselors encourage them to talk about their problems. Some students also resent having test results given to them in groups; in particular, they are sensitive about having others hear their ability and aptitude test scores. Although they themselves often tell their classmates how they did on these tests, they resent having their teachers and counselors tell, and they look upon such action as breaking confidence with them. Some also deeply resent coercion exerted on them by their classmates to reveal test scores.

A GUIDANCE COURSE

One of the most popular techniques for providing pupils with information is a guidance course, sometimes called an orientation course, designed for either eighth- or ninth-graders. Typically the course is required of all pupils and attempts to acquaint them with their abilities, aptitudes, and interests, to familiarize them with the various curricular and extracurricular offerings, to introduce them to the study of occupations, to encourage them to *begin* thinking about a vocational choice, and to help them develop an education plan. Sometimes the course introduces them to the study of adolescent psychology and principles of mental hygiene. Usually, however, a more systematic study of the principles of mental hygiene is incorporated in a general psychology course offered for eleventh- and twelfth-graders.

Required course work has been used successfully for guidance purposes, especially when the teacher provides appropriate educational and occupational information. Warren Gribbons [8] appraised the effectiveness of a group guidance unit [9] with eighth-graders. The pupils were presented with a method of appraising their abilities, values, and interests and were assisted in relating this information to educational and occupational choices. Primary attention was focused on *immediate* decisions concerning choice of high school curriculum and its relation to educational and occupational opportunities. When the data obtained from pupils in post-treatment interviews were compared with those obtained in pre-treatment interviews, Gribbons found that these eighth-graders had increased significantly their awareness of: (1) factors to consider in curriculum and occupational choices; (2) their ability and inadequacies in relation to making curriculum and occupational choices; (3) their general scholastic ability; and (4) their interests and values, and the relevance of these for occupational choice. The pupils also demonstrated considerable gains in knowledge about educational and vocational requirements.

Very recently another study was reported on the materials described in the previous paragraph. Benjamin Shimberg and Martin Katz found that experimental subjects in group guidance courses earned significantly higher scores in an objective test designed to appraise mastery of information presented in the text than did their controls. Their conclusions may be summarized as follows:

8 Warren D. Gribbons, "Evaluation of an Eighth Grade Group Guidance Program," *Personnel and Guidance Journal*, XXXVIII (1960), 740–45.

9 Martin R. Katz, *You: Today and Tomorrow* (Princeton: Cooperative Test Division, Educational Testing Service, 1959).

While the accumulated weight of these evaluation studies suggest that group guidance courses using *You: Today and Tomorrow* may result in pupils' increased self-understanding and greater awareness of the factors to consider in educational and occupational planning, there is no basis for concluding that such courses substitute for individual counseling.

Group activities can contribute economically to the effectiveness of a school's guidance program by communicating basic information, concepts, and attitudes that are useful to all students and thus enhance students' readiness to profit from individual counseling.

The skilled counselor will then be able to use his time more efficiently in helping individual students solve their *unique* problems. It is here that he brings to bear the full weight of his professional training. Schools seeking to strengthen their total guidance program should consider making maximum use of limited counseling time through a balanced program including group as well as individual guidance.[10]

There are a number of reasons why all group guidance courses have not been as effective as the one described by Shimberg and Katz: (1) teaching materials are inadequate; (2) the staff did not understand the objective of the course; (3) they did not feel adequately prepared to teach it; (4) they questioned the value of grades in such a course and they lacked acceptable criteria for assigning grades; and (5) they were not able to motivate pupils who saw no need for the course. Obviously some of these problems could be prevented by careful planning and in-service education of teachers.

AN OCCUPATIONS COURSE

Many schools that do little else in guidance set aside time in a required course for a vocational guidance unit, or teach an occupations course.[11]

Even before the child enters the junior high school, he usually visits several local industries with his class. Through these field trips he is taught about the products of local industries and the ways in which some citizens of the community earn a living. Pupils also learn about occupations by reading biographies and career books which they select from their school or city library.

10 Benjamin Shimberg and Martin R. Katz, "Evaluation of a Guidance Text," *Personnel and Guidance Journal*, XLI (1962), 131–32.

11 Max F. Baer and Edward C. Roeber, *Occupational Information: Its Nature and Use* (Chicago: Science Research Associates, 1958). Chapters 14, 15, and 16 deal with pertinent issues for the teacher responsible for a vocations course.

Usually a student makes a more formal study of occupations after he enters the secondary school. Many students are introduced to the study of occupations in the ninth grade. Other students study occupations in either the eleventh or twelfth grade. Whenever the school presents the material, the teacher should of course adapt it to the maturity of the students.

Most ninth-grade students are not ready to study specific jobs or to make vocational choices. They are ready to study the major sources of employment in their region and to learn about the job families in these industries. They should learn about living conditions and recreational opportunities in the area, too. They are ready at this stage to discuss what they hope to achieve in high school, and to outline *tentative* plans for their lives beyond high school.

In such an occupations course, ninth-graders should develop an educational plan [12] for their last three years of high school. The plan should include their tentative educational and vocational goals, a list of subjects they wish to take each year, and a list of extra-class activities in which they want experience.

Since students' goals change from year to year, naturally their educational plans will have to be changed too. As students' goals change, counselors should help them reflect on why they originally chose these goals and why they feel they should change them.

If the ninth-grade student is to achieve the understanding he needs, he certainly must study himself. Still more self-study will be necessary later when he thinks of himself in terms of specific occupations. Even the upper classman may do well to study himself in terms of job families. Few American youth will select one job and work in it throughout their lives.[13] It is important, therefore, that the student not only learn a great deal about the few occupations which appeal to him most but that he learn about other related occupations.

Since another chapter is devoted to educational and vocational planning, and since the setting in which information may be given best was discussed earlier, only the course outlines will be presented here.

12 Leslie L. Chisholm, *Guiding Youth in the Secondary Schools* (New York: American Book Co., 1950). Chapters 3, 4, and 5 would be very useful to workers who want information about the educational plan.

13 C. Gilbert Wrenn, "New Directions in American Society," Chapter 2 in *The Counselor in a Changing World* (Washington, D.C.: American Personnel and Guidance Association, 1961).

Ninth-Grade Vocations Course Outline
1. The educational opportunities provided in the school
   a. Special curricula offered and courses included in each
   b. Extra-class activities offered; others which can be made available
   c. Opportunities for students to participate in leadership and student government
2. Definition of expectations from high school
3. Study and development of the educational plan
4. The major sources of employment for graduates of the school
   a. The products produced
   b. The working conditions in each industry
   c. Living conditions in the area in which workers live
   d. Kinds of workers employed in each industry
5. Study of one job family which appeals to the pupil most

Twelfth-Grade Vocations Course
1. A study of self in terms of both school work and job experience
   a. Analysis of jobs and courses which the student liked best
   b. Analysis of jobs and courses in which he did well
   c. Analysis of jobs and courses which he disliked
   d. Analysis of jobs and courses in which he did poorly
   e. Study of jobs and courses he avoided and reasons for avoiding them
2. Identification and analysis of job preferences (use of interest inventories as well as independent analysis of stated interests)
3. Study of jobs and job families which seem to appeal to the student most
   a. Finding and studying occupational information
   b. Identifying the basic requirements and sources of satisfaction for the jobs
   c. The nature of the training program
   d. The nature of the entry jobs
4. The major sources of employment in the region
   a. The jobs currently held by recent graduates
   b. Other sources of employment in the region
   c. Opportunities for advancement
   d. Products made by these industries
   e. The working conditions on the job
   f. Living conditions of the workers

5. Finding jobs
   a. Agencies for helping youth
   b. Characteristics about which employers seek information
   c. Applying for the job
6. Selecting institutions for training beyond high school
7. Planning in terms of military service

A variety of group guidance procedures have been recommended for secondary-school students, but few of them have been evaluated by systematic research. Except for group counseling, more research has been done on the occupations course than in any other group guidance area.

Perhaps the most frequently quoted study of occupations is C. H. Stone's [14] evaluation of a vocational orientation course designed for University of Minnesota freshmen. Freshmen enrolled in this course were compared with other university freshmen not enrolled in the course. The members of the experimental group obtained more information about jobs than did members of the control group. But Stone also concluded that the course alone did not cause students to make more appropriate vocational choices in terms of their abilities, aptitudes, and interests than did mere residence in college. However, the course did seem to serve as a preparation for counseling and tended to reduce the amount of time necessary for the resolution of vocational and educational problems.

Edward Cuony and Robert Hoppock [15] evaluated the effect of a job finding and job orientation course for high school seniors. In a one year follow-up they found that the subjects in the experimental group earned significantly higher job satisfaction scores and better salaries than those in the control group. More of the experimental group also availed themselves of counseling than did the control group. In a five year follow-up on the original group, Cuony and Hoppock [16] found that members of the experimental group once again earned significantly higher job satisfaction scores than members of the control group. They also were employed significantly more weeks of the year than were members of the control group.

14 C. H. Stone, "Are Vocational Orientation Courses Worth Their Salt?" *Educational and Psychological Measurement,* VIII (1948), 161–81.
15 Edward R. Cuony and Robert Hoppock, "Job Course Pays Off," *Personnel and Guidance Journal,* XXXII (1954), 389–91.
16 Edward R. Cuony and Robert Hoppock, "Job Course Pays Off Again," *Personnel and Guidance Journal,* XXXVI (1957), 116–17.

Lowenstein and Hoppock [17] studied the effect of an occupations course taught to college-preparatory twelfth-graders. The course included follow-up letters to high school alumni, group conferences with people representing various occupations, personal interviews with persons in various occupations, self-appraisal with the aid of interest, achievement, and aptitude tests, visits to employment centers, library research on occupations, and case conferences. When they compared college transcripts and follow-up interview data for the control group with the same data for the experimental group one year after high school graduation, they found that the experimental group earned significantly better grades, spent less time in study, and devoted more time to extracurricular activities than their controls, and that a higher percentage of the experimental group had made a vocational choice.

A WORK-EXPERIENCE SEMINAR

Though the work-experience program is part of the instructional program, it makes a unique contribution to the information service. Clarence Fielstra [18] claims that these programs help youth in three ways: (1) they provide vocational guidance by giving youngsters an opportunity to observe and sample a variety of work in order to ascertain their interests and suitability for selected occupations; (2) they give students work-experience in a supervised setting where they can receive assistance in developing desirable work habits and attitudes; and (3) they provide vocational training in the occupations for which their courses are preparing the students. Work programs also make school experiences more meaningful to some youngsters who see little value in continuing their education, and may otherwise quit school.

The work-experience seminar is an important part of an *effective work-experience program*.[19] It gives students a chance to raise questions about problems they meet on the job, to share experiences and exchange ideas, to develop increasing awareness of and under-

17 N. Lowenstein and Robert Hoppock, "High School Occupations Course Helps Students Adjust to College," *Personnel and Guidance Journal,* XXXIV (1955), 21–23.
18 Clarence Fielstra, "Evaluating the Work Experience Education Program in Santa Barbara County Schools," *Educational Leadership,* XVIII (1961), 231–35.
19 Mary E. Oliverio, "Experience of Work: Prerequisites to Its Success," *American Vocational Journal,* XXXVI (1961), 15–16.

standing of human behavior, to examine the employers' expectations and their own work attitudes, and to integrate classroom learning with job experiences. Frequently, students profit from role playing difficult situations: role playing helps them better to understand the work situation and those who are involved in it; it gives them a chance to try out some of their ideas for coping with the situation; it encourages classmates to react to each other's methods for meeting problems; and it encourages them to face their problems and to take some positive action.

Obviously, careful self-study and vocational planning should precede placement in a work station, but these activities should not stop with placement. The decisions the student arrives at should be looked upon merely as steps in the process of growing up, as necessary choices but not final ones—to be reviewed from time to time as the individual learns new things about himself and about occupations. We are living in a rapidly changing world. Many important jobs that are done by skilled craftsmen today will soon be done by machines, and new jobs requiring new skills will open up. Work-experience programs must take cognizance of this prospect, and use the services of well-qualified counselors to prepare students for the change.

SPECIAL UNITS IN REQUIRED COURSES

At present, these units cover a wide variety of topics: adolescent psychology, dating, etiquette, mental hygiene, developing an educational plan, developing a vocational plan, and learning to get along with others. The schools present these topics, and related ones, in various ways. Family living units are usually taught in home economics courses, although boys, who of course need this information too, usually do not get it this way. Some of these topics are dealt with in social problems courses. Frequently, the high school biology course includes a unit on sex, which is designed to help students obtain the information they need. Perhaps the most common procedure is to include these units in such required courses as English or social studies.

Some teachers are pleased to have the opportunity given by such units to demonstrate their personal interest in their pupils. Others resent the time lost from regular subject matter. On the other hand, even some of those English teachers who fall within the latter category are willing to use these topics, and other similar topics suggested under "Voluntary Discussion Groups," as subjects for themes.

Like the guidance course, most of these guidance units reach all the pupils. Those who teach these units meet essentially the same problems as those who teach the required guidance course.

COLLEGE DAYS

Many high schools set aside time for students to obtain certain educational information they need from the representatives of colleges and other post-high school institutions. Usually arrangements are made for each representative to meet in groups all the students who are interested in his institution. It is also common practice for representatives to schedule individual conferences for some students.

Students should have an active part in planning these guidance experiences. A student-faculty workshop committee is one good way of involving the students in the planning. Early in the planning, the committee should poll the student body to determine the extent of student interest in college days and to identify the institutions that should be invited to send representatives. The committee chairman should invite representatives and maintain an accurate record of the names of representatives, and of the students who are to see each. He also should schedule meeting space for each representative.

Before setting a date for the workshop, the chairman should give institutions a chance to indicate preferred dates; then he should notify the institutional representatives of the date and the approximate number of students each can expect to see. If there is to be a speech at a general session to open the workshop, the committee should select the speaker, invite him, and brief him for his assignment. Some schools also make it a regular practice to invite students' parents as well as the recent graduates of their high school who are attending or have attended the institutions participating in the workshop.

Once the committee has completed the planning for the workshop, provision should be made for students to discuss in classes or homerooms how to appraise an institution and what they need to know about the institution that they expect to attend. After the workshop is over, the committee should seek the assistance of pupils, staff, and institutional representatives in evaluating the workshop. Finally, the committee should recommend changes for improving the next workshop and suggest what should be done next to enable the students to reap the full benefit of the workshop.

CAREER DAYS

Career days are very similar to college days except that the purpose is to provide students with occupational information and to introduce them to persons employed in their preferred occupations. The same general procedures should be followed in involving students in planning these workshops and in polling students to determine which occupations should be represented. After the committee members have determined which occupations should be represented, they should early in their planning ask students to select the sessions they wish to attend. Many students also can profit from individual counseling and voluntary discussion groups concerned with choice of vocation prior to career days. In addition to selecting the occupational representatives and briefing them, the committee should select and instruct student chairmen, hosts, and hostesses. When small schools conduct career days in cooperation with other high schools, of course it is important to plan the program cooperatively.

The workshop sessions should be chaired by students. In a one-hour session the guest speaker or consultant should probably devote not more than fifteen or twenty minutes to a lecture. This allows him enough time to give an overview of the job, to describe how one is trained for it, to explain how an applicant obtains his first position, and to show how the job fits into a family of jobs. It also gives the students a chance to warm up to the consultant. Prior to the meeting, students should have formulated questions which they will ask immediately following the lecture. Otherwise, the consultant may feel that he must lecture for the rest of the period. Students who have been prepared for the conference will keep the consultant busy the remainder of the hour. A final summary by the student chairman ties the session together and provides the consultant with an opportunity to correct any false impressions the chairman and group may have received from the discussion.

When the day is over, there is still need for follow-up work with consultants and pupils. The committee must send letters of appreciation to the consultants and make provision for evaluation of the program by the students. Much of what career days should achieve will not come to pass if students do not have an opportunity to discuss and evaluate the program. Time should be set aside in homerooms or specified classes to help students analyze what they have learned. The committee should also help students to define other questions and to learn how they can find the answers. Sometimes students can answer these questions by reading carefully chosen pamphlets and books. At other times they will profit by referral to appropriate persons or agencies in the community. Some students require the help of a well-trained counselor in order to make objective self-appraisals, to clarify their values and goals, and to plan a training program that will help them achieve their goals.

Career days and college days appear to have certain obvious advantages. They also have disadvantages. If poorly planned, the days lose much of their effectiveness. Because consultants have personal loyalties to a trade, a profession, an employer, or an institution, there is always a possibility that they will give students biased information. There is also the danger that the favorable publicity which accrues from these workshops will satisfy the public and many of the school staff to such an extent that they are not motivated to improve their guidance services. It must be kept clearly in mind that career and college days are only a small part of a good guidance program.

CAREER CLUBS

In almost every school we find teachers working with informal student groups, such as the mathematics club, the art club, the science club, and the industrial arts club. Often these groups form around the teacher of a favorite subject. Occasionally, pupils seek out a teacher who has a hobby which coincides with their own: such might be the case with a photography club in a school that has no photography course.

Special study in the subject of their choice, though interesting in itself for club members, should lead on to the study of jobs which have a direct relationship to the subject, including skilled and semi-skilled occupations as well as professional and managerial occupations. Graduates of the school who are employed in a related field make effective speakers for these clubs. They are able to provide useful occupational information and to help students identify entry jobs.

Since all the students who enjoy study in the subject will not want to pursue vocational or professional preparation in the field, advisers should help their students explore the avocational as well as the vocational outlets related to the subject.

THE HOMEROOM

The homeroom, at first glance, appears to be a natural place for the information service and for leadership development. In student government it can provide grass-root participation in solving school problems. It also can be where students are given basic educational, occupational, and social information and where students can discuss the kinds of topic which will be described later in connection with student forums.

There are a number of reasons why the homeroom has often failed to provide the experiences for which it was intended. All too often the homeroom period is too short to accomplish anything significant. Frequently homeroom teachers have known neither what the school officials expected of them nor how to go about doing what they believed they should do. Sometimes teachers see their students only during the few minutes of the homeroom period.

Where homeroom programs have been successful, most of the following conditions have been met:

—The school principal had some clear-cut expectations for the homerooms which are consistent with good guidance practices, and he was able to select teachers for this responsibility who were interested in developing good homeroom programs.

—Where the number of qualified teachers who exhibited interest in the homeroom program was insufficient to staff homerooms for all the grades in the building, the principal provided a homeroom experience for only the first grade in the building—e.g., the seventh grade in a junior high school.

—Teachers who were selected as homeroom teachers were assigned a proportionately lighter teaching and/or extracurricular activity load.

—In-service education was provided by the guidance personnel—especially when the program was begun.

—Students were asked to state first and second choices for homeroom teachers, and these choices were carefully considered in making assignments.

—A student was always assigned at least one course with his homeroom teacher. At the junior high school level, the schedule was usually arranged so that students spent three consecutive periods—two regular classes and a homeroom period—with the homeroom teaher. Where this was not possible every day, at least once a week a full class period was set aside for a homeroom program.

—Some of the best homeroom teachers were permitted to have two homerooms, one in the forenoon and another in the afternoon.

—Students helped select the discussion topics and conducted the discussions. Actually, the discussions had much in common with the student forums described in this chapter.

—The members of the homeroom brought problems to the attention of their student council representative; he also reported student council actions back to his constituents in the homeroom.

Voluntary Discussion Groups

VOLUNTARY discussion groups are recommended for adolescents for many of the same reasons that group counseling seems to be effective with pupils of this age: (1) pupils can attend sessions with those whose opinions and reactions they value most; (2) they want to have their judgment respected; (3) they have less reason to be suspicious of the leader's motives when they feel that the decision on whether they participate is theirs; and (4) they can participate in those discussions which they believe are most relevant for them.

Best results are usually achieved when the *purpose of the discussion groups and their value for students* can be carefully described for students in a setting in which they can ask their questions about the process, its value, and what will be expected from them, and then decide when, if ever, they wish to participate in such discussions. This approach is based upon these principles: (1) not all pupils recognize the need for the same information, and in fact may not need certain information because they have obtained it previously; (2) when students who choose at first not to participate hear about a discussion group from peers who have attended and profited from the sessions, they too are motivated to attend; and (3) information can be best accepted and used when the pupil recognizes a need for it.

Who takes the initiative for organizing the first such group? The school counselor who is best qualified in use of group work procedures and who has been most successful in leading discussion groups assumes this responsibility. In addition to presenting the idea to the pupils and selecting the pupils for the first group, he should conduct in-service education seminars for those who are selected by the guidance director to assume this responsibility later, and arrange for these staff members to observe (preferably via a one-way vision mirror) the discussions with the demonstration groups. He also should encourage them to help him evaluate his success with those groups for whom he serves as discussion leader (a play back of tape recordings of the discussions can be useful for this).

Where can pupils be contacted? One place is the study hall. Increasingly, today, pupils are contacted during their supervised study periods within regular classes. After having cleared the program with the principal, but prior to approaching individual teachers, the demonstration leader should describe the purposes of the discussion groups to the teaching staff, explain how they are conducted, give some examples of the questions for which students seek information, and answer the students' questions. When he must contact most students in supervised study periods, he should work with teachers who teach the required courses. (This prevents the unnecessary loss of study time which occurs when pupils hear the presentation in more than one class.) Usually, then, students who elect to participate in discussions are excused from the study hall or from the supervised study periods for the group discussions. Because of students' tight schedules, there are always some students for whom discussion groups must be arranged before or after school.

What are some kinds of questions for which students seek information in these discussion groups?

For occupational information
1. How can I decide what I really am most interested in?
2. What should I consider in choosing an occupation?
3. Where can I get information on jobs in our community?
4. To what extent does my choice of occupation determine where I will live?
5. How do I go about getting the job I would like most?
6. What are some of the common problems young people meet on their first job? How can they solve them?
7. For whom is the work-experience program planned? Who should be in it? How are students chosen for it?

For educational information
1. What should I consider in selecting my school subjects and extracurricular activities?
2. How can I decide whether I should go to work or to college?
3. Why attend college?
4. Who should go to college?
5. Who should take a terminal junior college program?
6. Who should attend business and vocational schools?

7. How should I choose a college?
8. How can I get ready for scholarship and admission testing programs?
9. What are my chances for scholarships, loans, and other financial aid?
10. What are the possibilities for me to work my way through college?
11. What can I do to increase my chances for getting off to a good start in college?
12. How can I improve my school work now?

For social information

1. What are other junior high (or senior high) school young people like?
2. What do my parents have a right to expect from me? What should I expect from them?
3. What are the advantages and disadvantages of going steady?
4. How can I get into extra-class activities that I would like most?
5. What can we do to improve the extra-class program?
6. What can we do to improve the social program in the school?
7. What do girls expect from boys?
8. What do boys expect from girls?
9. What is there to do outside of school in this town?
10. How can I get across to my parents how I feel about certain things?
11. What can I do to understand and accept people who are different from me or see things differently than I do?

By now, perhaps, those who would like to try this technique have other questions that they would like answered: How do the students let the leader know what they would like to discuss next? How many students are admitted to a group? How often do these groups meet? Where do they meet? When the leader presents the idea to students he suggests a number of topics, encourages them to select some for the first few sessions, and tells them how to submit future topics to him (e.g., in a question box in his office or homeroom). Usually one session is devoted to each topic or question. Sometimes as many as three sessions will be devoted to a topic. To answer the last three questions cited above: (1) 10–15 are admitted to each group; (2) students are not excused from supervised study more than once a week; and (3) they meet in a library conference room or classroom.

Does participation in these student-centered groups actually help students? The evidence suggests that it does. For example, Donald Hoyt [20] used University of Minnesota freshmen to compare the effectiveness of small group discussions on choice of occupation with individual counseling. No significant differences were found between these two experimental groups. Members of both experimental groups became significantly more certain of their vocational choice and more satisfied with their vocational choice than their controls, but only those who participated in the group discussion made more realistic choices than controls after treatment.

K. M. Miller and J. B. Biggs [21] found that participation by eleventh-graders in undirected discussions concerned with their feelings about people who were different from themselves in their own and other countries increased their tolerance of these other nationalities.

Earlier Gerald Wieder [22] conducted a similar study with college students. His purpose was to compare the effectiveness of two methods of instruction (student-centered versus lecture-discussion) in modifying attitudes associated with racial, religious, and ethnic prejudice. Those who were enrolled in the lecture-discussion section in practical psychology did not modify significantly these attitudes, but those enrolled in the student-centered section did. Those enrolled in the student-centered section also improved significantly their acceptance of self scores.

FILM DISCUSSIONS

Films and film strips are often used to present occupational and educational information. Films also may be used both to present social information and to stimulate pupils to think about a question raised by one or more of the pupils. For example, films like *Shy Guy, You and Your Family,* and *You and Your Friends* encourage discussion among students and make the topic more real for them.

20 Donald P. Hoyt, "An Evaluation of Group and Individual Programs in Vocational Guidance," *Journal of Applied Psychology,* XXXIX (1955), 26–30.
21 K. M. Miller and J. B. Biggs, "Attitude Change Through Undirected Group Discussion," *Journal of Educational Psychology,* XLIX (1958), 224–28.
22 Gerald S. Wieder, "Group Procedures Modifying Attitudes of Prejudice in College Classroom," *Journal of Educational Psychology,* XLV (1954), 332–44.

Besides having experienced some of these feelings themselves, they usually know others like the character on whom they are asked to focus their attention. Though they get ideas from the solution suggested by the film, they must realize that they do not have to accept that solution. In fact, it is usually a good idea to stop the film before the solution is presented and ask the students to suggest what they think the others in the film could do to help the character whom they have selected to help. This gives the students a chance to test their ideas, to get others' reactions, and to get ideas from peers. It also gives them ideas against which they can appraise the film's suggestions for helping the character.

STUDENT FORUMS

Another method for providing secondary-school students with an opportunity to discuss important topics of their own choosing is student forums.[23] Typically, the forums are conducted during an activity period. They have been handled in a number of ways, but they are usually most effective when planned and administered by a student-faculty committee. In fact, the idea may be presented to students by a student member of the committee in homerooms. Once the idea has been accepted by both faculty and students, the student-faculty committee provides a place where students may leave their suggested topics and the names of students whom they believe would have some ideas or questions on the topic. The student-faculty committee studies the students' suggestions, selects the topics for discussion, and names a panel for each topic. Then they advertise the forum program in the school newspaper and on school bulletin boards. Since the meeting space is usually limited, the committee sets a limit on attendance and arranges some place, such as homerooms, where students can pick up their admission passes.

Though it is profitable for the forum committee to meet with each panel to suggest sources of information, to review all the proposed topics related to the one selected for discussion, and to answer questions, the panel should realize that they are responsible for the discussions when they appear before the forum. For the first few forums a student member of the forum committee may serve as panel chairman. Successful participation on forum panels is a

23 Merle M. Ohlsen, "Group Guidance Through Our Pupil Forum," *The Clearing House*, XV (1941), 529-30.

good criterion for selecting the subsequent panel chairman. At the beginning of a discussion each panel member takes two or three minutes to comment on the issues, to present some of his own personal reactions, or to provide information; then the chairman invites the audience to participate. After a few sessions the pupils realize that this truly is their forum. When they recognize that the topics discussed are actually the ones that they or someone they know suggested, they participate in the discussions with enthusiasm and behave very well. Because the forum is something planned by them for themselves, they feel that they have to make it work. Rarely does a faculty member of the forum committee have to step in to help the student chairman maintain good order. Even students who often cause trouble in their regular classes try to behave well in the forums.

PARENT DISCUSSION GROUPS

Sometimes the best way to help pupils is to conduct discussion groups for parents. For example, parents of gifted children often need help in understanding their gifted child and their unique responsibilities to him, and in providing a stimulating environment for the development of his potentialities. Because they are stimulated by other parents' comments and questions, and motivated by their interest and enthusiasm for doing something, this help often can be given better in groups than in individual conferences. The author was impressed recently with the work a high school counselor did with parents of future students (parents of eighth-graders enrolled in an eight-year elementary school) even though these parents should have been given this information earlier. Before describing what was done, it should be noted that the high school is located in an industrial area and the percentage of students who are likely to attend college is relatively low. Prior to contacting the parents the counselor had selected pupils whose scores on mental tests placed them in the top five percent of the elementary-school population for at least two of the three mental tests administered in that school. When he called the parents to arrange for the group sessions he told them why they were chosen and what he hoped to accomplish in the sessions, and he found out what evening would be best for them. Most parents agreed to attend at least one meeting. The author observed the first of three sessions conducted for four couples. Two of the fathers were semi-skilled laborers, one a small neighborhood grocer, and one a physician. All of the wives, except the doctor's wife, were employed at least part-time in clerical and service occupations. Only the physician had graduated from college. After introducing the parents to each other, the counselor's opening remarks were essentially these:

You are very fortunate indeed to have a child who learns as easily as your eighth-grader does. But if your child is to become what he can become, he will need more than ease in learning. You must be interested in how well he does in school, you must expect much from him, and, without nagging him, you must encourage him to choose a challenging occupation when he is old enough to make that choice, and help him to develop educational plans which will enable him to achieve that occupational goal. Though he doesn't have to make a vocational choice now, he should be making general educational plans for high school and college. Perhaps some of you feel that it is unrealistic for your child to look forward to college or perhaps you wonder whether you will lose him by encouraging him to enter a profession. These may be things that you would like to discuss. However, what we discuss is for you to decide.

During the three sessions the parents discussed these topics: who should go to college? what were the possibilities for financial aid? did it really pay for pupils to attend college? what could they do to help their children do well in high school? what should parents expect of high school students? Perhaps the three most important outcomes were an improved understanding of: (1) their child and what to expect from him; (2) what the high school staff members were trying to do and why they needed parents' assistance; and (3) higher education and what it could do for their child. The permissive atmosphere within the group and the counselor's ability to help them examine their doubts about the value of education contributed most to helping the group achieve these benefits. The fact that each had a gifted child gave them something in common. It also gave them a feeling of equality—something the doctor's wife found difficult to accept at first. The doctor's sincere effort to understand the other parents and his ability to share his personal evaluation of college also helped the counselor present the case for higher education for gifted students.

Parent discussion groups also have been effective for other purposes. For example, one high school offered adult classes for expectant parents, parents of preschool children, parents of primary-school children, parents of upper-elementary-school children, parents of junior high school youngsters, and parents of senior high school students. The discussion leaders were the high school counselors and the school psychologist. Though the leaders prepared good bibliographies, and occasionally made good use of guest speakers, perhaps the primary benefits came from giving these parents a chance to discuss the problems that bothered them, and a chance to exchange ideas with other parents. Through these experiences they obtained an improved understanding of their children and what to expect from them, and they discovered how some of their attitudes and behavior influenced their children. Some also learned how better to relate to their children and to cope with problems that worried them.

The Orientation Service

ORIENTATION is designed to help pupils prepare for and adjust to new situations as they progress through school—e.g., home to kindergarten, kindergarten to first grade, elementary to junior high school, junior to senior high school, and senior high school to college or employment. As the author sees it, orientation is a part of the information service, and it is appropriate to discuss it in this chapter.

. . . the immediate purpose of the orientation work is to help the new student feel emotionally secure in his new school environment by making him feel wanted; by giving him as quickly as possible the information needed about school routine, regulations, plant and personnel; and by securing from him the information needed in order to guide him into the right activities, curricular and noncurricular . . .[24]

Harold Dillon [25] concluded that students who leave school prior to graduation may do so because school personnel have failed to help them adjust to a new school situation. A good orientation program is an introduction to the new situation.

Most of these programs contain these general features, with individual variations: visits to the new school, visits by counselors to the schools, printed material, and conferences with parents and students.[26]

24 Jane Warters, *High School Personnel Work Today* (New York: McGraw-Hill Book Co., Inc., 1956), p. 265.
25 Harold J. Dillon, *Early School Leavers* (New York: National Labor Committee, 1948).
26 Emery Stoops and Gunnar L. Wahlquist, *Principles and Practices in Guidance* (New York: McGraw-Hill Book Co., Inc., 1958), p. 81.

Although most school principals recognize the need for orienting new pupils, few of them are completely satisfied with their program. The most common weaknesses in the programs are: (1) trying to prepare pupils for problems which they have not yet met—and which, consequently, have little meaning for them; (2) not knowing what *pupils feel* they need to know; (3) providing pupils with appropriate information on academic and extra-class activities, but failing to convey to them a desire to get to know them as persons; (4) failing to recognize the need for a continuing program over a period of time; and (5) failing to evaluate the program with systematic research.

Like every other situation in which pupils need information, this one involves more than obtaining the right data and communicating them to the pupils. Those who participate in the orientation program must try to look at things through the pupils' eyes—try to assess how pupils feel, and to help them find out what *they feel* they need to know. Giving new pupils the information they need and telling them what is expected in the new setting is, even then, only part of the story. The more difficult part is to communicate the fact that people in the new setting care about each of the new pupils as persons, want to get to know them, and want to help them get off to a good start.

Obviously, these goals cannot be achieved by a few contacts with the new school at the end of a school term, or by a short orientation program for new pupils at the beginning of the school term. It is a continuous program which must be carried on over a period of time. It also requires the involvement of pupils as well as staff. Those pupils who have already made a good adjustment can do much to help new pupils make the necessary adjustment for success in a new setting. For the lowest age levels, just prior to entry to kindergarten and first grade, best results are usually obtained by small group sessions with parents, in which the parents are given help in preparing their children for school. At the elementary-school level classroom teachers, and at the secondary-school level homeroom teachers, have many opportunities to identify new pupils who need assistance, and to provide the assistance needed. They also are in a good position to enlist pupils' assistance and to prepare them to help new pupils. The student council also can provide excellent leadership in orienting new pupils. Some pupils, however, need the assistance of an understanding and well-qualified counselor.

To what extent have orientation programs been successful? What research evidence do we have? Though a number of studies have been done, the real influence of specific programs is difficult to assess. In part this is true because so many variables are involved. Sometimes little effort has been made to control the important variables.

Harold Kobliner [27] developed a pre-entrance orientation course for sixth-graders and evaluated its effectiveness. The course included a visit to the junior high school, a talk by the junior high school counselor, conferences with seventh- and ninth-grade students, the showing of slides of junior high school activities, and group discussions about junior high school. The experimental group was compared with a control group on the following data: (1) absence rate, (2) attitudes toward school, (3) teacher's ratings of behavior, (4) grades, (5) social acceptance, and (6) number of problems checked on the Mooney Problem Check-List. However, the results were not significant; chance could account for any differences noted between the two groups.

Charles Williams [28] studied the effectiveness of a three-semester-hour orientation course in the problems of first-year college women. Both the experimental and control group completed the Mooney Problem Check-List at the beginning and end of the semester. Only the experimental group reduced significantly the number of problems checked. In fact, in two areas the control group checked more problems in post-testing than in pre-testing.

Harold Richardson and Henry Borow [29] tested the hypothesis that first-year university male students who receive group orientation to educational-vocational counseling adopt a more effective and realistic role in counseling than do students who, though comparable in other respects, do not receive such preparation. Although the results favored the experimental group, the data failed to support the hypothesis. However, the researchers did find that the experimental group scored significantly higher on the attitude-information

27 Harold Kobliner, "The Effects of a Pre-Entrance Orientation Course on the Adjustment of Sixth-Grade Pupils for Junior High School," *Dissertation Abstracts*, XX (1959), 588–89.

28 Charles C. Williams, "An Experimental Study to Determine the Effectiveness of the Freshman Orientation Course at North Texas State College," *Dissertation Abstracts*, XIX (1959), 341–42.

29 Harold Richardson and Henry Borow, "Evaluation of a Technique of Group Orientation for Vocational Counseling," *Educational and Psychological Measurement*, XII (1952), 587–97.

test than the control group did; the control group also reported more dissatisfaction with counseling than did the experimental group.

No one seems to question either pupils' need for educational, occupational, and social information or their need for orientation to new school experiences, but perhaps guidance workers should devote more attention to evaluating the effectiveness of what they are doing. To expect to help everyone is unrealistic, but all of us must be willing to replace or to try to improve those guidance techniques which do not seem to help youth. With the shortage of guidance personnel we must make every effort to use staff time efficiently.

SUGGESTED READINGS

1. BAER, MAX F., and EDWARD C. ROEBER. *Occupational Information.* Chicago: Science Research Associates, 1958.

   This book was written for school counselors by men with successful experience in publishing and using occupational information in schools. It describes good sources of information and suggests how to use the information with clients.
   a] What criteria should be used in evaluating occupational information?
   b] What kinds of information can schools obtain from the United States Department of the Interior?
   c] Why should a student want to consult the Army's *Occupational Handbook?*

2. HOPPOCK, ROBERT. *Occupational Information.* New York: McGraw-Hill Book Co., Inc., 1957.

   This book was written as a text for training personnel workers, especially school counselors, in selecting and using occupational information.
   a] What should counselors know about occupations?
   b] What should clients know about occupations?
   c] Where can clients obtain occupational information?
   d] What criteria may be used to appraise occupational information?

3. NORRIS, WILLA, FRANKLIN R. ZERAN, and RAYMOND N. HATCH. *The Information Service.* Chicago: Rand McNally & Co., 1960.

   This text discusses ways of using information to help pupils. Its authors present unique objectives of the information service for elementary, junior high, and senior high school pupils, they describe the major classification systems, they list sources for various types of information, and they define criteria for evaluating these materials.
   a] What are the primary objectives of the information service?
   b] What do students need to know about occupations?

c] What are some of the nonmonetary rewards of an occupation that students should know about?

d] What are the objectives of the information service in the elementary schools?

4. SHARTLE, CARROL L. *Occupational Information, Its Development and Applications.* New York: Prentice-Hall, Inc., 1959.

This is one of the good books which have been revised many times to better help professional personnel workers to understand and to use occupational information.

a] What is occupational information?

b] What do counselors need to know about occupations?

c] What is the difference between a job and an occupation?

d] How do values seem to influence school achievement and choice of occupation?

e] What can one learn about an occupation from the *Dictionary of Occupational Titles?*

5. WRENN, C. GILBERT. *The Counselor in a Changing World.* Washington, D.C.: American Personnel and Guidance Association, 1962.

This is one of the most important projects that has been sponsored by any professional group in the last ten years. It discusses technological changes and industrial changes, social changes, and changes in school practices which are anticipated in the next fifteen to twenty years, and examines how these are apt to influence the role of the counselor.

a] What changes are anticipated in occupational trends?

b] What important social changes can we expect in the next fifteen to twenty years?

c] How will social changes influence school practices, and especially the counselor's role?

11

Educational-vocational Planning

THE RIGHT of each individual to choose his life work is a respected tradition in the United States. As a nation we value hard work and individual success. We are committed to the idea of helping each person develop his interests, abilities, and aptitudes in his own way. Choice of occupation is one method for an individual to convey to others how he wants to be perceived and to implement his self-image.

From the time a child first tries to communicate with others, he is developing an image of himself, and this image is not easily changed even at age sixteen or seventeen. From those whose acceptance, love, and recognition he seeks, he has learned to honor certain behavior, to reject other behavior, and to use these criteria to evaluate himself and his own actions. Sometimes he is pleased with himself and at other times he is disappointed. If, however, he has grown up within a wholesome environment, he has learned to accept himself as he is, with both his weaknesses and his strengths, and to plan for the future accordingly. Though he tries to correct those weaknesses that he can correct with a reasonable effort, he does not brood about the others. He realizes that he does not have to be perfect to be accepted and to achieve his goals in life.

Neither should he feel that he must choose his occupation from a field in which there is a labor shortage. Counselors should inform youth of our nation's manpower needs, but should not put pressure upon them to select their life work in such a field. Manpower needs change, and an individual has a right to develop in his own way. Furthermore, only the dependent client tends to accept decisions that are made for him. Most adolescents are deeply involved in the struggle for independence when they make their first vocational choice, so any such pressure is not likely to be effective. Though some appear to accept the counselor's advice on a particular choice of occupation, they often fail to prepare for and enter the recommended field. Those who exert pressure also overlook the fact that most young people are deeply concerned about our nation's welfare and are inclined to give special attention to those fields in which they are needed even if no pressure is put upon them to do so.

Theories of Vocational Choice

JUST as a self-image develops gradually over years, so does the readiness for realistic vocational choice. According to Super, vocational choice is a developmental process which extends over a period of time:

This process may be summed up in a series of life stages characterized as those of growth, exploration, establishment, maintenance, and decline, and these stages may in turn be subdivided into (a) the fantasy, tentative, and realistic phases of the exploratory stage, and (b) the trial and stable phases of the establishment stage . . . The process of vocational development is essentially that of developing and implementing a self concept: it is a compromise process in which the self concept is a product of the interaction of inherited aptitudes, neural and endocrine make-up, opportunity to play various roles, and evaluations of the extent to which the results of role playing meet with the approval of superiors and fellows . . . The process of compromise between individual and social factors, between self concept and reality, is one of role playing, whether the role is played in fantasy, in the counseling interview, or in real life activities such as school classes, clubs, part-time work and entry jobs . . . Work situations and life situations depend upon the extent to which the individual finds adequate outlets for his abilities, interests, personality traits and values; they depend upon his establishment in a type of work, a work situation, and a way of life in which he can play the kind of role which his growth and exploratory experiences have led him to consider congenial and appropriate.[1]

Super looks upon vocational development as one aspect of individual development much as his colleagues in psychology have looked upon social, emotional, and intellectual development for some time:

> Work, like social life and intellectual activity, is one specific medium through which the total personality can manifest itself. Like other aspects of development, vocational development may be conceived of as beginning early in life, and preceding along a curve until late in life. Thus the four-year-old who plays carpenter or storekeeper is in a very early stage of vocational development, and the septuagenarian who no longer teaches or does research but still attends scientific meetings or writes his professional autobiography is in a very late stage of vocational development.[2]

Super's theory of vocational choice also takes cognizance of individual differences in abilities, aptitudes, interests, and values: certain characteristic patterns of abilities, interests, and personality traits are required for each occupation; both occupations and people change over a period of time; and every individual is qualified for a number of occupations. Finally, he sees vocational choices as a means of implementing the self-image.

A recent study supports Super's notion that one chooses his vocation to implement his self-concept. Meryl Englander [3] found that elementary-school teaching majors perceive elementary teaching as a means of perpetuating their respective self-images and attaining those things which people desire in a vocation, while noneducation

---

1 Donald E. Super, "A Theory of Vocational Development," *American Psychologist*, VIII (1953), 187.

2 Donald E. Super, *The Psychology of Careers* (New York: Harper & Row, Publishers, 1957), p. 185.

3 Meryl E. Englander, "Q-Sort: A Means to Explore Vocational Choice," *Educational and Psychological Measurement*, XXI (1961), 597–605.

majors perceive elementary teaching as a vocation quite different from what they expect and desire for themselves.

Ginzberg and his associates also described vocational choice as a developmental process:

> The process of occupational decision-making can be divided into three distinct periods: the period during which the individual makes what can be described as a fantasy choice; the period during which he is making a tentative choice; and the period when he makes a realistic choice. The first coincides in general with the latency period, between six and eleven, although residual elements of fantasy choices frequently carry over into the preadolescent years. The second coincides by and large with early and late adolescence; . . . To some degree, the way in which a young person deals with his occupational choice is indicative of his general maturity and, conversely, in assessing the latter, consideration must be given to the way in which he is handling his occupational choice problem.
>
> It requires a considerable degree of maturity to realize that one must make a decision which will commit one to a course of action and that it is neither expedient nor desirable to postpone it. It is also evidence of maturity to realize that one's intellectual and emotional development cannot be erased and that one must act in terms of it rather than seek ways of escaping from it.
>
> Implicit in making a firm vocational decision is the willingness of the individual to keep stable his image of himself. His next step is to concretize this image by becoming increasingly aware of specific objectives, possibly even to establish a time sequence with respect to these objectives. The young adult is much more aware than the adolescent of the need to consider carefully the demands of the reality situation. He no longer has the wide margin of freedom to explore what he would like to do and how he would like to do it. His best chance for finding a satisfactory solution of his problem at this stage is to deal effectively with the current concrete demands. He no longer has to decide between medicine and physics, but must discover what to do to gain admission to medical school or graduate school.[4]

But though he must make certain decisions, he can postpone others within the broad areas in which he hopes to work.

Ginzberg [5] also recognizes that vocational choice is not a single decision, but a series of decisions made over a period of years. However, he sees the process as largely irreversible. Because educa-

4 Eli Ginzberg, W. S. Ginsburg, Sidney Axelrod, and J. L. Herma, *Occupational Choice* (New York: Columbia University Press, 1951), pp. 60, 70.
5 *Ibid.*, pp. 185–98.

tion as well as other exposures can be experienced only once, time cannot be relived; later decisions are limited by previous ones. The process ends in a compromise between interests, capacities, values, and opportunities.

Anne Roe believes that both the individual and the society are more flexible than Ginzberg has indicated that they are:

> It is true, as Ginzberg and his associates have emphasized, that there are irreversible elements: one type of education cannot be exchanged for another in retrospect; time spent on one job means that there is that much less time to spend on another, and so on. Nevertheless, both individuals and society are more flexible than Ginzberg seems to consider them. Individual occupational histories show shifts. Some of these may seem minor at the time, but they may mean personally significant changes, even within the framework of a superficially similar job, that lead to more congenial activities. The same job is rarely done in the same way by two different persons, and most jobs other than fully routinized assembly line or clerical ones, can be approached in different ways, or organized somewhat differently in accordance with individual peculiarities. They not only can be, they inevitably will be.[6]

According to Roe's own theory, an individual's choice of occupation is closely related to the psychological climate in which he was reared. Out of these early experiences, she believes, a person develops certain needs, interests, and values which influence his choice of occupation. Two recent studies attempted to test specific hypotheses which developed out of Roe's theory. Alden Utton conducted a study to test the following hypotheses:

> (1) . . . that those subjects employed in occupations oriented toward persons would manifest greater altruistic love of people than those subjects employed in occupations which were primarily nonperson-oriented, and (2) . . . that the subjects employed in person-oriented occupations would recall their early childhood environment as having been warmer than that of subjects employed in nonperson-oriented occupations.[7]

His data supported the first hypothesis, but not the second. However, he did find that the highly interested social workers and occu-

---

6 Anne Roe, *The Psychology of Occupations* (New York: John Wiley & Sons, Inc., 1956), p. 253.

7 Alden C. Utton, "Recalled Parent-Child Relations as Determinants of Vocational Choice," *Journal of Counseling Psychology*, IX (1962), 49–53.

pational therapists did recall their family atmosphere as having been significantly warmer than that of workers who were less interested in their profession.

On the basis of Roe's theory, Switzer, Grigg, Miller, and Young [8] predicted that ministerial students would remember their parents as more overdemanding than chemistry majors would think their parents were, and that chemistry majors would remember their parents as more rejecting than ministerial students would think their parents were. Their findings failed to provide any systematic support for their predictions.

Although as a nation we are very proud that an unskilled laborer's child can become a professional man or woman, and that we respect the individual's right to make his own choice of occupation, still the early home and community experiences do tend to limit a person's choices. Hollingshead [9] concluded that most persons find it almost impossible to do better than their fathers did—in fact, children from the lower class even had great difficulty obtaining employment. Erland Nelson [10] found that teachers', journalists', and physicians' children tended to select their father's occupation, whereas farmers' and laborers' children did not. Samson and Stefflre also studied the relation between the student's (high school seniors) first choice of vocational objective and his father's vocation:

> The primary overall tendency revealed here is for children to pick occupations at higher levels than their parents' but there is also a significant secondary tendency for the parents' occupations to influence the child's choice of objective . . . Circumstances will probably prevent many children who are desirous of mobility from moving away from the occupational level of their parents.[11]

These authors also cited the need for research evidence that might explain why children from the lower class make proportionately few choices of professional objectives and why upper-class children

8 D. K. Switzer, A. E. Grigg, J. G. Miller, and R. K. Young, "Early Experiences and Occupational Choice: A Test of Roe's Hypotheses," *Journal of Counseling Psychology,* IX (1962), 45–48.

9 A. B. Hollingshead, *Elmstown Youth* (New York: John Wiley & Sons, Inc., 1949).

10 Erland Nelson, "Fathers' Occupations and Student Vocational Choices," *School and Society,* L (1939), 572–76.

11 Ruth Samson and Buford Stefflre, "Like Father—Like Son," *Personnel and Guidance Journal,* XXXI (1952), 38, 39.

tend to avoid manual objectives. An apparent explanation is that a person does not choose something with which he is unfamiliar.

The studies reviewed above suggest that an individual's vocational choices are determined by the breadth of his experiences and the attitudes which he developed during the process of growing up.

According to John Holland's [12] theory, an individual orders his preferences for six major environments as he matures, and this ordering of preferences determines the person's range of vocational choice. When, for example, there is a well-defined hierarchy (one preference clearly dominates all others), the individual can make a choice of vocation with a minimum of conflict or vacillation, but where the hierarchy is ambiguous (two or more competing preferences), there is vacillation or no choice. Holland's six major occupational environments are: (1) motoric environment, e.g., occupations such as machine operators, aviators, or truck drivers; (2) intellectual environment, e.g., philosopher or chemist; (3) supportive environment, e.g., counselor, teacher, or social worker; (4) conforming environment, e.g., bank tellers, file clerks, or secretaries; (5) persuasive environment, e.g., business executives, politicians, or salesmen; and (6) esthetic environment, e.g., artists, poets, or musicians. If this theory is supported by research, it may prove very useful in encouraging an initial choice of a broad field of work, with eventual refining of the choice as the individual matures. Certainly this approach is not new. It was the basis upon which Kuder developed the ten interest areas for his interest inventory. It was also the basis on which the occupational groupings of interest were developed for the Strong Vocational Interest Blank.

Man has many important goals, and his early home and community experiences probably influence the choices he makes in defining these other goals much as they influence his choice of vocation. His choice of a marriage partner, of friends, of church, of political party, of residence, and of automobile all reflect the image of himself that he is trying to convey to others. The extent to which this public image agrees with his private image of himself may also be an indication of his mental health. If he finds his goals personally satisfying and if he believes he can achieve them, they are appropriate; but if he has created them to reassure himself, to answer some doubts he has about himself, they are unhealthy.

12 John L. Holland, "A Theory of Vocational Choice," *Journal of Counseling Psychology*, VI (1959), 35–44.

Choice of goals probably has symbolic meaning for the individual. J. R. Cautela [13] very effectively uses the cases of two college students to illustrate how the symbolic meaning of occupations influenced their vocational decisions. Segal [14] utilizes psychoanalytic theory to determine how accounting students and creative writing students differed in certain personality characteristics. For example, his data show that accounting students made a vocational choice earlier than did creative writing students, and that creative writing students were more able to respond to emotionally toned situations than were the accounting students. Dipboye and Anderson [15] investigated the importance of manifest needs in occupational behavior. Among other things, they concluded that an individual must consider not only the congruency between his needs and the potential of an occupation to satisfy them, but also the potential which his total environment has for satisfying his peculiar needs. Thus, an individual must consider all of his goals in making decisions with reference to each one.

Helping Girls Achieve Vocational Maturity

THE special problems that girls confront in making vocational and educational plans have been neglected even by researchers in their studies of the development of vocational maturity. Such research is badly needed, though there are special difficulties involved in studying the development of vocational maturity among females. While studies of women might begin at approximately the same age as similar studies of men, they must be conducted over a longer period of time and extended farther into adult life. They must cover the time a young woman establishes her family, and continue to the time she enters or returns to her out-of-home career, if she does so.

Increasing numbers of women are being employed, and more will continue to be employed, outside of the home.[16] Increasing effort will be made to identify some of our brightest girls and to attract

13 J. R. Cautela, "The Factors of Psychological Need in Occupational Choice," *Personnel and Guidance Journal*, XXXVIII (1959), 46–48.

14 S. J. Segal, "A Psychoanalytic Analysis of Personality Factors in Vocational Choice," *Journal of Counseling Psychology*, VIII (1961), 202–10.

15 W. J. Dipboye and W. F. Anderson, "Occupational Stereotypes and Manifest Needs of High School Students," *Journal of Counseling Psychology*, VIII (1961), 296–304.

16 C. Gilbert Wrenn, *The Counselor in a Changing World* (Washington, D.C.: American Personnel and Guidance Association, 1962), pp. 23–25.

them into responsible positions in business, industry, and the professions. With the shortage of college-educated manpower, it is imperative that we make effective use of the talents of those women *who decide to seek employment outside of the home.*

Those most concerned with this problem have been professional women who were interested, and properly so, in obtaining equal rights for women. Because of this interest, however, they have often failed to differentiate between their role as a campaigner for equal rights for women and their role as counselor or academic advisor. While failure to make this distinction is understandable, it seems to have interfered with their success in helping promising young women find a career outside of homemaking or in addition to homemaking.

On the other hand, society's influence has not encouraged girls to take seriously the choice of an out-of-home career. Most scholars agree that a happy marriage and family are more highly valued by our society than is a girl's success in an out-of-home career. At least most high school and college girls are convinced that this is so. Even those who have made vocational plans that involve both an out-of-home career and marriage usually discover that when financial support is limited, the family will elect to educate the boys in the family in preference to the girls. Such choices suggest to girls that their parents do not believe that out-of-home careers are very important for girls. Consequently, girls tend to be more concerned about their success in love, marriage, and a family than they are with the choice of an out-of-home occupation.

To illustrate some of the problems counselors face in helping intellectually gifted girls make vocational choices, the author would like to cite a series of discussions he had with a group of twenty intellectually gifted undergraduate university women—each of whom, at one time or another, had been encouraged to do advanced graduate work. During the discussions these students expressed some feelings that may help school counselors understand why such girls react as they do when counselors try to encourage them to use their abilities in challenging occupations: (1) we believe that homemaking is an honorable career, and what is more, the women we admire most are good homemakers; (2) we cannot accept as female models most of the women who have encouraged us to do advanced graduate study; (3) we find honors courses interesting and challenging and we believe that we could enjoy advanced graduate study, but we are not willing to substitute a career outside of the home for marriage and a family; (4) though we cannot get enthusiastic about some of the routine household chores, we are not certain that we care to jeopardize our success as homemakers by employment outside of the home; and (5) we resent the pressure to seek employment outside of the home; we believe that we have the right to make the choice that we feel is best for us.

Whether one likes it or not, these feelings influence girls' choices. Counselors must accept and try to understand these feelings, including the girls' right to be full-time homemakers; they must try to help girls discuss their feelings and take account of these feelings in making their vocational choices; and they must try to introduce those interested in a career out-of-the-home to women who have solved these problems in various ways. Where, for example, a girl believes that her need for a college education is being overlooked in order to provide a college education for her brother, the counselor can help the girl discuss how she feels about this, what the intellectual challenge means to her, why she needs it to realize her full potential as a person, and how she can convey these feelings to her family. On such occasions she wants understanding, not pity.

For many girls, especially for the intellectually gifted, the financial reward may not be sufficient reason to seek employment outside the home (and the material things the money buys can be a source of guilt). The need for intellectual challenge and for self-realization has appeal for many bright girls; the fact that they can make a significant contribution also has great appeal. For those who have a deep commitment to becoming successful homemakers, even these attractions may not be sufficient; they must be convinced that they can have a career outside the home without jeopardizing their marriage. Discussing their doubts with an understanding counselor helps, though for many even this is not sufficient. Before they can accept a career outside of the home, they must understand how they can fulfill their family responsibilities and enjoy their family life.

Lest the reader misunderstand, the author is not arguing for putting pressure on girls to seek out-of-home careers. He is merely reporting that increasing numbers of women are seeking employment outside of the home and that society must make the best possible use of these resources. Far too many bright women who are employed in out-of-home careers are doing work which does not begin to use their full potential. Careful vocational and educational planning

while they are still in high school should increase the chances of using the full potential of those who decide to follow an out-of-home
career.

In addition to all the problems with which a boy is confronted in
developing educational and vocational plans, a girl must answer to
her satisfaction questions [17] such as: How important are marriage and
a family for me? Am I a good marriage prospect? To what extent
should I take account of my chances for marriage in making educational and vocational plans? How do I really feel about an out-of-
home career? To what extent should I be willing to reevaluate my
educational and vocational plans in order to take account of the
needs and wishes of my fiance or husband or children? If I decide
to give full-time attention to my family while my children are
young, how can I take this decision into account in developing my
plans? To what extent should I consider part-time employment in
developing my plans? Such questions are not easily answered and,
once answered, they must be raised over and over again in light of
new information and new opportunities. Though counselors must be
careful not to force these questions upon girls, they must convey to
the girls that they can understand why the questions are difficult to
answer and that they are willing to help them think about the answers. Neither should this be perceived as the responsibility of only
female counselors. Many girls prefer to discuss these questions with
male counselors.

Though Hugh Bell [18] used three male cases to illustrate effectively
ego-involvement in vocational decisions, his findings certainly apply
to females. He concluded that the counselor must consider the degree of ego-involvement and be patient with the client as he struggles to understand himself, the forces influencing his choices, and
the opportunities available to him. When girls really examine the
kinds of question raised here, there will be ego-involvement in
choice of vocation. Unfortunately, far too many girls never really
seriously consider choice of vocation; they perceive the choice
merely as a matter of selecting a job to provide the necessary income
until they marry or have children. To make the best possible use of
their talents and to help them achieve job satisfaction, girls must

17 Obviously, many of these questions must be examined by boys too, but
the answers do not influence a boy's choice of vocation in the same way they
do a girl's choice.

18 Hugh M. Bell, "Ego-involvement in Vocational Decisions," *Personnel
and Guidance Journal*, XXXVIII (1960), 732–36.

give the same serious attention to educational and vocational plans that we have normally expected boys to give to these decisions.

Implications of Theory and Research for Practice

VOCATIONAL choice is no longer perceived as a single choice, but as a series of choices which occur as the individual passes through various stages in the process of achieving vocational maturity. This new perception has implications for school guidance practices pertaining to the study of occupations, use of tests, educational planning, school curricula, and counseling procedures.

What are the implications for the study of occupations? Adults should give more attention to elementary-school children's interest in occupations. Though these children are still in the fantasy choice stage, parents, teachers, and counselors should foster their interest in occupations. Unfortunately, only a limited amount of material appropriate for these children is available. Research similar to that of J. Harlan Shores [19] is needed; however, it should focus attention upon what elementary-school children would like to know about occupations. Once these data are available, publishers should be encouraged to prepare pamphlets to answer children's broad questions on the world of work as well as their questions on specific occupations.

Super's [20] findings suggest that junior high pupils may need a different type of occupational information than is generally available today. He reported that ninth-graders were ready for vocational exploration, but not for vocational choice. If careful examination of the occupational information reveals that it was designed to help those actually making vocational choices, then a different type of material will be needed to help those who are exploring vocations. Here, too, research is needed to determine what these pupils want to know about occupations. Even if the present occupational information provides pupils with the facts, it will not be accepted and used effectively unless the pupils perceive it to be appropriate and relevant. More material also should be written for junior high school pupils on job families. Even the material on specific occupations

19 J. Harlan Shores, "Reading Interests and Information Needs of Children in Grades Four to Eight," *Elementary English,* XXXI (1954), 493–500.

20 Donald E. Super, "The Critical Ninth Grade: Vocational Choice or Vocational Exploration," *Personnel and Guidance Journal,* XXXIX (1960), 106–09.

which has been developed for junior high pupils should place more emphasis on the relationship between each specific occupation and closely allied occupations than is commonly done today. With increasing amounts of automation, as well as all the other socioeconomic factors which will influence employment during the next two decades, more attention also must be given to job families in developing materials even for those who are making vocational choices.

What are the implications of the research evidence and the new theories of vocational choice with respect to use of tests? When the school counselor was primarily concerned with helping each student make a reasonable vocational choice and develop educational plans to achieve that particular goal, it was not as important for the student to understand test results as it is today. Although good counselors have always tried to help their clients obtain and understand the information required to make intelligent choices, until very recently a counselor's success has been judged in terms of whether the objectives selected were realistic, not whether his clients understood the information provided. With the acceptance of the notion that vocational choice is a process which involves a series of choices, many of which will be made after the students graduate from high school, the school counselor must help his clients understand and accept themselves as they are so that they can make wisely the choices they will be required to make after they leave school. The research studies reviewed in Chapters 6 and 7 suggest that it is very difficult to help students understand and accept test results. The evidence also suggests that a counselor must be able to detect and help students discuss feelings about test results, and that successful test interpretation requires a better understanding of human behavior and better counseling skills than most educators have realized.

Test results also must be supplemented with nontest data, and better tests are required to provide students with the information they need. However, we must also realize that at least part of the instability of test scores can be accounted for by the students' immaturity. Super [21] reported that ninth-graders' aptitudes, interests, self-knowledge, and attitudes are still developing and changing, some of them only slightly but some of them considerably. Therefore, when a student makes educational and vocational decisions,

21 *Ibid.*, p. 109.

the counselor should recognize the importance of having relatively recent test data; he cannot rely on test scores taken several years earlier. Though such scores may be reasonably accurate for most students, the counselor has no way of knowing whether the scores accurately describe his particular client at present.

What are the implications of research evidence and new theories for curriculum development? High school teachers, counselors, and administrators are confronted with growing pressure from colleges to increase the number of graduation requirements for students in the college preparatory curriculum.[22] Changes resulting from this pressure force students to make educational decisions before they are mature enough, and aside from depriving youngsters of the chance to explore widely before making decisions, there is a tendency to treat these decisions as irreversible. The curriculum makers must resist the pressure to make curricula inflexible. They also must make every effort to provide both challenging and varied school experiences. For example, course offerings should be broad enough to provide students with the opportunity to take courses in the various fields. Schools also should provide opportunities for students to explore their vocational roles through extra-class activities, work-experience programs, and part-time employment.

Even if there were no shortage of technical and professional personnel, teachers and counselors should be concerned about identifying, motivating, and guiding all gifted and talented youth. There are at least two good reasons for this, and both have implications for curriculum planning: first, our nation is committed to helping every individual develop his abilities, aptitudes, and interests in his own way, and second, reasonable self-actualization is a necessary condition for mental health. Not only must the gifted and talented be identified while they are in school, but they must be identified early in order to provide proper educational experiences for the development of their interests, aptitudes, and abilities, in order to help them understand and accept themselves and their gifts, and in order to help parents understand and accept their children's gifts and assume responsibility for helping develop them. A good testing program

22 Three recent publications discuss these changes and their implications for school practices: (1) J. B. Conant, *The American High School Today* (New York: McGraw-Hill Book Co., Inc., 1959). (2) *Facing Facts About College Admissions* (New York: The Prudential Insurance Company of America, 1962). (3) Sidney Sulkin, *Complete Planning for College* (New York: McGraw-Hill Book Co., Inc., 1962).

is essential to fulfill these objectives, but perhaps harder to provide is the quality program required to challenge and motivate these children, and the time and effort required to help parents understand and meet their responsibilities.

What are the implications of the research evidence and the theories of vocational choice for educational planning? There will probably always be some good college prospects who will decide very late in their high school careers that they want to go to college. For example, let us consider the case of a high school senior who completed a technical vocational course before he accepted his unusual intellectual ability and made plans to attend college to prepare for a new vocational goal. Some counselors are inclined to feel that it is too late for such a student to make such a radical shift in plans. Instead, the counselor must try to understand how the change occurred, how the client feels about abandoning the old goal, and why the new goal is meaningful for him now—and help him prepare for the new goal. Unfortunately, some high school counselors have too readily accepted Ginzberg's notion that the choice process is largely irreversible. Though the original vocational choice in this case was irreversible in the sense that the student did have to take considerable post-high school work in order to meet college admission requirements, the advantages which accrued to the individual, and to society, should certainly be worth it—especially when one considers the choice in terms of a productive work life of approximately forty-five years.

Another implication is that parents often blame school personnel for failing to prepare their children to meet college admission requirements. Counselors can avoid much of this criticism by careful educational planning and by enlisting parents' participation in developing educational plans. Parent discussion groups designed for this purpose were described in Chapter 10. Another effective approach is an annual spring registration which encourages parents' participation in the selection of school subjects and extra-class activities. (See FIGURE 3.)

Effective use of this card calls for parents' approval following careful choice of school subjects in terms of the student's educational and vocational goals. Teacher advisers may be used for this purpose. Usually, best results are obtained when students are given a choice of adviser. This gives the student a chance to select someone he knows and feels is interested in him (often he selects a

FIGURE 3   Registration Card

```
┌─────────────────────────────────────────────────────────────────┐
│                                                                   │
│  REGISTRATION CARD              Date _____      │
│                                                                   │
│  Name _____   │
│  Address _____   │
│  Attended _____ School last year    Grade _____   │
│  ═══════════════════════════════════════════════════════════════  │
│                                                                   │
│  Vocational goals: _____    Subjects:                    │
│  _____    1. _____   │
│  _____    2. _____   │
│  Educational goals: _____    3. _____   │
│  _____    4. _____   │
│  _____    5. _____   │
│  Extra-class activities:             6. _____   │
│  1. _____    If it were offered, I would take: │
│  2. _____    _____    │
│  3. _____    _____    │
│  4. _____    _____    │
│  ═══════════════════════════════════════════════════════════════  │
│                                                                   │
│                                                                   │
│       Signature of Adviser              Signature of Parent       │
│                                                                   │
└─────────────────────────────────────────────────────────────────┘
```

teacher who teaches his favorite subject), and the teacher, knowing that the student chose him, is motivated to do an especially good job. Perhaps some are wondering what the counselor's responsibility for registration is: he is responsible for in-service education of teacher-advisers and for helping those who have no educational or vocational plans to make at least tentative plans.

Another practice that usually prevents registration errors is mimeographing different forms of the registration card for each grade and curriculum. Working with groups enrolled in the same curriculum, the administrator can list all required courses on the registration card.

With this kind of planning and parent participation, there is less likelihood that parents will blame the school later, and when they do, the registration cards for each year can be used to help parents see how school personnel have tried to help students select courses and extra-class activities in terms of their stated goals.

Though most students are not ready to make even tentative vocational choices at the end of the eighth grade or at the beginning of the ninth grade, many are ready to make at least tentative plans with reference to college. Even those who are good college prospects but have never seriously considered college are more willing to consider it with an open mind at this age than they usually are a year or two later. Sometimes students reject the idea of going to college because parents have talked too much about college. For other students it is their parents' and friends' doubts about college that make them look upon it with disfavor. With the present concern for the intellectually gifted, there is also a real possibility that school personnel will neglect those for whom college is neither essential nor appropriate; they too must make appropriate educational plans in order to achieve their vocational goals.

Finally, what are the implications of the new approach for counseling procedures? Inasmuch as choice of vocation is now accepted as a series of choices instead of a single choice, and many persons will be required to make new vocational choices as adults during the next two decades, it is more important than ever that students obtain from vocational counseling self-respect, independence, improved understanding of themselves, competence in identifying and coping with the forces that influence their choices, and improved skills in solving problems. Helping clients make realistic choices will continue to be an important criterion in evaluating vocational counseling, but increasing attention must be given to helping clients understand themselves and to teaching them to make independent decisions. Rather than advising and pointing out relationships, the counselor must try to help each client discover for himself such things as: (1) the relationship between the job requirements and his ability to do the job; (2) the relationship between tasks required on the job and the things which he enjoys doing; (3) the relationship between his vocational choice and his other important goals; (4) the extent to which his total environment has potential for satisfying important needs and interests which are not apt to be satisfied on the job; and (5) the questions for which answers should be sought prior to making a choice. When a student challenges the validity of the information pertaining either to his own qualifications or to the requirements of the job, the counselor should help the student examine these feelings by responding to the feelings. The best way to help the student understand himself and learn to take independent action is to help him obtain the information he feels he needs, to react to the information, and to examine ways of making the decisions he needs to make.

But someone will surely say, "Many students are too immature to make their own decisions. Some will make unreasonable choices. Should not the counselor try to prevent these failures?" This question may be answered with another question, "Can the counselor really prevent failure?" Some students have made such deep personal commitments that they cannot change their goals readily. Many of these students would rather experience failure than give up without trying to achieve their goals. Moreover, some poor risks *do* succeed. Thus teachers and counselors should be cautious about making dogmatic statements concerning a student's chances for achieving success. The available research evidence suggests that such statements are inappropriate. Instead, the counselor should allow the student the privilege of deciding whether he wants to gamble on the odds for success reflected in the data.

Other adolescents do not seem to be able to make a vocational choice. A number of factors could account for this inability: (1) day to day existence in a home in which there is little planning, (2) dependence on parents or other adults for direction, (3) lack of a strong identification figure, (4) no one expecting very much from them or caring very much about them, (5) adults' failures to encourage their early interest in occupations, or (6) lack of opportunity for self-appraisal and exploration of occupations during early high school years. Some of these youngsters do whatever adults suggest without really understanding the significance of their choices. Others are inclined to postpone vocational choice too long, and may never make a choice while they are in school unless the school personnel can help them develop some readiness for decision. Those who leave school before they make a choice often drift into their life work without any real vocational planning.

It is important that those who do not expect to continue their formal education when they leave high school at least be offered assistance in making a vocational choice, and that the counselor try to help these students see this initial choice as one choice in a series which they will be required to make. Some high school principals are so committed to this point of view that they automatically refer every drop-out to a school counselor. The extent to which these referrals are successful tends to be determined by the way the referrals are made. Most of those who drop out of high school have already developed a hostile attitude toward school, and therefore are difficult to reach and to help. If, in making the referral, the principal says something like, "Most students who quit school seek employment. If you would like assistance in choosing an occupation and in finding a job, one of our counselors would be glad to help you, and I should be happy to introduce you to one of them," he increases the chances of the student's accepting the counselor's help. If, in contrast, a student who is quitting school is referred to the counselor with the statement, "Next you must talk with a counselor and obtain his signature on this card," it is most difficult to develop a counseling relationship. And by the same token it is difficult to help the student make a vocational choice. As a matter of fact, the most permissive approach tends to encourage students to remain in school. When, in a permissive atmosphere, the student studies himself, his interests, his preferred occupations, and the training required for each occupation, he frequently finds that his preferred occupation requires more education. This kind of experience is much more convincing to the high school student than a lecture on the merits of a high school education.

Some students elect to continue their education beyond high school because they cannot make a vocational choice. While they are broadening their understanding of the culture and the problems of modern life, they should be encouraged to study themselves and to explore ways of earning a living. Others continue their education beyond high school to acquire a general education, usually a liberal arts education. Among these, there are always a few who do not have to be concerned about earning a living; others, who have made vocational choices, realize that their chosen occupations require little, if any, vocational or professional training.

Still others continue their education beyond high school to prepare themselves for specific vocations or professions. They believe they know how they want to earn a living, and they need help in selecting subjects and extra-class activities that will help them achieve their goal. They also need assistance in making choices that will help them understand themselves and the world around them. They, too, can profit from general education.

In selecting schools and colleges, a student in each of the above groups should take cognizance of his own special situation. This means, of course, that the student should know what he wants from a college before he selects one. After he has decided what he wants, he is ready to look for the institutions which will best prepare him for his goal. Group techniques which the counselor may use to aid students in these decisions were described in Chapter 10. Suggestions for working with students on an individual basis may be found in Chapters 3 and 4.

Finally, school counselors should try to convey to the students and the staff what guidance services are provided to help students develop educational and vocational plans. All along the way educational planning should be integrated with vocational planning. Whenever a student selects subjects and extra-class activities, he should consider the values to be derived from each in achieving his vocational objectives. He also should think of the contributions each may make to his personal development. When choosing subjects and activities, he should consider which will help him learn to live a happier life and to contribute to his community, as well as which ones will help him achieve his vocational goal.

SUGGESTED READINGS

1. GINZBERG, ELI, W. S. GINSBURG, SIDNEY AXELROD, and J. L. HERMA. *Occupational Choice*. New York: Columbia University Press, 1951.

   This book reports on a study of the determinants of vocational choice. Four chapters are especially relevant: 7, 8, 9, and 13.
   a] How do children's reasons for vocational choices change as they mature?
   b] What elements seem to influence vocational choice?
   c] What essential decisions are high school students required to make that influence choice of vocation?

2. HOPPOCK, ROBERT. *Occupational Information*. New York: McGraw-Hill Book Co., Inc., 1957.

   Three chapters are recommended here: 7, 8, and 9.
   a] What factors influence occupational choice?
   b] How may a counselor help a pupil take account of psychological factors in choosing an occupation?
   c] How do one's needs influence his choice of occupation?

3. ROE, ANNE. *The Psychology of Occupations*. New York: John Wiley & Sons, Inc., 1956.

   This book was written for students preparing to enter vocational guidance, counseling psychology, and clinical psychology. Suggested chapters are 1, 21, 22, and 23.

a] To what extent does sex determine occupational role?
b] What elements seem to determine a worker's level of aspiration?
c] How does choice of occupation influence other aspects of living?

4. SUPER, DONALD E. "Preliminary Appraisal in Vocational Counseling," *Personnel and Guidance Journal*, XXXVI (1957), 154–61.

This paper suggests ways of using nontest data to supplement test data in vocational counseling. It also presents a number of good ideas which can be used to develop hypotheses for research.
   a] What is the primary danger of counselors becoming preoccupied with gathering information for clients?

5. SUPER, DONALD E. and PHOEBE OVERSTREET. *The Vocational Maturity of Ninth-Grade Boys*. New York: Columbia University Press, 1960.

The second monograph in Super's career pattern studies, this volume analyzes the vocational maturity of ninth-grade boys. Suggested chapters are 6 and 9.
   a] What variables are associated with vocational maturity?
   b] What are the implications for educational planning?

Vocational Placement and Follow-up

F VOCATIONAL counseling is to be effective, it must be supported
by effective vocational placement. Adequate placement services
are needed to help students implement their vocational choices
and apply the vocational skills and knowledge obtained subsequent
to making a vocational choice. Without adequate placement services
students tend to take whatever job they can obtain, usually through
the help of people close to them. For example, Lloyd Reynolds [1]
reported that most of his research subjects found jobs with the assistance of relatives and acquaintances. Regis Leonard [2] also found

1 Lloyd G. Reynolds, *The Structure of the Labor Markets* (New York:
Harper & Row, Publishers, 1951), p. 129.
2 Regis J. Leonard, "Occupational Experiences of Trade School Graduates,"
Occupations, XXVIII (1949), 28–31.

that most of the subjects in his study obtained jobs through personal contacts, and that only 43 percent of the graduates of these particular vocational programs obtained employment in the field for which their training had prepared them. Margaret Andrews [3] found that when youth first leave school, they often are idle and many shift aimlessly from one job to another.

Unemployed young people are a serious threat to our nation's economy and a source of discontent and crime. In fact, this problem has become so serious that special federal legislation was passed recently to cope with it.[4] Though federal aid may be needed for the training program, schools must take responsibility for the counseling and training of these youth, and must cooperate with other agencies in placing them.

A well-coordinated follow-up service is needed to obtain from recent graduates a realistic picture of what lies ahead for present students, to help former students reappraise their educational and vocational plans, to appraise the school's program, to obtain ideas for improving the program, and to obtain the information the school requires to adapt its adult education program to meet better the needs of its former students and the community.

Responsibility for Placement

THE mere fact that students need a service is not sufficient reason for the schools to provide it. Whenever there is evidence that students need a service which is not being provided adequately, school personnel should help define the required service and help the community leaders decide who should be assigned responsibility for it. Inasmuch as most school districts have either a State Employment Office located within their district or a nearby one which services their community, the task of job placement seems to be one of those instances in which the responsibility should be shared. If however, adequate service is to be provided and conflict is to be avoided, employees of both agencies must understand what each agency should be expected to do. Usually, best results are obtained when policies are established by an advisory committee, made up

3 Margaret E. Andrews, *Providing School Placement Service* (Chicago: Science Research Associates, 1957), p. 6.

4 The Juvenile Delinquency and Youth Offenses Control Act (Public Law 87–274) was passed in 1961, and the Manpower Development and Training Act (Public Law 87–415) was passed in 1962.

of representatives selected from members of the student councils, and adults who work in school placement, the State Employment Office, labor, business, and industry.

First, let us consider what assistance can be expected from the State Employment Office. It can provide: (1) information on the labor market for both local and national conditions; (2) information on local job openings, including part-time and summer employment as well as full-time regular post-school jobs; (3) information on opportunities for on-the-job training in business and industry; and (4) information on apprenticeship opportunities.

School personnel can (1) help students understand themselves; (2) help them make a tentative vocational choice; (3) encourage them to explore vocational roles through extra-class activities, work-experience programs, and part-time employment; (4) help students identify their salable skills, help them evaluate specific jobs, and help them solicit placement data from the school staff; (5) cooperate with local representatives of the State Employment Service in appraising an individual's job competencies, in teaching youth how to apply for jobs, and in locating persons for specific jobs; and (6) do follow-up studies to assess former students' success on the job, in training programs, and in post-high educational programs.

The school placement officer should arrange for a representative from the local offices of the State Employment Office to register all students seeking jobs and to test them. These things can be done without cost to either the school or the students. Originally, the objective of the United States Employment Service was to develop relevant tests for every major job family. Though this objective has not been achieved, much useful data can be obtained from this battery which can be used in helping students make vocational choices, explore job competencies, and discover abilities and aptitudes required for training programs.

If a school is to have an effective placement service, a member of the staff must be assigned responsibility for its part of the work, and it must provide a well-balanced guidance program. Of the six responsibilities listed above, the first three are provided primarily by the other guidance services: counseling, child study, information, orientation, and educational-vocational planning. For the third, a good high school program also is essential. These other services were discussed earlier; hence, the rest of this section is focused upon (3), (4), (5), and (6).

A WORK-EXPERIENCE PROGRAM

At present, most of these programs are provided at the senior high school level. However, the development of vocational education in community junior colleges has given rise to a marked increase in such programs at the junior college level. Except for the programs developed for the mentally handicapped, most of the programs have been designed to provide supervised work-experience in semi-skilled and skilled trades, and in clerical, secretarial, and sales occupations. Usually the responsibility for the various phases of the programs is assigned to staff members in business education and industrial education. These persons must be competent in their own vocational skills and must be able to establish a good working relationship with organized labor as well as with management.

For a work-experience program to be effective, student self-appraisal, vocational counseling, and some vocational training should precede it. While students are participating in the work-experience program, their on-the-job training should be supplemented by further vocational training and supervision by a competent employer at the work station and by a school staff member. In addition to helping students to increase their job skills, and to solve whatever other problems they meet, the school supervisor should encourage students to appraise their job skills and to become acquainted with related occupations. To achieve these objectives, the coordinator of every work-experience program must have a reasonably good knowledge of each student's skills; an adequate, and well-qualified, school staff to supervise students on the job; a variety of good work stations in which to place students; and well-qualified counselors to whom he can refer students for vocational counseling. For these reasons, the work-experience program should be closely integrated with the school placement and counseling services. Frequently, one of the work-experience coordinators also serves as placement officer.

PART-TIME EMPLOYMENT AND
SUMMER EMPLOYMENT

Most jobs can provide meaningful experience for youth. Among other things, work-experiences teach young people to be punctual, to assume responsibility for specific tasks, to make certain relatively independent decisions, and to adapt to new and different types of people. Some jobs also introduce youth to a variety of occupations and to people from various socioeconomic strata, teach new job skills, and provide satisfaction from a job well done.

Whenever possible, students should be encouraged to take jobs that enable them to explore preferred occupations. Though they can get such work much more often than is common today, there are three primary reasons why it is not always possible, especially for certain types of professional occupation: (1) there are too few such part-time and summer jobs which provide experience with professional workers for high school students; (2) those jobs which do exist are rarely reported to school placement offices; and (3) other jobs pay better wages. With the assistance of professional persons, more such jobs can be located, but the wage problem would still exist: for example, a future doctor can earn more in construction work than he can as a hospital orderly. Many students need the additional money. All the placement officer can do is help the student locate employment and help him examine the relevance to himself of each job; the student must choose.

Some adults have been encouraged to help young people find summer jobs because they fear idle youth. When young people do not have something worthwhile to do, they often get into trouble; consequently, many communities have organized local campaigns to obtain jobs for them. Labor leaders, business and industrial leaders, school placement officers, state employment officers, and local newspaper publishers usually cooperate in these projects.

LOCATING JOBS

Local offices of the State Employment Service tend to have a better coverage of available jobs than schools do, but additional jobs are often discovered by supervisors of work-experience programs and school placement officers. These agencies should exchange job listings regularly, and school personnel should arrange for students to register in the State Employment Service.

It is not sufficient to know that there is a job opening in a given plant. To locate the best prospects for each job and to help the student evaluate the job, placement officers need an accurate description of it. Often this is difficult to obtain at first, but eventually employers come to see the mutual advantage of developing good job descriptions. Where local placement offices have been able to attract and hold good personnel over a period of time, employers tend to improve their description of jobs for which they are seeking employees.

EVALUATING JOBS

Evaluating jobs is the primary responsibility of the school placement officer, but often this responsibility is shared with the student's counselor. Even the choice of a part-time job should be looked upon as a means of implementing a vocational choice. When the problem is seen in this light, it is obvious why the student's counselor is often asked to aid the student in evaluating a given job. The evaluating process always should involve an analysis of the job duties, including the competencies required, and a comparison of these with the student's competencies, interests, and vocational goal. Sometimes such analyses call for a reappraisal of a student's interests, abilities, and aptitudes—something that certainly requires the assistance of the counselor. Students also should be encouraged to continue appraisal of the job as they work at it, and to take note of related jobs which have special appeal for them. When the placement officer knows of specific jobs in a work setting that is directly related to a student's vocational goal, he should encourage the student to note these jobs in particular and call the employer's attention to the student's goal.

APPLYING FOR JOBS

In order to present his salable skills, a student must know them. Though he should have learned them in vocational counseling, he may need to review them with his counselor's assistance just prior to applying for a job. Voluntary discussion groups (see Chapter 10) may be used to help students figure out how to describe their salable skills, and to provide assistance in writing letters of application, in filling out application blanks, in scheduling appointments for interviews, and in preparing for interviews. Role playing also may be used to supplement the discussions. Representatives of state employment services and major employers may be used effectively as consultants for these discussion groups.

Another interesting innovation is use of assimilated interviews with former students to prepare students for personal interviews. The interviews may be conducted in the former student's place of employment or at school. In either case, the student makes application and is interviewed for a specific job. After the interview, the former student discusses the success with which the student sold himself and his job competencies, and suggests ways the student can improve his presentation. Of course, the student is also encouraged to ask questions about any other problems that worry him concerning employment.

Administration of the Placement Service

IN ORGANIZING a school placement service for a school system which has more than one high school, one is confronted with the problem of whether to have a centralized service or separate services in each school. Over a decade ago Leon Lerner [5] noted a trend toward centralized placement services. Most experts also agree that at the least an officer should be designated by the superintendent to coordinate the school placement activities. To retain the chief advantage of decentralized placement, some school systems have designated a placement officer in each school, who helps students identify their salable job skills, helps them evaluate specific jobs, helps locate candidates for jobs, and solicits and organizes placement data for the central offices. Each of these activities requires a thorough knowledge of the students and faculty and their personal cooperation, knowledge possible only in the small community of a decentralized system. On the other hand, a coordinator of placement for the entire school system can provide leadership for in-service education of all school placement officers, can provide definition of policies for the entire system, and can represent the school in its relations with employers, organized labor, and the local State Employment Office.

THE COUNSELOR'S ROLE

What should be the counselor's role in placement? His primary responsibility here is to help his clients understand themselves, identify their salable skills, define vocational goals, and examine the relevance of specific jobs for their vocational goals. However, there are at least two reasons why a school counselor should not also serve as a placement officer: (1) he has unique professional skills for which there is a shortage of qualified workers and (2) the judgments which a placement officer is required to make interfere with

5 Leon L. Lerner, "Placement in Public Schools," *Occupations*, XXVII (1949), 322–25.

his effectiveness as a counselor. A good placement officer must screen candidates for jobs, and often he is called upon to give his own personal appraisal of candidates. Knowing this, students would be reluctant to discuss with him those topics which might expose their negative characteristics; thus, his effectiveness as a counselor would be reduced by his acting in a judgmental role as a placement officer.

If, however, a school has enough certified counselors to assign one to full-time placement, he should be well qualified for the job. Since those responsible for work-experience programs often have completed some of the basic graduate work in counselor education and have broad contacts with the employers and organized labor, they, rather than counselors, are commonly designated as placement officers.

PLACEMENT RECORDS

Unless the placement officer is careful, he can let the development and maintenance of placement records consume most of his time. Obviously, he cannot collect all the data that everyone would like to have on a prospective employee. And he must be very careful as to how he uses the data he does collect. A student's cumulative folder includes confidential data which was provided to help school personnel understand the child as a student; therefore, a placement officer should share no information with a prospective employer without first obtaining clearance with the faculty and the student.

What should be included in the placement record? This question may quite properly be discussed with the advisory committee on placement. Usually, the placement officer solicits a personal statement from the student and personal evaluations from certain teachers and former employers.

A student's statement should include a brief personal history and a description of his goals. Some employers also ask employees to describe their major strengths and weaknesses. Though some students have difficulty writing a concise personal statement, and some will require the placement officer's assistance, the task usually helps them organize their thoughts for completing application blanks and for personal interviews in the future.

If the school maintains a good cumulative folder for each student, the placement officer can use it to write a brief school history for the placement record. The history should include a description of the student's vocational objectives, his job skills, and his interests, abilities, and aptitudes as they were exhibited on tests (though not reported as specific test scores), in academic work, in extra-class activities, and in work-experiences. Evidence of leadership also should be noted. More precise suggestions for summarizing the data in the cumulative folder were given in Chapter 6.

Personal evaluations may be character references, evaluations of job skills, or both. Civic leaders are often asked to write character references. Though teachers and employers may be asked to appraise personal characteristics too, they are expected to focus attention on work habits and job skills; this is especially true of teachers of vocational subjects. Sometimes they are asked to record their appraisal of a student on a rating sheet, on which space is also set aside for additional comments. The rationale for using rating sheets and suggestions for developing them were presented in Chapter 8.

Follow-up Service

THE purposes to be achieved by a well-organized follow-up service are presented on the first page of this chapter; this section will discuss guides for conducting follow-up studies, using the data, and administering the service.

PLANNING FOLLOW-UP STUDIES

Follow-up studies should be planned with the same care and precision as research studies are. Before any attempt is made to collect data from former students, the following questions should be answered satisfactorily: (1) What purposes may be served by a follow-up study? (2) What data are needed to fulfill these purposes? (3) How do we expect to use these data to improve the school program and the guidance services for students? (4) Will our instruments provide the data we need? (5) Were the instruments developed with sufficient care, and properly field-tried, before being used with the entire sample? (6) Would we do better to use a sample from the defined population rather than to try to obtain data from everyone? (7) What provisions have been made to follow-up on those who fail to respond? (8) What consideration was given to obtaining data on forms which can be easily adapted for machine processing and statistical analysis?

To insure the careful planning required for successful follow-up studies, the proposal which answers the above questions should be developed and distributed to the entire faculty for discussion at a regular faculty meeting prior to launching the study. If the faculty has an executive committee, the proposal should be discussed with the committee prior to submitting it to the faculty. It also should be discussed with the student council. For the first study, at least, a consultant can help develop the instruments, select the sample, and plan the data processing. On the other hand, school personnel must be wary lest the expert delete important items from the instrument merely because they cannot be easily handled on the data-processing machines.

J. W. M. Rothney [6] made the following suggestions for conducting follow-up studies: (1) follow-up studies should be planned with students while they are still in school (more are apt to respond to and recognize the value of such studies when they understand why they are conducted); (2) contacts should be maintained with students between graduation and follow-up studies; (3) the follow-up questionnaire must be carefully prepared; (4) the mailing date should be selected with care; (5) correct addresses are important; and (6) follow-up letters must be carefully planned.

A SAMPLE STUDY

Most high school seniors are inclined to believe that a follow-up study of recent graduates will provide them with a realistic picture of what might lie ahead for them. The plan described here was developed by seniors enrolled in a work-experience seminar. After they had developed the proposal with the assistance of their instructor and he had cleared it with the faculty, they presented it to the entire senior class (eighty-nine students).

At a special meeting, the class discussed every step of the plan and the responsibilities to be assumed by each class member. Students who presented the plan felt that it could not succeed without full cooperation from every senior. After the class had approved the undertaking, each senior selected the names of alumni, from the two previous graduating classes, to whom he would send follow-up letters and questionnaires. Since each senior selected only those alumni whom he knew personally, those who selected names as-

6 J. W. M. Rothney, "Follow-up Services in the Small Secondary School," *High School Journal*, XL (1957), 274–79.

sumed responsibility for obtaining the current addresses for everyone on their lists. In their English class the next day the seniors wrote the following paragraphs, which everyone incorporated in his personal letter:

Our senior class has decided to try to find out what recent graduates are doing now. We feel that your answers will give us the best possible picture of what we can expect when we graduate. I chose you because I felt we knew one another well enough so you would make a special effort to answer my letter. I know we can count on your help.

Attached to this letter you will find a page on which I wish you would write your answers to our questions. You will also find enclosed an addressed, stamped envelope.

All the answers will be summarized by two seniors whom we have chosen because we felt they would do a good job and not tell anyone anything they learned about any individual. We want frank answers. We are sure you can trust these two seniors. Please complete this task for us today.

The following questions were included in the questionnaire attached:

1. What are you doing now? If you are working, describe the nature of your work. If you are in school, tell what you are preparing to do.
2. How did you decide to do what you are doing now?
3. If you have a job, tell how you obtained it.
4. What is the starting annual salary for jobs like the one you have?
5. What do most people in jobs like yours earn after one year?
6. Do you hope to make your career in this work?
7. If you are neither in the job in which you expect to make your career nor studying for it, how do you hope to get into that work?
8. Among the many things which you might have learned in high school, which would be most helpful for you to know now?
9. If you could turn the clock back to the second semester of your senior year, what would you do differently?
10. Where do you work?
11. Where do you receive your mail?

Slightly better than eight out of ten questionnaires were returned within two weeks of the mailing date, but very few additional ones were returned in response to follow-up letters. Three factors seemed to account for these unusually high returns: (1) correct addresses were obtained; (2) the seniors understood the relevance of the study for themselves and were deeply committed to it; and (3) the seniors knew well those to whom they addressed letters.

Since the school was quite small, machine processing of data was not essential. After the questionnaires were returned, the two seniors summarized the findings. Except for the last question, which was used by the principal's secretary to obtain correct addresses for alumni, the students summarized the responses for one question at a time. Usually they found the responses could be classified into one of four or five categories, which they defined with the assistance of the teacher. For question number one, the school counselor also noted whether the stated goal in the follow-up agreed with the student's goal when he left school. On all other answers, then, students could compare the two groups: those who were actualizing their goals with those who were not. When they completed their analysis of the data for each class they made an oral report to the senior class, filed a written report in the library for students' further study, and submitted a copy to the faculty for their use.

Perhaps some readers will wonder whether this follow-up questionnaire is typical. In those schools which summarize responses by some data-processing machine, most of these same questions may be asked but answers must be arranged for easier processing. As for the data requested, a number of common items were not included in the above questionnaire: (1) schools attended, curriculum pursued, degrees or certificates earned, and dates received; (2) positions held; (3) marital status; (4) children; (5) organizational memberships, including offices held in each; and (6) suggestions for improving the high school program.

Perhaps some readers will also wonder whether the questionnaire method is the best possible one. Other methods which have been used are personal interviews, telephone surveys, news notes sent in response to alumni newsletters, and analysis of news items in local papers. Though the questionnaire is far from a perfect method, it is the most common one used, and perhaps the most practical one for many schools.

APPRAISAL OF THE RESPONDING SAMPLE

What can one conclude from the data obtained from a mailed questionnaire? Who responds to such questionnaires? To what extent do they accurately represent the total population? F. K. Shuttleworth [7] obtained a significant difference between responses on early incomplete returns and responses on final complete returns. He reported that the following factors seemed to account for the biased returns: the respondent's success, the time required to complete the questionnaire, concern about confidences being kept, whether the questionnaire was sent to current addresses, and the respondent's perception of how results were to be used to help or hinder his success.

A decade later, Rothney and Mooren [8] studied sampling biases in a follow-up study of graduates from four Wisconsin high schools six months after graduation. The first mailing (double post card) brought 56 percent returns, the second mailing another 23 percent, the third mailing (which was accompanied by a form letter) brought 10 percent more, and finally the fourth mailing (which was accompanied by a personal handwritten letter) brought 6 percent more. The remaining 5 percent were visited in their homes. Had they been satisfied with incomplete returns, their results would have been biased in favor of those who returned their questionnaires first. The following kinds of people tended to return their questionnaires first: the girls, those who received intensive individual attention, those residing in industrial communities, the better students, the more intelligent students, those who continued their education beyond high school, and the employed—especially those who were employed in the better jobs. In other words, incomplete returns would tend to present an unduly favorable response because the proportion of responses was weighted in favor of the satisfied and successful. In a later paper to which a reference has already been made, Rothney also said that follow-up studies which are based upon 60 percent returns or less tend not to include responses from those

who were in prison, whose marriages had been broken, who were considered failures by themselves and society, who had been lowest ranking students in their high school classes, who held grudges against school and school personnel, and who were dissatisfied with their current status.[9]

7 F. K. Shuttleworth, "Sampling Errors Involved in Incomplete Returns to Mail Questionnaires," *Journal of Applied Psychology*, XXV (1941), 588–91.

8 J. W. M. Rothney and R. L. Mooren, "Sampling Problems in Follow-up Research," *Occupations*, XXX (1952), 573–78.

9 *Op. cit.*, p. 275.

What do these studies suggest for practices? (1) Students should be told about the follow-up studies while they still are in school; better still, they should be encouraged to help plan the studies and assist with the collection of the data so that they can learn from firsthand experience how the results are used to improve the school program and its guidance services. (2) The questionnaire must be carefully constructed to insure that pertinent data are obtained and that the questions are asked in a manner which will encourage the former student to answer honestly and to return the questionnaire. The suggestions which were made in Chapter 8 with reference to constructing personal history questionnaires certainly apply here, too. (3) The questionnaire should be accompanied by a covering letter (preferably a handwritten letter from someone the recipient knows) which explains how the results will be used, why they need responses from everyone, and how confidences will be kept. (4) Though schools may wish to send questionnaires to everyone to exhibit an interest in all graduates who are members of the classes designated for study and to identify those for whom the school can still provide needed services, perhaps they should use carefully chosen sampling techniques *to select a predetermined sample* from each class for whom *complete returns would be obtained*. The use of a carefully chosen sample from the total population is common in polling today and has proven to be an effective practice. For example, polls commonly predict elections with a percentage of error as little as one or two percent. Schools, too, should use a sampling for such purposes as follow-up studies. Obviously, they cannot afford to telephone or to arrange for personal interviews for everyone in an entire class who fails to return a questionnaire, but they can afford to do these things for those few in a selected sample who failed to return their questionnaires.

ADMINISTRATION OF THE SERVICE

No one would argue with the idea that someone must be assigned responsibility for this service if it is to be done well. Usually one of three persons is assigned the responsibility: the coordinator of placement services, the director of research, or the director of guidance. Obviously, a case can be made for making each responsible for the follow-up service. Certainly, the administrator of this service must possess certain research competencies. The director of placement must maintain good contacts with former students in his regular placement work, so many people think he is in the best position to obtain good returns from former students. Others argue that his responsibility for placement may prevent some of the least successful from cooperating with him in follow-up studies. The primary argument for making the guidance director responsible for administration of the follow-up service is that he is most directly involved. He is in a position to use the data to improve the guidance services and to make recommendations for improving the school program. Whoever is assigned the primary responsibility for the follow-up service obviously must work closely with the others, with the students and with the faculty, to do this job well.

SUGGESTED READINGS

1. FROELICH, CLIFFORD P. *Guidance Services in Schools.* New York: McGraw-Hill Book Co., Inc., 1958.

    This is an introductory guidance text. Chapter 11 is recommended for our purposes here.
    a] Why should schools provide placement services?
    b] What are the primary arguments for a central placement office for an entire school system?

2. HUMPHREYS, J. ANTHONY, ARTHUR E. TRAXLER, and ROBERT D. NORTH. *Guidance Services.* Chicago: Science Research Associates, 1960.

    This introductory text presents and describes procedures for guidance services at all educational levels. Chapters 10 and 14.
    a] What must a counselor consider in following up on former clients?
    b] What can the school do to help a student increase his chances for getting a job that he wants?
    c] What are the responsibilities of the school placement officer?

3. HUTSON, PERCIVAL W. *The Guidance Function in Education.* New York: Appleton-Century-Crofts, 1958.

    Chapter 17.
    a] Where do young workers learn about their first jobs?
    b] What are the principal advantages of the Hunter plan for instructing students in job-finding skills?

13

Social and Leadership Development

THE IMPORTANCE of self-realization for good mental health has been stressed throughout this book. The author has discussed ways in which a student's mental health may influence his school and vocational success, and the ways his successes may influence his mental health. But man is involved in activities other than schools and jobs for which social and leadership skills are required, and these also affect his mental health.

For a long time educators have recognized the need for carefully planned social programs and extra-class activities to provide recreation and to help young people develop social skills. They have realized that the young person needs to learn to play as well as to work with others, and that carefully planned social experiences can be used to teach social skills and develop leaders.

Educators also have recognized the importance of developing leaders and of helping them fill useful roles as citizens. It is not sufficient to teach young people about their responsibilities as citizens in a democratic nation; while they are students they should be provided with experiences in which to develop leadership skills and the will to work for and contribute to the improvement of our local, state, and federal government.

Since the guidance department is usually given the primary responsibility for these activities, they are discussed here. There are several reasons why the guidance staff should be expected to provide leadership for the development of social and leadership programs: they should possess the personal qualifications, professional experiences, and knowledge of human behavior and group dynamics essential to select faculty sponsors, to help develop programs, to provide in-service education, and to appraise such programs. Eventually, most of the responsibilities for the social program and leadership development should be assigned to members of the teaching staff as was suggested for the information, orientation, placement, and follow-up services.

This chapter discusses the development and appraisal of social and extra-class programs, various types of leaders, leadership training in a school setting, leadership experiences which schools can provide, and the implications for using the study of group processes with students.

The Development of a Social Program

THE purpose of a social program is to provide meaningful social and recreational experiences for youth. To achieve this purpose, the members of the school staff must be acquainted with the school's traditions, the pupils' interests, and the activities appropriate for pupils of this age. They must be able to enlist the pupils' cooperation in identifying and appraising social and extra-class activities. The staff also should try to identify activities which will teach new social and recreational skills.

There are a number of ways of identifying meaningful social activities in and out of class. One of the best is through the suggestions of the youngsters themselves. When pupils realize that their suggestions are appreciated, they will pass them on to their teachers and counselors. Secondary-school students' suggestions for extra-class activities can be solicited during spring registration —especially when students are encouraged to select extra-class activities with the same care that they select school subjects, as was suggested in Chapter 11. The student council also can play an important role in soliciting students' suggestions for both extra-class activities and for social programs. Sometimes the student council merely asks students to submit suggestions. Other councils have helped the staff develop a questionnaire or interview schedule which the council members later used to solicit suggestions from a carefully chosen sample of the student body.

If a quality program is to be developed and maintained, it must be evaluated periodically. In addition to encouraging students to react to extra-class offerings during registration, and to suggesting meaningful new activities, the staff should solicit the student council's assistance in evaluating both the extra-class activities and the social program. Sometimes such evaluations reveal that even popular clubs are selected only because nothing else available really appeals to pupils. Such evaluations have also revealed that the activities provided meet the needs of only part of the school population. For example, pupils from lower-class homes rarely participate in either the extra-curricular activities or school social programs. This may be one reason why these pupils do not feel accepted in school, and why they often leave school before they graduate from high school.

Good ideas for improving extra-class activities and social programs can be obtained from the students. Furthermore, students appreciate the opportunity to make suggestions. At first, some may indicate that they are interested in activities for which they are not ready, but eventually they will learn that they can admit what they really enjoy. This is particularly true of junior high school pupils. For example, junior high school boys may ask for social dancing but not really enjoy dancing. These youngsters vary so much in social maturity that a variety of activities must be provided at most social events in order to provide meaningful experiences for everyone.

School traditions also influence extra-class activities and social programs. Often, there is strong student support for activities which were developed to meet the unique needs of students who have long since graduated. If the school is known for these activities, teachers, students, and parents tend to support them. Even when the staff members enlist students' assistance in developing and evaluating these activities, they must take account of tradition. Before activities which have become a part of school tradition can be dropped or changed, the pupils and the staff must try to understand the traditions, those who support them, and for what reasons, and why these particular traditions no longer serve the best interests of the present student body.

The Leader

WHEN we speak of school leaders we are usually thinking about the students who assume responsibility for one or more of the activities described above. Out of these groups emerge individuals believed to possess the unique characteristics which should enable them to help their groups achieve the members' goals. If these leaders are to succeed, they also must possess, to some degree at least, the ability to recognize and use the problem-solving skills of the entire membership.

Since the guidance worker's goal is to try to identify potential leaders, to provide leadership training, and to provide leadership experiences for pupils, a brief review of the literature on leadership is included here as background for this discussion.

Early research on leadership tried to identify the unique characteristics of persons in leadership positions. Though these studies demonstrated that leaders possessed some common characteristics, recent studies indicate that the leader must take account of the setting in which he functions. An excellent summary of the findings on factors associated with leadership is provided by Ralph Stogdill.[1]

1. Capacity (intelligence, alertness, verbal facility, originality, judgment)
2. Achievement (scholarship, knowledge, athletic accomplishments)
3. Responsibility (dependability, initiative, persistence, aggressiveness, self-confidence, desire to excel)
4. Participation (activity, sociability, cooperation, adaptability, humor)
5. Status (socioeconomic position, popularity)
6. Situation (mental level, status, skills, needs and interests of followers, and objectives to be achieved)

A person does not become a leader by virtue of the possession of some combination of traits, but the pattern of personal characteristics of the

1 Ralph M. Stogdill, "Personal Factors Associated with Leadership: A Survey of the Literature," a paper in *The Study of Leadership*, ed. C. G. Browne and T. S. Cohn (Danville: The Interstate Printers and Publishers, Inc., 1958).

leader must bear some relevant relationship to the characteristics, activities, and goals of the followers. Thus, leadership must be conceived in terms of the interaction of variables which are in constant flux and change. The factor of change is especially characteristic of the situation, which may be radically altered by the addition or loss of members, changes in interpersonal relationships, changes in goals, competition of extra-group influences, and the like. The personal characteristics of leader and of followers are, in comparison, highly stable. The persistence of individual patterns of human behavior in the face of constant situational change appears to be a primary obstacle encountered not only in the practice of leadership, but in the selection and placement of leaders. It is not especially difficult to find people who are leaders. It is quite another matter to place these persons in different situations where they will be able to function as leaders. It becomes clear that an adequate analysis of leadership involves not only a study of leaders, but also of situations.[2]

Stogdill used the term "figurehead" to differentiate between the leader and others who may hold status positions. W. H. Cowley was one of the first to make this distinction. He differentiated between leaders and headmen as follows: "A leader is an individual who is moving in a particular direction and who succeeds in inducing others to follow after him . . . A headman is an individual who, because of his ability or prestige, has attained to a position of headship." [3] In some instances the leader is elected to provide general leadership for a group for a specified term, but in other instances he is informally chosen by the group to help them solve an immediate problem for which they believe he possesses essential knowledge and personal skills.

Within the school setting, headmen are often elected as presidents of student organizations which have no real purpose. Electing someone to such an office represents the members' way of giving status to the designated person. Sometimes faculty sponsors also are headmen. They are appointed by the principal to achieve the principal's objectives for a group rather than to help the group define and solve the problems that are important to them. The problem of what to do about these groups, and of how to define the sponsor's role, is discussed later in this chapter; it is sufficient to say here that when both people try to accomplish something, the leader's task is much easier than the headman's task.

2 *Ibid.*, pp. 56–57.
3 W. H. Cowley, "Three Distinctions in the Study of Leaders," *The Journal of Abnormal and Social Psychology*, XXIII (1928), 145–46.

Both Cowley's and Stogdill's definition of the leader's role states that the leader is expected to get something done. According to Cowley, the leader may be described as effective even when he manipulates the group into helping him achieve his goals, whereas Stogdill implies that to be effective the leader must help members achieve their common goals. But even for Stogdill democratic methods are not essential for effective leadership.

Joan Criswell [4] concludes that the leader is not completely at the mercy of task requirements or his own and others' needs. However, the leader must be able to assess and use these data in the course of problem solving.

Tannenbaum, Weschler, and Massarik describe the leader's role as follows:

The leader assesses followers and situation as a preliminary to action. In doing so, he forms a mental image of the barriers and facilitating circumstances that bear on the desired goals of his leadership behavior. He further visualizes (sometimes explicitly and sometimes implicitly) those action pathways open to him which he believes will lead to leadership effectiveness. However, the psychological map that is available to him undoubtedly is a combination of accurate and inaccurate notions regarding relevant and irrelevant items. Whatever the nature of its components, this map provides the basis for the course which the leader follows in his attempt to exert influence through communication. [5]

For both Helen Jennings [6] and Bernard Bass [7] members have an active part in the problem-solving process. Jennings describes leadership as a process in which one individual has a major role, but in which relatively many share. Though Bass describes leadership as an interaction between members of a group, he recognizes that leadership involves organizing activities, recognizing resistance to change, and coping with resistance.

Thomas Gordon believes that for most effective results demo-

4 Joan H. Criswell, "Nature of Leadership," *Adult Leadership*, X (1961), 103–04, 119.

5 Robert Tannenbaum, Irving R. Weschler, and Fred Massarik, *Leadership and Organization: A Behavioral Science Approach* (New York: McGraw-Hill Book Co., Inc., 1961), pp. 39, 40.

6 Helen H. Jennings, "Sociometry of Leadership," a paper in *The Study of Leadership*, ed. C. G. Browne and T. S. Cohn (Danville: The Interstate Printers and Publishers, Inc., 1958).

7 Bernard M. Bass, *Leadership, Psychology, and Organizational Behavior* (New York: Harper & Row, Publishers, 1960).

cratic leadership is essential. He argued the case for democratic leadership as follows:

> The challenge that democracy faces is to discover a conception of leadership more consistent with the fundamental democratic principles we have learned to cherish. When discovered, it will need to be so injected into the blood stream of the social organism that it will reach every group and institution in our society.
>
> It is our thesis that society is searching for a kind of leadership that puts human values first. Traditional leadership, based as it is upon authority and power, has often restrained the individual through submission to that authority, and consequently has failed to release all the creative and constructive forces within the individual . . .[8]

Since Gordon describes the leader's role differently than the others have, perhaps a review of his basic attitudes toward members would be helpful. He has great confidence in and respect for the individual. He also believes that the group can be trusted; that individuals join a group to actualize their own capacities; that the group should provide each member with an opportunity to grow, develop, and create; that the best solution to a group's problems will result from the use of its members' combined resources. He recognizes that at first, when members perceive the leader as someone who possesses more status and power than they do, that even the group-centered leader will have to act differently than he will later; but Gordon believes the leader must help members to become increasingly self-directing and to assume increasingly greater responsibility for themselves. Gordon accepts the importance of diagnosis but recommends that the leader, instead of himself making the diagnosis for the group, should help members discover and use their own resources for making diagnosis. His goal is to replace the single leader with as many potential leaders as there are within the group. The leader listens with understanding to every speaker, trying to see things as the speaker sees them, and he tests his understanding by mirroring back what the speaker says. He also tries to detect and to convey linkage between what individuals say. Except for the fact that he focuses attention on the group's task instead of the therapeutic needs of individual members, Gordon's description of the leader's role is very similar to the author's description of the

8 Thomas Gordon, *Group-centered Leadership* (New York: Houghton Mifflin Company, 1955), p. 7.

counselor's role in group counseling (see Chapter 5). In other words, the group-centered leader is an active member of the group. He makes a sincere effort to help the members solve their problems, but he does not try to get them to accept his solution.

Since some have confused democratic leadership with laissez-faire leadership, the difference between the two must be clarified. Theoretically, the laissez-faire leader believes that a group should govern itself with a minimum of control, whereas both the autocratic leader and the democratic leader recognize the need for structure and limits. However, the two differ with reference to how these should be developed and enforced. The democratic leader believes that the members must help him decide what can be expected from each one, including the leader, that the members must define their objectives within the limits of the organization, and that they must define the regulations which they need to operate effectively; the autocratic leader, on the other hand, decides these things himself or tries to manipulate the members into accepting his ideas.

Why, therefore, would anyone confuse laissez-faire leadership with democratic leadership? Both let members help solve problems. However, these two types of leader behave very differently in their groups. The laissez-faire leader is passive. Frequently he believes that he is democratic, but often he is basically autocratic; however, he lacks the courage and self-confidence to act, so he defers to the group. In contrast, the democratic leader has real confidence in the group and in himself. He believes that he needs the resources of the entire group to make the best decisions and to implement these decisions. The author believes that a democratic leader can also contribute information and ideas, and even participate in the evaluation of alternative solutions. If the group is to make the best possible use of all of its resources, it certainly needs the leader's contributions too.

On the other hand, there is a danger that the members will just accept the leader's ideas, letting him make the decisions. Little wonder that this happens. In most groups there are persons who previously accepted the challenge to participate in decision-making, but who were eventually penalized by the leader when they disagreed with him. Naturally, they are suspicious when another leader asks them to participate in solving the group's problems, fearing that reprisals may befall them again. If a leader wishes to function democratically, he must prove to the members that he really wants and needs their assistance, and that he can accept the contributions of even those who disagree with him. This requires time and patience on the leader's part; members must discover that they can trust the leader, and that he respects them and their ideas. Though, for these reasons, he may limit his contributions at first, eventually he should be able to contribute what he knows and thinks. He also must be able to help others make their contributions.

Although we have been examining the leader's role in formal organizations, many groups also have an informal organization. Both can contribute to helping a group fulfill its purposes. Whenever a person accepts responsibility in a formal organization, he gives up some aspects of personal freedom for rewards which the formal organization provides. Often an informal organization arises to restore, in part, the freedom surrendered. If the needs of individual members are not met in the formal organization, participation in the informal organization may be motivated by members' need to fight the formal organization. An informal organization also may develop out of honest differences in opinion concerning what is best for the entire group.

To illustrate what serious problems can arise when an informal organization develops to satisfy needs that are not met in the formal organization, Bass describes the case of a department head in an industrial plant:

> If a department head fails to meet regularly with his group to discuss mutual actions and problems, he may be surprised by the development of active cliques sharing their guesses about various motives and future actions. The informal organization may serve to disrupt the formal relations established by authority. Communications by the informal interaction is less likely to be accurate. Material unfavorable to the formal system is likely to be disseminated informally . . . A group of technicians from different departments may band together to share grievances concerning their dissatisfaction with an immediate supervisor and his boss, leading eventually to some deleterious action.[9]

This sort of thing also happens in schools. For example, most of us can recall hearing colleagues discuss issues in the faculty lounge which they should have discussed in the regular faculty meeting, or seeing students organize informal pressure groups to cope with

9 *Op. cit.,* p. 85.

problems which they should have discussed in the student council. When the leader of the formal group discovers such activity, he is often tempted to penalize the leader of the informal group. Such a response rarely solves the difficulty, especially when serious problems are involved. For a better solution, the leader of the formal group should try to discover why the members of the informal group did not feel that they could present the issues before the formal group and get a fair hearing. With effective leadership, such divisions should not arise. Members should know how to get their point of view before the group, and should be secure enough to present it.

A Leadership Training Program

WESCHLER, Klemes, and Shepard outlined the principal goals for leadership training, and made an excellent case for emotional understanding as well as intellectual understanding in leadership training:

There are several aims in this type of training. First, each trainee should get a better picture of the kind of person he is, of the impact he has on others, and of the characteristic behavior he employs to protect himself against real or imagined threats. As a result of the training process, he is likely to discover some of his "blind spots"—those problem areas in his personality which he is unable to perceive without gross distortion and which frequently operate to his detriment in relating to others.

Second, the participants should check the accuracy of their perceptions as to what other people are like. Many trainees tend to think in stereotypes, which if strong may drastically color their perceptions. Participants learn to recognize individual differences, to accept them for what they are, and to understand better how their own needs and desires distort perceptions of others.

Third, the participants should obtain more factual information, useful and pertinent in this area. This may include some theory and research data on individual differences, personality, leadership, communication, and group dynamics.

Fourth, each trainee should develop new "human relations" skills, including ways of dealing with conflicts and tensions. As participants put into practice their understanding of themselves and others, they learn how to communicate effectively, how to interview and listen, how to inform and evaluate, how to praise and discipline, and how to motivate. These specific skills can usually not be acquired until some of the insights mentioned above have first been attained.

Finally, the participants should be helped to become more aware of "group process," those forces unique to a group which ultimately may result in its success or failure. They should learn to recognize functional and blocking members' roles; they should become aware of, and learn to deal with, "hidden agenda," those personal or situational pressures which simmer underneath a surface of good manners and friendly interchange; they should become acquainted with procedural skills which allow a group to get its work done in the most expeditious manner.[10]

Inasmuch as different types of persons become leaders, use different leadership approaches, and provide leadership for quite different groups, it is obvious that they will meet different kinds of problem. To meet the needs of these various leaders in a school setting, the author has achieved best results with the type of voluntary discussion groups described in Chapter 10. Usually those who are invited to participate in the discussion groups are assigned to groups on the basis of two criteria: (1) the type of organization for which they are leaders and (2) their previous leadership experience and training (e.g., a group is often organized for new leaders who have had no previous leadership training, or a special group may be organized for those who are interested in obtaining leadership positions). Discussions focus attention on the problems which confront the leaders within their various groups. Harry Grater [11] used a similar method very effectively in a leadership training program at Michigan State University. He used Gordon's group-centered leadership with thirty undergraduates who were enrolled in two sections of a leadership training course. The students discussed the problems they faced as leaders of student groups. Grater concluded that the change in perception of self rather than the change in perception of ideal self accounted for the significant reduction in the discrepancy between ideal self and real self.

Leadership Experiences

AT THE beginning of this chapter Stogdill's review of the research on the personal characteristics of leaders is cited. Many of these attitudes, abilities, and skills are learned in a wholesome social en-

10 Irving R. Weschler, Marvin A. Klemes, and Clovis Shepard, "A New Focus in Executive Training," *The Study of Leadership*, ed. C. G. Browne and T. S. Cohn (Danville, The Interstate Printers and Publishers, Inc., 1958), pp. 441–42.

11 Harry A. Grater, "Changes in Self and Other Attitudes in a Leadership Training Group," *Personnel and Guidance Journal*, XXXVII (1959), 493–96.

vironment without any formal leadership training. For example, Barr and Hoover [12] found that high school leaders grew up in a different home atmosphere from nonleaders. Leaders had a voice in family decisions, they were allowed more freedom in choosing moral standards, their homes provide recreational opportunities for themselves and their friends, and parents used praise and reason as corrective measures. The father of female leaders also was able to spend most evenings with the family. Leaders also had work-experience both in and out of the home.

From Barr and Hoover's results one may infer that parents who are interested in developing leadership attitudes, skills, and abilities must respect their children as individuals, exhibit confidence in them, and teach them responsibility and independence. The classroom teacher also should try to exhibit these attitudes, and provide opportunities for their students to learn them. Usually they are best learned in a pupil-centered classroom in which students' ideas are respected, their assistance is sought in developing and maintaining a wholesome learning atmosphere, and they are encouraged to participate in classroom discussions. Appropriate social experiences also contribute to the development of leadership. Learning to adapt to and interact with various types of people in various settings provides useful skills for leaders.

Outside of the classroom it is also important for pupils that their teachers exhibit the attitudes described above when serving as sponsors (or advisers) for service and activity groups. Unfortunately, these sponsors are often expected to achieve the school principal's objectives for the group, instead of helping the group define and achieve their own objectives. Where most effective, the sponsor serves as a consultant rather than the power behind the throne. For example, the sponsor explains why the leader needs an agenda and how he may solicit items for it, but he does not make out the agenda for the student leaders. He also helps the leader diagnose problems within the group, and use all the human and material resources effectively in achieving the group's objectives. The sponsor does not do things for the group or make decisions for its members, but tries to help them learn to take responsibility and to do things for themselves.

12 John A. Barr and Kenneth H. Hoover, "Home Conditions and Influences Associated With the Development of High School Leaders," *Educational Administration and Supervision*, XLIII (1957), 272–79.

J. C. Jurjevich's [13] paper described a situation in which an interested staff member served effectively as a consultant for a student group. The students sponsored discussions concerned with solving a noon-hour recreation problem, and apparently solved it very effectively. He concluded as follows:

These youngsters wanted a chance to live as citizens of their school and to have a voice in the policies and matters which concerned them. They provided leadership which brought many more students into a common social action. This kind of leadership is essential in democratic life—the kind of leadership which permits and encourages everyone to contribute as much as possible in the pursuance of common goals.[14]

The student council, one of the very best groups for the purpose, should provide just this kind of leadership training and experience.

While everyone agrees that young people need student council experiences, some teachers and administrators have been so threatened by what seems the students' "struggle for power" that they have not been able to work with the council effectively. Too many students elected to the council, on the other hand, have never known exactly what they were to do. They have found themselves caught between the pressure of obtaining privileges for students, and the administrator's limits on their activities. Sometimes, the council members are confused by their loyalties to opposing influences. At other times, they feel they must fight for the best interests of those whom they represent. The battle for power results.

Both the students and the faculty recognize the necessity for defining limits. It is best, therefore, for them to discuss this problem frankly and then set up machinery for solving it. Usually this can be done best if a student-faculty committee, appointed by the principal with the approval of the council, studies the problem and presents recommendations to the faculty and student council. When both groups have approved the recommendations, the principal should include them in student and faculty handbooks, and the student council should incorporate them into the constitution of the council.

If the student-faculty committee has defined appropriate guides,

13 J. C. Jurjevich, "How to Educate for Democratic Leadership," *High School Journal*, XLIII (1960), 346–51.

14 *Ibid.*, pp. 350–51.

council behavior should reflect the following characteristics and relationships:

—Council members know what the school expects the council to do, and they know what to expect from one another.
—Council members realize that they can speak their minds without fear of reprisals. They trust and accept one another and their advisers. They also recognize the responsibilities associated with each of their privileges.
—The principal rarely, if ever, has to apply his veto power to council action. The students try not to put the principal "on the spot," and he in turn tries not to embarrass them.
—Students and faculty members frequently visit the council and bring problems to the council members. Council members feel that they are welcome, whenever an occasion requires that they meet with the faculty.
—The student body knows about and is interested in what the student council is doing. The council reports to the student body regularly on council activities.
—The council makes provision for evaluating their activities and for improving their effectiveness.
—Students conduct school elections on a businesslike basis, and the student body selects council members with great care.
—The council makes provisions for spring elections so that outgoing council members can help new members organize the new council.
—The adviser for the council is selected by the council and approved by the faculty.
—The council meets regularly and keeps accurate minutes of its meetings.
—The council is affiliated with the regional, state, and national organizations.

Even though the student council has good working agreements with the faculty, it is still a good idea for the adviser to encourage the members of each newly elected council to consider how they will work together. In their organization meeting, council members may appropriately ask themselves questions like these:

—What are the principal things we want to accomplish this year?
—How do these problems relate to our responsibilities as they are defined in our constitution?
—Should we suggest changes in the constitution?
—What can we expect from one another in attacking these problems? What special responsibilities should we expect from our officers? What should we expect from our advisers? What can they expect from us?

—How do the other students feel about these issues which require our attention? How do the teachers feel about these issues? How can we enlist the help of students and faculty? How can we keep both groups informed?

—How can we make it easier than it now is for students outside the council to get problems before the group? How can we make it easier for teachers to get problems before the group?

Applying the Study of Group Process To Leadership Development

EFFECTIVE leaders must develop some understanding of group dynamics. While they are working with their groups, they must be able to determine why the groups are effective sometimes and ineffective at other times. To understand this they must be able to recognize behavior which suggests difficulty, to diagnose the source of the difficulty, to recognize and use the problem-solving resources within the group, to enlist the cooperation of members in solving problems, and to take appropriate action. This section discusses techniques which student leaders can use to involve members in improving the effectiveness of their groups.

A thorough study of the place of evaluation in the group process is inappropriate here. However, it is relevant to consider briefly how a group can identify the problems which prevent members from achieving their goals.

There are two obvious places where the study of group process may be introduced: (1) during the first few sessions, when the members are defining working agreements or operational rules, and (2) at some point when the members feel they are "bogged down." In either case, the group should, of course, agree on the approach to be used and any specialized resource persons needed.

THE OBSERVER

The group *observer* is a student specialist appointed by the leader to try to discover why things go well sometimes, and why the group bogs down at other times. He keeps a running account of what happens. When the members request a report, he tries to present his observations so as to encourage the members to take positive steps for improving the group process. He looks for the answers to questions like these:

—Are the members aware of what they are trying to accomplish?

—What evidence do I find that suggests that they are either achieving or failing to achieve their objectives?

—Who contributed to the group discussion? How was the participation distributed among the membership? What was the nature of the contributions (e.g., did they ameliorate, block discussion of certain issues, clarify various feelings and ideas, evaluate others' contributions, provide information, seek information, or provide support for others)?

—Do the members seem to understand one another? How do they feel about what is being accomplished in the group? (Data for the answers to these questions may be obtained from the end-of-meeting reaction sheet, described below.)

—How do they feel about one another? (Data may be obtained from the end-of-meeting reaction sheet.)

—How does the group make decisions on controversial issues?

—How do the members respond to personal conflict within the group? Who helps to resolve the conflict? How is it resolved?

—What is the elected leader's role in the group? What other leader roles have evolved?

—What special roles does the leader assign to members for the purpose of studying the group process? How does the group accept these specialists?

—How do the members seem to feel about devoting time to evaluating the experiences of members in the group?

—How have the members put into practice the changes recommended for improving group efficiency?

END-OF-MEETING REACTIONS

End-of-meeting reaction sheets can supplement the observer's report to the group. These sheets should be distributed by the observer at the close of a session, and should be explained by him for the group. He should urge members to say exactly what they think, and to submit their statements unsigned. When the members sense that they can afford to be frank and that the group uses their suggestions for improving the group process, this technique can be very useful. The following set of questions has functioned well for this purpose:

END-OF-MEETING REACTION SHEET

1. How do you feel about this session?

    (   ) a. It was one of the poorest I ever attended.

    (   ) b. It was less successful than most such meetings.

( ) c. It was as successful as most such meetings.

( ) d. It was better than most such meetings.

( ) e. It was one of the best I ever attended.

2. How do you feel toward the other members of the group?

( ) a. I am not sure how I feel about the others.

( ) b. They did not seem to be interested in what I had to say, but most of them seemed to accept me as a person.

( ) c. They did not seem to be interested in what I had to say, and most of them did not seem to accept me as a person.

( ) d. They were interested in what I had to say, and most of them accepted me as a person.

( ) e. They were interested in what I had to say, but most of them did not seem to accept me as a person.

( ) f. If none of the above apply, write your reaction to the others here.

_____

_____

3. Among the kinds of behavior usually associated with effective leadership, which were exhibited in this group?

( ) a. The leader encouraged other members to contribute their ideas.

( ) b. He exhibited respect for and confidence in other members.

( ) c. He helped other members discover and use their own resources.

( ) d. He helped members clarify their goals.

( ) e. He listened to others with understanding and acceptance.

( ) f. He recognized resistance to change and dealt with the resistance.

( ) g. He recognized and used facilitating circumstances.

( ) h. Members of the group exhibited improvement in their daily effectiveness.

( ) i. Members seemed to know what they could expect from each other and from the leader.

( ) j. Members seemed to feel they were accomplishing something.

( ) k. When the leader shared his ideas with the group, he expected his ideas to receive the same critical evaluation that those of others receive.

4. What did you like most about the session?
5. What changes would you suggest for improving the session?

THE RECORDER

The *recorder* is a student specialist who is appointed by the leader to keep a running account of what the group discusses: the topics on which agreement is achieved and action is taken, those on which there is disagreement, and those which the group identifies but does not examine. Like the observer, this student reports to the group whenever a member requests a report. However, his report is quite different from that of the observer: while the recorder's report stresses what the group accomplished, the observer's report attempts to explain how the group accomplished what it did. Both of these students should be prepared for their responsibilities by the leader and the faculty sponsor. The members of the group must perceive both recorder and observer as servants of the group rather than as power figures in the group.

SUGGESTED READINGS

1. BENNE, KENNETH D., and BAZIDAR MUNTYAN. *Human Relations in Curriculum Change.* New York: Holt, Rinehart & Winston, Inc., 1951.

    Part 3 of this excellent book of readings on the group process is recommended.
    a] Read the paper, "Functional Roles of Group Members," by Benne and Sheats; then select a particular meeting and study the roles played by the members of the group.
    b] How could you use the fifteen questions on pages 83–84 to help members study efficiency?

2. BROWNE, C. G., and T. S. COHN (ed.). *The Study of Leadership.* Danville: The Interstate Printers and Publishers, Inc., 1958.

    This book of readings brings together a fine group of papers for those interested in identifying and training leaders. Perhaps the best papers for our purposes are: "Leadership: A Conception and Some Implications" by Irving Knickerbocher; "Sociometry of Leadership" by Helen H. Jennings; "Personal Factors Associated with Leadership; A Survey of the Literature" by Ralph M. Stogdill; "Patterns of Aggressive Behavior in Experimentally Created 'Social Climates'" by Kurt Lewin, Ronald Lippitt, and Ralph K. White; "Leadership and Change" by C. G. Browne; "A New Focus in Executive Training" by Irving R. Weschler, Marvin A. Klemes, and Clovis Shepard; and "Role Playing in Leadership Training" by A. A. Leveright.

a] What is the function of the leader?

b] How may leaders precipitate change?

c] In what ways do youth react differently to autocratic, laissez-faire, and democratic leaders?

d] Why must those concerned with leadership training take account of feelings as well as content and skills?

e] How can the results of leadership training be evaluated?

f] How can role playing be used in leadership training?

3. GORDON, THOMAS. *Group Centered Leadership.* Boston: Houghton Mifflin Company, 1955.

This book was originally planned as a brief mimeographed report designed to present the author's experiences with a group of religious leaders. Later, the theoretical rationale for group-centered leadership was added to develop it into a book. Suggested chapters are 1, 3, and 8.

a] What are the primary arguments for democratic leadership?

b] What are the leader's major responsibilities?

c] Why do people join groups?

d] How do groups solve problems?

e] How do the group-centered leader's attitudes differ from those of the typical leader?

f] How do group-centered groups differ from leader-guided groups?

Applying Guidance Methods in Discipline

EFFECTIVE teachers know that school discipline involves more than administering restraints. The eventual goal of all disciplinary action in the school should be self-discipline by the pupil; a pupil learns self-discipline only gradually through experiences which help him to balance his needs for independence and his recognition of the rights of others. The child best learns both rights and responsibilities in a permissive atmosphere in which he has a chance to participate in solving problems that have meaning for him. Arnold Gesell and Francis Ilg describe this process as follows:

> The authoritarian schoolroom, like the authoritarian home of an earlier day, has become inconsistent with the spirit of democracy. Since the sec-

ond Great War we realize that the sources of the democratic spirit are to be found in the homes and the schools of the people—in the interpersonal way of life which prevails in the parent-child and teacher-child relationships. Do not children need discipline? Yes, but discipline being a mode of government can be either autocratic or democratic in method. It can defy the laws of development. It can humanely defer to them.[1]

Defining and Enforcing Limits

VERY early in life, the child learns that there is some behavior even his parents cannot tolerate. When he discovers that he cannot always do what he would like to do, inescapably he feels some frustration. But limits, of course, must be placed on the individual's behavior in order to protect the best interests of the group as well as those of the individual.

Parents and teachers sometimes forget that how they enforce these limits makes a difference. They need to remember that the child must understand his boundaries before he can be expected to live within them. Sometimes, even after he has learned, he forgets. As the child matures he raises questions about the limits, and eventually he should learn how to examine them and how to change those which are no longer appropriate.

In enforcing limits on the behavior of an individual pupil for the good of the whole class, the teacher should recognize that merely suppressing the child will not solve the problems which account for his unacceptable behavior. So long as serious unsolved problems are lodged within him, his effectiveness will be impaired and he will continue to create discipline problems in the classroom. The child whom the teacher sees as a problem has taken months or years learning to be what he is. Somewhere in his personal history there is an explanation for his unacceptable behavior. All those who work with the child must cooperate to find that explanation.

Truant Evelyn is a case in point. Her fifth-grade teacher was so concerned about Evelyn that she sought the help of a guidance consultant from the State Department of Public Instruction when he visited her school. A careful survey of the facts by the two of them and Evelyn's fourth-grade teacher showed that the girl's truancy

1 Arnold Gesell and Francis Ilg, *The Child From Five to Ten* (New York: Harper & Row, Publishers, 1946), p. 34. Reprinted by permission of author and publisher.

began during the last part of the fourth grade, when she began having trouble with arithmetic. A recounting of the events showed that Evelyn often went home sick during the morning recess that was followed by the arithmetic class. Occasionally, she presented other good excuses for missing arithmetic classes. Several times she just "skipped" school. When she returned to school, she was always cooperative.

At the teacher's request, the guidance consultant agreed to interview Evelyn. During a series of three conferences, he learned that Evelyn was anxious to do well in all her subjects, that she did well in third-grade-level arithmetic, but that her mother had convinced her that she would always do poorly in mathematics, just as both her parents had. On the basis of these conferences, the guidance consultant, with Evelyn and her teacher, planned a program of remedial work in arithmetic. The remedial program convinced Evelyn that she could learn arithmetic, and the quality of her work improved. When Evelyn learned how to solve her problem, she also accepted the school's regulation on regular school attendance.

Had nothing been done about Evelyn's problem, she might have left school at her first opportunity, or she might have avoided future mathematics courses. At the very least, she was underestimating her ability to learn arithmetic, and the correction of this false perception was itself important for her.

Once her teacher knew why Evelyn was truant and what remedial instruction Evelyn needed, she found that for several reasons it was relatively easy to correct the situation: first, Evelyn's problem was discovered early; second, cooperative study of the child, with the aid of a trained specialist, revealed the source of the difficulty; third, the specialist obtained additional information and insight through his interviews and then helped to interpret the facts and to plan remedial instruction; and finally, Evelyn wanted to do well in all of her subjects, while her teacher was willing and able to help her succeed. Unfortunately, all discipline problems cannot be corrected this easily. Many require intensive work with the parents and the child. Still other discipline problems, however, can be solved even more easily than Evelyn's. But whatever the behavior problem, whatever its seriousness, the child must be understood before he can be effectively helped.

A sound philosophy of discipline implies a flexible balance between the extremes of no-control and over-control. At the earliest possible moment, children should be encouraged to participate in the definition of reasonable limits for themselves. To maintain good working conditions and to avoid the chaotic classroom, however, the teacher may find that there are times when he must assume police powers. Direct control by the teacher can be most effective when he is fair, considerate, consistent, and sincerely interested in helping pupils live in accordance with well-defined standards. However, the teacher's responsibilities do not stop there. He should use direct control only until his pupils assume the responsibilities which he may reasonably expect from them. When pupils do not recognize their responsibility, the teacher should describe the problem and request their help.

In addition to defining reasonable limits, both teachers and parents must show confidence in the child's respect for the limits. All too frequently, they question the child's wish to act appropriately: they say what they expect, and in the same breath they tell him what they will do when he ignores the limits. These threats suggest to the child that they do not believe in him, that they expect him to let them down. A threat is also a challenge to the child to see if whoever has made the threat will really carry it through. Far better results are obtained by believing in the child until he lets one down; then, of course, prompt action should be taken by the responsible adult to enforce the limits. Usually the child will live up to the adults' expectations; without a threat he has no way of determining whether the risk involved is worth ignoring the limits. Though there is an advantage in his not knowing for sure what the responsible adult will do when he ignores the limits, it is important that he realize that the adult will do something—that the limits will be enforced.

The principles stated above apply to adolescents too, but special attention must be given to the unique problems confronting the adolescent in his struggle for independence. At times he demands the right to decide things for himself, and at other times he feels so unsure of himself that he solicits suggestions and advice from adults whom he respects. He tends to be sensitive to criticism and others' judgment of his worth because he is often criticized by adults who do not try to understand him; he is unsure of himself, and he feels guilty when he fails to live up to his code (he is idealistic). Usually he wants to do the right thing. He needs to be loved, trusted, and respected. He also needs reasonable limits for which he will assume increasingly greater responsibility, but which *will be enforced until he is able to be self-disciplined.*

His acceptance of limits is further complicated by a strong need to be accepted by his peers. Often the desire to be accepted by peers and to prove that he can take independent action causes him to do things which he prefers not to do. On such occasions he needs the assistance of an understanding adult to help him evaluate and cope with these forces.

Many adults have difficulty defining and enforcing limits for adolescents. If instead of demanding respect, the adults would try to see matters as the adolescent sees them, try to convey this desire to understand him, encourage him to help define reasonable limits, exhibit some faith in his ability to do what is expected, and take prompt action when he fails to do what is expected, better results would be achieved. But adults are threatened by many phases of an adolescent's behavior, and they often question whether he can be trusted to assume the responsibility of which he is capable. Some adults expect the worst, and by their accusations give the adolescent ideas for doing things he probably would never have thought of doing. Perhaps they are afraid that he will do some of the things that they did or almost did when they were adolescents. When he challenges them or defies them and disregards the limits, adults often question whether he respects and loves them. When action is required they are reluctant to act because they are afraid he will leave home or quit school. This reluctance makes them appear weak, and causes him to lose respect for them. If they really care about him and his welfare, and if the action taken is fair, he will accept it. Usually he realizes when he needs help in living with the defined limits.

Sometimes discipline problems arise when expectations vary considerably from teacher to teacher. School administrators long ago recognized the importance of some common expectation for a given school. This applies to the home situation as well. Many times a group of parents can avoid discipline problems with their adolescents by agreeing among themselves on some of the basic expectations for their children. If, for example, an adolescent's friends are all expected to be home at about the same time, the adolescent finds it easier to come home on time and not to resent it. The kinds of voluntary discussion group described in Chapter 10 help students discover such common expectations. These groups also can be used to help parents define similar expectations.

Thus, for effective discipline, pupils should have a part in deciding what they may expect from one another and from their teacher or parents, and how to live with, or change, the regulations resulting from these decisions. Effective discipline, therefore, like effective teaching, is pupil-centered.

Understanding and Treating Discipline Cases

As the teacher answers the following questions he becomes better acquainted with himself as well as with the child. Sometimes, indeed, he finds that his own personal needs play an important part in creating his conflicts with the child.

> 1. *What did the child do the last time that he misbehaved in my presence? What was it that he did that disturbed me? Has this same sort of difficulty arisen in other classes? Who was the target for his aggressive behavior?*

When a pupil misbehaves, according to the teacher's standards, he is trying to satisfy some unmet need. (This idea will be discussed again under question 4.) Careful study of what he says and does may unveil the story behind the act. Usually the teacher is most effective when he makes it easy for the child to express his negative feelings. At the same time, the teacher should help the child learn where to express these feelings, and how to express them in a frank, yet considerate manner. The child may also release his negative feelings through talking with his teacher or a counselor.

On the other hand, the "misbehaving" child may not be harboring negative feelings at all. He may have suffered a disappointment, as Jimmy did with his spelling. Jimmy had worked hard to get ready for the spelling test; nevertheless, he missed several words. He was so disgusted that he slammed his book down on his desk and knocked his ink bottle into Jane's lap. With ink spilled all over her new dress, Jane was both angry and hurt.

Obviously, Jimmy's teacher had to do something. At the same time, she wanted to let Jimmy know that she understood how he felt. She said, "This looks like one of those cases where someone has been hurt and we shall have to do something about it. When a fellow works as hard as you did, it is pretty disappointing not to do well on the test, isn't it, Jimmy?" Jimmy agreed, but timidly, because he was himself startled by what he had caused. After a moment he told Jane he was sorry, and when he had helped blot up as much ink as possible, he volunteered that he and his mother could wash Jane's dress. Because Jimmy was obviously sorry, and because their teacher approached the incident so calmly, Jane did not remain excited long. So, through the teacher's ability to understand the boy's motives, the incident was handled quickly and constructively.

> 2. *Outside of the incidents in which discipline problems arise, how do I feel about this child? Is he the kind of youngster I like or the kind who annoys me?*

If the teacher likes the child, he may let him get away with too much. If, on the other hand, the teacher rejects him, the child may sense this attitude and either fight back or withdraw.

With the help of the school counselor, the teacher can learn to examine his feelings about the child, and so learn better to evaluate his influence on him. As the teacher grows accustomed to working with others in close study of children, he will feel freer to discuss his attitudes toward a particular child. The attempt to view the child apart from discipline-problem situations and the practice of evaluating the teacher's influence on the child will make it easier for the teacher to accept the child, even while rejecting what he sometimes does.

> 3. *What did I do when he misbehaved in my presence the last time?*

It is not sufficient for the teacher merely to examine his general feelings toward the child. He also must examine his attitudes and actions as they relate to a specific incident. For instance:

> a. *Did I want to punish him or did I accept his behavior as normal for a child of his age?*
>
> Rarely do teachers purposely punish their pupils to "get even with them," but occasionally they do so without realizing it.
>
> When the teacher knows what to expect from his pupils and when he tries to see the situation with the pupil's eyes, he makes the child feel he is understood. And it is easier for the child to accept restraints from someone who he believes understands him and someone whom he loves and respects.

Adults should remember that although the child may often need to be reminded of duties, he resents nagging. In reminding the child of duties, the teacher should use such expressions as, "I thought maybe you had forgotten that you were supposed to do . . ." In contrast, nagging teachers use many "do's" and "don'ts."

b. *Did I give him a chance to describe the situation as he saw it? Did I try to help him see how his behavior affected the rest of the group?*

c. *What did I do to correct the child? Did my actions embarrass him? What methods have worked well with the child previously? Which ones seemed to "put him on the spot"?*

In reviewing every discipline case, the teacher should scrutinize the educational value of his corrective methods, for sometimes they do not teach the lessons which he believes they should. Sarcasm and public humiliation are but two examples of disciplinary methods which, although they usually produce conformity, also hurt the child and make him hate the teacher. Sometimes under such pressures the child fights back and embarrasses the teacher.

d. *What did I do to help him before this discipline crisis arose? Did I try to obtain help from any of my colleagues?*

When a teacher discovers a potential discipline problem before he is forced to take action, he often can prevent the problem. He is also better able to understand the reasons for the difficulty and to consult with colleagues. Sometimes when he takes action during a crisis he does things about which he feels guilty and ashamed; consequently, he becomes defensive when colleagues try to help him reexamine what happened and what he could have done differently.

e. *Was I fair to the child? Did I try to understand him? Was his punishment appropriate? Did I treat him differently than I do others in the class?*

f. *Am I afraid to admit that I am wrong when I am wrong?*

Even though it is difficult, the teacher must admit his errors. He should accept the fact that he makes mistakes, and he should try to correct them. He may ask the pupils to help him make the desired changes. Such actions tend to win the support and respect of pupils.

g. *Can I afford to let my pupils know me as I am?*

The teacher who believes in himself, and can afford to let his pupils know him as he is, is able to create a wholesome classroom atmosphere. When he is ashamed of his behavior, he tells pupils that he is sorry; when pupils do things that please him, he expresses his pleasure; and when they disappoint him, he tells them why and requests their cooperation in rectifying the difficulty. Though a teacher may partially conceal his true feelings, some of his pupils probably will sense when something is wrong, though they may not be able to correctly identify the trouble. For instance, a pupil may feel that the teacher is rejecting him when, as a matter of fact, the teacher may be feeling guilty about the way he has treated the pupil.

For example, Miss Sorenson had a rough day in school, following a long evening of hard work on the teachers' welfare committee. When Susan spilled the finger paints, after repeated warnings to be careful, this was too much. Miss Sorensen blew her top. Among other things, she told Susan to clean up the mess and go sit on the other side of the room until she could act her age. Very shortly Miss Sorensen was ashamed of herself for making such a fuss over a minor incident and, in her shame, avoided speaking to Susan for several hours. Unfortunately, Susan interpreted the behavior which resulted from Miss Sorenson's guilt feelings as feelings of rejection.

Had Miss Sorenson told Susan how she really felt and why she acted as she did, Susan would have understood and quickly forgotten the incident. Certainly she would not have questioned Miss Sorenson's acceptance of her.

4. *What unsatisfied needs are suggested by the child's behavior?*

Reflection on the child's behavior just before and during the discipline crisis frequently reveals that one of the basic needs described in Chapter 2 is not being satisfied. Sometimes, one or two needs will be more important to him than to his classmates because he is more mature or less mature than they. For example, in most seventh grades there are some early maturing girls who are more aware of their sex needs than their classmates are. Consequently, they are more interested in the dating type of parties than are other students, especially boys.

5. *Do I have any reason for believing this child is not well?*

Of course the teacher cannot expect to correct medical problems with remedial work or counseling, nor can he expect a sick child to perform satisfactorily. Some sick children are aggressive, others are restless, and still others are sleepy and unresponsive. As was mentioned in Chapter 2, the physical conditions in the room make a difference, too—and these the teacher can correct.

6. *Do I know of anything worrying him?*

Some disturbed youngsters show their need for help through anti-social behavior. They need help, not punishment.

7. *How do the members of his family feel about one another?*

Does the child live in a broken home? Is he an accepted member of his family? Even though both parents live in the home, it still may be "broken" in the sense that the parents have to a great extent rejected each other.

8. *Is there anything unusual about the child's family life that may account for his unacceptable school behavior?*

If the family group chooses to live by unusual values, this is often reflected in a child's behavior in school. Some parents cling to beliefs about rearing and educating children which are so at variance with those usually held by educators that the child does not behave as his teacher would normally expect a child of his age to behave. There are also parents who neglect their children by actually failing to provide food, clothing, shelter, and protection, and parents who do not spend time doing things with their children or who do not try to understand them.

The teacher must be sensitive to still another factor that determines a child's behavior: parents from different social classes give recognition for different types of behavior. What the teacher considers to be antisocial behavior, the child's family may accept as perfectly appropriate. As a simple example, fist-fighting among boys may be accepted, even admired, by a father. But despite these differences, most parents respond favorably when the teacher seeks their help in achieving what is best for their child. Rather than reject the parents, the teacher must try to understand and cooperate with them.

> 9. *How is the child disciplined at home? How does he feel about the restraints in the home and the methods of enforcing them?*

G. B. Watson [2] demonstrated that many unhappy children came out of strict homes and that the children who came from these homes were more shy, did more quarreling, more stealing, more daydreaming, and had more sex curiosity than the children who were raised in liberal homes.

> 10. *Did the child know what I expected from him and his peers? Did he know what he should expect from his peers and from me?*
>   a. *Did the child understand the regulations which the pupils and I developed? Has my behavior been consistent in helping the pupils enforce these regulations? Was it reasonable for me to expect the child to conform to these regulations?*
>   b. *Did I allow the child to be put into a situation which he was not prepared to meet?*
>   c. *Did I remember that even adults deviate from what is expected from them when they work under the stress of an emergency?*
>
> 11. *How does this pupil "rate" with his classmates? Who are his friends?*
>   a. *Who talks to him?*
>   b. *Who works with him?*
>   c. *Who gets into trouble with him?*

If the child cannot win recognition in the group through behavior which is accepted by the school authorities, he may attempt to attract the attention of classmates through undesirable behavior. Some of this behavior may be essentially an attack upon the teacher as a symbol of authority in the school. The teacher could easily misinterpret this type of aggressive behavior as a personal attack upon himself; when he understands why the child acts as he does, he can accept such behavior more readily.

2 G. B. Watson, "Fresh Evidence on an Old Problem," *Child Study,* XXI (1944), 99–101.

It is the teacher's job to help the child discover what members of the group expect from him and how to earn recognition from them through desirable behavior.

12. *How has the composition of the group contributed to this discipline problem? Has the combination of youngsters increased this pupil's chances for getting into trouble?*

Methods for studying this question and the previous one more closely are presented in Chapter 8.

13. *What are the working conditions in my classroom?*
    a. *Are they conducive to work?*
    b. *Have I forced youngsters to work alone when group work may have been more appropriate?*
    c. *Have I permitted the pupil to work alone on special projects or activities which are important to him?*
    d. *Do I make the schoolwork interesting, meaningful, and useful to my pupils?*
    e. *Do I have adequate facilities to do the job I am attempting to do? What facilities would help improve learning conditions within my classroom? How can I better adapt my teaching to the facilities I have?*

14. *What is the quality of the child's schoolwork?*
    a. *Does he get into more trouble while he is working on certain lessons than on other lessons?*
    b. *Does he know how to do the assigned tasks?*
    c. *What have I done to make him feel that I am interested in his success with schoolwork, and that he may come to me for help?*
    d. *Is there a possibility either that I expect better schoolwork than he can do or that I fail to provide him with work which is challenging?*

If the teacher expects too much from the child or the task is too difficult for him, he is likely to give up and waste his time. If the teacher expects too little from him, he will finish his work early, and also waste time; or if he finds the work far too easy, he may not think it worth doing. In all these cases, the resulting idleness creates discipline problems.

The Responsibility for Discipline

THE person to whom the principal assigns the responsibility for enforcing the school's rules is the *discipline officer*. He is the person to whom teachers refer behavior problems that they feel they cannot handle by themselves. Teachers confer with him privately before sending him students with behavior problems. In smaller schools the principal is himself the discipline officer. In larger schools, especially secondary schools, the principal assigns the responsibility for discipline to the assistant principal, attendance officer, dean of boys, or dean of girls. Unfortunately, there are still some schools in which the responsibility for discipline is assigned to a counselor.

Though the principal has assigned the responsibility for discipline to one staff member, the entire teaching staff must share this responsibility. Obviously, an effective learning atmosphere must be maintained in the classroom. The best working atmosphere exists when the teacher helps his pupils develop the rules for their classroom, helps them become acquainted with the other school regulations, and helps them learn how to change rules and assume personal responsibility for enforcing them.

While the principal may assign the responsibility for discipline to others, the final responsibility for protecting pupils' and teachers' best interests remains his. Some cases, usually the most difficult ones, eventually land in his lap; he must help the persons involved to discover ways of meeting their problem. When the behavior of pupils throughout the school is unsatisfactory, the principal should recognize it as an all-school problem which demands careful study by both staff and students; in such a case he works with a faculty committee and student groups, such as the student council, to plan a frontal attack on the problem of irresponsible behavior.

A variety of situations arise in which the discipline officer is called upon to solve problems that are beyond the scope of classroom teachers. When there is a conflict between a teacher and a pupil it is usually handled by the discipline officer. His task is to try to understand both teacher and pupil, and to help them not only to resolve the immediate problem but also to prevent similar conflicts from arising in the future. He can use the suggestions presented in the previous section as he tries to understand the pupil and his teacher and to help them discover a solution.

Sometimes parents believe that their child has been treated unfairly, and they come to school to defend him. Since there is a possibility that the treatment has been unfair, the discipline officer (and often the principal becomes involved in the case) should listen to the parents and try to understand them. Even when the parents are angry, the discipline officer should help them express their feelings. He should also indicate that he is concerned about the best interest of both the pupil and the teacher, and that he fully expects to talk with them too. While it is important to give everyone a chance to express his feelings, the release of feelings alone will not solve the problem; eventually, those most directly involved must agree cooperatively on a solution.

As for the teacher, there is no reason why he should feel that he always has to be right. Rather, he should expect to be treated fairly. If the discipline officer defends the teacher's actions when the teacher is clearly wrong, he gives the child and his parents reason to question the social justice in the school. But the discipline officer need not and should not criticize the teacher's inappropriate behavior in front of a pupil and his parents. Instead, he should focus attention upon finding a solution to the problem. Usually, after considering the problem in light of the circumstances, parents recognize the teacher's difficulties and are willing to admit that the teacher did as well as, or better than, they could have done under similar circumstances. However, parents accept the teacher's actions more readily if the discipline officer is fair-minded than if he defends the teacher's questionable behavior.

When the teacher's actions are not appropriate, the principal should discuss the situation with the teacher in a *private* conference. (If the case was previously handled by a discipline officer, this person also would be invited to the conference.) Though the principal may be tempted to avoid such conferences because they may be difficult, and even embarrassing, for both him and the teacher, he must try to help the teacher analyze what happened and try to help him determine how to handle similar incidents in the future. A school staff recognizes very quickly whether such efforts are designed to help them; if so, they are not only appreciative, but they also seek the principal's assistance with discipline problems before it becomes necessary for them to send pupils to his office.

Developing reasonable limits and enforcing these limits is an important service which contributes greatly to the pupils' emotional and social adjustment. Even the pupils themselves sense this. When the discipline officer acts promptly, exhibits courage and strength, and is fair, he is accepted and respected by most of the pupils. They recognize the need for someone to enforce the rules of the school and to limit the activities of those who cannot discipline themselves.

But despite the importance of discipline, and the need for staff members to share the responsibility for discipline, the counselor functions best in a nonjudgmental role and should not be assigned such responsibility. He should be the person whom pupils feel they can take into their confidence, the person with whom they can discuss even violations of school regulations without fear of reprisals. Pupils must believe that the counselor is unequivocally a trustworthy confidant.

Few studies have attempted to assess the effect of assigning the counselor responsibility for discipline, but most of the leading scholars in this field agree with the above point of view, and three relatively recent studies seem to support it.

Ralph Jensen [3] obtained reactions from a random sample of 20 percent of 8,000 ninth-, tenth-, eleventh-, and twelfth-graders who had talked with their counselors in the Phoenix high schools. The students were shown six problem areas and were asked to indicate to whom of the following people they would go for assistance with the problems: friends, parents, teachers, counselors, and dean of boys or dean of girls. From his data Jensen concluded:

Deans of boys and deans of girls who are known by the students to be responsible for school discipline received few choices. It would seem that students would definitely avoid seeking help from individuals who assume authoritative roles.[4]

Allen Ivey [5] investigated the effects of combining counseling with teaching a college course in personal adjustment planned for freshmen. He found that students preferred to discuss problems of a serious and confidential nature with someone other than their teacher.

3 Ralph E. Jensen, "Students' Feelings About Counseling Help," *Personnel and Guidance Journal*, XXXIII (1955), 498–503.

4 *Ibid.*, p. 503.

5 Allen E. Ivey, "A Study of Two Types of Guidance Staff Organization and Their Relation to Student Perception and Use of College Guidance Services" (unpublished dissertation, Harvard University, 1959).

Norman Gilbert [6] compared high school students' (tenth- and twelfth-graders) perceptions of actual and ideal student-counselor relationships in three different school districts in which the degree of responsibility for discipline varied: (1) counselors had no responsibility for discipline; (2) counselors had no formal responsibility as discipline officers but they did spend approximately half of their time teaching guidance courses; and (3) every counselor was also a discipline officer. Though tenth-graders described the ideal counseling relationship somewhat differently than did seniors, students in the various schools generally agreed on their perception of the ideal student-counselor relationship, and their perception agreed very well with the scholar's description of the relationship—as most effective when least linked with discipline. The extent to which their counselor's role was authoritarian influenced negatively their perception of their relationship with him. Significant differences between systems were noted in the following dimensions: (1) the extent to which the counselor was able to understand and follow the student; (2) the extent to which the counselor acted superior to the student; (3) the security of the counselor in the relationship; and (4) the extent to which the counselor assumed responsibility for directing the student or the student was permitted to direct himself.

Students from the school system in which the counselors had no responsibility for discipline described the student-counselor relationship as closer to ideal than students from either of the other two schools.

It seems, therefore, that the counselor is not as effective in his work if he carries responsibilities for discipline as he might be without these responsibilities, and that the principal should assign the responsibilities for counseling and for discipline to different staff members. Where there is only a part-time counseling position, it would be better for the counselor to have his day divided between teaching and counseling than between counseling and disciplinary duties.

We should not conclude from this that counselors and discipline officers cannot work together. They can when they understand each other's functions and when the pupils understand the functions of

6 Norman S. Gilbert, "A Comparison of Students' Perception of Counseling Relationships Among Schools in Which Counselor Duties Differ" (unpublished dissertation, University of Illinois, 1962).

each. However, no one should expect the counselor to violate the confidences of the pupils who have sought his help. He should maintain with pupils a relationship which would encourage all of them, even those involved in conflicts with the staff over discipline, to seek his assistance in working out their problems.

While it is best to free the counselor of responsibility for discipline, teachers cannot escape the conflicting roles of confidant and disciplinarian. The handicap of having responsibility for discipline is less serious when the pupil is helped to understand the worker's dual role. When the pupil selects as his counselor a qualified staff member who also has discipline responsibilities, it should be made clear to the pupil that the staff member is functioning in his capacity as counselor, that is, in a nonjudgmental role. The problem to be discussed at the interview is the pupil's problem, and he is responsible for solving his problem in his own way. If, on the other hand, the staff member must call the pupil before him for disciplinary reasons, then the staff member is functioning in a judgmental role. The discipline problem is the staff member's, and therefore he must assume the responsibility for solving it.

School Prevention of Juvenile Delinquency

A FULL treatment of juvenile delinquency cannot be included here, but it is important to discuss the ways in which good school discipline and counseling can help to solve this serious problem.

If educators are to deal effectively with juvenile delinquency, they must understand the conditions which seem to contribute to it. The Interim Report of the United States Senate's Subcommittee to Investigate Juvenile Delinquency described these conditions as follows:

Studies indicate that young people of school age who are beyond the age required for school attendance and who drop out, constitute a group particularly at a disadvantage at present in finding employment. Inquiry has also shown that at least a portion of that group—jobless, idle, and without funds—becomes particularly vulnerable to delinquency. A number of reasons may be given for the large number of students who leave school before completing the secondary or high school level. These include: family difficulties, teacher-pupil friction, lack of interest and ability to keep up with studies, ill health, marriage, parental influence, a desire for adventure, and sometimes, simply a desire for money to keep up with their economically more fortunate classmates.

Children in the category referred to as school "dropouts," therefore, are often potential delinquents. Too often they have received little in the way of special services of which they are in need. Statistics show there is a much higher percentage of delinquents among those who drop out of school as compared with those who remain enrolled in school.[7]

The delinquent has rarely, if ever, become deeply involved in a meaningful experience at school. At least he has not become ego-involved and achieved success in those school activities which either the school or the society honors and rewards. Usually his home and neighborhood have also failed to provide such experiences. Allport[8] concluded that failure to experience ego-involvement produces a reactive ego, and a reactive ego tends to perceive associates as adversaries rather than as collaborators. Such a youth finds outlets in complaints, scapegoating, and antisocial behavior. Often he is faced with threats and deprivations. Consequently, the delinquent gang fulfills a genuine need for protection and membership.

Before teachers, counselors, and discipline officers can involve potential delinquents in meaningful school experiences, they must understand these youngsters. But even this is difficult because most discipline officers, teachers, and counselors, as members of the middle class, have difficulty understanding the delinquent who usually comes from the lower class. Kvaraceus explained this phenomenon as follows:

> The dominant focal concerns of this subculture include: trouble, toughness, smartness or duplicity, excitement, fate, and autonomy. These may be contrasted with the focal concerns of middle-class culture laying heavy stress on child rearing, preservation of the nuclear family, ambition to get ahead, achievement through directed work efforts, schooling and improvement of the mind, deferment of immediate pleasures and gains for future goals, accumulation of material goods and conscientious maintenance of property.[9]

But even if the school staff knows about the delinquent's class values and his school behavior, they know only a part of the story; Kvaraceus believes that norm-violating behavior has its roots in

7 *Education and Juvenile Delinquency,* Interim Report of the Subcommittee to Investigate Juvenile Delinquency to the Committee in the Judiciary (Washington, D.C.: U.S. Government Printing Office, 1956).

8 Gordon W. Allport, "The Psychology of Participation," *Psychological Review,* LII (1945), 117–32.

9 William C. Kvaraceus, "Nature of the Problem of Juvenile Delinquency in the United States," *Journal of Negro Education,* XXVIII (1959), 193.

the neighborhood gang, the community, and the family, and that perhaps it is even condoned by the attitudes of the community's law-abiding citizens:

> In understanding the delinquent's behavior and in assisting him in buying and living by the legal-societal rule book, professional and lay workers will need to be aware of the delinquent's primary reference group, the interplay of forces within this milieu, and finally how the child can be weaned from his rule book and helped to adopt the code of conduct of another reference group . . .
>
> The adults in the community are explicitly and implicitly involved in the delinquency story. Norm violations by youngsters tend to fulfill a number of psychological functions for older and more law-abiding members of the community. In the sanctimonious cluckings of many parents can be heard a half-concealed vicarious thrill and delight in escapades of youth. One can almost sense the adult smack of his lips as he bemoans the "awful" norm-violating conduct of the less inhibited young. If delinquency is to be prevented and controlled, it will be necessary for many adults to inspect their own emotional needs, their own problems, and their own pleasures in the delinquency phenomenon.[10]

Should school people then conclude that they cannot do any good by trying to identify potential delinquents and working with them? No, the situation is not that hopeless. If a hardened criminal like Paul Crump [11] can be rehabilitated, then there is certainly hope for the potential delinquents whom we discover early. We can learn much from Warden Jack Johnson's patience, courage, and faith in men.

Although school personnel should be encouraged to do what they can to make school meaningful for every potential delinquent, they should recognize that such efforts will not solve the juvenile delinquency problem. Besides a good educational program and effective counseling services, a real reform requires a good program of school discipline and the cooperation of the entire community to cope with the sources of crime: e.g., unemployment, inadequate recreation, poor housing, irresponsible parents, and poor law enforcement.

What can school personnel do to provide meaningful experiences

10 *Ibid.*, pp. 192, 198.
11 Ronald Bailey, "Facing Death, A New Life Perhaps Too Late," *Life*, LIII (1962), 26–31.

for potential delinquents? First of all they must try to identify them as early as possible. Techniques for identification are described by Kvaraceus and Miller [12] and by Kuhlen and Collister.[13] Next, the staff must try to identify these pupils' interests and to relate these interests to intellectual and social experiences provided by the school. As was indicated in Chapter 13, new activities also should be introduced to meet the needs of these pupils. Meaningful social, extra-class, and leadership experience should be provided for all youth—not just the favored social classes. Wherever possible, opportunity should be provided for these pupils to have rich, meaningful experiences with youngsters they admire who have learned to conform to reasonable standards. If such efforts are to be successful, the staff must take account of the potential delinquent's success in such groups. With reference to the influence a group can have on an individual, Dorwin Cartwright wrote as follows:

> Now if we try to discover how the level of aspiration gets set, we are immediately involved in the person's relationship to groups. The groups to which he belongs set standards for his behavior which he must accept if he is to remain in the group. If his capacities do not allow him to reach these standards he experiences failure, he withdraws or is rejected by the group and his self-esteem suffers shock.[14]

Therefore, those who help the potential delinquent achieve membership in these groups which are selected to provide new and conforming experience also must communicate to him that they are interested in helping him succeed in these groups, and that he may turn to these teachers or counselors for additional assistance when he feels he needs it.

In order for such groups to be able to effect change, Cartwright reported that the following conditions must be met:

> (1) If the group is to be used effectively as a medium of change, those people who are to be changed and those who are to exert influence for change must have a strong sense of belonging to the same group. (2) The

12 William C. Kvaraceus and Walter B. Miller, *Delinquent Behavior* (Washington, D.C.: National Education Association, 1959).

13 Raymond G. Kuhlen and E. Gordon Collister, "Sociometric Status of Sixth Graders and Ninth Graders Who Fail to Finish High School," *Educational and Psychological Measurement,* XII (1952), 631–37.

14 Dorwin Cartwright, "Achieving Change in People: Some Applications of Group Dynamics Theory," *Human Relations,* IV (1951), 384.

more attractive a group is to its members the greater is the influence that the group can exert on its members. (3) In attempts to change attitudes, values or behavior, the more relevant they are to the basic attraction to the group, the greater will be the influence that the group can exert upon them. (4) The greater the prestige of a group member in the eyes of other members, the greater the influence he can exert. (5) Efforts to change individuals or subparts of a group which, if successful, would have the result of making them deviate from the norms of the group will encounter strong resistance. (6) Strong pressure for changes in the group can be established by creating a shared perception by members of the need for change, thus making the source of pressure for change lie within the group.[15]

Early in his school experience the potential delinquent must find genuine acceptance at school, and also have the school's goals for him reinforced in the home. Since many potential delinquents come from homes in which parents found school unrewarding, and perhaps even punishing, this reinforcement cannot be easily obtained. Parent discussion groups of the type described in Chapter 10 can provide the group climate which is essential to change parents' attitudes toward school. Recent unemployment and the special adult education encouraged by the Manpower Development and Training Act of 1962 also have attracted the attention of many such parents and have motivated them to reevaluate their attitudes toward school. If counselors will work closely with those in charge of these adult education programs, they may be able to attract such parents to school for parent discussion groups.

A number of studies have been reported on the efficacy of group counseling for nonconforming, antisocial youth. Some of the most pertinent papers were published by Caplan,[16] Daniels,[17] Franklin,[18]

15 *Ibid.*, pp. 388–90.
16 Stanley W. Caplan, "The Effects of Group Counseling on Junior High School Boys' Concepts of Themselves in School," *Journal of Counseling Psychology*, IV (1957), 124–28.
17 Marvin Daniels, "The Influence of Sex of the Therapist and of Co-therapist Technique in Group Psychotherapy with Boys: An Investigation of the Effectiveness of Group Psychotherapy with Eighth Grade, Behavior-problem Boys, Comparing Results Achieved by a Male Therapist, by a Female Therapist, and by Two Therapists," *Dissertation Abstracts*, XVIII (1958), 1489.
18 Girard H. Franklin, "Group Psychotherapy with Delinquent Boys in a Training School Setting," *International Journal of Group Psychotherapy*, IX (1959), 213–18.

Gadpaille,[19] Gersten,[20] Schulman,[21] Staples,[22] and Stranahan, Schwartzman, and Atkin.[23] Group counseling provides the climate in which potential delinquents can become ego-involved in the process of solving their own problems; from the group they can secure encouragement to try various methods of adjusting to expectations of society, obtain understanding and support, develop the will to act, and be motivated by group pressures to conform to reasonable limits. For youngsters who often have been deprived of membership in a cohesive, understanding, and accepting primary group, counseling within a group setting has much to offer. In spite of the success reported in the literature on counseling groups of delinquents and potential delinquents, the author's own personal experience with such groups strongly suggests that these kinds of youngster can be helped most easily when they are included in groups with other youngsters whom they admire, but who have already learned to conform to reasonable limits. The principles reported by Cartwright [24] earlier also support this notion.

Finally, as suggested earlier in this chapter, these youngsters should be encouraged to participate along with their classmates in the definition and enforcement of reasonable limits. Such experiences increase the chances that these youngsters will understand and accept the necessary limits.

The real significance of setting and enforcing reasonable limits is summarized by Kvaraceus and Miller:

19 Warren J. Gadpaille, "Observations on the Sequence of Resistances in Groups of Adolescent Delinquents," *International Journal of Group Psychotherapy*, IX (1959), 275–86.

20 Charles Gersten, "An Experimental Evaluation of Group Therapy with Juvenile Delinquents," *International Journal of Group Psychotherapy*, I (1951), 311–18.

21 Irving Schulman, "Modifications in Group Psychotherapy with Anti-social Adolescents," *International Journal of Group Psychotherapy*, VII (1957), 310–17.

22 Ethel James Staples, "The Influence of the Sex of the Therapist and of the Co-therapist Technique in Group Psychotherapy with Girls: An Investigation of the Effectiveness of Group Psychotherapy with Eighth Grade, Behavior Problem Girls, Comparing Results Achieved by a Male Therapist, by a Female Therapist, and by Two Therapists in Combination," *Dissertation Abstracts*, XIX (1959), 2154.

23 M. Stranahan, C. Schwartzman, and E. Atkin, "Group Treatment for Emotionally Disturbed and Potentially Delinquent Boys and Girls," *American Journal of Orthopsychiatry*, XXVII (1957), 518–27.

24 *Ibid.*, pp. 388–90.

Although symptoms manifested in norm-violating behavior may be similar in form, the underlying personality problems may be very different. If there is a common denominator, it is to be found in the idea that each child needs to be helped constantly to conform to limits which are reasonable for him and which are demanded by his community. This concept runs counter to the common myth that psychiatrists have urged complete self-expression; no sound psychiatrist has ever denied the need for the establishment of ego-limits.

Limit setting is a vital element in permitting and assisting every child to learn rules and regulatons and to abide by them. The child must learn what is expected of him, and this is true in every culture and subculture.

The child can learn limits from many sources, including his gang. One difficulty is related to the fact that limits often become identified with maleness or femaleness according to the emotional significance of persons with whom the child identifies in early life. This might involve one kind of "mother" in the lower-class type of female-based household and another kind of "mother" in the middle-class type of female-dominated household or classroom. Each situation presents its own variety of problems. A boy out on a window-breaking spree "for fun" may assess the relative weight of conflicting directives: "My mother (or teacher) says this is not the thing to do, but, hell, she's only a woman. The kids in my gang say to do it, so I guess I better."

A major basis for learning limits which one really accepts is identification, an important form of which is positive identification. This concept has many implications for parents and teachers. It is central to the question of how best to establish a strong two-way relationship between parent and child, teacher and student. This means that neither school nor parent can hope to help the delinquent in setting and living by limits unless the youngster senses that the relationship includes important elements of real affection.[25]

SUGGESTED READINGS

1. BARUCH, DOROTHY W. *New Ways in Discipline.* New York: McGraw-Hill Book Co., Inc., 1949.

    While Dr. Baruch addresses herself to the parent, her work has great significance for the teacher. She has done a scholarly job, but has at the same time made her knowledge about children meaningful to others. Because Dr. Baruch is able to help the reader go beyond verbalizing these concepts, this is one book every teacher will want to read.

    a] How might a child respond to lack of love?

    b] Why does Baruch feel it very important for a child to express his

25 *Op. cit.,* pp. 112–13.

negative feelings? What restrictions does she place on this expression?

c] What is your reaction to Baruch's attack upon parents' use of "reasoning with the child"?

2. KVARACEUS, WILLIAM C., and WALTER B. MILLER. *Delinquent Behavior.* Washington, D.C.: National Education Association, 1959.

This report on the Juvenile Delinquency Project was prepared to help teachers, guidance workers, and school administrators plan and implement programs to cope with juvenile delinquency. It has proven to be very useful for these purposes.

a] What are the primary causes of juvenile delinquency in the United States?

b] What are some of the most promising approaches for coping with the problem?

3. MOWRER, O. H. "Discipline and Mental Health," *Harvard Educational Review*, XVII (1947), 284–96.

Mowrer contends that it is not the disciplining of a child but the way in which it is done that makes him neurotic.

a] What would Mowrer have parents do differently in disciplining their children?

4. SHEVIAKOV, GEORGE V., and FRITZ REDL. *Discipline for Today's Children and Youth.* Washington, D.C.: Department of Supervision and Curriculum Development, National Education Association, 1944.

These writers have produced a pamphlet which is helpful to both parents and teachers. They state the basic principles of discipline and then show the relevance of the principles for those of us who work with children.

a] What should parents learn about discipline?

b] From the writers' guides on the use of punishment, select six and defend them.

c] To what extent is the teacher's personality an element in classroom discipline?

5. STENDLER, CELIA B. "Climates for Self-Discipline," *Childhood Education*, XXVII (1951), 209–11.

Stendler shows how pupil participation in formulating goals and evaluating progress toward these goals contributes to self-discipline. She also identifies types of children who cannot be self-disciplined.

a] Under what condition do children respond best to discipline? What kind of children respond best to self-discipline?

b] How can you identify children who cannot learn to discipline themselves?

c] Why is it so important for the teacher to understand the reasons for his emotional reactions to certain kinds of behavior?

SUGGESTED FILMS

1. *Helping the Child to Accept the Do's* (11 minutes), Encyclopaedia Britannica Films, 1948.

   This film illustrates some of the types of "do's" a child must accept, and how he reacts to them.

2. *Helping the Child to Face the Don'ts* (11 minutes), Encyclopaedia Britannica Films, 1948.

   This film does essentially the same thing for "don'ts" which the one cited above does for "do's."

   a] If you were the counselor in your building, how would you use these films for in-service training with your staff?

3. *Maintaining Classroom Discipline* (14 minutes), McGraw-Hill, New York, 1947.

   This sound film presents some of the fundamental issues involved in a teacher's maintaining a good learning atmosphere.

   a] How did you feel about what the teacher did?

   b] What would you have done differently? Why?

15

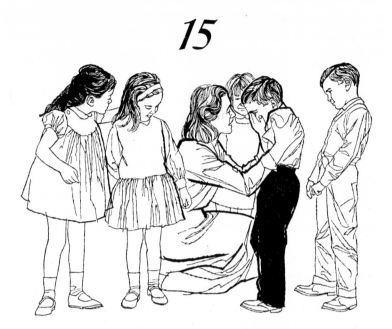

The Teacher's Responsibility for Guidance

THE TEACHER'S primary responsibility is to facilitate the mastery of knowledge, concepts, and skills; his guidance activities are auxiliary to instruction, and are performed in order to facilitate learning. However, the teacher's day-to-day contacts with pupils make him vital to guidance, even when guidance specialists are available. When the teacher shows concern for pupils' welfare, tries to understand and accept them, tries to provide challenging and satisfying learning experiences, helps them discover how well they are doing and where they need to improve, and tries to avoid hurting or disturbing them, he contributes to both their intellectual and their social-emotional development. Ideally, every teacher should respect each pupil as a person, deal with the pupil in terms of what is best for that pupil, and help each youngster learn to become increasingly self-disciplined and independent. Furthermore, the teacher is in a position to spot the early symptoms which suggest that a specialist is needed.

To fulfill these expectations, a teacher must be a reasonably well-adjusted person who is sensitive to his pupils' needs and has some facility for helping them satisfy their needs. Furthermore, he must possess the ability to appraise his impact upon his pupils and be willing to try to change to meet their needs.

This kind of teacher realizes that most pupils occasionally need individual help; and he lets his pupils know that he is willing to provide this help. He knows that different pupils have different potentialities in relation to the subject matter; he tries to ascertain the potentialities of each and to challenge them to the maximum without overtaxing the pupil. He tries to make the subject matter interesting and meaningful to each pupil in the light of the pupil's own background, so that each pupil will want to do the very best work of which he is capable.

He encourages his pupils to try to understand and to accept each other, and to work together in order to learn from each other. He also encourages his pupils to help define the rules by which they will live and he expects them to help enforce their own rules. Though he is capable of setting and enforcing appropriate limits, and his pupils realize this fact, he prefers to enlist their assistance; he respects them and tries to take advantage of every opportunity to make them increasingly responsible for themselves.

The teacher's ability to help his pupils develop a wholesome climate for effective learning is one of his most important contributions to guidance. After pupils discover that their ideas and opinions are respected and that the teacher can accept opinions that differ from his own, pupils feel free to say what they really think, admit what they do not understand, seek assistance when they feel they need it, and even ask about personal matters that have bothered them. Within this permissive, accepting atmosphere, pupils are able to help a classmate to explain and clarify his ideas, to defend his ideas when necessary, to learn to accept criticism from others, to realize when he has a contribution to make, and also to realize when he is merely seeking attention and perhaps wasting the group's time. Here pupils can afford to be themselves—to be what they are.

General support for this kind of personal relationship within the classroom was reported by Robert Bush:

Although most of the ratings indicate a positive feeling tone on the part of teachers and pupils toward each other, in 70 percent of the cases the feelings are not highly positive on both sides of the relationship. Perhaps the most revealing aspect of this inquiry into the nature of personal relationships between teachers and pupils is that the facts do not support the common view that a teacher's personal liking for pupils is more important than a pupil's liking for the teacher. The teacher must love his pupils, a dictum of ancient origin, is still popular. According to this view, it is not the business of teachers to secure love from their pupils, but to "learn" them, even if, perchance, it becomes painful. In older and harsher times, it was considered even desirable that learning should be not too pleasant. Contrary to this traditional belief, the findings of this study suggest that the personal liking of a pupil for his teacher is one of the most powerful factors in bringing about an effective learning relationship between the teacher and the pupil. This requires a teacher who is skilled, sensitive, and adjusted in the area of personal relationships and who is able to handle his relations with pupils objectively rather than as a source of meeting his own personal inadequacies. Learning is enhanced markedly when teachers make themselves personally acceptable to pupils.[1]

A teacher also has important contributions to make to each of the various guidance services; his responsibility for each of these services is discussed below.

Counseling

THE teacher should not be expected to provide counseling since that is a complex undertaking which requires special professional knowledge and skills. However, he should be expected to exhibit interest in his pupils and to listen to them attentively when they seek his assistance. Whether the pupil is worried about a grade, the loss of a pet, a family quarrel, or breaking up with his girl friend, the teacher should try to understand how the pupil feels and help him express his feelings.

Sometimes a pupil wants a private conference [2] but does not know how to arrange for it; therefore, the teacher must watch for

---

1 Robert N. Bush, *The Teacher-Pupil Relationship* (Englewood Cliffs, N.J.: Prentice-Hall, Inc., 1954), pp. 188–89.

2 Here the term "private conference" is used to distinguish between the conference a pupil has with a trusted adult, and counseling with a qualified counselor.

cues which suggest this need. For example, a pupil may come to school early, stay late, offer to help the teacher with room chores, or request assistance with an assignment as an excuse to see the teacher alone. A few even misbehave to attract the teacher's attention. If it is inconvenient for the teacher to see the child immediately, he should set aside a *specific* time for a later conference. Early in the school term the teacher also should tell pupils that it is appropriate for them to request private conferences. Usually such a statement enables most of them to ask directly for a conference rather than to use devious means of revealing the need for assistance.

What should the teacher attempt to accomplish in a private conference? How far should he go in attempting to help a pupil who is worried or upset? His goal should be to try to help the normal child who is temporarily bothered by a problem to understand himself better, and to discover ways of coping with his difficulty. If, however, this help requires more than one or possibly two sessions, the pupil should be referred to a counselor. The teacher should understand how the counselor attempts to help pupils, what he expects from them, what they may expect from him, and how he often helps them. These topics were discussed in Chapter 3.

The teacher must be relied upon to identify the pupils who have more serious problems. The counselor talks to them and decides whether he should attempt to help or should refer them to others for treatment. When a teacher discovers such a pupil (and the pupil has not initiated a conference with the teacher), he may either call the pupil in for a conference and make the referral to the counselor, or ask the counselor to see the pupil.

At the high school level, teachers have a valuable contribution to make as academic advisers. In this role they should help each student select those school subjects and extra-class activities which will help him achieve his educational and vocational goals, and which seem to contribute most to his social and emotional development. Though the adviser should try to understand the student and provide him with the information which he needs to make these choices, his role is usually more authoritarian than the counselor's role. At least he is expected to enroll a student in those courses which help him achieve his goals. When the student has no educational or vocational goal or needs help in changing his goals, he is referred to a counselor.

Although the teacher is not expected to do counseling, he should find Chapter 4 helpful in coping with the problems he meets in private conferences. Because beginning counselors, and perhaps teachers too, are inclined to advise, to reassure, and to probe for what they believe to be relevant information, teachers are urged to study carefully the material on these topics. The use of these techniques involves dangers of which most teachers may not be fully aware.

Child Study

To TEACH effectively, a teacher must know his pupils reasonably well. He must know what he can expect from each pupil, he must help each to discover what to expect from himself, and he must be able to help each pupil discover and diagnose his learning problems.

The teacher has much to contribute to helping other staff members, such as the counselor, to understand his pupils. During a single school day he often sees his pupils in such varied settings as the classroom, the lunchroom, the playground or gymnasium, the library, the hallway, or even at a school party. In the classroom, for example, he sees how the child performs academically, and how he plans his work. In the library some of the child's major interests may be discovered from the books he chooses. On the playground or in the halls, he sees many indications of the child's relations with his peers. From some of these contacts the teacher also may learn about the child's food and health habits and his general health condition. From the child's comments, the teacher comes to know something about the child's home life, and this understanding can be increased by contact with the parents at school or on a visit to the home. In order to contribute systematically to his colleagues' understanding of his pupils, the teacher must appraise the pupils' growth, record any significant behavior he observes (See the section on Staff Reports in Chapter 8), and participate in cooperative child study with colleagues (See the first two sections in Chapter 6). Sincere participation in case conferences is perhaps the most significant contribution a teacher can make to child study.

Important as it is for a teacher to understand his pupils, we must recognize that the typical teacher will not have the time fully to understand every pupil; still, he must continue to try to do so. Robert Bush[3] found that the teachers who know most about their pupils, and are aware of and sympathize with their individual needs

3 *Op. cit.*, pp. 189–90.

and interests, develop more effective relationships with them than do those whose major concern is knowledge of subject matter. Where the school principal exhibits a sympathetic concern for his pupils and teachers, and encourages teachers to participate in cooperative child study, teachers tend to carry the attitude over into their own classroom. Besides being an effective child study technique, the case conference encourages child study and helps teachers improve their child study methods.

Information Service

WHEN teachers are vitally interested in their pupils, they will help pupils obtain the information they need. A section of Chapter 2 (Understanding Physical and Emotional Changes), a section of Chapter 4 (Answering a Client's Questions), and the introduction to Chapter 10 discussed the conditions under which information is most readily accepted and used.

Obviously, teachers cannot be expected to be able to answer all the questions that their pupils ask, but they should be able to help their pupils find the answers to their common questions, and they should know where they can get assistance in helping pupils locate other needed information. Some teachers are inclined to answer pupils' questions when, instead, they should take advantage of the opportunity to teach independence by helping pupils find the information for themselves. In so doing they also reduce the chances of providing incorrect information. At the same time, a teacher must be careful not to convey indifference. While teachers help pupils learn to locate and use needed information on their own, they also must convey to pupils a personal interest in them.

In addition to helping pupils answer their various questions, teachers should help pupils discuss the information in self-contained classrooms at the elementary-school level, and in homerooms at the secondary-school level. Some teachers should be qualified to lead voluntary discussion groups of the type described in Chapter 10. A secondary-school teacher also should accept responsibility for devoting some time to discussing the vocational implications of his subject. Enrolled in almost every course are some pupils who like that course very much and do well in it; they appreciate knowing where they can use their knowledge and skill to earn a living. Such information also helps pupils who are not interested in the course to discover either the vocations they should avoid or reasons for trying to change their attitudes or performance in the course.

Orientation

PERHAPS the best assistance a teacher can provide with orientation is to help new pupils answer their questions. He also may serve as leader for homeroom discussions and for voluntary discussion groups designed to help pupils adapt to their new school situation.

Educational-vocational Planning

HELPING pupils define educational and vocational goals is primarily the school counselor's responsibility, but a teacher can contribute to this planning process by interpreting its nature to pupils, acting as a discussion leader for voluntary discussion groups, and serving as an academic adviser. He also can take pupils' special interests into account when assigning special projects, and can help pupils obtain information on occupations which are related to his teaching subject.

Job Placement

BY HELPING pupils become acquainted with the vocational implications of his school subject, the teacher encourages a pupil to look for his salable vocational skills, one of the first steps in job placement. Noting and appraising the development of these salable job skills is another important contribution the teacher can make to job placement. Responsibility for doing this is usually recognized and accepted by teachers of vocational subjects, but other teachers should do it too. Those who know a pupil best also should write letters of recommendation for student placement—both for job placement and for educational placement in college or some other post-high school institution.

Some teachers, especially those who teach vocational subjects, often serve as coordinators of the school placement service.

Follow-up

AS CHAPTER 12 indicated, the success which a school has in getting responses from former students is determined while students are in school. If former students understand the purpose of the follow-up studies and sense some genuine interest in them as individuals, they are much more inclined than they would otherwise be to provide the data requested in the studies. Teachers have an important role to play in interpreting the follow-up program and in developing the emotional climate for an effective response. The contacts they maintain with individual students and the ideas they contribute to the development of the program also are important. Where the data are obtained as suggested in Chapter 12, a teacher often has primary responsibility for the follow-up studies.

Social and Leadership Development

THE director of guidance is usually assigned responsibility for the extra-class program and for leadership development, but the teaching faculty usually sponsors most of the extra-class activities and the organizations which provide leadership experiences. Teachers play an important role in helping students to develop new activities, and to evaluate the various activities and student organizations. Although members of the guidance staff usually initiate leadership training programs, eventually these activities are also assigned to members of the teaching staff.

The Reluctant Participant

MOST teachers are genuinely concerned about their pupils' welfare, but not all teachers recognize and accept their guidance responsibilities. Most reluctance arises from teachers' being too busy. They hesitate to accept more responsibility when they feel they are already doing everything they can do or care to do. Some of these teachers are meeting their guidance responsibilities, but they do not realize it and they are afraid that still more time will be required. Others would like to participate in the guidance program, but they do not know what they can contribute to it. They also may question whether they have the professional competencies to do what is expected from them. If the guidance director will try to understand these teachers, help them provide the services they feel that they can provide within their time limits, and make available appropriate in-service education, most of them will accept their guidance responsibilities. Furthermore, the school principal must believe that guidance responsibilities are important and he must be patient with teachers as each tries to discover what he can do, and as each learns to provide these services.

Despite these measures, however, a few teachers in almost every school system will refuse to participate in the guidance program. Even some of these teachers are genuinely interested in their pupils and try in their own way to help their pupils achieve a good school adjustment. Others do only what is required; they are not interested in their pupils as persons. Fortunately, those in the last category are the exception. At least Bush found that most teachers wanted to improve their professional skills:

An outstanding fact of the study is that teachers were anxious to improve their professional skill and change their teaching practices when they were treated as individuals and supplied with basic facts concerning their teaching. Moreover, teachers remained objective even when confronted with unpleasant and negative facts relating to their competence. Several factors probably contributed to this situation:

1. Instead of working predominantly with groups of teachers, individualized observation and consultations were emphasized.

2. The data presented to the teacher were factual and objective.

3. The investigators scrupulously refrained from making value judgments concerning "good" or "bad" findings.

4. The teacher was given ample opportunity to study the findings and to draw his own inferences from the facts.

5. The teachers who participated in the study volunteered, and work with them was on a basis of professional equality.

6. The data remained strictly confidential between the investigator and the teachers.[4]

Several inferences may be drawn from Bush's findings: (1) teachers want to be understood too; (2) they can be helped best when they recognize their need for help; (3) they want to be respected and to be treated as an equal; and (4) they need a confidential relationship in which they can discuss the things that really concern them.

Most educators agree that teachers should have an important place in the guidance program, but many argue that the overworked teacher cannot be expected to take on even more work. However, effective participation in guidance may not take more time, for with a better understanding of his pupils, the teacher could save time

4 *Ibid.*, p. 191.

often spent on unproductive remedial work and on the working with certain types of discipline case. He also could be spared some of the anxiety and worry resulting from unsuccessful efforts to help or to control pupils with such problems. Furthermore, teachers should be encouraged to scrutinize their activities in an effort to determine which are most likely to produce best results for the pupils and to give the teacher most satisfaction. Some clerical and administrative duties are inescapable, though much time—spent on tasks that are not important or that might well be done by others—could be saved. Finally, a teacher experiences personal satisfaction when he sees a child's behavior improve as a result of his efforts to help the child.

SUGGESTED READINGS

1. ANDERSON, G. LESTER (ed.). *Learning and Instruction,* Forty-Ninth Yearbook of the National Society for the Study of Education. Chicago: University of Chicago Press, 1950.

   This yearbook presents a scholarly analysis of the aims of educators and the nature of human learning. Chapters 1, 2, 5, and 6 are most relevant for our purposes because they deal with what motivates children and how they learn interests, attitudes, and ways of adjusting to school life.
   a] What is the teacher's role in developing a favorable learning climate?
   b] How do children learn interests, motives, and attitudes?
   c] What elements seem to influence personal and social adjustment? What can the teacher contribute to improved school adjustment?

2. GORDON, IRA J. *The Teacher as a Guidance Worker.* New York: Harper & Row, Publishers, 1956.

   Chapters 1, 7, and 8.
   a] What does Gordon believe the teacher's role is in guidance?
   b] How can the teacher provide his pupils with real choices?
   c] How can a process observer be used to evaluate group processes within a classroom?
   d] What is the teacher's responsibility for counseling?

3. JOHNSON, EDGAR G., MILDRED PETERS, and WILLIAM EVRAIFF. *The Role of the Teacher in Guidance.* Englewood Cliffs, N.J.: Prentice-Hall, Inc., 1959.

   In addition to defining the teacher's role in guidance, this book, like Gordon's, makes a special effort to help the teacher understand his pupils. Suggested chapters: 1, 12, and 13.
   a] What is the teacher's unique role?
   b] What kind of help should a counselor expect from a teacher?

4. OHLSEN, MERLE M. (ed.). *Modern Methods in Elementary Education.* New York: Holt, Rinehart & Winston, Inc., 1959.

This book was written to help the beginning teacher solve the problems he meets in his day-to-day work. Chapter 1, "Learner-Centered Teaching," describes a relationship conducive to guidance within the classroom.
   a] What is unique about learner-centered teaching?

SUGGESTED FILMS

1. *Experimental Studies in the Social Climate of Groups* (43 minutes), State University of Iowa, produced by Lewin, White, and Lippitt at the Iowa Child Welfare Research Station, 1940.

   This film shows how a group of boys behaved when they were organized in clubs run on democratic principles, on autocratic principles, and on laissez-faire principles.
   a] How did behavior change when the leadership shifted from one type of government to another?

2. *The High Wall* (32 minutes), McGraw-Hill, 1952.

   This film, which shows how prejudices develop and which suggests ways of breaking down those prejudices, was produced under the joint sponsorship of the Anti-Defamation League of B'nai B'rith, the Departments of Public Information and Mental Health in the State of Illinois, and the Columbia Foundation of San Francisco.
   a] What are the social dangers of prejudices?
   b] How do prejudices affect mental health?
   c] What are some of the best ways of breaking down prejudices?

3. *Willie and the Mouse* (11 minutes), Teaching Films Custodians, 1946.

   This film tells the story of success and failure through the effect of each on two mice.
   a] Why did the two mice react to failure differently?
   b] What are the implications for the teacher?

16

The Administration of Guidance Services

I F THE members of the guidance staff are going to develop a good program, they must understand who is responsible for making the decisions, how to communicate effectively with the decision makers, and how to identify and deal with those who influence the decision makers. Thus, in order to achieve their objectives, the guidance director and his staff must understand the administrative structure of the school. This chapter describes that administrative structure and the problems of administering and coordinating guidance services in a public school setting.

Local initiative has been an important element in the development of the public schools in the United States. With this local initiative there developed a feeling of local ownership and pride in the schools, elements which have helped to maintain public interest in the school's program and its problems. Local control also has made it possible for local leaders to adapt, within the limits defined by state laws, the program to meet the special needs of their children.

On the other hand, local control, and primarily local financial support of the school districts, has had several disadvantages. Often, the schools in one district will suffer from lack of sufficient funds to carry on a minimum program while the schools in even neighboring districts have more tax resources than they need to carry on a good program. In other instances, there are not enough children living within the school district to maintain a high quality program economically. Frequently, local leaders resist both district reorganization and the increased state and federal control which they fear would accompany state and federal aid.

In spite of these weaknesses, the advantages of local control seem to outweigh its disadvantages. Furthermore, many of its weaknesses are being corrected: small school districts are combining their resources to employ needed specialists in such fields as guidance; intermediate districts, often counties, are employing specialists to supplement services offered at the local level; small inefficient districts are decreasing; legislation is being passed to improve the tax structure for school support; and local leaders are learning to deal with the vocal minority which may or may not be working for the best interest of all the children.

At every level certain forces influence decisions about special services such as guidance: public opinion, pressure groups, the legislature, the school board, and the professional leaders. Additional elements affect policies and practices at the local level: the quality of the staff, the nature of the student body, and the community's ability and willingness to finance the schools. All of these elements must be considered in initiating and improving guidance services.

School board members at both the state and local level, and even the state legislators, are obligated to take cognizance of public opinion, but they should be certain that they are obtaining an opinion which represents all segments of the population. Too frequently, both the board members and state legislators respond only to the opinions of a vocal minority. To cope with this problem more adequately than many have in the past, school administrators must help the elected representatives of the people tell their constituents how to communicate with the school board, encourage constituents from all segments of the population to submit their problems and their suggestions, publish the board's actions along with the debate on the issues, and try to avoid the temptation to conduct business in closed committee meetings and in executive sessions.

Every school district has its critics, but recently schools have been confronted by intelligent critics supported by influential citizens and clever advertising techniques. Often these critics have been manipulating school administrators into debating the issue on the critics' ground rules and time schedule. Consequently, school administrators have not had or taken adequate time to obtain the essential facts, to present them effectively to the public, and to analyze the weaknesses in their opponent's case. The administrators would not be forced into a defensive position if they would listen to the critics, take time to consider the criticisms in light of what is best for all of the children, force the critics to defend their program in terms of these best interests, ask the critics for specific suggestions for implementing suggested programs, and finally, use the critics' ideas whenever an objective judgment indicates that those ideas will improve the school program. Many of the critics do not have a program, and those who do are usually interested in only part of the total school population. But frequently the critics have good ideas for this part of the school population, and are sufficiently committed to help the schools improve educational programs for those children. Care must be taken not to permit such groups to manipulate schools into using an unfair share of the school's resources for improved programs for any special group. By actively responding to the various criticisms of the schools, administrators can adapt those suggestions which best serve the needs of all children, and make clear to the public the limitations of other suggested changes.

The Board of Education

ALTHOUGH local boards usually possess considerable authority, the primary authority for education rests with the state government. School boards must function within the limits granted them by the state legislature, and these limits may be changed at any time at the discretion of the state legisuature. On the other hand, since local autonomy is so deeply entrenched in American public education, it is unlikely that the local school board's powers will be changed drastically at any given legislative session.

Usually local school boards are granted the authority to establish schools, to employ a superintendent of schools, to define standards for the employment of school personnel, to establish salary schedules for personnel, to employ and to dismiss personnel upon the recommendation of the superintendent, to define the scope and purposes of local public education, to state policies for the admission and attendance of pupils, to purchase teaching materials and school supplies, to institute policies for the expenditure of school funds and the accounting for school funds, to buy school property, to contract for the construction of school buildings, and to levy taxes. Unfortunately, many school boards spend most of their time on business matters, and fail to give adequate attention to the educational program and the essential special services. Some school boards also attempt to administer the schools; instead, they should define school policies and hold the superintendent responsible for executing those policies.

The Advisory Council

WITHIN the past decade the aid of local advisory councils has been enlisted by many school boards for solving school problems. The councils also have served a useful function on a continuing basis for such special programs as vocational agriculture, business education, and part-time work experience. In every case these persons should be appointed by and their responsibilities should be defined by the school board.

There are some disadvantages in using lay advisory councils. After describing the advisory council's major contribution Van Miller and Willard Spalding cite its chief weakness:

Such a council is an effective device for this purpose [to bring the thinking of the community to bear upon problems of the school] in some places for a period of time. It [the advisory council] does not work well over a long period of time . . . It tends to gain power, which frequently brings it into conflict with the board which created it. There is little place for a continuing advisory council of laymen in a community where the board is fully alert to its responsibilities as a public body and lives up to them in a desirable way.[1]

1 Van Miller and Willard B. Spalding, *The Public Administration of American Schools* (New York: Harcourt, Brace & World, Inc., 1952), p. 101.

The School Administrator

THE school administrator serves four important functions: (1) leadership, (2) public relations, (3) regulation, and (4) business. The superintendent of schools fulfills these functions for the entire school system, the principal fulfills them for his building, and the guidance director fulfills them for the guidance personnel. Because most of his personnel are assigned to school buildings, the guidance director must fulfill his administrative obligations in cooperation with the various building principals.

In the *leadership role* the school administrator should select his staff with great care; bring new and stimulating ideas to them; make provision for them to exchange ideas; cite problems with which he needs their help; encourage them to bring problems to the entire staff for study; and assist each individual in diagnosing and solving his professional problems. He should solicit the aid of his staff in reviewing the educational needs of the community, county, or state, and should motivate his staff to improve the quality of their services. Of all of these functions, perhaps selecting staff members and motivating them to improve their services are the most important, for the quality of services provided by the staff depends on the worth of the individuals, and it soon declines if its members are not of the highest possible caliber and alert for ideas which will enable them to improve their work.

Every worker wants to know what is expected of him and what he can expect from his supervisor and colleagues, but for guidance workers, and especially counselors, such knowledge is critical. All too frequently, the principal, the teachers, the pupils, and the counselors (including the guidance director) have different perceptions of the counselor's role; therefore, the counselor will always disappoint someone in various ways and to varying degrees, depending on the extent to which his perception of his role disagrees with the others' perceptions. It is the guidance director's task to know the services for which he is responsible and to assign these responsibilities to individuals, taking account of the competencies of the individual and the compatibility of the different dutes. For example, Norman Gilbert's study [2] indicates that the responsibility for coun-

2 Norman S. Gilbert, "A Comparison of Students' Perceptions of Counseling Relationships Among Schools in Which Counselor's Duties Differ" (unpublished dissertation, University of Illinois, 1962).

seling and discipline should not be assigned to the same individual. But even careful assignment of duties is not sufficient. After the guidance director has defined each worker's role, he must help each worker understand the role, develop an image of it, and communicate this image to colleagues and pupils.

The staff in turn should help the superintendent provide leadership for its school board. If the staff members do not recognize this responsibility, the superintendent should alert them to it. To provide this leadership the staff should identify problems, make recommendations for solving them, and help the board solve the problems which the board refers to them. The staff also should be able to look beyond their immediate problems to help the school board to envision the overall purposes of education and to make long-term plans for the improvement of the schools under their jurisdiction.

In his *public relations role,* the superintendent and his staff should provide the school board and the staff with the information they need to interpret the school's programs for the public; inventory periodically the educational needs of the community, county, or state; inform the public how they can communicate to the school board their special educational needs and criticism of the faculty's practices and the school's program; conduct at the local level follow-up studies with former pupils; and inform the public of the school's needs. From the point of view of the staff in a local public school, the principal's most important public relations function is to interpret the school's programs for the public in general, especially for the parents, and to provide the teachers and counselors with information on the parents and their expectations from the school. Unfortunately, many administrators spend too much time trying to sell the public a bill of goods rather than providing accurate descriptions of the school's programs and its needs. If the programs are really good and the school's needs are genuine, the public will accept and support them insofar as they are able to do so financially. Furthermore, pupils' comments and behavior will provide the good school program with much favorable publicity, just as they will give the poor program much unfavorable publicity.

When the guidance director is called upon to interpret his program for the public or to present the case for additional services, he should take advantage of society's inherent interest in children and youth. Of this interest Wrenn recently said,

So deep is the concern that families sacrifice themselves for their children in many ways. They go to great lengths to provide for their children the best clothing, the best homes, the best community facilities for social development and recreation, and to provide for the greatest possible protection from exploitation and social perversion. (Unfortunately much of this parental concern consists of providing things for children, not loving and living with them.) Professional people in the various human behavior fields speak approvingly of the "child-centered" home and of the democratic family in which children are consulted on all matters which affect them. Youth tends to be for many a cherished period of life, one idealized and held apart.[3]

To be sure, not all Americans are interested in children and youth, but every community has a substantial majority who are, and the case that can be made for guidance appeals to them. Though a brief description of the guidance services is useful, parents are more interested in examples of the kinds of problems for which children and youth seek help and how they were helped. Such a presentation enables them to recall how they felt as children when they faced similar problems, and to understand why their children need guidance services today.

In his *regulatory role* the school administrator insures that the school functions in accordance with state legislation, that the school board's policies are followed, and that the quality of services meet *at least minimum standards*. For example, the superintendent is responsible for making certain that qualified personnel are employed, that the quality of teaching is satisfactory, that proper equipment and teaching materials are provided, and that funds can be accounted for. Where funds are provided by the state or federal government he must insure that certain special conditions are met—e.g., that only properly qualified students are admitted to the program.

Obtaining an adequately qualified staff is a critical problem for the guidance director. The shortage of qualified personnel has at times forced directors to accept persons who did not even meet minimum state qualifications. Sometimes higher salaries are required to attract good personnel. Whether these special considerations can be obtained or not, the guidance director must define each worker's

3 C. Gilbert Wrenn, *The Counselor in the Changing World* (Washington, D.C.: The Commission on Guidance in American Schools, American Personnel and Guidance Association, 1962), p. 3.

position with care, including qualifications of prospective employees, in order to obtain the best available people and to communicate the seriousness of his personnel problem to his superiors.

The administrator's primary *business responsibilities* usually include estimating the cost of the various educational programs and the potential school revenue, investigating the possibilities for increasing school revenue, budgeting funds for the programs, and supervising the expenditure of funds. Although these business responsibilities are important, they must not absorb so much of the school administrator's time that he neglects his *leadership, public relations,* and *regulatory functions.*

Perhaps some readers are wondering where supervision fits into the administrator's responsibility. Best results are usually obtained when it is incorporated with his leadership role. If, for example, the guidance director is to fulfill the leadership role, he must first help his counselors define their role and develop criteria, which they can use either by themselves or with his help, to appraise their effectiveness. This means that they should be encouraged to make tape, and where possible even video, recordings of their counseling sessions. These can be used both for self-study and for play-back with the supervisor. A counselor is most apt to seek this kind of help when he is secure enough to recognize his mistakes, when he wants to correct them, and when he feels that his supervisor respects him as an individual, wants to help him, and will try to understand why the counselor behaved as he did.

If a counselor does not seek the supervisor's assistance, the first thing the supervisor should do is to ask himself whether the conditions described in the previous paragraph were met. He also should ask himself the following question: Did my definition of our working relationship include a description of supervision?

Some counselors may not seek the supervisor's assistance because they do not believe he has anything to offer them. Some may doubt their competencies, and others may have little interest in improving their counseling skills. In the interest of the pupils, the administrator may have to function in his regulatory role for these counselors; he must try to assess the quality of their services and to improve it where it is deficient. This task is most difficult, for obviously, the supervisor cannot, nor would any good supervisor want to, force a counselor to make recordings for supervisory study. Other means of evaluation are discussed in the next chapter.

The Faculty

To DO the best possible job, every administrator must win the co-operation of his staff and be able to delegate some of his responsibilities to his colleagues. Usually, best results are obtained at every level when the administrator can build with the aid of his staff a friendly, permissive working atmosphere in which problems are attacked democratically. On the other hand, almost everyone will admit that some autocratic leaders have been successful: they have been successful because they selected a good staff, respected them as individuals, treated them fairly, won their confidence, and developed a program which most of the staff liked. Furthermore, a successful autocratic leader usually recognizes the value of consulting with his staff, thus making them feel that they have had a part in building and improving the school program even though they have not really participated in making the decisions. Of course some autocratic leaders allow the staff to vote on those issues on which they believe the staff will support them, in an attempt to convince their staffs and themselves that they too are democratic leaders. Nevertheless, one probably cannot expect members of the staff to function as democratic leaders within their own classrooms when their administrator is an autocrat. Moreover, the improvements which are made under the leadership of an autocrat tend to be associated with the leader and do not persist long after he leaves.

In contrast, the improvements which are made under a democratic leader tend to be carried on by the staff even after the leader leaves, because faculty members who participated in the decisions understand the reasons for them. Under democratic leadership, there is an opportunity for everyone's ideas to be considered, challenged, and appraised. Within such an atmosphere most individuals will become sufficiently secure to try out their own ideas and to ask for assistance with individual professional problems. Thus, when they have developed an idea and applied it in their daily work, they continue the practice until they develop a better idea. And they carry on the practice because they want to, not because they feel they must do so to please their leader.

Whether the administrator is autocratic or democratic, he must be able to create a climate in which the staff can provide quality service, will seek new and better ways of functioning, will help identify school problems, and will offer their suggestions for solving the problems. These are essential conditions for a good program.

The Guidance Committee

CHAPTER 6 explains how the guidance committee can be used effectively for cooperative child study and in-service education of the teaching staff. Here we shall be concerned with its use in the administration and coordination of guidance services.

The previous section stressed the advantages of involving the faculty in all the decisions which affect them. Perhaps more than anywhere else, ego-involvement of the faculty is essential for the development, administration, and coordination of guidance services. Through their cooperative efforts in helping their pupils, faculty members discover how children are helped, what the faculty can contribute to the guidance program, and how much personal satisfaction that contribution gives. They also assume responsibility for describing and defending guidance services to those colleagues who reject such special services.

Teamwork, such as the experiences on the guidance committee, makes life more meaningful to people. Allport[4] claims that it enlarges the ego-boundaries, causing selfish gratifications to give way to cooperative satisfaction. On the other hand, failure to provide ego-involvement can result in even the potential supporters of guidance services joining those who criticize all special services.

ITS RESPONSIBILITY FOR ADMINISTRATION

A chief responsibility of the guidance committee of an individual school is to provide continuity for child study. While its members are helping colleagues study their pupils, they often identify problems which they feel require attention. How they act will be determined by the way their function is defined. They may suggest solutions to the principal or refer the problem to another faculty committee. They may formulate a recommendation which then may become a building policy, or may be referred to the principal or faculty for action before it affects building policies. Or if the recommendation seems to have implications for the entire school system, it may be referred to another policy-making body or person for

4 Gordon W. Allport, "The Psychology of Participation," *Psychological Review*, LII (1945), 117–32.

action. It is clear that the building guidance committee is in a good position to discover problems and to develop school policies out of their experiences in helping pupils.

These experiences in helping colleagues study their pupils may lead the members of the guidance committee to discover the need for special services. When this happens, they often can help the principal develop job descriptions and rationales for the new positions. They also can help the principal select personnel for these new positions, and help interpret the new person's role to colleagues.

ITS RESPONSIBILITY FOR COORDINATION

Guidance services should be coordinated throughout the school system. This may be done by a guidance council, composed of representatives elected from each of the school guidance committees. Since efficient operation limits the council to not more than fifteen or twenty members, large school systems may have to define city districts from which guidance committees, meeting together, elect one person to represent the several schools in the district. Later, at district-wide meetings, each representative is instructed by the committees he represents. When working in this fashion, an individual school committee must be able to request, without first getting the sanction of a full district meeting, that the district representative carry an issue to the coordinating council and report council action back to the school committee.

As a consequence of experiences in helping pupils, school guidance committees have requested guidance councils to develop school policies and to make recommendations on such issues as the evaluation of the cumulative record, methods for transferring a pupil's cumulative record from school to school, testing programs, promotion policies, adequacy of the course offerings and the extra-class activities program, use of community guidance services, sources and use of occupational information, and reports to parents.

As building guidance committees identify problems, they also may wish to suggest ways of attacking them. Sometimes an examination of the problems reveals to a building committee the need for new policies for the entire school system. At other times a committee discovers new approaches which might well replace old ones throughout the school system. These they will wish to take before the coordinating council. It is usually a good idea for guidance committee members to discuss issues with their entire school staff before they make recommendations to the coordinating council. Through this approach the guidance committees keep their colleagues informed and involve all of them in formulating guidance policies.

Probably no one can define the various staff members' roles in guidance as effectively as the staff themselves can. Teachers, in particular, have much to contribute in formulating guidance policies, in identifying needed special services, and in helping the administrator select specialists for these positions. But if a guidance program is to thrive, it must have the support of the administration as well. Both the superintendent and the building principal, recognizing work in guidance as one of the important responsibilities of the school, must take an active part in the program and must secure financial support for it.

The school administrator must do more than merely tolerate the guidance program. He must understand its objectives, realize how it helps young people, insist that specialists' roles are so defined as to make best possible use of their services, and encourage teachers to practice principles of the guidance program in the classroom. He must encourage his staff to participate in solving the school's problems, in formulating school policies, and in coordinating guidance services. In a well-organized guidance program, teachers, specialists, and administrators work together to contribute to adjustment and development of potentialities of all the pupils. Finally, a well-qualified director of guidance must be assigned responsibility for the basic administrative roles: leadership, public relations, regulation, and business.

SUGGESTED READINGS

1. BAXTER, EDNA DOROTHY. *An Approach to Guidance.* New York: Appleton-Century-Crofts, 1946.

   This is a story of a guidance worker's experiences with students and teachers and an interpretation of the principles she used.
      a] What were the three most important obstacles faced by Molly? How did she overcome them?
      b] With which of her basic principles did you disagree most strongly? Why?

2. FRAZIER, ALEXANDER. "The Teacher and the Counselor—Friends or Enemies," *National Education Association Journal,* XXXVIII, 104–05.

a] What does the author believe to be sources of conflict between the teacher and the counselor?

3. GRACE, ALONZO G. (ed.). *Changing Conceptions in Educational Administration,* The Forty-Fifth Yearbook of the National Society for the Study of Education, Part II. Chicago: University of Chicago Press, 1946.

> *The title describes this yearbook very well.*
> a] What reorientation in school administration is needed?
> b] How can the school system be organized for staff participation in decision making?
> c] How may community participation be achieved in coordination and planning of school programs?

4. MILLER, VAN, and WILLARD B. SPALDING. *The Public Administration of American Schools.* New York: Harcourt, Brace & World, Inc., second edition, 1958.

> *This book does an excellent job of analyzing how decisions are made in the public schools. The following chapters are recommended: 3, 4, and 8.*
> a] What are the characteristics of a good school?
> b] What are the school board's primary responsibilities?

5. MORPHET, EDGAR L. (ed.). *Citizen Co-operation for Better Public Schools,* The Fifty-Third Yearbook of the National Society for the Study of Education, Part I. Chicago: University of Chicago Press, 1954.

> *This yearbook discusses the public's role in developing and administering good schools.*
> a] Why is cooperation needed today?
> b] What are some of the problems that develop out of efforts to enlist public cooperation in improving school programs?

6. ROEBER, EDWARD C., GLENN E. SMITH, and C. E. ERICKSON. *Organization and Administration of Guidance Services.* New York: McGraw-Hill Book Co., Inc., 1955.

> *This volume, completely revised in 1955, describes the basic guidance services, defines the guidance responsibilities of various guidance workers, and explains how to organize and administer a program which provides these services. Suggested chapters are 3, 4, 5, and 10.*
> a] What are the primary duties of the counselor?
> b] What are the teacher's responsibilities for guidance?
> c] Who should administer the guidance program?

7. SPURLOCK, CLARK. *Education and the Supreme Court.* Urbana: University of Illinois Press, 1955.

This useful book reviews for teachers and laymen the Supreme Court decision on education. Those who do not have time to read the entire book should read at least Chapter 13, "Summary and Conclusions."

a] What important decisions have been rendered with reference to guidance policies?

b] Can the state force parents to send their children to public schools?

17

Evaluation of Guidance Services

GUIDANCE workers must not take for granted that they are achieving their objectives; they must continuously appraise the quality of their services. When they fail to do so others do it for them, often with insufficient and inappropriate data. As a matter of fact, these services are evaluated every time a decision is made about personnel, supplies, and facilities. Over twenty years ago Grayson Kefauver and Harold Hand saw the problem clearly. They said:

> Old activities are dropped or revised and new ones are substituted or added, depending on the judgment of their efficacy. Informally, the staff, students, and parents make judgments as to whether or not the service is adequate.

Many of these evaluative judgments are based on informal observations.

It is not always possible to secure all the facts which are needed to make wise judgments. However, more facts could be gathered than are used in most situations. Teachers, guidance workers, and school administrators should be encouraged to secure and examine pertinent evidence of the value of their work . . . Periodically there is need of a more systematic analysis and appraisal of the guidance services. More data would be secured in such a stock-taking than is ordinarily possible in the normal operation of the program.[1]

Dressel discussed the essential nature of evaluation as follows:

Evaluation involves judging the worth of an experience, idea, or process. The judgment presupposes standards or criteria. Thus, the worth of a single element, such as an idea, may be judged on some absolute basis— for example, its truth or falsity. The worth of each of several alternative ideas may be judged by comparison—for example, by their relative simplicity, inclusiveness, or effectiveness. The worth of an experience may be judged by its educational impact—that is, by the extent to which it, in itself or in comparison with other possible experiences, results in certain desired changes in those having the experience . . . The issues to be resolved in clarifying the nature of the evaluation which takes place are concerned with the nature of the data, the range of considerations involved in making judgments, and the persons or agencies entrusted with making them. There is no issue regarding the presence or absence of evaluation. When one is faced with choice, evaluation, whether conscious or not, is present. Failure to engage systematically in evaluation in reaching the many decisions necessary in education means that decision by prejudice, by tradition, or by rationalization is paramount. . . .[2]

Most research conducted in the schools is concerned with the evaluation of the various guidance services. Guidance workers also are obligated to evaluate periodically the impact of the entire guidance program. The first part of this chapter is devoted to the evaluation of individual services, the second to the evaluation of the total program.

Research

WHEN faced with the problem of evaluating a specific service, school guidance workers can do one of two things: they can rely

1 Grayson N. Kefauver and Harold C. Hand, *Appraising Guidance in Secondary Schools* (New York: The Macmillan Company, 1941), p. 241.
2 Paul L. Dressel and Associates, *Evaluation in Higher Education* (Boston: Houghton Mifflin Company, 1961), p. 6.

on research findings of other investigators, or they can design a study to appraise the service for themselves in their own setting. Even when others' findings appear to be convincing, a worker may have difficulty accepting results which seem to question his practices. For example, it is easy to understand why some guidance workers find it difficult to accept negative findings on a specific technique, such as guidance classes, after they have invested a great deal of time and effort in that technique. If, however, they want to continue to use the technique in their school, they must demonstrate its efficacy. This calls for carefully planned and executed research.

Listed below are some criteria a researcher may use to evaluate a research proposal on a specific service:

—Have I defined the problem clearly, and developed a sound rationale for it?
—Have I defined clearly the various treatments and/or techniques?
—Do I have someone who is qualified to provide the treatment or the various treatments?
—Do I have adequate knowledge of related research and theory?
—Have the goals for this service been defined in terms of measurable outcomes?
—Have I stated criteria for evaluating the outcomes?
—Have I selected appropriate methods for evaluating change in terms of stated criteria?
—Have I selected experimental and control subjects with sufficient care?
—Have I selected appropriate statistical procedures for testing my hypotheses?

Before the author discusses each of the above criteria, he would like to state that he knows of no published research that meets all of them perfectly. If a guidance worker postpones evaluation of a service until his proposal meets every one of the criteria perfectly, he probably will not do research; on the other hand, he should compromise only when necessary. On this matter Mymon Goldstein writes as follows:

It must be granted that scientific discoveries can be made, on occasion, in spite of abundant experimental error . . . Nonetheless, error must properly be viewed as a matter of discomfort and admitted only when there is no alternative.[3]

3 Mymon Goldstein, "Some Characteristics of Research in Applied Settings," *American Psychologist,* XIV (1959), 275.

DEFINITION OF THE PROBLEM

It is easy to say that definition of the problem is simply a matter of the researcher stating what he expects to do and telling why it is worth doing. The actual defining, however, is much more difficult. As Harold Pepinsky [4] has said, it is a slow and painstaking process. The researcher must state precisely what service he hopes to evaluate, under what conditions, and for what subjects. To communicate effectively with his colleagues he must try to avoid professional jargon and any words that mean different things to different people. Where he cannot avoid the use of such words, he must define the terms as he uses them. Though important for communicating with colleagues, this process of defining the problem probably is most important to the researcher himself; it insures *that he sees* clearly what he is going to do before he attempts it.

. . . we should do a compulsive job of planning our research: how the data will be collected, how they will be analyzed, and even how they will be interpreted. Lacking careful planning, we may be tempted to improvise as we go along. This can lead us far afield from our original hypotheses. Pilot studies are strongly recommended as an antidote to the wandering research objective. Finally, we would do well to exercise restraint in discussing our results and in generalizing them. If we have decided in advance upon criteria for accepting or rejecting the original hypothesis, the obtained results should be integrated in light of that prejudgment. [5]

Considering his own professional competencies, the other problems that deserve study, and the demands for his services, the researcher must ask himself whether this particular research proposal is the one that most deserves his time and energy. For the audience to whom he expects to report his findings, he must state precisely what makes this particular problem worthy of study. A research proposal may involve a new service that is being introduced on a trial basis and therefore requires formal evaluation to determine whether it should be continued. It may involve a service which the members of the staff have asked to have evaluated by systematic research because they question it—either on the basis of others' research or on the basis of subjective appraisal. In either case the researcher is

4 Harold B. Pepinsky, "Some Proposals for Research," *Personnel and Guidance Journal,* XXXI (1953), 291–94.

5 *Ibid.,* pp. 292–93.

asking whether the service meets the needs of youth and fulfills the objectives defined for that service by the staff. Research is also initiated in the public schools to test some well-conceived theory and to compare various techniques, various definitions of roles, and various administrative arrangements. In order to develop a sound rationale for a particular study, the researcher must know the related research literature and the relevant theories, understand the problem himself, be able to sift out of the related literature the relevant material, relate that material to his problem, and communicate his purpose to his audience.

DEFINITION OF THE TREATMENT PROCESS

Where a service or technique is commonly understood, it need be referred to merely by name. One also may use another's definition, giving credit to the source. Of course, most readers also want to know the setting in which the treatment was provided and who provided it. The difficulty in referring to a type of treatment is that many of the guidance services are defined differently by different authorities. In these instances the investigator must state precisely how he defined the treatment. He also must try to determine whether the person who will provide the service can do what the definition of the service suggests that he will do.

The uses of the term "group counseling" illustrate how the same label may be assigned to very different treatments, often with the author not defining the treatment process. The varying uses of the term are revealed in the following three cases—each of which is called a group counseling experience. In one published study the leaders provided educational and vocational information to groups of approximately thirty students in guidance classes, and encouraged the students to discuss the information. The leaders were teacher-counselors who had very little special professional preparation. In the second study the leaders were well-qualified counselors who interpreted tests to students in groups of less than ten. The process was primarily one of giving students information about themselves and encouraging them to discuss the vocational relevance of the information. No effort was made to deal with students' feelings about their test results or to involve the students in the test interpretation process. In the third study, a well-qualified counselor helped students in groups of seven or eight discuss whatever bothered them. Insofar as process was concerned, he made no effort to distinguish between counseling and psychotherapy, but he did include in the counseling groups only those who were normal, reasonably well-adjusted youth.

For two of the three studies significant changes in clients' behavior were obtained, but since the treatment methods were so different and the qualifications of the counselors varied so much from one study to the next, one cannot make any generalizations concerning the success of group counseling from these three cases. If, however, each of the three authors had defined the treatment process, indicated the competencies of the counselors, and described the clients and the setting in which the service was provided, a reader would be able to judge the merits of each treatment method for himself.

THE GUIDANCE WORKER'S QUALIFICATIONS

Failure to describe the professional qualifications of the guidance worker who provides the service is a common weakness of research papers. For example, a recent paper compared the effectiveness of individual and group counseling when provided by the same counselors with similar clients. Though the design of the research was good, its author failed to describe the counselors' qualifications. Personal correspondence with the author indicated that all of the counselors were beginners who possessed minimum professional preparation. They had formal course work and supervised practice in individual counseling, but none of them had formal course work, supervised practice, or experience in group counseling. No significant growth was noted. But had individual counseling proven the more effective, no one would have known whether this was a result of the superiority of the technique or the better preparation of these counselors for doing individual counseling. A technique can be fairly appraised only when the treatment is provided by qualified personnel, and techniques can be compared only when those who use each technique are qualified to use it and recognize its potential worth.

KNOWLEDGE OF RELATED RESEARCH AND THEORY

For several reasons school guidance workers often find it difficult to do a thorough review of related literature: (1) they do not have an adequate library readily available, (2) they do not have the time needed, and (3) they often are pressed to complete the proposal quickly. Obviously, a professional worker can find no good substitute for keeping up with the literature in his field. One way for a school guidance worker to obtain the necessary time for review of related research literature is to spend a summer on a major university campus reviewing the literature and developing his research proposal. Here, consulting help is also available to assist with design, measurement, and statistical problems. Another alternative is to employ consultants. Still another way to obtain assistance is to serve as a cooperating school for university research projects.

What does a careful review of related literature contribute to the development of a good research proposal? It helps the investigator clarify and sharpen his problem, define the treatment process, identify hypotheses to be tested, and locate suggestions on research design, criteria for evaluating change, instruments to measure change, and statistical analyses of data. Sometimes a guidance worker will discover a study which is similar enough to the one he planned so that he can use the results for his purposes. Usually, he also discovers pitfalls in others' studies from which he can profit in designing his own.

DESCRIPTION OF THE GOALS

Whenever a new service is introduced, the staff should understand clearly what that service contributes to the school adjustment and development of the potentialities of the pupils it is designed to serve. Obviously, they should know the objectives of all the other guidance services too. Unfortunately for the researcher, these objectives are often defined in terms which do not readily lend themselves to systematic evaluation. If a service is to be evaluated, its objectives must be stated in terms of measurable outcomes, a benefit which accrues to schools in which the staff participates regularly in research.

DEFINITION OF CRITERIA

When the members of the staff have defined the objectives for a specific service in terms of measurable outcomes, the primary work has been completed for the definition of criteria. If the objectives for a service are not defined in terms which lend themselves readily to evaluation, criteria must be defined when research is initiated to evaluate it. At this point the investigator must ask himself how he would expect the service to influence pupils' school adjustment and the use of their potentialities. Then he must ask himself what criteria he will use to determine whether the expected benefits are observed in pupils. If, for example, the service is designed to help pupils to understand and to accept their abilities, then increased understanding and acceptance of their abilities would be the criteria used to appraise the effectiveness of the service. When these are achieved, one would expect to find increased congruence between test-estimates and pupils' self-estimates of abilities, aptitudes, and interests; one would also expect the definition of students' educational and vocational goals to be more consistent with their abilities, aptitudes, and interests than were their previous goals.

Jensen, Coles, and Nestor [6] conclude that criteria should possess the following characteristics: (1) they should be defined in such a way that they are understood by the consumer of the research; (2) they should be stable; (3) they should be relevant—accurate measurement of them should yield pertinent data; and (4) measures of them in the population should show variability.

In discussing research concerned with the evaluation of counseling, E. J. Shoben lists similar points:

. . . Until the operational criteria used in specific studies are related to the realities of the clients' actual world, their meaningfulness remains moot and controversial.

The second point deals with generality of the interpretation generated by the studies utilizing criteria of client improvement that are markedly restricted by their very nature . . .

. . . Thus we are brought full circle to our central point that research effectiveness must be concerned with the valuations the client makes of his experience of counceling and the valuations placed upon the client before and after his counseling experience by what Sullivan calls his significant others.

. . . Investigations of counseling effectiveness will bring proper returns only when they involve consideration of how the client deals with himself and his associates in the world beyond the clinic doors. This extra-clinical emphasis, stressing the psychological health values of the community, must ultimately be included in all our designs . . .[7]

Though Edwards and Cronbach also recognize the advantages of obtaining clients' reactions to counseling, they point out that these

6 Barry T. Jensen, George Coles, and Beatrice Nestor, "The Criterion Problem in Guidance Research," *Journal of Counseling Psychology*, II (1955), 58–61.

7 E. J. Shoben, "Some Problems of Establishing Criteria of Effectiveness," *Personnel and Guidance Journal*, XXXI (1953), pp. 289, 291.

reactions are not sufficient evidence of success or failure; they also caution researchers about using a general index of growth:

> In evaluating guidance some investigators might propose to measure how the client feels about his problem after counseling. This is relevant evidence, but it is equally important to know if the client has learned new ways of thinking about himself that will help him solve later problems.
>
> In therapy, an overall index is not a good criterion if progress of a patient away from anxiety is concealed by negative scores assigned for an increase in expressed aggression.[8]

Nonsignificant results often can be accounted for by the investigator's failure to define appropriate criteria for individual clients. Researchers also often make the mistake of appraising change with reference to some vague, general criteria. Edwards and Cronbach warn against use of an overall measure of adjustment just because such a general measure may not be relevant for a specific client, and also because when data are combined for various clients the net result may conceal growth for individual clients. The latter distortion may arise even when the investigator uses an appropriate device for assessing changes in clients. If, for example, both nonconforming and overconforming subjects were included in the experimental group, and an adequate scale were used to appraise growth of clients, the growth achieved by one of these two types of client could cancel out the growth of the other. The obvious solution to such a problem is to define criteria for each client prior to, or during the early stages of, treatment, and to use signed numbers [9] to appraise appropriately the growth for each client.

To appraise individual growth or change, the researcher must define specific goals for individual clients. Perhaps this should be done in the evaluation of other guidance services too. At least in counseling, clients usually reveal during the first interview some things they hope to gain from the experience. They reveal other goals as they progress through counseling. This writer believes that the

8 A. L. Edwards and L. J. Cronbach, "Experimental Design for Research in Psychotherapy," *Journal of Clinical Psychology*, VIII (1952), 55.

9 If, for example, the instrument selected for appraising adjustment defines increased conformity as improved adjustment, a negative sign is attached to the scores for those pupils who were judged to be too conforming prior to counseling. When, therefore, such a pupil obtains a score of -18 ($-[-18]$), it automatically is converted into a $+18$.

counselor too may define additional goals for or with his clients. If adequate appraisal of growth is to be achieved, then criteria must be defined in order to measure movement toward these goals. After the criteria are defined, appropriate instruments or observation techniques can be selected to evaluate growth in terms of these criteria. Support for this notion of appraising clients' growth in terms of clearly defined components of personality is also presented by D. S. Cartwright:

> We think that at the present stage of the science of evaluation, it is of major strategic importance to analyze that global dependent variable called personality change into its discriminable, independent components, if such exist. And we think they do exist. A good student with no study problems who experiences difficulty in interpersonal relations is not likely to improve his work efficiency very much as a result of counseling. He is very effective to start with. But he is likely to improve his interpersonal skills, for that is where he needs to change and can change for the better. And if he does come out with greater ease and facility in his relationships, who knows: he might even be less effective (or less compulsively effective) in his work. And "successful counseling" for him would likely mean very different changes in behavior from what it would for a student who started with nothing but study problems.[10]

Paul Dressel elaborates further on this same notion and ties it in with the development of hypotheses and research design:

> If we can define some of these possible effects, we can search for evidence that such changes take place in the individual counseled.
> Viewed in this way, an attempt to evaluate counseling would start with the formulation of an hypothesis probably based on some particular psychological theory. By stating this hypothesis in operational terms, it may become clear how the hypothesis is to be tested. Quite likely, this will result in some suggestions as to how the testing of the hypothesis is to be undertaken. Next, the instruments or procedures are selected or developed to carry out the necessary operations and finally, the particular sample and controls are selected through which these instruments or techniques are to be applied.[11]

10 D. S. Cartwright, "Methodology in Counseling Evaluation," *Journal of Counseling Psychology*, IV (1957), 263.
11 Paul L. Dressel, "Some Approaches to Evaluation," *Personnel and Guidance Journal*, XXXI (1953), 285.

SELECTION AND USE OF EVALUATION TECHNIQUES

If henceforth researchers would carefully define relevant criteria, they would correct one of the serious deficiencies in past research. With this accomplished, at least they would know what kind of evidence they need to appraise the growth of those for whom they expect to provide a specific guidance service.

Once criteria are defined, the researcher must either select from the evaluation techniques available or develop techniques that are appropriate for his purpose. While selecting evaluation techniques he must consider the validity and reliability of each. He also must ask himself whether the data obtained from each technique will lend themselves to the kind of statistical analysis that is required to test adequately his hypotheses. When he finds an instrument for which relevant measures of several criteria are reported in a single score, he must try to determine whether its items can be divided or revised to provide sub-scores for each of the relevant, independent components.

Timothy Leary [12] developed a theoretical system for personality evaluation which appears relevant for classifying techniques used for evaluation of the counseling services, and perhaps of other guidance services too. He defined five levels of personality based upon the source of his data. Level I, which he called public communication, concerns the interpersonal impact which the subject has on others—his social stimulus value. Typically, sociometric tests, behavior inventories, Q-sorts, and check-lists are used by classmates, friends, teachers, siblings, and parents to describe subjects' behavior. Level II he labeled as conscious descriptions. Usually, such self-reporting devices as autobiographies, check-lists, Q-sorts, behavior inventories and personality questionnaires are used to obtain the subject's view of himself and the world. Level III provides the subject's autistic, projective fantasy productions—the preconscious symbolization. Leary used the picture story type of projective test to evaluate subjects' adjustment, but the Rorschach may be used for this purpose too. For Levels IV and V he assigned the following labels respectively: unexpressed unconscious and ego ideal. Because Leary himself admits that Levels IV and V have limited usefulness at this time, they will not be discussed here. Fortunately, most, if

12 Timothy Leary, *Interpersonal Diagnosis of Personality* (New York: The Ronald Press Company, 1957).

not all, of the techniques used heretofore can be classified into one of Leary's three levels. Where instruments from these various levels contain the same components, some interesting possibilities are offered for studying the level at which the changes noted at one level seem to influence changes at the other levels.

Currently several counselor educators at the University of Illinois, concerned with appraising growth of clients participating in group counseling, are revising the content scoring system used by Broedel, Ohlsen, Proff, and Southard [13] to adapt it to conform to Marie Jahoda's [14] definition of mental health. Originally, they were concerned only with revising the questions used for content scoring of picture story protocols (Leary's Level III measure); then it occurred to them that they could develop a Level II instrument by converting each question used in content scoring into a description of human behavior written in first person, and a Level I instrument by converting each question into a description written in third person. By using these test items which deal with essentially identical components and for which data are obtained by pre-counseling, post-counseling, and follow-up testing, they hope that they might be able to study some of the patterns of change suggested above. Though much still must be done to assess the adequacy of these instruments as evaluation devices, this work shows how Leary's notion of personality levels can be applied in evaluating guidance services.

Leary's theory of levels has additional implications for research. A number of noted figures in psychology have suggested that conflict between levels of personality may account for maladjustment. Freud [15] contends that neurosis represents a conflict between the ego and the id or the ego and the super-ego, and that psychosis represents a conflict between the ego and the outside world. Jung [16] says that the various interacting systems within a maladjusted person are at war with each other. Karen Horney [17] takes the position

13 John Broedel, Merle Ohlsen, Fred Proff, and Charles Southard, "The Effects of Group Counseling on Gifted Underachieving Adolescents," *Journal of Counseling Psychology,* VII (1960), 83–90.

14 Marie Jahoda, *Current Concepts of Positive Mental Health* (New York: Basic Books, Inc., Publishers, 1958).

15 Sigmund Freud, *Collected Papers,* Volume II (London: Hogarth Press, 1957).

16 C. G. Jung, *Two Essays on Analytical Psychology* (New York: Pantheon Books, Inc., 1953).

17 Karen Horney, *Our Inner Conflicts* (New York: W. W. Norton & Company, Inc., 1945).

that it is not the conflict itself, but the degree of conflict, the degree of the subject's awareness or lack of awareness of the conflict, and the degree to which he can make choices between possible solutions of his problems, that differentiate the neurotic and normal person. Sullivan [18] believes that both interpersonal and intrapersonal conflicts interfere with the communication process, and that poor communication precipitates and perpetuates maladjustment. If these psychologists are correct in assuming that conflict between levels results in maladjustment, then counseling and psychotherapy should reduce the extent of conflict between levels.

W. A. Carlson [19] tested the hypothesis that counseling reasonably healthy adolescents would reduce the amount of conflict between personality levels. Though he failed to demonstrate that counseling did reduce conflict between levels, he concluded that the problem is worth further study. Included among his explanations for the lack of significant findings were: not long enough a treatment period, insufficient client motivation for change, and inadequate instruments to detect change.

Most of the devices used to evaluate changes in subjects fall into Leary's Level I or Level II type, and probably Level II (conscious description or self-reporting devices) is most often used. Where Level II types of instrument are used to evaluate counseling, clients are asked to describe themselves on personality questionnaires, check-lists, behavior inventories, and Q-sorts. Irving Berg [20] found most of the self-rating devices worthless because clients tended to report what they thought their counselors wanted to happen. When psychological tests and personality questionnaires were used, he found it difficult to tell whether the treatment or the tests were being evaluated. Obviously, much needs to be done to improve these instruments, and those who use them must take account of their weaknesses in interpreting data obtained from them; however, researchers will probably continue to use them. For something that touches one's personal life as much as guidance services do, it seems to be appro-

18 H. S. Sullivan, *The Interpersonal Theory of Psychiatry* (New York: W. W. Norton & Company, Inc., 1953).

19 W. A. Carlson, *The Relationship Between Success in Group Counseling and Discrepancy in Levels of Personality*, A Supplement to Cooperative Research Project No. 623 (Urbana: College of Education, University of Illinois, mimeographed, 1961).

20 Irving A. Berg, "Measures Before and After Therapy," *Journal of Clinical Psychology*, VIII (1952), 46–50.

priate to solicit the students' appraisals and reactions. Perhaps such inquiries should be conducted with more subtle and more effective devices than researchers have used in the past.

If guidance services are effective, important other people (classmates, friends, teachers, siblings, and parents) should be able to note changes in students' behavior outside of the setting in which the service was provided. Some believe that these changes will be noticed first, however, within the guidance setting. Consequently, other students who participate in the guidance experience and the leaders are often asked to describe changes noted in subjects. The establishment of an effective relationship tends to produce positively biased evaluations—evaluators look for what they wanted to happen. When students resisted the treatment, they tended to deny its benefits even when positive changes may have resulted. If items in the instruments focus attention on describing human behavior rather than on making value judgments about it, perhaps some of this bias can be eliminated.

Asking important other people to detect and to describe changes in students' behavior and attitudes involves another problem which is discussed by Broedel, Ohlsen, Proff, and Southard:

> . . . each client must learn to live with his new self, communicate this new self to important others, and teach these important others to understand, to accept, and to live with the new self. For example, it is difficult for the average teacher to believe that these hostile and uncooperative students have really changed and for the distressed parents to believe that these youngsters are willing to take responsibility for their work, and without nagging.[21]

Rating scales are commonly used to obtain evaluations from important other people (Leary's Level I). Of them, Berg writes as follows:

> The major virtue of rating techniques lies in their convenience and accessibility. They provide a comprehensive estimate of adjustment not obtained by other methods. In many clinical situations no other method is feasible. Unfortunately, the reliability of ratings is usually low, and the validity is difficult to establish. Careful construction and pretesting of such forms can remedy these defects substantially; however, the necessary effort seems to be put forth but rarely.[22]

21 *Op. cit.,* p. 170. 22 *Op. cit.,* p. 46.

Other people's appraisal of changes in students' behavior is also obtained by making content analysis of interactions. Though this method has been applied only to the evaluation of counseling, it offers possibilities for evaluating some other services too. It also has the advantage of not requiring a great deal of technical knowledge and clinical skills. Raimy,[23] Seeman,[24] Sheerer,[25] Snyder,[26] and Stock [27] did some of the most significant early studies which focused attention on the affect associated with clients' reference to self and others during counseling. The same approach may be used for every topic that has a direct bearing upon a pupil's problems. If, for example, a student has difficulty getting along with a particular teacher, the researcher would note (in making a content analysis of interactions from tape recordings or video tapes) every time the student mentioned that teacher and the affect (e.g., positive, negative, or ambivalent) associated with discussion of him.

Where content analyses are made of interactions during counseling, it may be appropriate to schedule, during follow-up testing, additional sessions with clients in which they are encouraged to discuss those topics which bothered them when they sought counseling. Heretofore, no such follow-up data have been obtained. If researchers are going to try to determine whether growth achieved during counseling is maintained, such further content analyses appear to be essential.

Other questions which may be answered by content analyses of interactions during counseling and of interactions of recorded follow-up sessions are: Was each client able to discuss the problems for which he sought help? With what affect was each of these relevant topics discussed? Did the affect which was associated with each topic change during counseling or during the follow-up ses-

23 V. C. Raimy, "Self Reference in Counseling Interviews," *Journal of Consulting Psychology*, XII (1948), 153–63.

24 Julius J. Seeman, "The Process of Non-Directive Therapy," *Journal of Consulting Psychology*, XIII (1949), 157–68.

25 Elizabeth T. Sheerer, "An Analysis of the Relationship Between Acceptance of and Respect for Self and Acceptance of and Respect for Others in Ten Counseling Cases," *Journal of Consulting Psychology*, XIII (1949), 169–75.

26 W. U. Snyder, "A Comparison of One Unsuccessful and Four Successful Nondirectly Counseled Cases," *Journal of Consulting Psychology*, XI (1947), 38–42.

27 Dorothy Stock, "An Investigation into the Interrelations Between the Self-Concept and the Feelings Directed Toward Other Persons and Groups," *Journal of Consulting Psychology*, XIII (1949), 176–80.

sions? For example, W. W. Wigell and M. M. Ohlsen [28] found that gifted, underachieving adolescents who had difficulty with authority figures began counseling by discussing authority figures with significantly more frequent use of negative affect than either ambivalence or positive affect, and concluded counseling discussing the topic with significantly more frequent use of positive affect.

Much work still must be done to establish satisfactory validity and reliability for the Level III type of evaluation technique. At this point it appears that content analyses of students' responses to picture story tests and incomplete sentence tests offer most promise for those who wish to use this type of evaluation.

Finding adequate evaluation devices to detect changes in normal youth is difficult for those who attempt to appraise guidance services. This is especially true of personality measures which were often designed for emotionally disturbed clients. When used to pre-test normal clients, such tests describe them as so healthy that there is little opportunity for post- and follow-up-scores to be improved. Furthermore, Carl Bereiter [29] concluded that present methods of test construction tend to produce tests that are insensitive to the differential changes that educational and guidance practices are supposed to produce. Where these tests are used, negative findings can be expected. However, this does not mean that the situation is hopeless. There are a number of techniques which the guidance worker can use to evaluate services, and new ones are currently being developed. For example, Bereiter described an approach to test construction which causes the test to converge on the factor of change rather than the factor of status.

When a researcher is forced to use inadequate evaluation techniques, he must do so only after he has made every effort to insure that no better ones are available; and when he interprets his findings he must take into account the quality of instruments used. If, instead of using whatever devices are readily available, a researcher will take the time to define criteria carefully, to select or to develop techniques which will evaluate relevant changes in subjects, and to administer the technique to every appropriate subject under the

28 W. W. Wigell and M. M. Ohlsen, "To What Extent is Affect a Function of Topic and Referent in Group Counseling?" *American Journal of Orthopsychiatry*, XXXII (1962), 728–35.

29 Carl Bereiter, "Use of Tests to Measure Change," *Personnel and Guidance Journal*, XLI (1962), 6–11.

specified conditions and at the proper times, the quality of research can be improved markedly.

SELECTION OF SUBJECTS FOR TREATMENT

Selecting subjects for the experimental group and for the control group often presents the following problems for those who attempt to evaluate specific guidance services within a school setting: (1) obtaining enough subjects who understand and see value in the service for them; (2) being able to define the population from which the sample is drawn and having enough information on subjects to determine the extent to which the results of the study can be generalized; (3) securing enough information on subjects to obtain data on the relevant variables prior to assigning subjects to experimental and control groups; (4) obtaining an adequate amount of the subject's time for pre-, post-, and follow-up-testing; and (5) enlisting the cooperation of teachers and administrators in order to provide adequate control of the subject's experiences outside of the experimental conditions.

R. M. Travers discusses the importance of the control group as follows:

One of the basic difficulties in evaluating the outcomes of guidance is in finding suitable control groups. . . . It should be noted that in order for the control group to serve its purpose, it must be similar in all important respects to the experimental group.

In the field of guidance, evaluation has been undertaken on many occasions by comparing the behavior of those who received guidance with the behavior of a control group which did not. Unfortunately, there are hardly any studies on record in which the control group and the group receiving guidance (experimental group) were adequately matched. The common tendency has been to match control and experimental groups on the basis of irrelevant factors. For example, one study was carried out in which the investigators studied a group that received guidance at the University of Minnesota Testing Bureau and an allegedly matched group which received no special guidance because the members of the group did not apply for any. The matching in this study was based on factors which had little relation to the purposes of counseling. Since the groups were compared in terms of their later adjustment, the control group and the experimental group should have been matched initially in terms of adjustment; and since this was not the case the outcomes of the experiment become almost impossible to interpret. It is hardly surprising under these circumstances that the counseled group showed better adjustment than the noncounseled group for, by applying for counseling, they had shown that they were individuals actually seeking an improvement in their adjustment to life. In this experiment the only meaningful control group would have been another group of individuals who by their behavior showed that they were actually seeking to improve their adjustment and who were not given personal counseling services.[30]

Further support for careful choice of subjects and control of variables in appraising the counseling service is offered by Edwards and Cronbach:

Cronbach sees the number of relevant variables in the clinical study as likely to be so large that enough cases to account for them will almost never be available. Edwards thinks a few well chosen organismic variables will clarify therapeutic conclusions and that in the long range research the specified types to complete the cells of more complex factorial designs can be obtained. The writers agree that effort to isolate effects due to organismic variables can have only a beneficial effect and that cases should be selected to represent as much variation as can be. It is far more valuable to study ten cases, two each of five identifiable subtypes, than to study a pool of fifty undescribed and undifferentiated people.

The considerations that apply to organismic variables apply also to situational variables. . . . Educational studies have found it necessary to give constant attention to the interaction between the teacher's feeling about a new method and his effectiveness in using it. Surely the therapist is a significant variable to be used in building the design.[31]

To illustrate this last point these authors discussed the between-counselor differences noted by Paul Dressel and Ross Matteson [32] and the impact of the counselor on the results they obtained. Their last point also has implications for definition of the treatment process as well as for the guidance worker's qualifications and attitudes.

Under the best conditions it is difficult to obtain adequate control subjects and to control the situational variables. For example, even when the investigator tries to match experimental and control subjects on relevant variables in order to compare the effectiveness of

30 R. M. Travers, "Critical Review of Techniques for Evaluating Guidance," *Educational and Psychological Measurement,* IX (1949), 222.

31 *Op. cit.,* p. 54.

32 Paul L. Dressel and Ross W. Matteson, "The Effect of Client Participation in Test Interpretation," *Educational and Psychological Measurement,* X (1950), 693–706.

individual and group counseling, and arranges for the experimental and control subjects to be placed in the same class section for four out of the seven school periods, he cannot be certain that he has controlled all of the relevant variables. Nevertheless, this kind of effort to control relevant variables should be made.

Today three methods are commonly used to obtain subjects for the control group who are similar to those in the experimental group: (1) have subjects serve as their own controls; (2) match experimental and control subjects on the basis of relevant variables; and (3) use statistical controls—e.g., analysis of co-variance. Prior to deciding which he will use, the investigator must decide on the statistical tests he feels are essential. If, for example, he decides to match experimental and control subjects, then certain statistical tests which require random sampling cannot be used. Where, however, he draws a large sample he may be able to divide the experimental and control groups by use of random number techniques, and he may be able to demonstrate by use of appropriate statistical tests that with reference to relevant variables chance can account for any differences between the experimental and control groups.

Even when chance can account for differences between experimental subjects and their controls on relevant variables, or when they are carefully matched on relevant variables, the investigator cannot be sure that the organismic variables are adequately controlled. This fact has encouraged many researchers to use experimental subjects as their own controls. One of the primary weaknesses of this method is that it usually does not permit the investigator to obtain follow-up data on the subjects as control subjects. After they are tested at the beginning and end of the control period, they are given the prescribed treatment; therefore, follow-up data cannot be obtained from them as control subjects. Whether the investigator uses subjects as their own controls or uses other subjects as controls, some clients who have accepted the need for a specific treatment must be forced to postpone or forego the treatment. Even when they are treated later, those who have been used as control subjects for research on effects of counseling tend not to be as good prospects as when they first recognized the need for the counseling. In other words, there is no easy solution to the problem.

At present, more time and effort is focused on evaluation of counseling than of any other service. Two approaches appear to offer considerable promise in solving the problem of experimental subjects: (1) selecting and screening clients for research projects through cooperative effort; (2) establishing research centers in cooperating schools.

Where university training centers have been developed to provide supervised practice in counseling for graduate students and have earned a reputation for good service to the schools, a wide variety of clients will be referred to such centers for counseling. From this pool of clients an investigator can select appropriate clients to evaluate a specific technique or to compare several different techniques. Where the type or types of client needed are carefully described, school counselors within a given system also can cooperate in locating a pool of clients for colleagues who wish to conduct research. In addition to providing a large pool of clients from which an investigator can select his experimental and control subjects, this approach usually has the further advantage of obtaining clients who know what to expect from counseling and have accepted the need for it.

For many years public schools have made significant contributions to teacher education—especially in providing centers for student teaching. Good cooperating schools also can make a major contribution to educational research. As members of the cooperating school staff assist their university colleagues in investigating problems important to school personnel, they become increasingly interested in evaluating school guidance services. Usually, university researchers take the initiative in establishing such centers. Guidance directors also should be encouraged to take the initiative in developing such research centers. Best results are achieved when such programs begin on a small scale in one or two of the schools within a school system. In selecting these schools, the guidance director should consider the quality of leadership, the faculty's attitude toward research, and the guidance workers' ability to accept and apply research findings. For individual projects, the guidance director must try to assess the researcher's acceptance by the staff and his ability to state clearly what he expects to do, why it needs to be done, and how the results may be used to improve the particular service involved. The guidance director also should try to assess the researcher's interest in helping the staff make the necessary changes suggested by the research findings. Where these conditions have been met, cooperating school personnel achieve genuine satisfaction from helping solve professional problems, and research scholars are encouraged to do their research in a school setting. School personnel obtain help in appraising their guidance services, and the research findings are more readily accepted by other practitioners because the research was done in a school setting.

STATISTICAL ANALYSIS OF DATA

Although the various elements to be considered in planning a research project have been discussed separately, a researcher must consider several of them simultaneously when he develops a research proposal. When, for example, he defines his hypotheses, he must ask himself whether they can be tested. In order to test his hypotheses he must be able to define relevant criteria, to select evaluation devices which will provide essential data for the criteria and lend themselves to statistical analyses, and to select appropriate statistical procedures to test the hypotheses. When he selects his sample, he must also ask himself whether this method of choosing his experimental and control subjects will enable him to use the statistical procedures he has chosen. Where data are to be programmed for computer analysis, he must consult with the statistical service that he intends to use in order to insure that his data are collected for most economical handling and best statistical treatment. Frequently, such consultation not only saves time and money but it also provides the researcher with the benefit of new and improved statistical tests which can be made.

Two of the most common mistakes researchers make in selecting statistical procedures are: (1) they do not know or they ignore the conditions that must be met in order to use a given statistical test and (2) they seek help with statistical analyses of their data after all the data have been collected. If consultants are to be used most effectively, their assistance should be sought during the planning stage. Where consultants are employed in planning the research, arrangements can often be made for having statistical tests constructed by some nearby statistical service. Most major universities have such services, and members of the staff are willing to provide assistance with analysis of data. Not only does this service save precious time for guidance workers, but it encourages them to do research. Lack of confidence in their ability to do the statistical analyses discourages many guidance workers from doing research.

Self-Study of Guidance Services

THE self-survey is designed to appraise the impact of the entire guidance program upon the lives of the pupils. It draws upon the appraisal of individual services and it seeks new data on the overall effect of the guidance program. The necessary conditions for an effective local survey must be examined before a self-study is initiated. First, an evaluation of guidance services is pointless unless there is commitment to make the necessary changes suggested by the data obtained. Frances Wilson wrote about this readiness for change as follows:

Within each school there is need for courageous self-evaluation, which implies an ability on the part of the school staff to recognize their own weaknesses, to find favorite "brain children" faulty, and traditional methods unsound. If unencumbered growth is to result in any institution, there is need for discarding the outmoded, the unsound, the impractical, and refining the promising, as well as providing for needs that have been unmet. The individual school is, in many ways, in a better position to analyze successfully the strengths and weaknesses of its own program than are the members of a survey committee. Sometimes, however, this very closeness acts to blur perspective, rather than to sharpen the powers of appraisal.[33]

When members of a guidance staff are seriously threatened by an evaluation, they tend to defend present practices rather than to make the necessary changes required to improve the services. Like the pupil who seeks counseling, a guidance worker feels more secure and accepts more responsibility for his own growth when he asks for help than when it is thrust upon him. Therefore, the members of the guidance staff should participate in the self-study and help formulate the recommendations which grow out of it. Since teachers have an important part to play in any good guidance program, they should be represented on the local survey (self-study) committee, too.

Besides evaluating the quality of existing services and determining what additional services are needed, a self-study should examine the

33 Frances M. Wilson, *Procedures in Evaluating a Guidance Program* (New York: Bureau of Publications, Teachers College, Columbia University, 1945), p. 161.

qualifications of the staff with reference to their assignments, the use of staff time, the need for better definitions of jobs, the places where better use could be made of personnel by redefinition of jobs or changing assignments of certain personnel, and the need for new personnel. By being represented on the committee, teachers will become better acquainted with guidance services and the responsibilities of the various personnel, and will know in explicit detail why new persons are employed and what to expect from them. When the need for new positions is discovered in this manner, and the members of the survey committee are encouraged to help define the positions, they understand and accept the need for their services.

Occasionally, the administration and the teaching staff are dissatisfied with their guidance services and believe that these services cannot be improved without changes in the guidance staff. Under such circumstances, either the administration or the teaching faculty, preferably both, may request an evaluation of these services. The evaluation should be conducted by a committee made up of representatives from the teaching and administrative staffs, and those members of the guidance staff who choose to participate. In such a case, of course, the committee may recommend the transfer of some guidance staff members to other assignments instead of recommending only redefinition of jobs and employment of additional guidance staff.

Frequently, the superintendent of schools will employ outside specialists to evaluate guidance services throughout the school system. Such a consultant can help the local staff to formulate criteria for use in evaluating guidance services, help them to select and to develop evaluation techniques, and to summarize and to interpret their findings. But administrators should expect little from an evaluation conducted by outside specialists who gather the necessary information and write recommendations without the assistance of the local staff. Best results usually are obtained by a school when the consultant functions as the counselor functions. The consultant must believe in the local staff members' ability to obtain the facts and to make the best recommendations for their school, and must convey this feeling to them. Instead of giving advice, the consultant should help the local staff members decide what they need to know, help them determine how and where they may obtain the needed information, and help them clarify the problems which arise in formulating recommendations. At every step he should help staff members examine the data and the issues, but he should not solve their problems for them.

The consultant should recognize that the staff, just like pupils who are receiving counseling, can use information effectively only when they see the need for it. Facts which the consultant forces staff members to consider often influence only the staff members' official system of values; such information, though perhaps used in formulating recommendations, will not often change professional behavior.

The remainder of this chapter is devoted to a discussion of techniques which can be used by the local staff for their self-study and for the development of study questions which they can use in constructing their own instruments.

SURVEY INSTRUMENTS

Kefauver and Hand [34] conducted one of the first comprehensive appraisals of school guidance services, and many of the techniques which they used are still used by schools to determine what data they collect and how they will collect it. Later, with Hand's assistance, Victor Houston and Harry Lovelass [35] developed a series of three instruments which schools can use for self-surveys. Just prior to the publication of the Illinois Consensus guides, two other useful guides for self-studies were published: (1) Criteria for Evaluating Guidance Programs in Secondary Schools [36] and (2) North Central Association Self-Study Guides.[37] Recently, two similar self-study guides were published for the evaluation of counseling: (1) Survey of Illinois School Services in Counseling [38] and (2) Interviewing Rating Scale.[39] If no one of these guides meets the needs of the

34 Op. cit.

35 Victor M. Houston and Harry D. Lovelass, Consensus Study Number 3 —Program of Guidance Services (Springfield, Illinois: Illinois Curriculum Program, Office of Superintendent of Public Instruction, 1951).

36 A. L. Benson (ed.), Criteria for Evaluating Guidance Programs in Secondary Schools, Form B (Washington, D.C.: U.S. Office of Education, Division of Vocational Education, 1949).

37 North Central Association, Commission on Research and Service, Subcommittee on Guidance, "Report on the Self Study Survey of the Guidance Practices in North Central Association High Schools for the Year 1947–48," North Central Association Quarterly, XXIII (1949), 276–303.

38 Counseling Services in the Secondary Schools of Illinois, Allerton House Conference on Education, Study Group IX, Role of the Counselor (Urbana: University of Illinois, 1958).

39 Robert P. Anderson and Gordon V. Anderson, "Development of an Instrument for Measuring Rapport," Personnel and Guidance Journal, XLI (1962), 18–24.

local survey committee, members can obtain ideas from them to develop their own instruments.

Before a committee selects or develops its devices for collecting data, its members must decide what data are required to evaluate the guidance services. To make this decision they must describe over-all objectives or goals for the entire program as well as the objectives for each service, define criteria for evaluating the various objectives, determine from whom data will be sought and—where appropriate—how the population may best be sampled, decide what statistical analyses of data are essential, and determine in what form data should be collected in order to lend themselves to appropriate statistical analyses. Wherever possible, the local survey committee should encourage guidance workers to evaluate the various services by carefully planned research studies. In other words, the local survey committee should try to apply research principles in planning and carrying out their self-studies.

EVALUATING THE EDUCATIONAL PROGRAM

For good school adjustment, there is no substitute for good school policies supported by good teaching in a carefully planned educational program. Therefore, the survey committee appointed to evaluate guidance services must examine certain elements of the educational program, even though they cannot be expected to do a thorough evaluation of the entire program. Listed below are some of the kinds of question for which the committee should seek answers:

—To what extent do teachers seem to understand the basic needs of their pupils? What are they doing to help their pupils satisfy these basic needs?

—Do school policies take cognizance of pupils' needs? Are there any school policies which interfere with helping pupils satisfy their needs? What adjustment problems do these unsound policies create? To what extent do school policies encourage teachers to help pupils satisfy their basic needs?

—Do teachers help pupils develop good work habits and efficient study skills? To what extent do teachers help pupils develop proficiency in basic skill subjects?

—Are secondary-school offerings adequate to meet the needs of all the students? What provision does the school program make for general education? Do students have adequate opportunity to become acquainted with our culture, its history, and the problems of modern man? How and by whom are students prepared to meet their responsibilities as citizens? How adequately does the school program prepare students for their vocational goals? How adequately does the school program prepare students to meet their educational goals?

—What provisions are made for the identification and education of exceptional children?

EVALUATION OF INDIVIDUAL SERVICES

Throughout this chapter the author has advocated the evaluation of each guidance service by systematic research. Obviously, no one can expect the survey committee to do this for every service. Therefore, a few of the most relevant questions for which the survey committee may wish to seek answers are listed under each service.

Counseling. For this service, consideration also will be given to devices which the counselor can use to appraise his own counseling skills. One is the Anderson and Anderson's Interview Rating Scale,[40] to which earlier reference was made. Counselors also may wish to use Charles Southard's [41] scale to analyze five dimensions of the counseling relationship: communication, status, security, emotional distance, and responsibility. For most effective use he suggested that the scale be completed by both the client and the counselor immediately after an interview. Norman Gilbert [42] also used Southard's scale to compare counselors' relationships with clients in different settings.

A counselor tends to be assigned more than his share of administrative chores because he is accessible to the principal; for this reason, periodically he should keep a log to determine how he uses his time. After he has selected a week at random for study, he should keep a detailed record of what he does and how much time he spends on each activity each day, including time spent at school outside of the normal working day. In order to analyze the use of his time in some systematic fashion, he may find it useful to classify his activities in such categories as (1) counseling (this listing should be limited strictly to time spent talking to individuals or to or-

40 *Ibid.*, pp. 20–24.

41 Charles W. Southard, "Effect of Student-Selection of Adviser on Rapport," *Personnel and Guidance Journal*, XXXVIII (1960), 614–20.

42 Norman S. Gilbert, "A Comparison of Students' Perceptions of Counseling Relationships Among Schools in Which Counselors' Duties Differ" (unpublished dissertation, University of Illinois, 1962).

ganized groups such as those described in Chapter 5), (2) counseling related activities (e.g., studying the cumulative folder in preparation for an interview, screening tests for a client's use, or soliciting assistance of the staff in case conference to understand the client better), (3) conferences with teachers, (4) conferring with parents, (5) arranging for referrals to other personnel or agencies, (6) academic advising, (7) planning group guidance activities, (8) conducting group guidance activities, (9) performing clerical duties, (10) doing committee work concerned with school policies, and (11) performing general administrative duties.

If a counselor does not reserve time for counseling, he may not even be aware of how little time he is devoting to it. Counselors should, of course, give first priority to counseling pupils and to helping teachers understand their pupils.

Listed below are some questions for which the survey committee may wish to obtain answers from the pupils and the staff:

—What should pupils expect from counselors?
—What do counselors do?
—How do they help pupils?

In addition, the committee may wish to ask the staff what services they would like from the counselor, and what the counselors could do to improve their services to the pupils.

Counselors are usually asked such questions as:

—What do you think the pupils should expect from you?
—What do you think the staff should expect from you?
—How do you spend your time?
—For what purposes are pupils counseled?
—How have you helped these pupils?
—Who makes referrals to the counselor, and for what purposes?
—What proportion of the pupils are self-referrals?
—How do you decide whom you counsel?
—Who do you think are best bets for successful counseling?
—To whom have you referred pupils this year, and for what purposes?
—What record do you keep on conferences with your clients? Who is permitted to see these interview notes?
—What are the important things you do?
—What things are you expected to do that interfere with your developing a satisfactory relationship with either pupils or the staff?

—What changes should be made in your job description in order to make you more effective?

Child study. Questions to be answered on this service usually include the following:

—What do teachers feel they need to know about their pupils in order to teach them effectively?
—What additional information is needed by guidance workers?
—To what extent are all the needs of these staff members met by the child study service?
—What do teachers contribute to child study?
—By what means do teachers make their contributions?
—Who decides what data are included in the cumulative folder, and who maintains the folder?
—What tests are given? Who selected each? For what purpose was each test given? Who is expected to use and interpret each of them? What steps are taken to insure that those who are expected to use and interpret each test are qualified to do so? To what extent are tests actually used for the purposes for which they were selected?
—Are appropriate nontest data used to supplement tests? When a test is chosen, what is done to insure that appropriate nontest data can be obtained to supplement the test results?
—To whom are test scores released and/or interpreted?
—For whom have tests actually been interpreted? What precautions have been taken to insure adequate interpretation?
—To what extent has the child study service increased pupils' understanding of themselves?

Information service. The survey committee usually wants these questions answered about this service:

—For what questions do pupils want answers concerning themselves and their environment? Which of these questions should be answered by parents? How can the school help parents better meet their responsibility? Which of these questions should be answered in regular class work? For which should pupils be encouraged to find answers for themselves by reading? For which should they be encouraged to seek the assistance of a teacher or counselor?
—What materials are available for pupils' use? Are the materials appropriate for their use? What additional materials are needed?
—What proportion of the pupils actually use the materials?
—With what success have the materials been used by pupils? Have pupils

obtained satisfactory and accurate answers to their questions? What testing has been done to assess the accuracy of the information that students obtained by seeking answers to their questions?

—Are the materials organized for pupils' most efficient use? How may the materials be better organized for their use?

—What organized efforts are made to provide pupils with the information they need outside of the usual classwork (e.g., guidance classes)? What are the objectives for these activities? What has been done to evaluate their success? For example, how do the pupils react to them? What do they think the activities do for them? How do they think that they could be improved?

—To what extent are pupils prepared for new school experiences by adequate *orientation?*

Educational-vocational planning. Such questions as those listed below are usually asked by the survey committee:

—What proportion of the students who graduated from the high school last year had plans for post-high school prior to graduation? For what proportion of these students did their post-high school plans seem to be appropriate? What proportion of them actually followed through on the plans which they made while in high school? How many of them succeeded in their post-high school work?

—For what others would post-high school education also have been appropriate? Why didn't they plan for further education? What else could the school have done for them?

—What proportion of the students who entered high school with last year's class failed to graduate with them? Why did they leave school? What are they doing now?

—What proportion of those who left school last year (both drop-outs and graduates) had made a vocational choice? For what proportion was the choice a reasonable one? For what proportion were their educational plans appropriate for their vocational choice? What proportion are either employed in a job related to their goal or preparing for their vocational goal?

—What provision does the school make for helping former students examine and revise educational and vocational plans?

Placement and follow-up services. The following questions should be answered for these services:

—What is done to help students obtain summer employment, part-time work, and regular jobs related to their vocational goals?

—What provision does the school make for a work-experience program?

—To what extent are placement efforts coordinated with local and state employment services?

—What is done to help students better present their salable vocational skills?

—What percentage of the students who graduated in the class five years ago are employed in the vocation of their choice (their goal while in high school)? What percentage are employed?

—What follow-up studies have been conducted recently? For what purposes were they conducted? What conclusions seem to be justified from the data obtained? How were the data used?

Social and leadership development. Questions for which the self-survey committee should seek answers from pupils and the staff concerning this service are:

—What organized social activities do the schools provide? What efforts have been made to determine whether these activities are appropriate for the pupils for whom they were planned?

—What has the school done to identify meaningful extra-class and social activities for its pupils?

—How do the pupils feel about the extra-class and social activities which are available? Which activities do they find inappropriate and do they wish dropped; and which new ones should be added?

—On the basis of what criteria are leaders and potential leaders identified?

—What leadership training is offered for leaders and potential leaders? How have sponsors for these programs attempted to evaluate them?

—What leadership experiences do the schools provide? Are others needed? If so, what types of experience are most needed?

EVALUATION OF ADMINISTRATION

Leadership. The following questions should be asked with reference to this role:

—Are guidance positions clearly defined, and are compatible duties assigned to individual workers? Do job descriptions include adequate definition of professional qualifications of workers? Are staff members selected with care?

—Are members of the staff encouraged to share ideas, to grow on the job, and to contribute to the development of appropriate school policies?

—To what extent have individuals assumed responsibility for their own growth? How has the administration encouraged this self-development?

—What provision has the administration made for in-service education of the guidance staff? What part has the staff had in the development of this in-service education program? How do they react to this program? What specific improved practices have resulted from it?

—Who has responsibility for supervision of guidance services? What supervision is actually done?

Public relations. These questions should be answered by the staff as well as administrative officers:

—To what extent do parents, teachers, and pupils understand the various guidance services and realize who provides each?

—Who has the responsibility for speaking for guidance services and for releasing news stories to the public?

—What kind of working relationship does the guidance department have with referral agencies in the community? What use is made of these referral agencies?

—What organized efforts have been made to obtain reactions to guidance services, especially from pupils and parents?

Regulatory role. Answers should be sought to these questions:

—Are school policies followed in providing guidance services and in spending funds?

—Are qualified persons employed for the various guidance positions?

—What provision is made for determining whether quality of services provided meets at least minimum standards?

Business responsibility. Questions which should be asked about this phase of the administration are:

—To what extent are guidance services adequately financed?

—To what extent are guidance services adequately housed?

Like the rest of the faculty, guidance workers want and appreciate an adequate and attractive place to work. They need appropriate rooms for individual and group testing, rooms where pupils can use educational, social, and occupational information, space for small group meetings, for guidance classes, for private conferences, and for adequate storage of records. Obviously, they can share most of this space with other members of the faculty. If, however, pupils are to seek counselors' help, counselors must have private conference rooms or offices in which pupils feel they can talk freely without being overheard. For most efficient use of guidance records and of clerical staff, these offices should be located near the principal's office.

From the material presented in this chapter it is evident that evaluation of guidance services is time-consuming and difficult. But such evaluation must be made to insure that the needs of youth are adequately met. Only with careful evaluation of guidance services can administration insure that guidance workers use their time to provide those services that contribute most to improved school adjustment and to the best possible adjustment of pupils after they leave school.

SUGGESTED READINGS

1. BARNES, FRED P. *Practical Research Process: A Guidebook in Research Methods for Practitioners in Education.* Springfield: Illinois Curriculum Program, Office of the Superintendent of Public Instruction, 1958.

   This pamphlet was written to encourage practitioners to do research, and to help them with the problems they face in conducting research. Though most of its examples concern teachers' problems, its suggestions can be readily adapted to evaluation of guidance services. Barnes presents excellent case materials to illustrate his points.
   a] What are the essential steps in planning a research project?
   b] How does one formulate hypotheses?
   c] How can the practitioner design instruments to evaluate behavior change?
   d] What statistical tests lend themselves to the practitioner's problems?

2. FARWELL, GAIL F., and HERMAN J. PETERS (eds.). *Guidance Readings for Counselors.* Chicago: Rand McNally & Co., 1960.

   In this book of readings for students enrolled in the first course in guidance, Chapter 10 has much to offer on the evaluation of guidance services.
   a] What is unique about school counseling services?
   b] What are the major problems faced by those who try to evaluate guidance services by systematic research?
   c] What are the essential guidance services for the public schools? How can these services be evaluated?

3. JONES, ARTHUR J. *Principles of Guidance.* New York: McGraw-Hill Book Co., Inc., 1963.

   This is the fifth edition of a guidance text which has been read by more persons enrolled in the first course in guidance than any other book published. Its last chapter is recommended here.

a] What steps should be followed in evaluating guidance services?

b] In evaluating guidance services, why should evaluators look to the future as well as to the past?

4. McDANIEL, H. B., J. E. LALLAS, J. A. SAUM, and J. L. GILMORE. *Readings in Guidance.* New York: Holt, Rinehart & Winston, Inc., 1959.

Part V of this book of readings for counselors in training is relevant for those concerned about evaluation of guidance services.

a] What techniques may be used to evaluate guidance services?

b] What are the major limitations of current evaluation studies?

5. MILLER, CARROLL H. *Foundations of Guidance.* New York: Harper & Row, Publishers, 1961.

Because school counselors come into guidance with such varied academic backgrounds, Miller concluded that they need some common basic foundation early in their specialized preparation. This is precisely what he attempts to provide in this volume. Chapter 11, "The Fruits of Guidance," is a recommended reference for consideration here.

a] What criteria have been used to evaluate guidance services?

b] What conclusions may be drawn from previous efforts to evaluate guidance services?

c] Why may it be inappropriate to expect guidance services to reduce the drop-out rate?

6. ROBINSON, DONALD. "Evaluation as a Function of Student Personnel Administration," *Journal of College Student Personnel,* VI (1962), 20–22.

a] Why must administrators accept evaluation as a function of student personnel administration?

b] What form should the evaluation take?

7. WILSON, FRANCES M. *Procedures in Evaluating a Guidance Program.* New York: Bureau of Publications, Teachers College, Columbia University, 1945.

Though the entire book offers much, the last chapter is most pertinent here.

a] What are the essential conditions for a successful self-survey?

b] How may public opinion polls be used in evaluating guidance services?

Appendix

Use of Statistics in Child Study

ERTAIN basic knowledge of statistical concepts is essential in order to understand and use test results. Since most students have not had a course in educational statistics when they enroll in their first guidance course, a brief discussion of these statistical concepts is presented here.

Unfortunately, some guidance workers are convinced that they cannot learn statistics. But they need not approach the subject as reluctantly as they often do; the knowledge of statistics that the guidance worker needs for child study is not difficult to attain, though its mastery does require close and persistent attention. Anyone who mastered ninth-grade algebra reasonably well, or who can enlist the assistance of a mathematics teacher in reviewing the relevant material from ninth-grade algebra, can cope with the mathematics presented here. Only the basic statistical concepts used in child study are discussed, including a consideration of relevant formulas and the purposes for which each may be used by guidance workers.

The Frequency Distribution

A FREQUENCY distribution is one of the simplest methods for organizing test data in order to compare an individual with the others in his group. Further, as we shall see, preparing a frequency distribution is often the first step in other statistical processes.

The following scores, copied directly from the teacher's record book, were earned on a unit test by students in a tenth-grade mathematics class: 83, 75, 96, 128, 116, 100, 107, 94, 125, 113, 87, 97, 101, 92, 93, 106, 106, 100, 82, 120, 101, 99, 73, 94, 114, 110, 114, 102, 95, 102, 103, 77, 110, 98, 85, 113, 95, 109, 116. Obviously, when the scores appear in unorganized fashion like this, it is not easy to compare one score with the others. The basic method of preparing a frequency distribution is to arrange all the scores from high to low, and then tabulate the number of pupils who earned each of the scores. With a short list of scores this procedure is satisfactory, but where the list is long and cumbersome, it may be more convenient to tabulate the scores in *intervals*. If that is to be done, the first step is to decide the number of intervals to be used, and the size of each. Teachers usually find that approximately fifteen intervals are sufficient; accordingly, the *range* of scores from high to low would be divided into fifteen parts. In our example of the mathematics test scores, the highest score was 128 and the lowest was 73; therefore, the *range*—the difference between the highest and the lowest—was 55. That range divided by 15 yields slightly less than 4. But the interval size is preferably an odd number (so that each interval will have a midpoint that is a whole number). Therefore, in this case our interval is 3.

Next we take the multiple of our interval size which is nearest the high score. The multiple of 3 nearest 128 is 129. That figure becomes the midpoint of the highest interval: in our example, the highest interval is thus 128–130. Proceeding downward and tabulating the scores, we get the frequency distribution illustrated in FIGURE 4. Note that there are several intervals into which no scores fell in this case, and some into which only one score fell. Note also that because we used an interval-size of 3, slightly smaller than the range

FIGURE 4   A Frequency Distribution

128-130 /	98-100 ////
125-127 /	95-97 ////
122-124	92-94 ////
119-121 /	89-91
116-118 //	86-88 /
113-115 ////	83-85 //
110-112 //	80-82 /
107-109 //	77-79 /
104-106 //	74-76 /
101-103 ////	71-73 /

of scores divided by 15, we actually set up twenty intervals. If fewer than fifteen intervals had been satisfactory, an interval-size of 5 could have been used in this case.

Most importantly, we can see from this frequency distribution that a heavy concentration of pupils scored near the middle of the range. A frequency distribution like this one presents such information quickly and effectively, and can thus serve as a general base with which the teacher may compare an individual pupil's performance with that of the group. We shall see next that the frequency distribution forms the basis for several types of graphic representation of data; however, when you do not wish to report the data to someone else but rather wish to use it yourself for comparing pupils (for example, in assigning grades), it is usually unnecessary to go to the trouble of preparing a graphic representation once you have tabulated the frequency distribution.

Since the frame of reference for most elementary-school pupils is their present classmates, a teacher should develop local norms on standardized tests for his class. Making a frequency distribution is the first step in this process. The next step is to divide the scores into the five-point scale described in Chapters 6 and 7: (1) the bottom 10 percent—did very poorly; (2) the next 15 percent—didn't do as well as most; (3) the middle 50 percent—did as well as most; (4) the next 15 percent—did better than most; and (5) the top 10 percent—did very well. With this breakdown of scores a teacher is able to interpret a pupil's scores in terms of the pupil's reference group. He also is able to get some idea of how his pupils compare with most pupils of their age and school grade. Of course, rough norms of this type also may be developed for a school system.

Graphic Representations

THE *histogram*, more familiarly known as the *bar graph*, is a method of picturing the data in the frequency distribution in order to bring out the *differences* in the distribution. The *frequency polygon*, or *broken line graph*, is used when the *continuous* relationship of the data is to be emphasized. FIGURES 5 and 6 are the histogram and frequency polygon based on the test scores from the tenth-grade mathematics class mentioned above. The straight line at the left of each of these graphs is called the *vertical axis;* at the lower left

FIGURE 5   A Histogram

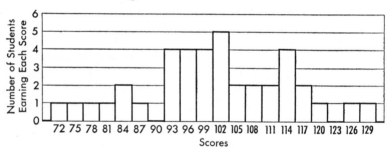

FIGURE 6   A Frequency Polygon

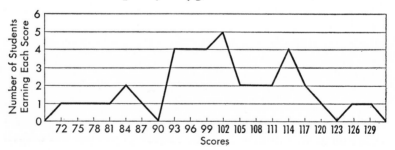

corner it intersects the *horizontal axis*. Up the vertical axis, equally spaced points mark the number of students who received any given score; along the horizontal axis equally spaced points mark the midpoints of the intervals used in the frequency distribution. Over any particular midpoint on the horizontal axis of the histogram, the height of the bar reveals the number of students whose scores fell within that interval. On the frequency polygon, the point on the graph directly above the midpoint of each interval reveals the number of scores which fell within the interval. For example, there were four students whose scores were between 92 and 94, so over the midpoint 93 in Figure 5 is a bar at the height of 4, and in Figure 6 a point at the same height.

For accurate representation in graphs of this sort, the units along each axis must be spaced equally. When practical, the units along each axis should begin with zero at the point where the axes intersect. However, so long as equal units are used, it is acceptable, as in Figures 5 and 6, to picture only the range of scores, when beginning the axis at zero would produce an impractically large graph.

EXERCISE

1. Verbal directions for mathematical operations can make difficult reading even when the mathematics is simple. The best way to understand such directions is to follow them with paper and pencil. The above instructions for tabulating a frequency distribution, if not clear to you now, will be quite clear if you set up a frequency distribution based on an interval of 5 for the same test scores.

Frequency Analysis for Diagnosing Learning Problems

A TEACHER may use another type of frequency analysis in studying test responses to identify concepts and skills that he should teach again before leaving the unit tested. This time let us use a new set of test responses; these were obtained from an eleventh-grade American history class. An example of such frequency analysis is Figure 7, which shows the items each student missed on this multiple-choice examination. It gives a graphic picture of the concepts which students have and have not learned. With this picture and a copy of the test, the teacher can group the items missed according to the topics covered by the test. Many times students miss a whole group of the items because they do not understand the one main idea which is basic to these items. That idea needs reteaching. Then, too, this technique gives the teacher a graphic picture of the difficulty level of his test items. Of the twelve items missed most frequently in this test (3, 6, 7, 9, 12, 13, 18, 19, 23, 28, 29, 30), four had to do with one of the major issues discussed in the unit, and another two were missed frequently because the questions were poorly stated; even though none of the remaining six items fell into any particular pattern, this graphic picture helped the teacher identify other content for remedial teaching.

In constructing a table for analysis of errors, all the teacher needs is a large piece of graph paper on which he can write the test-item numbers along the horizontal axis and the pupils' names in the left-hand margin along the vertical axis. Taking each pupil's answer sheet, one moves across that pupil's row marking an "x" in the column for each item the pupil missed. In FIGURE 7, the number

FIGURE 7 Table for Analysis of Errors (American History Class)

	1	2	3	4	5	6	7	8	9	10	11	12	13	14	15	16	17	18	19	20	21	22	23	24	25	26	27	28	29	30	Total Test Scores
Betty A.			X	X			X			X	X	X				X	X		X		X							X	X		17
Ralph A.	X		X		X	X		X		X		X				X			X									X	X	X	17
Harold B.			X	X			X	X			X	X			X				X											X	21
Gwen B.				X	X	X	X	X			X	X		X		X		X	·		X	X				X		X	X	X	15
Jim C.				X		X																						X			27
Barb D.	X	X			X		X		X		X					X			X									X	X		20
Mary E.												X				X			X									X			26
Bob G.			X	X	X	X				X								X										X	X	X	21
Bob H.		X			X	X				X	X					X							X	X			X	X	X		21
Helen H.			X		X			X		X						X				X							X	X			23
Jane I.		X				X			X		X	X											X	X	X						22
Pam J.	X		X			X			X	X			X		X		X		X	X			X	X				18
Peggy J.			X	X		X			X	X		X	X	X		X		X	X	X		X	X	X				16
James J.									X		X				X						X	X	X	X			25
Lee L.		X	·		X			X			X				X					X	X		24
Joan M.		X		X	X		X		X		X	X			X				X	X	X	19
Betty M.			X		X	X		X		X		X			X				X	X	X	21
Linda N.		X		X			X	X			X	X			X				X			22
Ruth N.	X			X	X	X			X	X								X	X		22
Dot O.		X	X	X	X		X							X				X	X		22
John Q.		X			X		X	X	X		X			X			X		X	X	X	20
Mary S.	X	X		X	X		X		X	X			X			X		X	X		19
Andy S.			X		X	X	X	X	X		X					X	X		23
Katie S.		X		X	X	X			X	X						X	X		22
Marj T.		X		X	X	X			X	X	X	X		X	X	20
Gil V.		X		X	X	X	X			X				X	X	23
Anna V.		X		X	X	X			X				X	X	23
Gini W.			X	X	X	X	X			X				X	X	22

1 2 3 4 5 6 7 8 9 10 11 12 13 14 15 16 17 18 19 20 21 22 23 24 25 26 27 28 29 30
Test Item Numbers

recorded in the right-hand margin represents each pupil's total test score.

Use of Averages

THERE are several kinds of "average": the *mean*, the *median*, and the *mode*. When people talk of "the average high school student," the "average American's standard of living," or "an average personality," it is not always clear to the statistician which of these "averages" is meant. For that reason, "average" is a very imprecise term, which should not be used in statistical work.

The three different types of "average" are used for somewhat different purposes, but all three are "measures of central tendency," that is, measures which can be used to represent a group's "typical" or "usual" aspects. A teacher or counselor needs a measure of central tendency whenever he wishes to compare an individual's performance with that of the rest of the group. He also needs a measure of central tendency as a starting point whenever he wishes to examine the variability of scores within a class.

MEAN

The *mean* is the type of "average" which pupils in elementary school learn to compute. The rule for computing the mean is the rule most people think of when "averages" are discussed: add all the items, then divide that sum by the number of items. While this rule can be stated simply without using its mathematical formula, discussion of its formula will provide an easy introduction to certain symbols we will use again.

$$M = \frac{\Sigma X}{N}$$

Here is what these symbols denote:

M = the mean
N = the number of items
ΣX = the sum (Σ) of all the individual items (X)

For example, returning to the tenth-grade mathematics test scores which we used in preparing FIGURE 4, we find that the sum of these 39 scores is 3,931. Dividing this sum by 39 produces a mean of 100.8 or, when rounded off to the nearest whole number, 101.

When people speak of "the average yield of grain per acre," "the average amount of money spent for clothes by women in Illinois during 1963," "the average height of nineteen-year-old males in the United States on May 1, 1963," and "the average weekly income of mine workers in Montana during 1962," they probably have in mind the mean, which is the more precise term; and if the mean is what they are referring to, they have chosen the correct measure of central tendency for their purposes. In schools, the mean should be used in speaking of such cases as "the average per pupil cost for operating elementary schools in Champaign during 1962," "the average grade point," "the average height of the college varsity basketball players," and "the average number of years spent in teaching by those who leave the profession with less than ten years of service."

Whenever a person needs a measure of central tendency that takes into account every score, he should use the mean. However, the fact that the mean does take into account every score is also one of its weaknesses, for it allows a few very high or few very low scores to influence the mean so greatly that it will not identify the typical individual.

Consider, for example, the distribution of scores on a biology test as seen in FIGURE 8. We need only to glance at the frequency distribution to recognize immediately that the typical student in this biology class probably made a score of 50; yet the mean for these scores is 54.3. Four students made scores which were so much higher than the rest that they pulled the mean up to a point on the scale

FIGURE 8   A Distribution of Biology Test Scores

79 /	71	63	55 /	47 //
78 //	70	62	54 /	46 /
77	69	61	53 //	45 /
76	68	60	52 ///	44
75	67	59	51 ////	43
74	66	58	50 ЖЖ	42
73	65	57	49 ЖЖ //	41
72 /	64	56 /	48 ///	40 /

below which five out of six of the scores fall. When a guidance worker sees that extreme measures are having this effect and that he needs an estimate of typical performance, he may wish to use the *median* because it is not affected by these extreme measures.

MEDIAN

The measure of central tendency which represents "the typical individual" or "a typical product" is the *median*. Before identifying the "typical person" it is necessary to define "typical" in terms of a well-defined trait. For example, a teacher might want to know how much "everyday business mathematics" the typical high school senior knows. This question first calls for definition of everyday business mathematical skills and concepts. The second step is to find or construct an acceptable test to measure these skills and concepts. Finally, a typical senior should be defined in terms of a specific student population. Once the worker has established what is being discussed, then he can use the median score as a measure of the typical student's general proficiency in business mathematics.

The median is the middle score in a distribution of scores arranged in numerical order. Using the tenth-grade mathematics test scores as an example once more, we find that their simple frequency distribution is 128, 125, 120, 116, 116, 114, 114, 113, 113, 110, 110, 109, 107, 106, 106, 103, 102, 102, 101, 101, 100, 100, 99, 98, 97, 96, 95, 95, 94, 94, 93, 92, 87, 85, 83, 82, 77, 75, 73. The middle score is 101, which is therefore the median. Had there been an even number of scores, we would have found the midpoint between the two middle scores. For example, the median of 12, 8, 4, 1 is 6 since 6 is halfway between 8 and 4.

The median is used instead of the mean in a variety of situations. The newspaper man who is interested in the reading levels of his audience uses it. He knows that if people are to read his paper, he must have the material written on the reading level of his typical buyer—his run-of-the-mill reader. In the school setting, the teacher adapts his instruction to the typical, or median, student, with special work for the groups at both extremes of the class. Of course, in identifying this median the teacher must describe these typical students in terms of specific traits, for obviously a student who is typical in algebra would not necessarily be typical in art.

Sometimes the mean and the median are represented by the same score. They were essentially the same in the sample problem involving tenth-grade mathematics test scores; in contrast, they were quite different in the biology test scores.

MODE

The score (or the interval, if intervals are used in the frequency distribution) that occurs most frequently in the distribution is the *mode*. Graphically, the point on the horizontal axis above which the curve is highest is the *mode*. For example, examination of FIGURE 5 shows that the interval with a midpoint of 102 represents this point. In FIGURE 8 the mode is 49. In school testing, the mode is the score earned by the largest number of pupils.

In every *bell-shaped curve* the mean, median, and mode are all associated with the same score. The normal curve, for example, is one such single humped curve with the high point at the mean which is also the mode and the median.

The mode is less useful in teaching than the other two measures of central tendency. But outside of the school setting, the mode is useful in several ways. Take the shoe-store operator who, in stocking his store, would be more interested in the popularity of style, quality, and size of a shoe than he would be in either a median or a mean shoe style, quality, or size. He would read the shoe trade publications and study his sales in order to find out which shoes were ordered most frequently. He might also keep a record of customer demands in order to stock his shelves more heavily with the size, quality, and style of shoes for which he had the best market. The teacher also uses this idea to identify for remedial instruction those items most often missed on a test.

EXERCISES

2. Find the median, the mean, and the mode for the American history test scores in FIGURE 7.
3. Find the median for the biology test scores in FIGURE 8.

ANSWERS

2. Median, 21.5; mean, 21; and mode, 22.
3. Median, 50.

Statistical Yardsticks

IN ORDER to understand more fully the descriptions of human characteristics that can be expressed as numbers (test scores, height, weight, age, etc.), teachers or counselors need techniques for studying the variability (or "spread-outness") among measures. A very simple device for studying this variability is the *range*. The range (difference between the highest score and the lowest score) was introduced in our discussion of frequency distributions. While the range does help the staff member understand the relationships among scores (especially when studied along with the high score, the low score, the median, and the mean), it is obviously not a very stable measure because it is based on only two pupils' scores. To have one or both of these pupils absent may produce a very different range with the same test.

PERCENTILES

Another statistical yardstick which the teacher or counselor can use in studying the relationships among measures is *percentiles*. *Percentiles* are points along a scale, which divide scores into a hundred groups, as if a frequency distribution were being set up with one hundred equal intervals. (Similarly, *deciles* divide the scores into ten groups, and *quartiles* divide them into four groups.)

In dividing scores into a hundred groups, the first step is to arrange the scores into an arithmetical sequence. When we discussed the median, we arranged the tenth-grade mathematics scores thus: 128, 125, 120, 116, 116, 114, 114, 113, 113, 110, 110, 109, 107, 106, 106, 103, 102, 102, 101, 101, 100, 100, 99, 98, 97, 96, 95, 95, 94, 94, 93, 92, 87, 85, 83, 82, 77, 75, and 73.

Even though the task of dividing the scores into a hundred groups should be a simple counting problem, it is not always that easy. An easier way (though on first reading it may sound complex) is to take each score and determine what percentage of the cases fall *below* it. If we take the score of 87, for example, we find that 6 scores are *below* it. Since there are 39 scores altogether, 6/39 or 15 percent of the cases fall below 87. We say, therefore, that the 15th percentile in this distribution of raw scores is the score of 87; the percentile rank of 87 is 15. In this same group of scores there were 32 scores below the score of 114. Since 32/39 = 82 percent, the 82nd percentile in this distribution is the score of 114. This process is repeated for every distinct score. The steps are:

1. Find the number of scores below a given score.

2. Determine what percentage that number is of the total number of scores.

CUMULATIVE FREQUENCY CURVE

A *cumulative frequency curve,* sometimes called an *ogive,* is a special graphical representation. FIGURE 9, an ogive, is based on the mathematics test scores. The vertical axis on the left represents the number of students who earned scores up to and including the scores indicated on the horizontal axis. One student earned a score of 73.

FIGURE 9 A Cumulative Frequency Curve: Scores on Tenth-Grade Mathematics Test

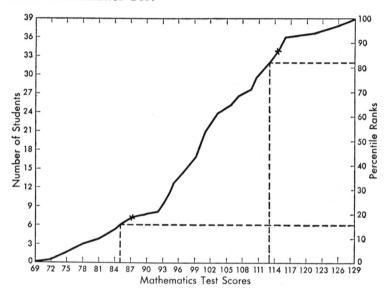

Therefore, over the score of 73 we mark a point opposite 1 on the left vertical scale. The next student earned a score of 75. Since this is a *cumulative* frequency curve, we mark a point opposite 2 on the vertical scale above 75 to show that two students earned scores up through 75. Working in this same fashion, we mark off 7 on the vertical scale above 87 because seven students earned a score of 87 or lower. (Since, however, only one student earned a score of 87, six scores were below 87.)

Now we can demonstrate a convenience of the cumulative frequency curve: percentile ranks can be read from it directly, without laborious computation of percentages. First, we need a new vertical axis (on the right side of FIGURE 9) on which 100 units divide up equally the distance between zero and the total number of scores. This has the effect of classifying the individual points on the curve into 100 different groups. But since we use only those scores which fall *below* a given score in computing its percentile rank, to find the percentile rank of the score 87 *we drop back* to the next earned score (85) in our list, and construct a perpendicular from 85 on the horizontal axis to the curve. From the point where the perpendicular intersects the curve, we draw a line, parallel to the horizontal axis, to the vertical axis on the right. The point where the horizontal line intersects the vertical axis defines for us the percentile rank for 87; it is the 15th percentile. Following this same procedure, we can verify our previous computation that 114 is the 82nd percentile. The broken lines drawn in FIGURE 9 demonstrate these steps in using the cumulative frequency curve to convert test scores into percentile ranks.

Though more and more schools are using percentiles in recording test scores, teachers should remember that real raw score differences are lost when one uses them. As one moves away from the mean, in either direction, the raw score differences between percentiles gradually increase. In FIGURE 9, for example, we see that 101 is at the 49th percentile [1] and that 99 is at the 41st percentile, while 129 is at the 97th percentile and 120 is at the 92nd percentile. The former represents a difference of 8 percentile points while the latter produced a difference of only 5 percentile points; yet the raw score difference near the mean is only 2, while at the outer extreme it is 9. In other words, the use of percentile exaggerates the small differences in original scores near the mean and diminishes the differences in scores at the two extremes.

STANDARD DEVIATION

Probably the most useful of all statistical techniques for studying variability among various measures is the *standard deviation* (usually abbreviated SD, as in this book, or σ). Because of its relationship to the normal curve, the standard deviation is one of the basic statistical tools for interpreting test scores and for research. It is also

---

1 Even though earlier we saw that 101 was the middle score in this distribution and therefore the median, computation of the percentiles places it at the 49th, instead of the 50th percentile as one would expect, because more than one student earned a score of 101.

a basic element in formulas used for predicting success on the job or in training programs.

The standard deviation has an impressive-looking formula, but it is not so complicated as it looks:

$$SD = \sqrt{\frac{\Sigma(X - M)^2}{N}}$$

Most of the symbols in that formula are familiar from our study of the mean:

SD means standard deviation.

$\sqrt{}$ tells us to take the square root of the expression underneath that sign.[2]

N is the number of measures or scores.

$\Sigma(X - M)^2$ tells us to square the difference between each score (X) and the mean (M), and add together (Σ) all those squared differences.

Therefore, to find the standard deviation, one subtracts the mean from each score, squares each of these differences, adds these squared differences, divides the total by the number of scores, and takes the square root of the average squared difference between the mean and each score.

TABLE 3 summarizes the preliminary computations for determining the standard deviation for the mathematics test scores. The mean which we computed previously was 101. Our next step is to add the column $(X - M)^2$, which produces a sum of 6,604. Then we divide that sum by 39 (the number of scores, N), getting 169.3. Rounded off to the nearest whole number, that becomes 169. The square root of 169 is 13, the standard deviation for these scores.

E X E R C I S E S

4. The mean of American history test scores in FIGURE 7 was 21. Compute the standard deviation.

5. The mean for the biology test scores in FIGURE 8 was 54. Compute the standard deviation.

A N S W E R S

4. 2.8

5. 9.0

2 The square root is found by an arithmetical process, rather similar to long division, and is usually taught at least once during the junior high school period. The square root of a number may also be found by referring to a table of square roots—many high school mathematics texts contain one—or by using

TABLE 3 Computation of Standard Deviations

SCORES (X)	$(X - M)$	$(X - M)^2$	SCORES (X)	$(X - M)$	$(X - M)^2$
128	27	729	100	−1	1
125	24	576	100	−1	1
120	19	361	99	−2	4
116	15	225	98	−3	9
116	15	225	97	−4	16
114	13	169	96	−5	25
114	13	169	95	−6	36
113	12	144	95	−6	36
113	12	144	94	−7	49
110	9	81	94	−7	49
110	9	81	93	−8	64
109	8	64	92	−9	81
107	6	36	87	−14	196
106	5	25	85	−16	256
106	5	25	83	−18	324
103	2	4	82	−19	361
102	1	1	77	−24	576
102	1	1	75	−26	676
101	0	0	73	−28	784
101	0	0			

The Normal Curve

MOST school staff members know the familiar bell-shaped curve, which we have come to call the normal curve, because so many statistics are distributed in approximately the manner pictured by it. Furthermore, teachers often assume that their measures of pupil growth are distributed in this fashion, and as a consequence they use the normal distribution as a guide in determining how many A's and F's, B's and D's, and C's they should give.

Not all statistical data, of course, are distributed as described by the normal curve, but most measures of human characteristics obtained from a randomly chosen group of sufficient size do display roughly a normal distribution. A common exception, which con-

---

a slide rule. The square roots that counselors and teachers must determine in order to use the standard deviation usually involve fairly small numbers. If, for instance, we were required to find the square root of 179, we could rather easily, by a process of trial and error, estimate the approximate square root. For instance, the square root of 179 is evidently between 12 ($12^2 = 144$) and 14 ($14^2 = 196$). Trying 13 yields a square of 169, which is close; 13.2 would next be tried, and would be found too small; 13.4 proves acceptable.

cerns teachers, is that of measures obtained from a small group of selected pupils. For example, some high school teachers teach elective subjects to small classes and forget that their pupils represent only the better pupils in that subject matter area. Obviously, if they attempt to assign grades on the assumption that student achievement is distributed normally, they will probably treat some students unfairly.

Even when a teacher deals with a cross section of the school population, he should not assume that measures obtained from a single class would be distributed normally. If, however, he combines measures obtained from several typical classes which are studying the same material, he usually can assume that the distribution will be roughly a normal one.

Teachers and counselors also use this concept of the normal curve along with such statistics as mean and standard deviation in summarizing test results and interpreting test scores. Authors of tests use this concept in developing and standardizing tests, and researchers use it in interpreting their data. As a matter of fact, researchers frequently must first prove that they are dealing with a normal distribution before they can use many of the statistical methods they need in order to analyze their data.

FIGURE 10 reveals that approximately 68 percent of the measures

FIGURE 10   The Normal Curve

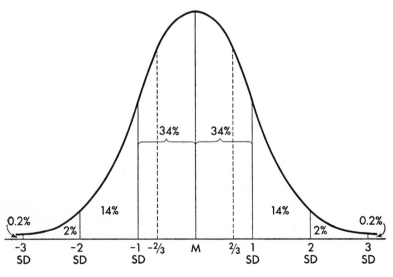

in a normal distribution fall within the area under the curve bounded by one *SD* (standard deviation) above and one *SD* below the mean. Approximately 14 percent of the measures fall within each of the next areas of the curve which are marked off between the perpendiculars at 1 *SD* from the mean and 2 *SD*'s from the mean. Approximately 2 percent of the measures lie between 2 *SD*'s and 3 *SD*'s from the mean. Less than .2 percent of the measures fall beyond 3 *SD* from the mean in either direction. One other interesting fact is that approximately half the measures fall within an area marked off by perpendiculars at ⅔ *SD* above and below the mean.

Z-scores, T-scores, and Stanines

IN CHAPTERS 6 through 9 we discussed test data, the ways in which they may be supplemented with nontest data, and the interpretation of test scores. However, we minimized the discussion of statistical tools. One technique for recording test data which we did not mention is the T-score. While, for a number of reasons, this is one of the best techniques for recording test data, it is also one which has not usually been taught for teachers' use. Before we can discuss T-scores further, however, we must understand thoroughly the concepts of standard deviations and of Z-scores.

Z-SCORES

To make the most meaningful interpretations of test scores, teachers and counselors need some standard yardstick for determining how a pupil's performance compares with the mean. The *Z-score,* or *standard score* as it is sometimes called, provides us with just that technique. It involves first converting raw scores into distances from the mean $(X - M)$, and then measuring these distances in terms of a common unit, *SD*.

The formula for computing Z-scores is:

$$\text{Z-score} = \frac{X - M}{SD}$$

(No new symbols are introduced in this formula.) Thus, in converting raw scores to Z-scores we subtract the mean from each score and divide this difference by the standard deviation.

Though very useful, Z-scores have one serious disadvantage: all the Z-scores representing raw scores *below* the mean (and this usually includes approximately half of the scores) carry a negative prefix. Some people are apt to be confused slightly by negative numbers. Worse still, if a teacher by mistake should drop the minus sign, there would be serious error in the pupil's test results. To overcome the inconvenience of negative numbers but still preserve the advantages of the Z-score (to be shown later), we can use the related *T-score.*

T-SCORES

The formula for computing T-scores is:

$$\text{T-score} = 50 + 10\,\frac{X - M}{SD}$$

Another way of saying the same thing is:

$$\text{T-score} = 50 + 10\,(\text{Z-score})$$

To convert a raw score into a T-score, we subtract the mean from the raw score, divide the difference by the standard deviation, multiply the quotient by 10, and add 50 to the product. Let us use the mathematics scores again in demonstrating the method:

$$M = 101 \qquad SD = 13$$

For the test score 125, the T-score is:

$$\text{T-score} = 50 + \frac{10(125 - 101)}{13}$$
$$= 50 + 18$$
$$= 68$$

Or using a score below the mean, 82, which would have a negative Z-score:

$$\text{T-score} = 50 + \frac{10(82 - 101)}{13}$$
$$= 50 - 15$$
$$= 35$$

Teachers, who are busy people, may not have time to convert test scores into T-scores. Fortunately, there is a short cut: after the mean and standard deviation have been computed, it requires very little time to convert raw scores into T-scores. Starting with the raw test scores, one can compute the mean and standard deviation and then follow these steps:

1. Assign the mean [3] a T-score of 50.

2. Find $\frac{2}{3}$ of the standard deviation and round this product off to the nearest whole number. Subtract this number from the mean and assign it a T-score of 43.

3. Add $\frac{2}{3}$ SD to the mean and assign it a T-score of 57.

4. Find $1\frac{2}{3}$ SD and round this number off to the nearest whole number. Subtract it from the mean and assign it a T-score of 33.

5. Add $1\frac{2}{3}$ SD to the mean and assign it a T-score of 67.

6. Using these five key T-scores, estimate T-score equivalents for each of the remaining test scores. For the extremely high scores and low scores, use the formula for computing T-scores.

If we use the tenth-grade mathematics scores to demonstrate how this method works, we find that $M = 101$, $SD = 13$ and

1. 101 has a T-score of 50.

2. $\frac{2}{3}$ SD = 8.7, rounded off = 9. When we subtract 9 from 101, we get 92 (T-score of 43).

3. When we add 9 to 101, we get 110 (T-score of 57).

4. $1\frac{2}{3}$ SD = 8.7 + 13 = 21.7 (which, rounded off, becomes 22). When we subtract 22 from 101 we get 79 (T-score of 33).

5. When we add 22 to 101, we get 123 (T-score of 67).

6. If we estimate the T-score equivalents for the raw scores between two of these key points, 79 and 92, we can demonstrate how a teacher can estimate the T-scores for all the remaining scores. The T-score for 79 is 33 and the T-score for 92 is 43. Since 85 is almost halfway between these two scores, assign a T-score of 38 to both 85 and 86. Now we can assign T-scores within these two groups with reasonable accuracy.

TEST SCORES	T-SCORES	TEST SCORES	T-SCORES
79	33	86	38
80	34	87	39
81	35	88	40
82	36	89	41
83	36	90	41
84	37	91	42
85	38	92	43

[3] If you study the formula for computing a T-score, you will discover that the mean always has a T-score of 50. You will also find that when $(X - M)/SD = -\frac{2}{3}$, the T-score equals $50 + 10 \left(-\frac{2}{3}\right)$, or 43.

There are four T-scores for five numbers; thus, one T-score must be assigned to two raw scores. Any one of several techniques may be used. For example, a teacher may number consecutively until he reaches the middle raw score and then assign that T-score to the next two raw scores to solve the problem.

Though the interpolations will not be completely accurate, they do represent the raw scores far more reliably than do either letter grades or percentiles. That, as the next paragraphs will show, is basic and sufficient reason for going to the trouble of computing them.

Most schools require teachers to assign grades. To do so efficiently and fairly, each teacher must keep a record of the students' performances and be able to assign weights to them. If, for example, a teacher plans to grade his class on the basis of scores on five tests given during the semester, he must decide how much he wants each score to count. If he knows that the tests were equally difficult, that the total number of points was the same, and that the tests covered equally important concepts, then he can weight them equally and use the sum of the five raw scores in reaching a decision. If, on the other hand, he decides that some of these conditions are not met, then he must weight the scores in some way. He can use T-scores for this purpose. Because they preserve the raw score differences in the original scores, he can appraise the students' status more fairly by recording T-scores than by recording either letter grades or percentiles. It fairly often happens, for example, that a student earns a very high C on all five tests and still earns more raw-score points than one who earns three low B's and two low C's; yet this fact would not be known if only letter grades were recorded.

If, for example, the teacher decided that the second, third, and fourth tests were of equal importance, he would use the T-scores recorded for these. Should he decide that the first test was only half as important as any one of those three, he would divide the T-scores for the first test by two prior to adding up the scores. Finally, he might decide that the last test was twice as important as any one of the three tests given before it: he would, therefore, double its T-scores. Then the weighted T-scores for each pupil could be added together. We can summarize these decisions algebraically as follows: $\frac{1}{2}T_1 + T_2 + T_3 + T_4 + 2T_5$. Frequently teachers also want to consider other data, such as other written work and class participation, in computing grades. If teachers know how much they want each performance to influence the decision on grades, they can use a T-score to weight each one as they wish.

STANINES

Recently, test publishers have introduced the use of stanines for grading, and some colleges have introduced them to replace letter grades. Therefore, teachers and counselors must understand them too.

When one uses stanines he divides the total range of standard scores of a normal distribution into nine units. Except for the two extremes, each stanine is defined as one-half SD. Stanine 5 includes those scores within one-fourth SD above and below the mean (approximately 20 percent of a normal population). Stanine 6 (approximately 17 percent of a normal population) is the half SD above stanine 5, and stanine 4 (also approximately 17 percent) is the stanine below 5. Stanines 7 and 3 each include approximately 12 percent of a normal population, and stanines 8 and 2 each include about 7 percent. Every measure which is more than $1\frac{3}{4}$ SD above the mean is included in stanine 9, and every one which is more than $1\frac{3}{4}$ SD below the mean is included in stanine 1. For a normal population there are usually 4 percent in each of the two extreme stanines.

If we were to use the tenth-grade mathematics scores as examples again, we would have to divide the SD of 13 by 2, giving us a half SD of 6.5. Then we must decide whether we round it off to 6 or 7. If the scores are distributed normally and if we round it off to 6, then we will not include 20 percent of the scores in stanine 5 (101 $\pm$ 3). In this case, all scores between 98 and 104 would be assigned to stanine 5. If we use one-half SD as 6, then the scores included in each stanine would be as follows: 4 (92–97), 6 (105–110), 3 (86–91), 7 (111–116), 2 (80–85), 8 (117–122), 1 (below 80), and 9 (above 122).

Stanines are based upon the same statistical concepts as T-scores and Z-scores. When they are used instead of the usual five letter grades, they require the faculty to make finer discriminations in grading than is usually required at present. On the other hand, some argue that they require the faculty to make finer discriminations in grading than they can make with reasonable reliability. Where stanines are used in grading, there is an obvious advantage of converting test scores into stanines: it enables the staff readily to compare mental test scores and achievement test scores with grades.

Correlation Coefficients

WHAT is a correlation coefficient? It is a mathematical index that indicates the extent to which the measures for a given individual move up and down the scale together. Although it is expressed as a decimal, it does not indicate the percentage of the time that the different measures for a given individual fall within the same relative position in the range of scores for the entire group.

For example, a tenth-grade biology teacher computed T-scores for the semester examination for one section of his class. He also obtained T-scores for these same students' semester examinations in English and geometry, for a standardized reading test, and for a mental test. These T-scores are reported (along with their Z-scores) in TABLE 4 (p. 495).

By scanning the various columns, we see that most students who earned high scores on one test also tended to earn high scores on the others, but of course there were exceptions. To obtain a visual picture of the extent of the relationship between geometry test scores and mental test scores the teacher prepared FIGURE 11.

From FIGURE 11 (p. 496) it is evident that there is not a perfect positive relationship between the biology test and mental test scores. As a matter of fact, only one student received the same T-score on both tests (52, 52), although two others earned very similar scores (27, 28 and 42, 43). Nevertheless, there does appear to be considerable positive relationship between these two measures.

If there were a perfect positive relationship between the scores in FIGURE 11, then all the "x's" would have fallen on the broken line diagonal drawn from the lower left corner to the upper right corner, and the *correlation coefficient* would be 1.00. With a correlation coefficient of 1.00, when we know where one measure falls, we can always predict exactly where the other will fall. If, for example, there were a perfect correlation between the scores in FIGURE 11, then a student who ranked fifth from the top on the biology test also would rank fifth from the top on the mental test.

If, on the other hand, in each pair of scores one is as much above the mean as the other is below the mean, there would be a perfect negative relationship and all the scores would have fallen on the other diagonal in FIGURE 11. With a perfect negative relationship the correlation coefficient is −1.00. Here, too, by knowing where

TABLE 4   Test Performances of a Tenth-Grade Class

STUDENT'S NAME	BIOLOGY T	Z	ENGLISH T	Z	GEOMETRY T	Z	MENTAL T	Z	READING T	Z
N.A.	51	(0.1)	45	(−0.5)	40	(−1.0)	35	(−1.5)	40	(−1.0)
R.A.	48	(−0.2)	61	(1.1)	60	(1.0)	70	(2.0)	49	(−0.1)
M.B.	49	(−0.1)	45	(−0.5)	38	(−1.2)	44	(−0.6)	55	(0.5)
P.C.	70	(2.0)	72	(2.2)	60	(1.0)	60	(1.0)	55	(0.5)
A.D.	52	(0.2)	49	(−0.1)	55	(0.5)	47	(−0.3)	41	(−0.9)
C.D.	54	(0.4)	75	(2.5)	65	(1.5)	59	(0.9)	70	(2.0)
M.D.	57	(0.7)	53	(0.3)	61	(1.1)	48	(−0.2)	50	(0.0)
H.F.	42	(−0.8)	40	(−1.0)	35	(−1.5)	43	(−0.7)	36	(−1.4)
M.F.	40	(−1.0)	39	(−1.1)	32	(−1.8)	45	(−0.5)	35	(−1.5)
R.M.	52	(0.2)	44	(−0.6)	53	(0.3)	60	(1.0)	50	(0.0)
S.M.	51	(0.1)	59	(0.9)	53	(0.3)	55	(0.5)	61	(1.1)
F.N.	60	(1.0)	45	(−0.5)	54	(0.4)	46	(−0.4)	56	(0.4)
A.O.	52	(0.2)	37	(−1.3)	44	(−0.6)	34	(−1.6)	43	(−0.7)
E.O.	27	(−2.3)	35	(−1.5)	40	(−1.0)	28	(−2.2)	44	(−0.6)
A.R.	62	(1.2)	46	(−0.4)	60	(1.0)	57	(0.7)	52	(0.2)
J.R.	55	(0.5)	56	(0.6)	51	(0.1)	46	(−0.4)	42	(−0.8)
J.S.	65	(1.5)	47	(−0.3)	46	(−0.4)	61	(1.1)	72	(2.2)
M.S.	41	(−0.9)	49	(−0.1)	51	(0.1)	48	(−0.2)	55	(0.5)
H.T.	52	(0.2)	59	(0.9)	46	(−0.4)	59	(0.9)	54	(0.4)
J.T.	40	(−1.0)	54	(0.4)	55	(0.5)	62	(1.2)	47	(−0.3)
M.T.	42	(−0.8)	40	(−1.0)	59	(0.9)	61	(1.1)	59	(0.9)
B.V.	41	(−0.9)	48	(−0.2)	47	(−0.3)	48	(−0.2)	49	(−0.1)
B.W.	52	(0.2)	52	(0.2)	59	(0.9)	52	(0.2)	49	(−0.1)
L.Y.	60	(1.0)	60	(1.0)	58	(0.8)	50	(0.0)	55	(0.5)
W.Y.	30	(−2.0)	40	(−1.0)	26	(−2.4)	40	(−1.0)	69	(1.9)

one measure falls, we can predict exactly where the other will fall. In this instance, we would find the second measure in the same relative position starting from the opposite end of the scale: where one measure was fifth from the top, the other measure would be fifth from the bottom.

Between any two sets of measures of the same group of students, one will find a correlation coefficient between 1.00 and −1.00. Ability to predict one measure from the other depends on the degree of relationship. As the correlation coefficient approaches zero, the accuracy of the prediction decreases until knowing one measure is of no help in predicting the other.

One may use any of a number of formulas in computing a correlation coefficient. However, we shall consider here only the three

FIGURE 11   A Scattergram for Tenth-Grade Students' Test
Scores in Biology and Mental Ability

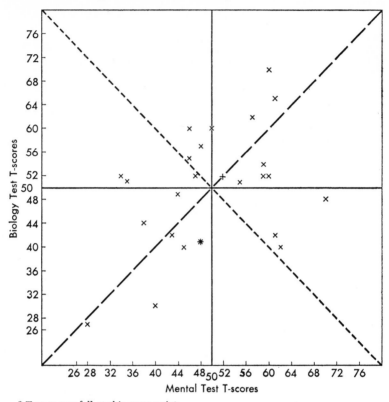

* Two scores fell at this same point.

least complicated methods: (1) the Z-score product method, (2) a
variation of the Z-score product method in which raw scores may be
used, and (3) the rank-order method. We have a mathematical
formula for determining the relationship between pairs of scores,
such as those collected in TABLE 4.

$$r_{xy} = \frac{\Sigma Z_x Z_y}{N}$$

Here r_{xy} is the symbol for the degree of relationship (correlation
coefficient) between two sets of data.

To determine the average Z-score product, which is the coefficient of correlation, we find the sum of all the Z-score products, then divide it by the number of pairs of scores. TABLE 5 shows these Z-score products and the computation of this coefficient of correlation.

Our sets of data in this instance are biology and geometry test scores: so Z_b stands for biology Z-scores and Z_g stands for geometry Z-scores. To compute r_{bg}, according to this formula, follow these steps:

1. From TABLE 4 take each student's Z-scores for biology and geometry, and find their product.

TABLE 5 Computing the Coefficient of Correlation for Biology and Geometry Test Scores

STUDENT'S NAME	Z-SCORES BIOLOGY (Z_b)	Z-SCORES GEOMETRY (Z_g)	$Z_b Z_g$
N.A.	0.1	−1.0	−0.1
R.A.	−0.2	1.0	−0.2
M.B.	−0.1	−1.2	+0.12
P.C.	2.0	1.0	+2.0
A.D.	0.2	0.5	+0.1
C.D.	0.4	1.5	+0.6
M.D.	0.7	1.1	+0.77
H.F.	−0.8	−1.5	+1.2
M.F.	−1.0	−1.8	+1.8
R.M.	0.2	0.3	+0.06
S.M.	0.1	0.3	+0.03
F.N.	1.0	0.4	+0.4
A.O.	0.2	−0.6	−0.12
E.O.	−2.3	−1.0	+2.3
A.R.	1.2	1.0	+1.2
J.R.	0.5	0.1	+0.05
J.S.	1.5	−0.4	−0.60
M.S.	−0.9	0.1	−0.09
H.T.	0.2	−0.4	−0.08
J.T.	−1.0	0.5	−0.5
M.T.	−0.8	0.9	−0.72
B.V.	−0.9	−0.3	+0.27
B.W.	0.2	0.9	+0.18
L.Y.	1.0	0.8	+0.80
W.Y.	−2.0	−2.4	+4.8

$$14.27 = \Sigma Z_b Z_g$$

2. Add up all these products.

3. Divide the sum of the products by N, which is 25 in this example ($14.27 \div 25$). The answer is $r_{bg} = .57$. Though this figure is correct, it is somewhat higher than we would normally expect.

E X E R C I S E

1. Let E represent the English examination scores, M the mental test scores, and R the reading test scores; then compute r_{bm}, r_{br}, and r_{er}.

A N S W E R

1. $r_{bm} = 41$; $r_{br} = .20$; $r_{er} = .35$.

Because we are already familiar with Z-scores, the formula

$$r_{xy} = \frac{\Sigma Z_x Z_y}{N}$$

was discussed before presenting another formula for the computation of correlation coefficients. With this second formula, we begin the computational process with raw scores instead of Z-scores; otherwise, it is based upon exactly the same mathematical concepts:

$$r_{xy} = \frac{\dfrac{\Sigma XY}{N} - M_x M_y}{(SD_x)(SD_y)}$$

1. ΣXY indicates that our first step is to find the product of each of the pairs of raw scores for each individual; then we add these products.

2. Since the formula indicates $\Sigma XY/N$, our next step is to divide this sum of the products by the number (N) of pairs of scores.

3. $M_x M_y$ indicates that our third step is to find the mean for each of the two sets of raw scores and then find the product of the two means.

4. Then, we subtract the product of the means ($M_x M_y$) from the quotient found in step 2: $\Sigma XY/N$.

5. Next we compute the standard deviation for both sets of scores and then find the product of these two SD's.

6. The final step is to divide the difference which we found in step 4 by the product we found in step 5.

Though this method does take some time, it certainly is not diffi-

TABLE 6 Reading and Arithmetic Test Scores for Fifth-Graders

PUPIL'S NAME	READING SCORE (X)	ARITHMETIC SCORE (Y)	XY
M.A.	53	35	1855
H.B.	49	50	2450
D.B.	40	37	1480
R.B.	30	49	1470
P.B.	41	54	2214
C.B.	26	35	910
P.C.	45	37	1665
J.C.	42	47	1974
A.C.	54	34	1836
D.C.	55	45	2475
R.D.	38	51	1938
B.D.	51	48	2448
J.D.	49	46	2254
W.D.	47	32	1504
R.E.	49	25	1225
C.E.	20	25	500
K.F.	43	39	1677
M.F.	40	38	1520
J.G.	42	35	1470
T.H.	17	21	375
A.H.	38	33	1254
C.H.	31	41	1271
L.H.	20	14	280
S.H.	21	29	609
B.H.	60	43	2580
M.H.	55	44	2420
P.H.	59	50	2950
G.J.	48	41	1968
J.J.	57	47	2679
E.K.	49	56	2744
A.M.	57	54	3078
K.M.	41	26	1066

$$\Sigma XY = 56,139$$

cult; it does not introduce either new mathematical symbols or new concepts, and it surely requires less time than the first method.

For the example presented in TABLE 6, $\Sigma XY = 56,139$, $M_x = 42.72$, $M_y = 39.41$, $SD_x = 12.18$, and $SD_y = 10.38$. Therefore

$$r_{xy} = \frac{\dfrac{56,139}{32} - (42.72)(39.41)}{(12.18)(10.38)} = .56$$

Another mathematical technique for studying the way in which sets of measures vary one with another is the rank-order method. It is a simple technique which can be used with smaller groups of students than those with whom the Z-score product method was used. Normally, it would not be advisable to use the Z-score product method with an N smaller than 30.

The formula for the rank-order method is:

$$r = 1 - \frac{6(\Sigma d^2)}{N(N^2 - 1)}$$

To apply this formula we proceed as follows:

1. Rank the students on the first set of measures starting with 1 for the highest score; then do the same with the other set.

2. Find the difference (d) between the two ranks for each student. Square each difference (d^2). (See TABLE 7.)

3. Find the sum of the squared differences (Σd^2) and multiply the result by 6.

4. To determine $N(N^2 - 1)$, find the product of the number of pairs of scores (N) and the number of pairs squared minus one ($N^2 - 1$).

5. Divide the product in step 3 by the product in step 4:

$$\frac{6(\Sigma d^2)}{N(N^2 - 1)}$$

Subtract this quotient from 1.

To illustrate how this method works, let us suppose that we had only half the pupils included in TABLE 6. Hence, we shall begin with M.A. and take every other case.

When, therefore, we substitute in the formula, we get

$$r = \frac{1 - 6(419)}{32(1024 - 1)} = .92$$

Normally we would expect this correlation coefficient to be much closer to .56, since it was based upon part of the same scores. Quite by chance, the odd number scores were much more highly correlated than the even number scores. When one

TABLE 7 Illustration for Computing Rank-Order Correlations

PUPIL'S NAME	RANK IN READING	RANK IN ARITHMETIC	DIFFERENCE IN RANK	DIFFERENCE SQUARED
M.A.	6	12.5	−6.5	42.25
D.B.	13	10.5	2.5	6.25
P.B.	12	1.5	10.5	110.25
P.C.	9	10.5	−1.5	2.25
A.C.	5	4.5	·5	.25
R.D.	14.5	3	11.5	132.25
J.D.	7.5	7	·5	.25
R.E.	7.5	15	−7.5	56.25
K.F.	10	9	1	1
J.G.	11	12.5	−1.5	2.25
A.H.	14.5	14	·5	.25
L.H.	16	16	0	0
B.H.	1	8	−7	49
P.H.	2	4.5	−2.5	6.25
J.J.	3.5	6	−2.5	6.25
A.M.	3.5	1.5	2	4

$$\Sigma d^2 = 419$$

uses only part of a small sample, he always runs the risk of obtaining biased results.

So far, we have considered only the extent to which pairs of measures vary together in a linear relationship—that is, along a straight line. There are occasions when two measures do vary together, yet do not follow a straight line; this is a *curvilinear* relationship, one example of which is the relationship between a man's age in years and the time it takes him to run a mile. From the time the child learns to walk until he is somewhere between fifteen and thirty years of age, he can gradually reduce his running time with practice. Then there will be a gradual increase in running time until he becomes so feeble that perhaps he is lucky if he can walk the mile at all. When a guidance worker discovers such relationships from an examination of a scattergram, he should use the special formula developed for studying curvilinear relationships.[4] That formula, however, is beyond our scope here.

4 E. F. Lindquist, *Statistical Analysis in Educational Research.* (Boston: Houghton Mifflin Company, 1940), p. 239.

Significant Relationships

SINCE guidance workers are usually interested in using these indices in making predictions, they should realize how much the probability of accurate prediction is increased with various levels of correlation.

When is this index significant?

.00 to .20 is of *negligible significance*. When $r = .20$, the chances for predicting the rank of one score, knowing the other, is only 2 percent better than chance, 2 percent better than 50–50.

.20 to .40 is of *slight significance*. When $r = .40$, the odds are only 8 percent better than chance.

.40 to .60 is of *moderate significance*. When $r = .60$, the odds for correct prediction are 20 percent better than chance.

.60 to .80 is of *substantial significance*. When $r = .70$, the odds are 29 percent better than chance; but when $r = .80$, the odds are 40 percent better than chance.

.80 to 1.00 is of *great significance*. When $r = .90$, the odds are 56 percent better than chance; yet when r is increased to .95, they are as high as 69 percent better than chance.

Studying the odds for better-than-chance predictions should make us cautious in predicting on the basis of test results. To use a mental test score, for example, in predicting a high school student's potential for success in college is reasonable, but we should realize that the correlation between most mental test scores and college grades is about .40. That means that in making such a prediction we can do only 8 percent better than chance guessing. If, however, we use a student's rank in his class along with a mental test score, then we usually obtain a correlation of approximately .60. In other words, our guessing is now 20 percent better than chance. These points are made not to discourge use of tests but to stress the need for cautious interpretations.

Even with fairly high correlation coefficients, it is obivous that we should not make the kind of extreme positive and negative statements that some workers are prone to make. The figures given above on the significance of a correlation coefficient should cause guidance workers to avoid statements like these: "Go ahead with your plans. You will do well in your chosen field; there just is no doubt about it," or "You should change your plans. These test scores indicate that you will never make it." It is unlikely that anyone will have supporting evidence to justify such absolute statements. However, the staff involved may have evidence to justify saying, "Most students like you do well in this work," or on the other hand, "Most students like you seem to have a pretty hard time making a go of it in this work." Sometimes, indeed, a guidance worker has the research evidence to support a statement of odds for success. In such a case, the worker could say to the first student above, "Of forty-eight students with records like yours, all but two have been successful in this work."

The mere knowledge that there is a significant relationship between two sets of data does not account for or explain the relationship. In fact, sometimes a third variable is involved which is related to both, and which may account entirely for the correlation obtained. If, for example, we obtained measures of mental ability and height for a randomly selected group of children between ages four and fourteen and computed a correlation coefficient for these data, we would obtain a significant coefficient. When, however, age is held constant, the correlation coefficient would be reduced markedly because both mental ability and height are correlated with age. Though a high correlation coefficient enables a teacher or counselor to predict one variable when he knows the other, he should be aware of the possibility that a third variable may account for the relationship. Such understanding enables him to use data more intelligently in helping pupils.

Use of Correlation Coefficients

UNDER what circumstances will teachers and counselors use a correlation coefficient in child study? Whenever they are called upon to help select tests or to interpret tests, they should be concerned about the reliability and the validity of the tests. Both reliability and validity are reported as correlation coefficients; therefore, teachers must understand this concept in order to select and use tests. They also are expected to use correlation coefficients in predicting success in courses, in training programs, in college, and in vocations. Such coefficients can at least be used to help them identify the variables which should be considered independently or as combined scores to make these predictions.

What is meant by the *reliability* of a test? If a test measures consistently whatever it measures, we say that the test is reliable. This definition of reliability was first introduced in Chapter 6, but now we can say more precisely what it means: usually the builders of tests compute a correlation coefficient by which they study the relationship of scores produced by the odd number and even number items and, after correcting the correlation coefficient with a special formula, report this index as an estimate of test reliability. Although it might appear more logical to study consistency by computing the correlation between test and retest results, several factors have discouraged this approach. First, learning usually takes place between testing periods. Also, students may try to respond exactly as they did before, or they may try to recall what they did before so that they can try another of the alternatives the second time. All of these factors would produce inconsistencies which would be the result of differences in the pupils rather than of the inability of the test to measure consistently.

Validity coefficients are coefficients of correlation too. A coefficient of validity is an index of the relationship between scores on a test and some measures based upon a criterion defined by the author of the test. Typically, the criterion used is only another estimate of the trait being measured by the test. If there is a high correlation between the test scores and the criterion measures, then test users need only be sure that the criterion is positively related to what they want to measure. If there is a low correlation, then even if the criterion is concerned with what test users want to measure, they should ask themselves whether there is another test which will do a better job for them.

To illustrate how correlation coefficients are used in predicting success in specific courses, let us consider the selection of students for ninth-grade algebra. Today such predictions are sometimes made at the end of the seventh grade in order to select students for advanced placement. When teachers examine the research evidence, they usually find that the highest correlation coefficients with grades in algebra are obtained for seventh-grade mathematics grades, algebra aptitude test scores, and mental test scores. These findings suggest that all three scores be considered. After the teachers have selected the variables which seem to be most relevant, they might very well convert these measures into T-scores which can be given various weightings based upon the ability of the various scores to predict success. If such weightings were experimented with over time, the predictions could probably be improved. With such data, teachers could prepare a table that would show for each score the percentage of the students who failed and passed algebra; or adding a little more detail, they could show a grade distribution in algebra for students making each combined score. Knowing the odds for success, they would be in a better position to help a student decide whether he should take algebra as an eighth-grader.

Mental test scores are also useful in helping students predict their success in college. Better predictions can be made, however, by using rank in the high school class together with mental test scores. As was said a few pages earlier, the counselor cannot assure the student's success in any college. But he can, through a knowledge of the college's standards and use of the data mentioned above, help the student discover whether his chances are *relatively* good or *relatively* poor. If the school has maintained a record of its former students' success in the colleges to which most students have gone, then the counselor can explain to the student how former students who performed at about his level did when they attended the college. While this information helps the student estimate his chances for success, it does not determine what he will do, for of course there are matters other than these which also influence his success.

The vast majority of students leave school before graduating from high school, or go to work immediately following graduation. Many industrial and business concerns are interested in placing these young people in the right jobs. Sometimes the employers cooperate with the schools in giving part-time work experience to students while they are attending school in order to help these young people find appropriate jobs after leaving school. By working together, the school and the employer can often define through research those variables which can be used to predict students' chances for success on the various jobs available to them.

We see, therefore, that educational statistics are basic tools which enable the guidance worker to summarize, to compare, to analyze, and to interpret data which have been or should be collected on pupils. Each statistic can be used for certain purposes and only when data appropriate to its use have been collected. Hence, the user must know for what purpose a statistic can be used and under what conditions.

SUGGESTED READINGS

1. BLOMMERS, PAUL J., and E. F. LINDQUIST. *Elementary Statistical Methods in Psychology and Education.* Boston: Houghton Mifflin Company, 1960.

This is the third edition of an excellent elementary text which was originally written by Lindquist.

2. WALKER, HELEN M., and JOSEPH LEV. *Elementary Statistical Methods.* New York: Holt, Rinehart & Winston, Inc., 1958.

This is a revision of another excellent text which was published originally by the same senior author in 1943. Both this text and the one mentioned above discuss the basic statistical concepts that teachers and counselors need for child study, and neither requires extensive background in mathematics to be understood.

AUTHOR INDEX

SUBJECT INDEX

Homeroom guidance, 322–23
Hostile client, *see* Clients, hostile

Ideal counseling relationships, 68
Independence, development of, 51–53
Information service, 302–34, 467–68;
faculty-planned groups, 311–23; staffing of, 309–11; voluntary discussion groups, 323–30, 420
In-service education, 194, 223–24, 225, 275–79, 350, 422–24
Intellectually gifted, *see* Gifted and talented children
Intelligence quotient, 235
Interest inventories, 286–98
Interests, study of, 286–98
Interview record, 72–73, 134–40, 179
Iowa Tests of Basic Skills, 246
Iowa Tests of Educational Development, 246

Job, location of, 19, 359, 360
Job evaluation, 361
Job placement service, *see* Placement services
Job skills, 19, 352, 358, 359, 361
Juvenile delinquency, *see* Delinquency

Kuder Preference Record—Vocational, 293, 295, 296, 297, 298, 301, 308
Kuhlmann-Finch Tests, 248

Leader, characteristics of, 374–75; definition of role of, 375–80
Leadership: experiences, 381–85; of formal organizations, 379–80; of informal organizations, 379–80; training, 371–72, 380–81; with social development, 371–89, 422, 469
Learning atmosphere, 416, 417
Learning efficiency, 416
Learning problems: diagnosing of, 218–19, 222–23, 416, 477–79
Limits, 41, 53, 391–95, 412, 416
Local control of schools, 426–29
Lorge-Thorndike Intelligence Tests, 249

Maintaining Classroom Discipline (film), 414
Matrix table for sociometric data, 269–71
Mean, 479–80
Median, 481–82
Mental age, 235
Mental health, 5–7, 17, 20, 21
Mental hygiene movement, 7–10
Mental tests, 229–41, 247–49
Michigan Plan for Filing and Indexing Occupational Information, 308
Minnesota Counseling Inventory, 284

Missouri Plan for Filing Unbound Information on Occupations, 308
Mode, 482
Mooney Problem Check Lists, 284

Nagging parents, 27
National Defense Education Act, 12
National Manpower Council, 16
Needs: for acceptance, understanding, and love from others, 42–46; to belong, 42–46; for clothing, 32–33; for essential physical requirements, 30–35; for health, 30; for housing, 32–33; for managing feelings of fear and guilt, 53–56; for recognition from others, 46–49; relation of to performance, 28–30; for self-acceptance, 37–42, 89, 336; for sex, 33–37; for understanding physical and emotional changes, 35–37; for understanding responsibility to others, 49–51
New York State Department Plan, 309
Nondirective counseling, 70–73, 78–80
Normal curve, 487–89

Occupational information, 306–21
Ogive, 484
Orientation service, 330–33, 421

Parent conference, 104–05
Parent discussion groups, 328–30, 349
Pauses, 109–11
Percentiles, 483–84
Performance tests, 218
Personal history, 26, 103, 105, 256, 258, 259–61
Personal history questionnaire, 258
Personal themes, 262–63
Personality: assessment, 342, 449; levels, 450–53; tests and inventories, 253–57, 450–53
Physical and emotional change, understanding of, *see* Needs: for understanding physical and emotional change
Physical needs, 30–35
Placement services, 20, 356–64, 421
Principal's role in guidance, 430–33, 434, 437
Private conferences, teacher's, 257–58, 417–19
Probing, 53–54, 74, 84
Problem-solving, 6–7
Projective tests, 255, 450
Psychodrama, *see* Role playing
Psychotherapy I: The Counselor (film), 101
Psychotherapy II: The Client (film), 101
Public relations, 431–32, 470